DATE DUE

MY 1 5'00			
JE 9'04			
JY 20 04			

DEMCO 38-296

International Conflict

International Conflict

*A Chronological
Encyclopedia of Conflicts
and Their Management
1945–1995*

Jacob Bercovitch and Richard Jackson

*University of Canterbury,
Christchurch, New Zealand*

Congressional Quarterly Inc.
Washington, D.C.

To Gillian and Michelle

©1997 Congressional Quarterly Inc.
1414 22nd Street, N.W.
Washington, D.C. 20037

Cover: Paula Anderson
Book design: Naylor Design, Inc

Printed and bound in the United States of America

Library of Congress Cataloging-in-Publication Data
Bercovitch, Jacob.
    International conflict: a chronological encyclopedia of conflicts and their management,
    1945–1995 / Jacob Bercovitch and Richard Jackson.
        p.   cm.
    Includes bibliographical references and index.
    ISBN 1-56802-195-X
    1. World politics—1945- —Encyclopedias. 2. Conflict management—History—20th century—
    Encyclopedias. I. Jackson, Richard, 1966-
    . II. Title.
    D842.B46 1997
    909.82'5'0202—dc21   97–30556

Summary Contents

Contents

Tables, Figures, and Maps

Tables

Figures

Maps

Preface

This book is a product of the International Conflict Management project begun more than a decade ago at the University of Canterbury in New Zealand. The project was designed to accumulate as much reliable information on international conflict management from 1945 to 1995 as was possible. To that extent, we can honestly say the book represents the culmination of many years of work.

The intellectual origins of the project owe much to J. David Singer's Correlates of War project. We wanted to explore conflict management in the same systematic fashion that Singer and his associates brought to their study of conflict and war. We presented some of the results of our investigations in a series of articles and papers. In this volume we follow a different path: Our primary goal is to present a comprehensive, chronological account of international conflict from 1945 to 1995 and to shed some light on its occurrence and its management.

We began by developing a list of the interstate armed conflicts, internationalized civil wars, and militarized disputes since 1945. This task involved synthesizing past studies on war and carefully examining the *New York Times Index, Keesings Archives,* and newspaper accounts from the *New York Times, The Times* (London), and Reuters Online Service for the period in question.

We considered conflicts only if they conformed to a strict set of specifications. First, we included conflicts between states that involved actual military hostilities or *significant* shows of force, such as large troop mobilizations along border areas, occupations of disputed territory, or the firing of warning shots. This criterion allowed us to include cases such as the Cuban Missile Crisis (see conflict 082), which, although it caused no combat deaths, posed a grave threat to international peace and security and had political effects and ramifications equal to that of any major war. The defining criterion here was the crossover from employing diplomatic or political means of addressing a conflict to using *credibly threatening* military force. The decision to use force is the critical moment that turns a mere conflict into an *armed* international conflict or militarized dispute. It is a crucial moment because the decision to use force is the final step along the path to putting at risk the physical survival of the opposing state, or at least threatening its territorial integrity.

Second, in the cases of internationalized civil conflicts, we included only those cases with *verifiable* and *significant* international aspects, such as the use of foreign troops, the use of foreign territory to launch attacks, large-scale efforts at agitation and subversion, and logistical and military support to internal groups by outside states. For example, the United States gave significant logistical support to the contra rebels in their insurgency against the leftist Nicaraguan government. It also provided advisers to train the contras and even went as far as mining Nicaraguan ports. We have therefore included the contra war in Nicaragua (1980–1994, see conflict 190), even though it was primarily a civil conflict.

Further, we also included cases of secession, or attempted secession, where the seceding party was accorded international recognition, even if it failed to win full independence. This decision permitted us to include important conflicts like the Biafran war (1967–1970; see conflict 118), the East Timor–Indonesian conflict (1975–; see conflict 156), and the ongoing war in Chechnya (1992–; see conflict 273). All of these conflicts were seen to be major threats to international peace and security, and the international community made efforts to resolve them peacefully. For example, the British Commonwealth sought to mediate in the Biafran war, and the Organization for Security and Cooperation in Europe (OSCE) has actively tried to mediate in the Chechen war since 1994.

Finally, we included militarized disputes that had the potential for wider and more serious conflict owing to the threat they posed to international peace and security. Most militarized disputes also occurred in unstable regions. That is to say, armed border incidents between traditionally hostile neighbors (for example, Israel and Lebanon, Peru and Ecuador) were included because the potential for escalation was extremely high. With political incidents, the threat to international peace and security is low and occurs in the context of otherwise friendly relations. A political incident poses no real threat to the territorial integrity of the opposing state nor to its physical survival. Political incidents were therefore not included in the data here.

Once chosen, each case was scrutinized to discover the issues in conflict, which parties were involved, what course the hostilities took, how many fatalities resulted, what the outcome was, and how the conflict was managed. The aim throughout was to discover patterns and variables that would shed some light on how international conflicts could be better managed to minimize their destructive aspects.

The result is *International Conflict: A Chronological Encyclopedia of Conflicts and Their Management 1945–1995*. In "Understanding International Conflict" and "Managing International Conflict," we examine the basic elements, issues, and techniques in international conflict and conflict management. There, we explore patterns in conflict and conflict management, illustrated with diagrams and tables. "Conflicts from 1945 to 1995" provides chronological descriptions of each of the 292 conflicts, covering history, issues, circumstances, players, management, and outcome. Extensive cross-references trace related conflicts throughout, and a lengthy bibliography, divided by region, provides more details and information about the conflicts.

Our method of naming and dating the conflicts may require some explanation: At the head of each conflict summary, we have named the principal country (or countries) involved. On the line below are brief descriptions of the fighting (territorial dispute, ethnic-based violence, secessionist warfare, and so forth), followed by the dates of the conflict in parentheses. For example:

032. Argentina-Chile
Border conflict; the Beagle Channel dispute (July 1952–1968)

The dates in parentheses represent the first and last *identifiable* violence directly related to the conflict. In the corresponding description, however, we focus on major incidents worth writing about. In the Beagle Channel dispute, for example, our summary ends with a 1958 flare-up. We elected not to describe the 1968 incident.

Acknowledgments

We are grateful to a number of people who have helped and encouraged us throughout the project. First and foremost, we must thank Margery Boichel Thompson, who was then director of publications at Georgetown University's Institute for the Study of Diplomacy, encouraged us to pursue our project and was able to kindle interest in the book from publishers. Shana Wagger and the team at CQ Books deserve our thanks for their patience, professionalism, and quiet encouragement throughout the entire project. Christopher Karlsten managed production of the pages. Our manuscript editor, Kris Stoever, was a model of unsurpassed thoroughness and reliability. The library staff here at the University of Canterbury has been most helpful with our many requests for interlibrary loans, online searches, and access to primary sources such as the *New York Times*, *The Times* (London), Reuters, and *Keesings Archives*.

Judith Fetter, Andrew Hampton, Jeff Langley, André Moore, and Simon Tucker provided able research assistance over the years. Special thanks are due to Allison Houston, who has been with us from the very beginning and been responsible for so many aspects of the project. Her computer and programming skills are much appreciated. To Jill Dolby we extend heartfelt thanks for all her secretarial help.

We are grateful to Robert Litwak of the Woodrow Wilson Center, Frederic Pearson of the Center for Peace and Conflict Studies, Wayne State University, and Randolph Siverson of the University of California, Davis, who carefully read through and reviewed earlier drafts of the manuscript. They offered a number of useful suggestions, many of which we sought to incorporate. We are responsible, however, for any errors, shortcomings, or omissions the book might possess.

Finally, we wish to express our gratitude to the University of Canterbury (Research Grant 2202062) and the Department of Internal Affairs, Peace and Disarmament Educational Trust for providing the financial assistance we needed to undertake and complete this project.

Understanding International Conflict

Of all the social processes, conflict is perhaps the most universal—and also, potentially, the most dangerous. A feature of every society and every form of relationship, conflict can be found at every level of human interaction, from sibling rivalry to genocidal warfare. Within our own selves we face conflicting emotions and impulses while responding daily to situations of conflict in our personal relationships. The groups we belong to—schools, clubs, companies, churches, associations, unions—continually undergo conflict. There are internal conflicts, such as the infighting between old and new members of an association, and external conflicts with other groups, which might include strikes by unions against employers or environmental groups remonstrating with oil companies. The largest human group—the state, or nation—also encounters conflict. Sometimes it is internal, as when different groups oppose the government or its policies. It might be external at other times, as when two states go to war.

Conflict is not only universal but also normal and necessary in the sense that every single person and every group has its own needs, expectations, and ways of behaving that it regards as appropriate. Given this diversity, and given that we live in a world of limited resources and opportunities, it is not surprising that conflict is a normal part of life. In fact, we could argue that conflict is necessary for our growth, both as individuals and as groups. It is only through conflict and its resolution in productive and creative ways that new ideas emerge, higher levels of understanding are reached, and obstacles surmounted.

In other words, conflict should not be viewed as a wholly negative phenomenon. Individuals face a myriad of conflicts every day, and for the most part, these are settled in a positive, or at least nonharmful, manner. It is only when we use coercion or violence—physical or psychological—that conflict devolves into something negative and destructive. Although this is a relatively rare event in terms of the total number of conflicts that occur every day, it is frequent and destructive enough to warrant careful study.

We recognize that conflicts, unless properly understood, may pose the greatest threat to the international environment, and we see this book as part of an effort to generate socially useful knowledge, in particular, knowledge about international conflict—its scope, patterns, outcomes, and management. We do not presume that such knowledge will enable us to move apparently intractable conflicts toward a solution. Yet we do believe that lack of knowledge about international conflict may preclude its successful management.

Conceptual clarity and a measure of verbal precision are preconditions for understanding conflict. If we seek to describe a range of behavior, we must begin by distinguishing it from related phenomena. This is particularly important with conflict, which is a ubiquitous process and easily confused with other processes such as aggression, violence, coercion, and so forth.

What Is Conflict?

In everyday language, conflict denotes overt, coercive interactions in which two or more contending parties seek to impose their will on one another. *Fights, violence,* and *hostility* are the terms customarily employed to describe a conflict relationship. The range of conflict phenomena is, however, much wider than that. The term *conflict* is used to describe inconsistencies as well as the process of trying to solve them; it has physical and moral implications; it embraces opinions as well as situations and a wide range of behavior. Conventional usage of the term then, does not capture the full range of conflict phenomena.

We define conflict as a process of interaction between two or more parties that seek to thwart, injure, or destroy their opponent because they perceive they have incompatible goals or interests. The conflict relationship is characterized by a specific set of attitudes and behaviors, and the conflict process implies a level of interdependence and dynamism between the parties. Conflict attitudes engender conflict behaviors which in turn induce a further hardening of attitudes in a cyclical fashion.

The different strands and components of a conflict relationship may be thought of in terms of three interrelated elements: (a) a specific conflict situation, (b) motives and the parties' cognitive structure, and (c) the behavioral-attitudinal dynamics of a conflict process; these can be considered jointly or separately. A *conflict situation* refers to a circumstance that generates incompatible goals or values among different parties. *Conflict attitudes* consist of the psychological and cognitive processes that engender conflict or are subsequent to it. And *conflict behavior* consists of actual, observed activities undertaken by one party that are designed to injure, thwart, or eliminate its opponent.

International Conflict

When we speak of international relations, we imply a level of interaction, or behavior, and an interdependence among actors. The interdependence we refer to is among nations. Their organization determines the configuration of the international system and the extent and intensity of conflict within that system. Interdependence can be negative (e.g., Greece-Turkey) or positive (e.g., United States–Canada). *Negative interdependence* implies a preponderance of competitive interests in the relationship, resulting in suspicious and hostile attitudes where conflict is defined as a win-lose situation. *Positive interdependence*, on the other hand, is characterized by largely cooperative interests.

International conflict, like peace, is a process rather than an end state. It is active and dynamic rather than passive and static. Its behavior consists of one nation's organized and collective effort to control, influence, or destroy the persons and property of another nation. International conflict is also a multicausal and multifaceted phenomenon. Its occurrence should not (unless it is violent) be taken as an interruption of "normal" interactions, but as a natural and probable consequence of the existence of actors with different values and interests. Given a system with fairly autonomous and diverse units, linked in a relationship both competitive and cooperative, the potential for conflict is unbounded. This does not mean that every relationship displays conflict. International conflict depends on a diffuse set of structures, attitudes, and feelings.

Although other kinds of conflict may be annoying or disruptive—such as public transport strikes at the municipal level—they rarely produce numerous casualties or large-scale violence. They can also be resolved by the parties themselves, or by legal authorities. That is, they are regulated. The same is not true of states, which exist in an anarchical environment without enforceable laws or norms, where conflicts are unregulated and can quickly spiral out of control. In such an environment, some conflicts will inevitably escalate into large-scale violence or war. Most international conflicts, however, are resolved peacefully and constructively through regular channels of diplomacy and international forums such as the United Nations. Very few conflicts escalate to the point of war. Here we want to look at the fifty-year period after World War II not only to ascertain the pattern, characteristics, and descriptions of conflict, but also to determine how conflict was managed.

International Conflict, 1945–1995

Since 1945 somewhere between 15 and 30 million people have been killed as a result of war-related violence or by the famine and disease brought on by war. Most of those deaths have occurred in the eighty or so major conflicts in Africa, Asia, and the Middle East. The wars in Korea (1950–1953), Vietnam (1964–1975), Bangladesh (1971–1974), Sudan (1963–1972, 1983–), Afghanistan (1980–), Iran and Iraq (1980–1989), and Mozambique (1975–1992) each killed more than a million people. Others, like the genocidal ethnic conflict in Rwanda in 1994 and the Angolan civil war (1975–1995), have each resulted in at least half a million deaths. On top of this, more than two hundred other armed conflicts between states have been recorded.

Although many of these have not resulted in tremendous casualties, they have had other destructive effects, such as creating enormous refugee populations; economic and environmental dislocation; political instability; tension; ethnic hatred; and food crises.

These 290 or so international conflicts have for the most part been related to the two main fault-lines of the postwar period—namely, the East-West conflict (which divided states into the communist Eastern bloc or the democratic Western camp) and the North-South conflict (which divided the advanced industrial countries, or the Northern states, from the developing world, or the Southern states).

The Cold War

The cold war split the world into two hostile camps, or spheres of influence, after the late 1940s, with each sphere dominated by one of the superpowers—the United States and the Soviet Union. Both countries vied for influence in zones outside their control, and many of the conflicts from 1950 to 1989 reflect this competition. In the Vietnam War (1964–1975), U.S. forces fought directly against communist forces supported by the Soviet Union. In the Afghanistan conflict (1980–), the Soviets fought directly against U.S.-backed mujahedin rebels.

Other conflicts that exhibit signs of this rivalry include the Korean War (1950–1953), the Cambodian conflict (1979–), the Ethiopia-Somalia wars (1972–1985), the civil wars in Angola (1975–1995) and Mozambique (1975–1992), and many of the conflicts in Central America, such as Nicaragua (1980–1994), El Salvador (1977–1992), and Guatemala (1954–1995). In each case, one or both superpowers intervened with a significant show of force, producing a crisis with a high potential for escalation.

Decolonization

The other major postwar fault-line, the North-South divide, produced a series of conflicts related to decolonization. In some cases, the conflicts were essentially wars of independence from European colonial powers like Britain, France, Portugal, and the Netherlands. Algerian nationalists fought a particularly vicious war of independence from France in the 1950s and 1960s, while other wars of independence were fought in India (1945–1948), Mozambique (1961–1975), Angola (1961–1975), Rhodesia/Zimbabwe (1967–1980), South West Africa/Namibia (1966–1990), French Indochina (1945–1949), and Malaya/Malaysia (1948–1960).

In other cases, war broke out when new states emerged from colonial domination and upset local power balances. Israel's war of independence (1948–1949) and subsequent conflicts with its neighbors resulted directly from British decolonization. In some instances, conflicts grew out of colonial policies that failed to consider local sensibilities and conditions. The ethnic violence between the Hutu and Tutsi tribes, which has plagued Rwanda and Burundi since their independence, can be directly linked to Belgium's colonial policies, which not only played tribal animosities off each other but also drew boundaries for the new nations with no regard for tribal land settlements. The intense violence between India and Pakistan following independence was largely caused by the haphazard boundary demarcations during the 1947 partition of the Indian Subcontinent.

The end of the cold war in the late 1980s led to the end of a number of conflicts. The Soviets withdrew from Afghanistan, and the Americans stopped aiding the mujahedin rebels. The United States and Soviet Union both withdrew support from the warring parties in Angola and Mozambique and forced them to the negotiating table. Wars ended in Cambodia, Nicaragua, and El Salvador, and the U.S.-led Coalition forces forced Iraq out of Kuwait in the Gulf war (1990–1991). It seemed as if a new era of peace had begun, especially since the threat of global nuclear annihilation was gone.

Ethnic Conflict

Unfortunately, the collapse of the Soviet Union and the end of superpower rivalry have not produced the tranquility envisioned at the end of the cold war. In fact, the breakup of the Soviet Union has led to a whole host of long-submerged conflicts in the 1990s, which can be largely characterized as wars of nationalism or ethnic-based conflict. The war in the former Yugoslavia (1989–1995) involving Serbs, Croats, and Bosnians is the most vivid example of this, but similar wars in Georgia (1989–), Chechnya (1992–1995), Armenia (1990–), and Tajikistan (1992–) are also examples. In each case, ethnic groups vie for power and resources in a spiral of violence laced with hatreds and grievances that often go back centuries. Other ethnically based conflicts can be seen in the Sudan civil war (1983–) being waged between the Muslim Arabic northerners and the Black African Christians and animists in the south, and in Rwanda (1990–), Burundi (1988–), Liberia (1989–), Moldova (1990–1992), Bougainville (1988–), and the Philippines (1970–1995).

Another important characteristic of post–cold war conflicts is that they are largely within, and not between, states. As such, they are called *civil conflicts*. The fighting in the former Yugoslavia erupted when Serb militias sought to prevent Croatia and Bosnia-Herzegovina from seceding from the federation and setting up their own new states. Thus, all the fighting took place within the borders of what used to be Yugoslavia, although at times it threatened to spill over into neighboring states and it involved many outside powers in the search for a settlement.

Types of International Conflict

International conflicts can be categorized in various ways. Here we divide them into four main types, which help to explain their causes and the form they take. These are (a) conflicts between states (interstate conflict), (b) internationalized civil conflicts, (c) militarized disputes, and (d) political incidents. How does one distinguish among these different kinds of conflicts?

Interstate Conflict

Interstate conflicts usually involve territory held in dispute by contiguous states. Somalia and Ethiopia, for example, have gone to war several times over the Ogaden region (1964, 1972–1985, 1987–1988)—an area ruled by Ethiopia but inhabited by Somali tribes. The coveted region lies on their mutual border and has long been claimed by Somalia. Very few wars are fought by states situated a long distance apart, although the Falklands war (1982) between Britain and Argentina is an exception. It continues to cost Great Britain millions of pounds every day to maintain a military presence on these distant islands.

In some cases, states will go to war when they have competing ideologies, or when they feel insecure. In 1980 opposition to Iran's brand of Islamic fundamentalism was partly why Iraq attacked its Shiite neighbor and rival in what became one of the world's bloodiest conflicts. Occasionally, interstate conflicts can escalate and bring in other states, resulting in a regional conflict that affects many countries in a given geographical area. This was the case in Indochina in the 1960s and 1970s, southern Africa in the 1980s, and the Middle East since 1948.

Interstate conflicts may also arise from rivalries whereby states feel threatened or intimidated by their opponents. They may engage in a dangerous cat-and-mouse game of provocation and escalation that often results in an armed conflict. In these cases, a pair of rivals might have four or more wars over a twenty-year period and many lesser incidents and periods of tension. India and Pakistan have been rivals since their independence in 1948 and have gone to war more than six times since then. Ecuador and Peru are another pair of rivals that regularly clash over a piece of territory in the Amazon. Israel and its neighbors have constantly maneuvered against each other since the Jewish state gained statehood in 1948. Other bitter historical rivals include Iran and Iraq, Greece and Turkey, China and Vietnam, Somalia and Ethiopia, and Chile and Argentina.

Internationalized Civil Conflict

The second type of international conflict occurs when another state becomes involved in a violent civil conflict, either directly by invasion, or indirectly by actively supporting a faction in the other country. Examples of direct intervention in a civil conflict include Saudi Arabia's invasion of Yemen on the side of the royalists, and Egypt's invasion on the side of the republicans in Yemen's 1962–1970 civil war. Also, in 1965 the United States invaded the Dominican Republic on the side of the government, which was then fighting a civil war against the constitutionalists, who wanted to restore Juan Bosch, a former president ousted in a military coup.

Indirect support, on the other hand, can take many forms. In some cases it can involve sending arms and providing training and advisers for one faction in the conflict, such as the United States' aid to the contra rebels fighting the Nicaraguan government (1980–1994). It can also involve allowing rebels to use territory from which to launch attacks. Zambia's support for the

Rhodesian rebels allowed the Zimbabwe African People's Union (ZAPU)—one of the African nationalist factions fighting Rhodesia's white-minority government in the war of independence (1967–1980)—to have bases and training camps on Zambian territory. ZAPU guerrillas would then launch attacks across the Zambezi border into what was then Rhodesia and then cross back into the relative safety of Zambia.

In extreme cases, superpower rivals can fight proxy wars by supporting opposing factions in a civil conflict. Thus, the United States supported Jonas Savimbi's National Union for the Total Independence of Angola (UNITA) guerrilla group in Angola, while the Soviets backed the governing MPLA (Movimento Popular de Libertação de Angola). This way, the superpowers could strike at each other indirectly without risking all-out war. A similar conflict took place in El Salvador (1977–1992), but here the government was supported by the United States while Cuba and the Soviet Union backed the left-wing rebels.

Some civil conflicts last for decades and take the form of guerrilla insurgencies. Often the guerrillas live in dense forest in border areas and move across borders at will, attacking government targets and then disappearing into the jungle again. The insurgencies in Burma (1949–) by ethnic Karen guerrillas and in Colombia (1965–) by Marxist insurgents have gone on for decades, as neither side has the ability to completely defeat the other. Other civil conflicts result from attempts by particular ethnic groups living in one area to break away, or secede, and form their own state. The Biafran war (1967–1970), the 1975 invasion of East Timor by Indonesia, and Western Sahara's efforts to resist Morocco's territorial claims since 1974 are all examples of this. In each case, states outside the conflict gave their recognition and support to the seceding party, and some even provided military aid.

For the most part, civil conflicts result from different ideologies, such as the communist insurgents in Guatemala who opposed the right-wing government and its policies, or from ethnic factors, such as many of the conflicts in the former Soviet republics, where Chechens, Ukrainians, Abkhazians, and ethnic Russians coexist in close quarters. In all cases, they became international conflicts when a second or third state intervened in a significant way, thus posing a risk to international peace and security. In other words, although the civil conflicts in Peru, in the Basque region of Spain, and in Northern Ireland have involved fighting, other states have not mounted a significant intervention. These conflicts do not, therefore, pose the same risk as internationalized civil conflicts.

Militarized Disputes

The third type of international conflict is the militarized dispute. This occurs when two states face off militarily, escalating a crisis or sparking an incident. Although such face-offs may not result in all-out wars, they create the potential for serious conflict and threaten international peace and security. In most cases, there is also some loss of life.

The most famous militarized dispute was the Cuban Missile Crisis of 1962, when the Soviet Union tried to station medium-range nuclear missiles in Cuba and the U.S. Navy threatened to sink any Soviet ships that entered the waters around Cuba. Although this crisis did not result in direct military conflict, it took the world to the brink of nuclear war. The persistent conflict between the Soviet Union and the United States produced a number of air incidents in the 1950s in which Soviet and United States jets shot each other down, threatened to escalate, and was controlled only by tightening the levers of deterrence.

Militarized disputes are important because they occur in the context of a tense and hostile relationship and are almost always preceded by a history of violence. Thus, they contain a very real risk of escalation into all-out war. Relations between rival states are usually characterized by numerous militarized disputes. Other important militarized disputes have occurred between states such as Zambia and Zaire (1982, 1983–1984), the United States and Cambodia (the *Mayaguez* incident in 1975), and Guatemala and Mexico (1982–1983, 1984).

Political Incidents

The fourth and final type of international conflict is the political incident. These are interstate disputes that escalate beyond the level of normal day-to-day conflicts between states, such as conflicts over trade, visas, diplomatic etiquette, and so forth. Usually, political incidents involve verbal and political demonstrations, such as denunciations, propaganda, name-calling, diplomatic insults, and maybe even threats and ultimatums. In a very few cases, armed incidents may even take place. Political incidents occur, however, between states that are normally friendly. Furthermore, the disputants tend to be democracies, and there is no history of violence nor the likelihood that the dispute will escalate into a war.

Examples of what we consider to be a political incident include the Anglo-Icelandic fishing dispute in 1972–1973. This involved several acrimonious verbal and political demonstrations, as well as the use of naval vessels to prevent boats from fishing in disputed waters. Although force was used in this case, there was no real threat of war, and the conflict occurred in the context of otherwise friendly relations between two democracies. In recent years, similar fishing disputes between Canada and Spain and Britain and Spain have also escalated into political incidents; these have been excluded from the book because, in our view, they posed no threat to international peace and security and do not qualify as true armed international conflicts (see below).

Patterns of International Conflict, 1945–1995

Our survey of the period from 1945 to 1995 found 292 international conflicts that conformed to these four categories—interstate conflicts, internationalized civil conflicts, militarized disputes, or political incidents. Further analysis of

Figure 1   Disputes initiated and in progress, by period

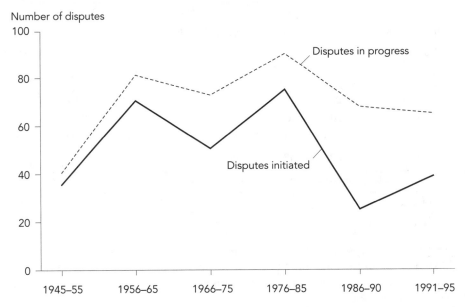

Number of disputes

these conflicts revealed some important facts. For example, the majority of conflicts took place from 1956 to 1985, during the era of decolonization and superpower confrontation (see fig. 1). Another feature of these conflicts is that both Europe and North America remained relatively free from conflict while the developing world was extricating itself from colonial ties and becoming prey to cold war adventurism. It is also clear that many post–cold war conflicts have grown out of the disintegration of the Soviet Union and the consequent collapse of Europe's cold war structures. While it lasted, therefore, the cold war kept the peace in Europe. It did not, however, prevent war elsewhere, nor did it guarantee a tranquil Europe in the twenty-first century—indeed, it was not designed to.

Another noteworthy pattern during this period from 1945 to 1995 is that while the absolute number of conflicts has risen, the number of conflicts *in progress* has been declining since the mid-1980s. The number of conflicts initiated dropped dramatically in the late 1980s (see fig. 1), when the Soviet Union was collapsing and commentators were quick to declare a new age of international peace. The years from 1991 to 1995, however, saw a sharp rise in new conflicts, as fragile states collapsed in Africa and as ethnic and nationalist rivalries sparked into war across eastern Europe and throughout what had been Soviet Asia.

Most conflicts flared in the traditional hot spots of Africa and the Middle East (see table 1). While Africa attempted to throw off colonial oppression, the Middle East played host to the superpower rivalry and tried to cope with the destabilizing effects of the establishment of the state of Israel. As we can see from figure 1, however, war is being utilized less and less, at least relative to the

Table 1 Dispute Initiation and U.N. Membership,[1] by region and period

	1945–55	1956–65	1966–75	1976–85	1986–90	1991–95	TOTAL
Latin America	4 (23)	10 (1)	4 (3)	14 (6)	3 (0)	3 (0)	38 (33)
Africa	4 (3)	16 (32)	14 (14)	23 (2)	12 (1)	10 (2)	79 (54)
S.W. Asia	6 (7)	8 (1)	3 (1)	8 (0)	3 (0)	2 (1)	30 (10)
S.E. Asia/ Pacific	11 (8)	13 (3)	10 (2)	13 (4)	2 (1)	7 (4)	56 (22)
Middle East	6 (10)	19 (3)	17 (3)	16 (1)	3 (0)	9 (0)	70 (17)
Europe	4 (27)	2 (1)	2 (1)	1 (0)	2 (1)	8 (19)	19 (49)
(TOTAL)	(78)	(41)	(24)	(13)	(3)	(26)	(185)

Note: The United Nations had 51 charter members when it was formed in 1945. The U.N. Security Council has 5 permanent members; 101 of the remaining U.N. members have also served on the Security Council at some time.

[1] Shown in parentheses.

number of new states joining the international system. That is, while the absolute amount of war may go up (or down), this is "normal" in the sense that the more states there are in the international system, the greater potential there is for conflict.

Although the potential for conflict is greater, this is not the same as saying that states are now more willing to use war as an instrument of foreign policy. Many of the conflicts in Africa in the 1970s and 1980s occurred between states that did not exist in the international system before the 1960s, and the wars in eastern Europe and what was formerly Soviet Asia are all between states that have only just joined international society.

When we look at types of international conflicts (civil disputes and interstate disputes) in the context of their system periods, it becomes clear how important interstate disputes became during the cold war period (see fig. 2). The cold war had the effect of suppressing many civil conflicts (except those exploited by the superpowers). It was only after the collapse of the Soviet Union in 1991 that many civil conflicts once again reemerged.

If we look at conflict in regional terms, Africa has suffered by far the most (see fig. 3). This is not surprising, as colonial policies in Africa often placed historically hostile ethnic groups together in a single state. The civil war in Chad (1982–) between Arabic Muslim northerners and Black African Christian southerners is a direct result of colonial boundary drawing that placed rival groups in a single state. Rwanda and Burundi were both deeply affected by colonial policies that favored one tribe over another, leading to postindependence rivalry and, eventually, genocidal conflict.

Similarly, the Middle East has suffered more interstate conflicts than any other region (see fig. 3) despite the fact that, with only seventeen countries, it has the second-fewest states of any region (see table 1). This can be accounted for by the emergence of Israel after 1948, which upset regional power balances and injected a great deal of instability into the region. Israel has been involved

Figure 2   Type of dispute, by period

Number of disputes

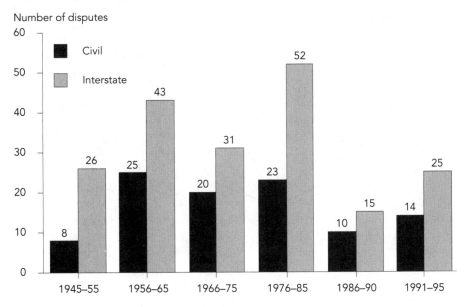

Figure 3   Type of dispute, by region

Number of disputes

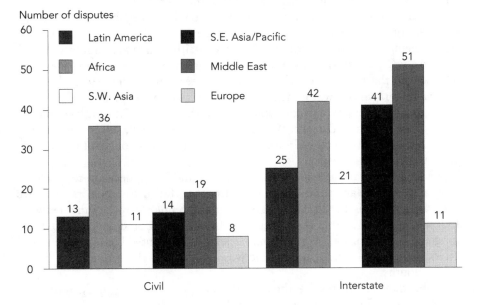

Figure 4   Duration of disputes (in months)

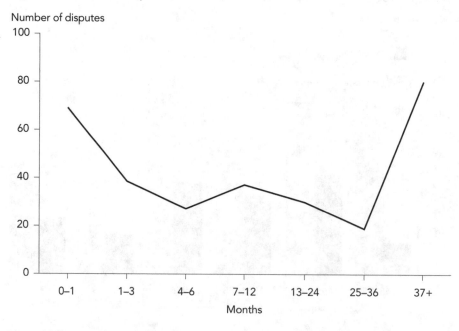

Number of disputes

in more than twenty conflicts since 1948. Also, the region's oil reserves and the Suez Canal make the Middle East strategically important—with a great deal of superpower maneuvering and intrigue being the result.

As for duration, international conflicts tend to be short and quickly resolved, or long and drawn out (see fig. 4). Few will last only a year or two before being resolved one way or the other—either they are caught early on and resolved peacefully, or they go on for many years with horrendous costs. The war in the former Yugoslavia demonstrates this clearly. Most observers believe the drawn-out war of attrition might have been avoided altogether had the Western powers, working in concert with the United Nations, tried harder early on to force a settlement. Without an early resolution, states begin to feel they have invested too much blood and treasure to give in, or that they can still win, and decide to press on.

These considerations were at work in Iran and Iraq's decision to pursue a long and costly war (1980–1989) after Iraq had failed to reach its objective soon after invading the Shatt al Arab Waterway. Similarly, the conflict between Indonesia and the Netherlands over West Irian (1962) could have resulted in a long and costly war of liberation, but because of the United Nations' quick and effective mediation, such an outcome was avoided and the conflict resolved in a few months.

States that do not resolve their conflicts early on tend to invest more and more in their effort to win, and in the end, these conflicts prove extremely costly in terms of human life. Although most conflicts resolve themselves before there have been thousands of fatalities, when conflicts go unchecked, fatalities

Figure 5   Number of disputes, by fatalities

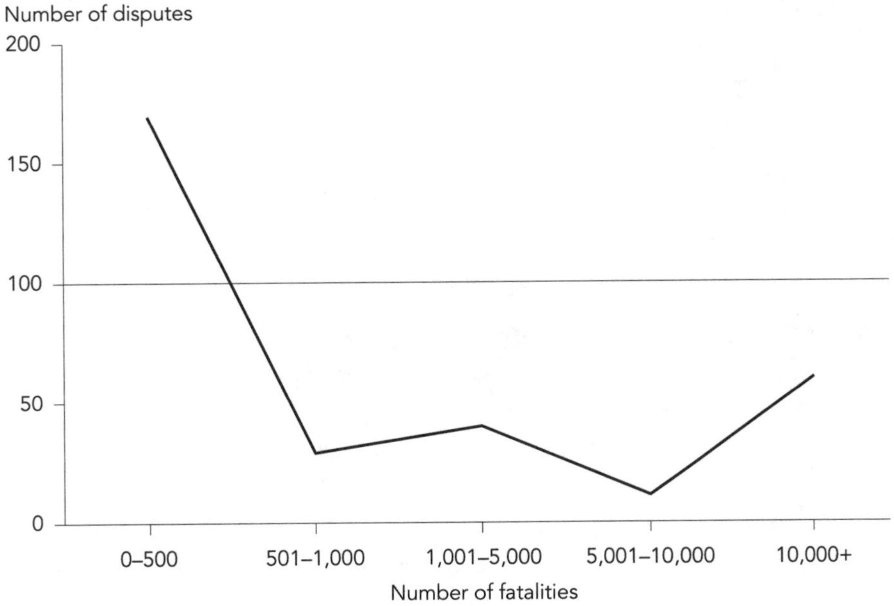

Number of disputes

may reach huge proportions (see fig. 5). Since 1945, sixty international armed conflicts have resulted in the loss of more than ten thousand lives. The Korean War, the Vietnam War, the Bangladesh war of independence, the Sudan and Mozambique conflicts, and Cambodia and Afghanistan have all cost more than a million lives each. Most of the dead were civilians, who were seen as legitimate targets, and many more died of disease and starvation brought about by war conditions.

When we look at why states resort to war, we see that territory and sovereignty are by far the most potent motivating factors (see fig. 6). The fundamental basis of every state is its territory and the control it has over that land. This makes it a most compelling issue whenever it is in dispute. States will go much further in defending their territory than they will over defending access to resources, for example. This is why most international conflicts that reach the point of armed confrontation are about territory. Even when the territory has little strategic or economic value, its symbolic value is sufficiently powerful to motivate states to go to war.

The Siachen glacier conflict between India and Pakistan (1984–) is a case in point. The area under dispute is remote, barren, difficult to get to, and many of the soldiers there die of the cold, avalanches, and accidents in the snow and ice. Despite this, both sides have invested vast amounts of resources and troops to continuing fighting, despite the unlikelihood of either side gaining a significant advantage. In contrast, no states went to war over the 1973 oil shocks, which involved access to vast supplies of essential resources.

The second most common reason a state gets involved in military conflicts

Figure 6   Primary issues of disputes

Number of disputes

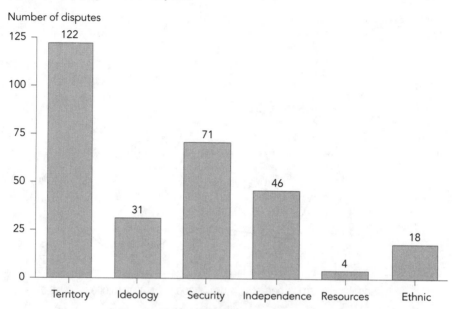

is where its security is threatened by interference from a rival state, or states, or from a group from within its own borders. Israel and South Africa have both launched attacks on other states because they felt their security was under threat. Israel attacked Lebanon in 1982 to protect its northern borders from Palestinian infiltrators, while South Africa launched raids into Botswana (1984–1986), Zambia (1987), and Lesotho (1982) to attack ANC bases.

Most conflicts, however, stemmed from more than one cause. Nearly all the conflicts we surveyed had multiple issues, especially those persisting for more than three years and involving large loss of life (see fig. 7). Over time, conflicts become reframed by the warring parties so that multiple interlocking issues are seen to be at stake; the struggle also becomes freighted with powerful symbolic meaning. The single-issue conflicts tend to be militarized disputes that were over quickly and involved few fatalities. For example, the *Mayaguez* incident between Cambodia and the United States (1975), the shelling incident between Taiwan and China (1994), and the Belize-Guatemala border incidents (1995) were all fairly simple conflicts in that they concerned single events that involved few fatalities.

Most states that resort to hostilities do so after a period of conflict that culminates in armed conflict. Few states that are friendly or that have few points of contact will end up in armed conflict with each other (see fig. 8). International armed conflicts represent a process that includes a relationship of conflict or rivalry that under certain conditions can lead to armed confrontation. Conflicts do not happen in a vacuum, and the roots of any war can almost always be traced back to a long history of antagonistic competition. Nearly all the conflicts were preceded either by antagonistic relations between the parties,

Figure 7   Issue complexity of disputes

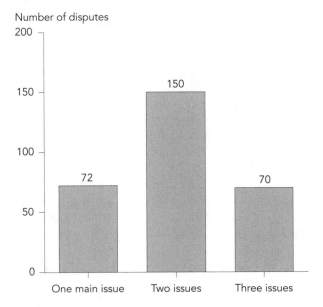

Figure 8   Previous relations of parties in dispute

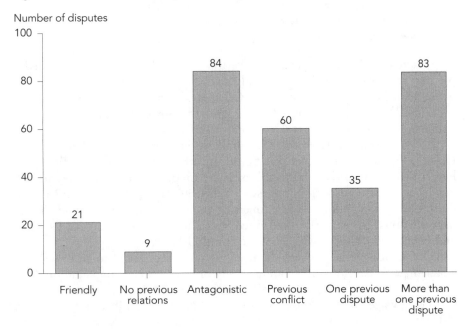

Figure 9   Dispute outcome

Number of disputes

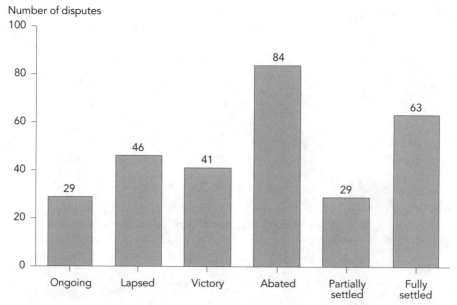

*Ongoing:*dispute continues without substantial progress.
Lapsed: dispute ends without agreement; issues no longer relevant.
Victory: dispute ends with one party winning.
*Abated:*potential dispute avoided before escalating into hostilities.
Partially settled: some issues resolved, although dispute persists.
Fully settled: all issues resolved.

or by actual violence. For example, Peru and Ecuador have long disputed a piece of territory in the Amazon, and their relations are characterized by frequent armed conflicts over the issue. Other rivals have been India and China, India and Pakistan, the United States and the Soviet Union, Ethiopia and Somalia, Vietnam and China, Uganda and Tanzania, and Iran and Iraq.

It is noteworthy that, of the 292 conflicts, only about 40 resulted in victories for one side or the other (see fig. 9). In other words, although the likelihood of victory is fairly remote (at least based on these statistics), states are still willing to initiate hostilities in pursuit of their goals. Of the few conflicts that did produce victory for one side, one side generally had a massive advantage over the other: for example, the United States' invasions of Grenada, Panama, and Haiti, and China's invasion of the Spratly Islands.

For the most part, however, the usual pattern is for states to go to war, for a stalemate to develop (either immediately or after a long campaign), and for negotiations to begin with the goal of ending the conflict. Case in point is the war being waged by the Polisario (Frente Popular para la Liberatión de Saguia el-Hamra y Rio de Oro) to free the Western Sahara from Moroccan control (1974–) has resulted in an impasse, despite Mauritania's support for the rebels.

Figure 10   Dispute outcome, by type of dispute

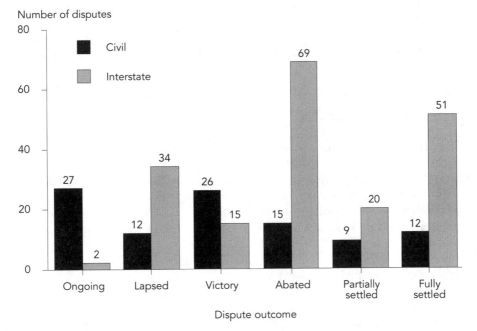

Ongoing:dispute continues without substantial progress.

Lapsed: dispute ends without agreement; issues no longer relevant.

Victory: dispute ends with one party winning.

*Abated:*potential dispute avoided before escalating into hostilities.

Partially settled: some issues resolved, although dispute persists.

Fully settled: all issues resolved.

Now, after twenty years of fighting, the United Nations is mediating the conflict.

Also of interest here is that nearly a third of these conflicts were at least partly settled through conflict management techniques such as mediation and negotiation. This is a significant achievement given the high number of international armed conflicts and their destructiveness—potential and real. Of more pressing concern are the (at this writing) thirty-one ongoing conflicts, of which many—such as Angola, Western Sahara, Afghanistan, Cambodia, Bosnia, and East Timor—have been extremely persistent and destructive. Furthermore, some conflicts have merely abated, making them potential flashpoints. Many of India's conflicts with its neighbors, and Israel's with the surrounding Arab states, fit into this category; it takes only a minor crisis to spark a major war. The war in Angola was thought to be over when elections were held in 1992, but UNITA's failure at the polls proved to be a flashpoint for further vicious fighting.

A comparison of conflict outcome with conflict type reveals the striking fact that nearly every ongoing conflict is civil (fig. 10), many of them brought on by the collapse of the Soviet Union. Also of concern are the many conflicts that have simply abated for the time being. These represent unresolved conflicts that no longer involve military hostilities. Many of these "rivalry relationships"—such as those between the Arabs and Israel, Ecuador and Peru, China and Vietnam, and others—are ripe for renewed military confrontation given the right circumstances.

The Need for Conflict Management

International conflicts can be very costly, particularly if they are not managed early on. We have already mentioned the millions of people, mainly civilians, who die because of fighting between states; other millions die as a result of starvation, disease, and exposure to the elements. War also produces vast refugee populations—millions of people on the move to escape the violence, without adequate food or shelter, who have to be cared for by neighboring countries and aid agencies. The U.N. estimates that there are presently some 28 million refugees worldwide. The war in Mozambique uprooted 1.7 million people, 1 million of whom fled to Malawi, one of the world's poorest countries that can hardly feed its own population.

Another cost of international conflict is the environmental damage caused by modern weapons. Dozens of Kuwaiti oil wells were blown up by retreating Iraqi forces in 1991, and devastating oil slicks ran up onto Gulf beaches. In Cambodia, the Khmer Rouge forces have strip-mined vast areas under their control in order to finance their insurgency with emeralds, while in the 1970s the United States defoliated Vietnamese forests using powerful Agent Orange chemicals.

Economically, conflicts are very costly. It costs money to finance armies and their offensives. War also diverts resources from health care, education, and infrastructural development. For example, it cost around $40 billion to finance the U.S.-led Coalition forces that defeated Iraq in the Gulf war (1990–1991). The postwar costs of reconstruction are also enormous. This is especially true in the poorer countries of Africa, Asia, and Latin America, where instability and insecurity have led to the financing of large armies at the expense of the poor.

States also lose out in trade opportunities in the event that neighbors close their borders and refuse any exchange. Even minor disputes can result in millions of dollars lost in trade opportunities as states have to reroute goods through other countries. For example, in the late 1960s, Zambia routed nearly all its copper exports through white-dominated Rhodesia (Zimbabwe). When Zimbabwean nationalist guerrillas, however, waged their war of independence (1967–1980), Zambian support for the rebel forces led to the closure of the then–Rhodesian-Zambian border. Zambia was therefore forced to devote vast sums to reroute its copper through other countries.

Finally, the international community usually has to donate millions or even billions of dollars toward emergency aid for postwar reconstruction. For example, more than a billion dollars has been pledged to rebuild the successor states of the former Yugoslavia.

Costs are also felt on the political level. Conflicts lead to tension, instability, and the threat of escalation. Routine governance becomes exceedingly difficult. The Middle East is an unstable region because the persistent, sporadic wars mean that politics can consist of little more than maintaining peace and security. In Africa, the social and political instability brought on by war erodes human rights and produces epidemics and famine. As a result, international companies are loath to invest in the region, and organizations like the OAU are unable to resolve conflicts.

Furthermore, armed conflicts represent the failure of international organizations, like the United Nations, and international policies to maintain peace. These failures contribute further to instability as states then feel that if the United Nations cannot solve their conflicts, they must take matters into their own hands.

These problems are further complicated by the proliferation of nuclear weapons. Although the threat of global nuclear war has evaporated with the end of the cold war, responsible nations rightly fear the emergence of unstable countries, and even terrorist organizations, with access to nuclear weapons. India and Pakistan came to the brink of nuclear confrontation over Kashmir in 1990, and it was only the United States' forceful intervention that averted further escalation. Iraq's attempts to acquire nuclear weapons are well known. Given the country's extremist leadership and foreign policy, it is horrifyingly possible to contemplate Iraq's use of such weapons.

These dangers underscore the urgent need to manage international conflict peacefully. As we have seen, it is not inevitable that conflicts between states escalate into hugely destructive and long, drawn-out wars. If they can be caught early on and managed effectively, they can be contained. In an attempt to do this, states and international organizations like the United Nations have developed a number of procedures and mechanisms to deal with their conflicts. These include direct negotiations, the use of mediators, arbitration by appointed international judges, conciliation by an investigating panel, or the help of international organizations like the United Nations, Organization of American States (OAS), and Organization of African Unity (OAU). These methods will be discussed in chapter 2.

Managing
International Conflict

International conflict is an immutable feature of international relations, with both good and bad corollaries. Its drawbacks—the staggering human and economic costs that threaten the order, stability, and very viability of international society—are obvious enough. At times, conflict has even threatened the existence of the international system, as with the Cuban Missile Crisis in 1962, when the superpowers came to the brink of nuclear war. But conflict can also bring about beneficial change. Examples include the guerrilla war waged by the South West Africa People's Organization (SWAPO), which eventually freed Namibia from South Africa's illegal and oppressive occupation (1966–1990). Conflict can also curb expansionist states, as with the Gulf war (1990–1991), which frustrated Saddam Hussein's designs not only on Kuwait but also on other states in the Gulf region.

Three postwar developments, however, have caused a shift in opinion about conflict: (1) the decolonization of the 1960s (whereby both the number of states and the potential for conflict proliferated), (2) the spread of nuclear weapons, and (3) the increasing destructiveness of conventional ones. Whereas conflict used to be an instrument of policy—one of the many ways by which an individual state might achieve its objectives—it was now viewed in a wholly negative light. The international system nevertheless had to find a functional equivalent to conflict—one that did not involve force (Claude 1964, 200).

War, then, has come to be seen as having such grave consequences that the international community has proscribed it until every other option has been exhausted (Claude 1964, 210). Even when states resort to war, their behavior is governed by certain norms. For example, only sovereign states possess the right to wage war, and traditional rules of war designate acceptable weapons, forbid the targeting of civilians, and dictate the treatment of POWs. In addition, the legitimacy of resorting to war in the first place is reserved for "just causes," and, once war has broken out, laws of neutrality contain its spread (Bull 1977, 188).

All social systems have established mechanisms for limiting and regulating conflict. Families have norms and informal rules; groups have customs and traditions; and states have legal and normative systems. Unregulated conflict is destructive and antithetical to the orderly functioning of social life. Without conflict-mitigating mechanisms, then, social systems break down into violence and anarchy and cease to function. The international system is no different. So, what methods, processes, or institutional arrangements are available to states (or nonstate international actors like ethnic groups or national liberation movements) that want to manage their conflicts without resort to violence? Just how effective are they?

In a section titled, "Pacific Settlement of Disputes," Article 33(1) of the U.N. Charter, states:

> The parties to any dispute, the continuance of which is likely to endanger the maintenance of international peace and security, shall, first of all, seek a solution by negotiation, enquiry, mediation, conciliation, arbitration, judicial settlement, resort to regional agencies or arrangements, or by other peaceful means of their own choice.

These methods will be considered below.

Dealing with International Conflict

Conflict management is often confused with *conflict prevention* or *conflict control*. This is regrettable. That is to say, conflict cannot be controlled; it can only be managed or resolved. To say that conflicts can be managed presupposes that conflicts are dynamic social processes that move from an incipient, latent stage to maturity and termination. It also suggests that conflicts have certain consequences for the parties involved as well as for the environment in which they occur.

The proper concern of conflict management is thus with increasing values and benefits and decreasing costs and harm. Conflict management is an attempt to inject some learning into the process of conflict, learning that can make it more productive and less costly. The primary purpose of conflict management is to arrest the escalation of violence and to create conditions that would permit benefits to accrue to adversaries who are considering peace. Of course, many factors influence conflict and its management. Among the most important of these are (a) the characteristics of the conflict parties, (b) the nature of the issues at stake, (c) the strategy and tactics employed by each party, and (d) the presence and activities of disinterested third parties.

Social systems have various procedures built into their structure for managing conflicts. Conflicts can be managed by institutional forms (e.g., collective bargaining), social roles (e.g., third parties), or social norms. Of these, legal regulation and bargaining and negotiation are perhaps the best-known methods. The international system has its own conflict-management procedures.

A conflict can be considered *settled* when hostile attitudes have been ameliorated and destructive behavior curtailed. A conflict is said to be *resolved* when the basic structure of the situation that originally gave rise to hostile attitudes and destructive behavior has been reevaluated, or perceived anew by the parties in conflict. Conflict management can therefore be directed either toward conflict settlement, or the more complex and durable outcome—conflict resolution.

When states have a conflict, they can either resort to violence (war or armed conflict) or employ one or more of the many peaceful methods of conflict management advocated by the United Nations. This is not to say that warring states have forfeited their ability to use peaceful methods. Often states will attempt violence first, only to realize that either the costs are too high for the potential benefits, or peaceful methods are a better way to achieve their goals.

Adversaries have three basic choices: They can (1) *manage* peacefully, (2) *confront* violently, or (3) *withdraw* from the conflict altogether. Morgenthau expresses these options as "diplomacy, war, and renunciation" (quoted in Sawyer and Guetzkow 1965, 466). Democratic states usually resolve their conflicts in a peaceful manner. Either that, or they can voluntarily withdraw from the conflict and renounce those actions that instigated the conflict. Again, these responses are common among friendly, democratic states like Britain and France.

Alternatively, states can go to war in an effort to physically overwhelm their opponent. The United States pursued this option in 1983 when it invaded Grenada; it did not even broach a peaceful solution. In the face of such attempts or threats of violence, states can simply submit. Haitian military leaders did this in 1994, acceding to U.N. and U.S. demands when the country was threatened with invasion by a much superior force.

States may also, as noted above, withdraw from the conflict and renounce their claims. This is often a useful choice if the costs of pursuing the conflict are higher than the expected gains of winning or compromising. In 1988 China took over the Spratly Islands after expelling the Vietnamese troops stationed there. Although Vietnam could have counterattacked, the potential costs of starting an all-out war with China would have been too high. As a consequence, they did nothing more than lodge a diplomatic protest.

Once states are in conflict—whether or not they have resorted to violence—they can peacefully manage their conflict in only two ways. First, they can try to solve their differences directly, or bilaterally, which will require them to negotiate in secret or out in the open. Second, they can enlist the support of a third party. Mediation, conciliation, adjudication, or referral to the United Nations are all examples of third-party intervention.

Another way to view peaceful conflict-management methods is to differentiate between legal and political conflicts. In other words, some conflicts lend themselves to a legal solution; others require political settlement. For example, when Iran nationalized its oil industry in 1951, the International Court of Justice (ICJ) was asked to rule on the legality of this move under international law. (Actually, the ICJ ruled on July 22, 1952, that it had no jurisdiction in the matter.) For those conflicts that cannot be settled by legal or quasi-legal procedures, a political solution is required. Distinguishing between political and legal issues in international conflicts is important, as the distinction bears directly on the effectiveness of legal methods of conflict management.

Approaches to Managing International Conflict

There are three approaches to conflict management. The first, advocated and pursued largely by states themselves, seeks to maintain the primacy of states in the international system through the use of bilateral negotiations. These negotiations keep the conflict-management process and outcome solely in the states' hands. Negotiation, mediation, and inquiry fulfill this need and are thus the most commonly utilized methods employed under the first approach. The parties in nearly all the 292 conflicts described in this book resorted to some negotiation or mediation, or both. States do not like to submit their conflicts to an outside power.

The second approach, advocated by both individuals concerned for international peace and order, and international lawyers, sees the establishment of international law as the panacea for international conflict. If states could be convinced or forced to submit their conflicts to international courts or tribunals, the thinking goes, the peaceful rule of law would prevail. This approach is at odds with the state-centered, bilateral approach, as arbitration and judicial settlement take away a great deal of control from states during the conflict-management process. This factor alone has made the legal approach unpopular. In most cases, states do not even subject their conflicts to such methods. Out of the hundreds of conflicts between states every year, the ICJ considers only a handful. Even then, when a state gets a judgment it believes unfavorable, it will ignore the ruling. When the ICJ ruled in favor of Chile in the Beagle Channel dispute (1952–1968), Argentina simply ignored the ruling and pressed its claims militarily.

The third, or "functionalist," approach sees the establishment of international organizations with specialized roles, such as the United Nations, as the most promising means of achieving peace and order in international relations. If states can cooperate in international organizations and use their peaceful-settlement mechanisms, these organizations might eventually perform functions like those of national governments and national legal systems, providing order in international society. Again, however, states are reluctant to relinquish any sovereignty to a body they cannot directly control. One example is Morocco, which has been fighting the Saharan nationalist group, Polisario, for control over the Western Sahara since 1974, and impeding U.N. attempts to hold a referendum there since 1992. It wants to run the referendum on its own terms, fearing the outcome of a U.N.-sponsored event.

These three approaches are mirrored in peaceful conflict-management methods: *diplomatic, legal,* and *political* means (Merrills 1991, ix). Diplomatic methods include traditional diplomacy, bargaining and negotiation, mediation, conciliation, and inquiry—all of which are determined and controlled entirely by the disputing states. Legal methods include arbitration and adjudication, or judicial settlement. Although the states sometimes negotiate the terms, methods, interpretation of outcomes, and so on, it is out of their hands once the legal method is under way. Political methods of conflict management are used by international organizations such as the United Nations, or a regional group, such as the European Union (EU) or the Organization of African Unity (OAU). The following section will examine these methods in a little more detail, focusing on their conceptual aspects, history, actual use in international relations, and their limitations.

Diplomatic Methods of Conflict Management

Diplomatic methods of conflict management may be thought of as a continuum, where adversaries will first try to solve their differences through normal diplomatic channels. If this fails, they may then progress to direct negotiations in a neutral environment. If unsuccessful here, they may then call in a third party to mediate, engage in conciliation, or hold an inquiry. In reality, however, states may choose to use one or all of these methods in any order, or even all at once. They may immediately negotiate, or a mediator may offer its services as soon as the conflict erupts.

Traditional Diplomacy

Traditional diplomacy refers to the official relationship between sovereign states and can be defined in the widest sense as the conduct of relations between states and other international actors by official agents and by peaceful means. Sir Ernest Satow has defined it more specifically as "the application of intelligence and tact to the conduct of official relations between the Governments of independent states. . . . [Traditional diplomacy is] the conduct of business between states by peaceful means" (quoted in Schuman 1969, 170).

Diplomacy became established in the seventeenth century when the international system was in its infancy. As interaction among emerging political units grew more intense, the need for permanent missions became obvious. These were first established in Renaissance Italy and by the eighteenth century had become common throughout western Europe. Today, most states have permanent diplomatic missions in the countries with which they have many interactions. Professional diplomats reside here and are a permanent link between the two states.

In a general sense, traditional diplomacy has several important functions. It eases both the negotiation of agreements and routine communication between the political leaders of states and other internationally recognized bodies. Diplomatic missions can also be used to gather intelligence, to reduce the effects of friction in international relations, and to symbolize the existence of the international society (Bull 1977, 170–172).

"Diplomacy is the continuing method of avoiding disputes" (Suter 1986, 8). Indeed, reducing friction and managing conflict is diplomacy's main function. When a conflict breaks out between two states, the senior diplomat, usually the ambassador or chargé d'affaires, is often expected to remain in close communication with the host government. These traditional diplomatic channels are then used to transmit messages between the disputing states in the search for a peaceful settlement.

Although traditional diplomacy is used every day to manage minor conflicts and misunderstandings, such as trade disputes, it is less well suited for managing violent conflicts. In fact, historically speaking, the onset of war usually led to the breaking off of diplomatic relations (Frankel 1969, 146). This practice continues to this day, where a conflict will escalate through several stages before all-out war is reached. A first stage involves expelling all the diplomats of the opposing country to signal the seriousness of the conflict. In this situation, traditional diplomacy is of little use in managing conflict because no diplomats are in place to talk with each other.

Other developments in contemporary international relations have also limited the usefulness of diplomacy for conflict management. First, ambassadors and resident diplomats are often unnecessary when heads of government can simply fly to another capital or talk directly with their counterparts. Modern transport and communications have made diplomats somewhat redundant. Second, states meet all the time in organizations like the United Nations and do not need to arrange special bilateral meetings. Many important diplomatic questions are now addressed in a multilateral context. Third, technical experts have replaced diplomats in negotiating agreements, while intelligence-gathering organizations have overtaken the diplomats' former function of gathering information and intelligence. Finally, the rules and conventions of diplomatic institutions have deteriorated in the postwar period. Diplomats are often vulnerable to physical attacks, surveillance, and other abuse (Bull 1977, 173–179).

For example, the U.S.-Iran hostage crisis (1979–1981) began when the Iranian government allowed radical students to ignore the traditional sanctity of embassies and to seize the diplomatic staff in complete violation of international agreements. Incidents involving the mistreatment of diplomats by host countries are now commonplace.

Bargaining and Negotiation. All these developments severely constrain the usefulness of traditional diplomacy in managing conflicts. As a result, states are often forced to turn to direct negotiation. In reality, negotiation is the principal means of handling all international disputes, including economic and trade disputes, and is employed more frequently than all other methods of conflict management put together (Merrills 1991, 2)—although this is not to say that negotiation is the most successful method of managing conflict. Negotiation is the process by which states exchange proposals in an attempt to agree about a point of conflict. It has been used for conflict management since relations between states began and has always been the primary method of attempting to solve disputes. As Suter has observed:

> Direct negotiation between sides in a dispute is the ideal way to resolve conflict on all levels. It is the most efficient method because it requires the least formality, eliminates the expense of third parties and helps avoid adversary proceedings which often aggravate hostility. The complexity of the communication problem may be reduced. . . . Privacy of discussion allows for flexibility and candour so important issues can be discussed with fewer risks. One of the major advantages of bilateral negotiations is that they can be more binding. Mutual consent to a resolution gives it legitimacy. (1986, 10)

This is not to say that negotiation is the perfect conflict-management method. Its record of failure in preventing, managing, or resolving many recent international conflicts is a testament to that. Most of the conflicts between 1945 and 1995 involved negotiation at some point, but many of these efforts did not succeed. In fact, negotiation has its limitations. For example, negotiations cannot even take place if the disputing states have broken off diplomatic contact and refuse to have anything to do with each other, or do not even recognize each other officially. A case in point is the conflict between Israel and the Palestine Liberation Organization (PLO), which for years refused to recognize each other or to speak officially. This prevented any attempts at conflict management until they commenced secret negotiations in Norway in 1993.

Also, negotiations are of little use when the states in conflict have few or no common interests and their respective positions are wildly divergent, as was true with the United States and North Vietnam during the Vietnam War (1964–1975). Despite many years of negotiations in Paris, they were unable to reach any accommodation. Negotiations need a strong motivation, a basic trust, and an overlapping field of interest. Further, the failure of negotiations can encourage the use of force by seeming to eliminate all other alternatives (Merrills 1991, 22–26). In the recently concluded conflict in Chechnya (1992–1995), the breakdown in talks between Russian and Chechen officials usually signaled the resumption of fierce fighting.

Mediation. When states reach an impasse in their negotiations, or cannot commence them (because there are no communication channels or few areas of mutual interest), they will often resort to mediation, which can be defined as a conflict-management method where an outside party helps adversaries to solve their differences peacefully. Outside parties can be individuals like former U.S. president Jimmy Carter, representatives of international organizations like the U.N. secretary-general Kofi Annan, or state officials like Madeleine K. Albright, the U.S. secretary of state. Essentially, mediation is the injection of a third party into negotiations designed to help the disputants find an acceptable solution.

Like negotiation, mediation has been employed by states for conflict management since states began to have conflicts; the method is widely used in international relations. Typically, the role of a mediator is to take the thread of negotiations into his own hands; to discuss with the parties, jointly and/or separately, their proposals for ending the dispute; to act . . . as a channel of communication between the parties if necessary; to suggest proposals of his own; to play an active role in narrowing the gap between the two sides; and possibly even to serve as the guarantor of the settlement ultimately reached, if any. (Northedge and Donelan 1971, 297)

For example, Cyrus Vance and Lord Owen, mediating in the Balkans conflict (1989–1995), would typically take the various faction leaders to a house in a neutral country like Switzerland. They would then give them carefully thought out proposals for ending the conflict. When appropriate, the Vance-Owen team would also separate the leaders into different rooms and shuttle messages between them. When the faction leaders were intransigent, Vance and Owen sought to win them over with promises of material aid or to intimidate them with threats of air strikes and sanctions.

For mediation to occur at all, however, willing mediators must step forward and disputants must accept the mediation and the mediators. In most instances, mediation occurs when (1) disputes are long, complex, and drawn out; (2) conflict-management attempts have failed; (3) both sides are eager to limit further costs and escalation; and (4) the disputants have a degree of willingness to cooperate and seek a peaceful solution (Bercovitch 1984.).

Conciliation. Although an important and effective method of conflict management, mediation is limited by the mediator's abilities and resources, the nature of the conflict (which may not be amenable to mediation), and ultimately, the adversaries' willingness and flexibility. If the disputants are inflexible and unwilling even to talk, then conciliation may be employed. Conciliation has been described as "an attempt to induce negotiations" (Bailey 1982, 167). But it may be described more formally as "a method for the settlement of international disputes of any nature according to which a commission set up by the parties, either on a permanent basis or an ad hoc basis to deal with a dispute, proceeds to the impartial examination of the dispute and attempts to define the terms of a settlement" (Merrills 1991, 59). That is, two states in conflict nominate officials to sit on a panel. The panel then gathers all relevant information on the conflict, examines it, and suggests ways to settle it. Another way to conceive of conciliation is to think of it as "institutionalized negotiation" (Merrills 1991, 67).

Theoretically, the line between conciliation and mediation is difficult to draw. Suffice it to say that conciliation formalizes the third-party intervention, institutionalizing it to a greater degree (Merrills 1991, 39). It is usually instituted by treaty. The conciliator's role is to propose either the rules governing the settlement—that is, the means by which the parties shall come to agreement—or the terms of the settlement itself (Suter 1986, 11). Historically, conciliation emerged out of treaty practice in Europe and reached its height between 1925 and World War II, when nearly two hundred treaties involving conciliation were concluded (Merrills 1991, 61). Since then, it has declined. In fact, when compared with other methods of conflict management, conciliation has never been widely used. Of the thousands of conflicts and disputes over the past seventy years, fewer than twenty cases of formal conciliation have been heard (Merrills 1991, 76). Informal conciliation through international organizations is used only slightly more often.

The reasons for the relative inutility of conciliation are many. First, many bilateral treaties restrict the categories of disputes open for conciliation to a small area of relatively unimportant issues. Areas of political concern, where conflicts are most likely to occur and most likely to be violent, are not covered by the treaties. Second, the expense and difficulties involved in convening and operating a conciliation often make other procedures more attractive. Third, conciliation is too elaborate for many minor disputes and lacks the political authority for major disputes. In short, conciliation has demonstrated some success only for disputes that were strictly legal and of minor importance (Merrills 1991, 76–77).

Inquiry. Another conflict-management method resembling conciliation is inquiry, which is "a specific institutional arrangement which states may select in preference to arbitration or other techniques because they desire to have some disputed issue independently investigated. In its institutional sense, then, inquiry refers to a particular type of international tribunal, known as the commission of inquiry" (Merrills 1991, 43). In other words, inquiry is the attempt by a third party to "establish the relevant facts and to elucidate those aspects of the dispute where incomplete or misleading information has been an unnecessary cause of contention" (Bailey 1982, 162–163).

Like conciliation, inquiry is a fairly recent and little-used addition to the range of conflict-management methods. This is because it is designed only for dealing with conflicts that revolve around disputed facts or information. Only four inquiries were conducted between 1905 and 1922. Another took place in 1962 but there have been no inquiries since then (Merrills 1991, 55). Although international organizations make much more use of it than suggested by these figures, the inquiry remains a relatively unimportant method of conflict management in international relations.

Legal Methods of Conflict Management

As has been mentioned, legal methods of conflict management represent the attempt to establish *international law* as the primary means of maintaining order in international society. A discussion of international law is necessary if we are to examine arbitration and adjudication. When we talk about law, we are referring to a "general rule which covers a specific class of cases, and which is backed by a probable sanction, stated in advance and widely accepted as legitimate" (Deutsch 1978, 201). International law then, may be conceived of as "a body of rules which binds states and other agents in world politics in their relations with one another and is considered to have the status of law" (Bull 1977, 127). Although, as we shall see, the status of international law differs from that of domestic law.

The functions of international law, and domestic law for that matter, are, first, to regulate interaction and interrelations in such a way that they can proceed in an orderly and efficient manner. For example, international law regulates the treatment of diplomats and the keeping of treaties. Second, international law fosters orderly change in the society of nations, permitting the system to adapt itself to changing circumstances without being violently disrupted. Third, it functions to limit and control the destructive or disorderly effects of conflict on the system. That is, it provides conflict-resolution mechanisms. Finally, from a more sociological perspective, we might say that international law functions to identify and embody the idea of a society of sovereign states (Delbruck 1987, 133–134; Bull 1977), in much the same way that domestic law provides a sense of identity and nationhood.

Because rules are so vital to the existence of society (no society can exist without them), the history of international law is as old as the international system itself. Among the many elements contributing to the development of international law, the most fundamental are the need to limit the use of force and the need for cooperation (Fawcett 1971, 19–20). After the medieval feudal system disintegrated and the first European states emerged, states cooperated or fought as they saw fit. Although the international system in the seventeenth and eighteenth centuries has thus been called anarchic, despite the reign of sovereign monarchs, certain basic rules of conduct, or rules of international law, were developed and observed. These were formulated primarily to regulate mutual relations in peace and conflict.

In the nineteenth century, when the idea of the state took hold, international rules of law developed at a fast pace. The Act of the Vienna Congress, the Peace Treaty of 1856 ending the Crimean War, the Acts of the Berlin Congress (1875, 1888), and the Act of the Brussels Congress (1890) were all important steps in codifying international relations. Furthermore, international rules of law provided criteria for settling disputes (Delbruck 1987, 128, 132). International law was refined and developed even further in the twentieth century. Most important, from the pioneering of the League of Nations following World War I, to the establishment of the United Nations in 1945, international law has sought to create centralized, authoritative mechanisms for regulating state relations and resolving conflict.

Contemporary international law, then, attempts to prohibit states from engaging in activities that are likely to disturb international peace and security. It also attempts to encourage those activities that are conducive to establishing a peaceful order, such as the regulation of economic, social, communications, and environmental matters (Delbruck 1987, 136–137; Bull 1977, 146).

Arbitration. International law provides two basic mechanisms for managing conflict—arbitration and adjudication. The Hague Convention for the Pacific Settlement of International Disputes (1907) offers the following definition: "International arbitration has for its object the settlement of disputes between states by judges of their own choice, and on the basis of respect for law. Recourse to arbitration implies an engagement to submit in good faith to the award" (quoted in Schuman 1969, 157). In other words, states in conflict agree to turn their dispute over to arbitrators who will decide between them on the basis of international law.

For example, when Chile and Argentina began to dispute the ownership of the Beagle Channel after World War II, they both submitted their claims to the ICJ. The ICJ judges investigated the relevant information and treaties and ruled that on the basis of international law, Chile was the rightful owner. Argentina later repudiated this ruling.

Arbitrators may use four sources of law to decide a dispute: (1) international conventions that have established rules recognized by the states; (2) international custom, as evidence of a general practice accepted as law; (3) the general principles of law recognized by civilized nations; and (4) judicial decisions and teachings by recognized experts (Bull 1977, 17). Furthermore, arbitration may proceed by means of ad hoc tribunals, or individual arbitrators. For example, in some cases, the states may establish a commission. In other cases, they may refer to a foreign head of state or specially qualified individual, or they may use a tribunal or collegiate body (Merrills 1991, 80–83). Normal practice is to have an odd number of judges, with each party having at least one of their own representatives on the panel.

The use of arbitration may be traced back to classical Greece. During the Middle Ages the pope often served as arbitrator. Interestingly, the pope also mediated the Beagle Channel conflict (1977–1984) between Argentina and Chile after Argentina rejected the ICJ's ruling and pressed its claims militarily. Although the arbitration system fell into disuse with the rise of the state system, it was revived in the nineteenth and early twentieth centuries (Suter 1986, 62). Even at its height, however, in comparison to other forms of conflict management, arbitration was never utilized to any great degree.

Adjudication. Like arbitration, adjudication (or judicial settlement) has also been little used by states. Adjudication refers to "the reference of a dispute to the World Court or some other standing tribunal, such as the European Court of Human Rights" (Merrills 1991, 80). In other words, the only essential difference between arbitration and adjudication is the manner in which the judges are chosen. They are identical in all other respects. In arbitration, states choose judges themselves, whereas in adjudication, states refer to established courts. The Permanent Court of International Justice (PCIJ), established by the League of Nations as the first such permanent court, heard only thirty-three contentious cases, while its successor, the International Court of Justice (ICJ), has heard little more than one case for every year of its existence (Northedge and Donelan 1971, 313–315).

Despite this sorry record, legal methods do have some advantages. In a general sense, legal methods supply a rational, orderly, and authoritative way of settling disputes. More specifically, the binding, impartial decisions handed down by arbitrators and adjudicators not only allow for states under domestic pressure to save face but also legitimize the successful party's claim in the eyes of the international community. Litigation is a good way to dispose of troublesome issues, and it gives states confidence in the process when they can choose judges. Permanent tribunals also relieve states of the need to set up new tribunals for every new dispute. In a general sense, legal methods discourage unreasonable behavior by reminding states that there are alternatives to violence. Surprisingly, arbitral awards are usually observed (Merrills 1991, 104–105, 153–154, 237–240).

The Limitations of International Law. Nevertheless, the legal methods of conflict management have serious limitations, and these are especially evident in three regards: enforcement, judicial scope, and the advent of nonstate actors. International law differs from the domestic law of nations because it has no enforcement machinery. If a state is determined to violate international law, no central authority or coercive machinery exists to prevent or punish that state. In other words,

> The difference between international law and the domestic law of countries lie[s] not in their character as law or in the kind of order they are designed to support, but in the actual distribution of power in the countries they serve, and in the degree to which that distribution has itself been reduced to order. A national community is one in which there is a very large number of weak units of power, so that sanctions against breaches of the law are normally effective and easy to maintain. . . . The international community is one in which there is a small number of units of power, of which some are enormous, most are considerable, and none are negligible. (Fawcett 1971, 15)

This problem strikes at the very heart of international law and means that observance of international law is based on considerations other than the threat of coercion. In international relations, self-enforcement is the basis for the observance of international law, and this self-enforcement proceeds from calculations that states make regarding their self-interest. The first calculation they make is that the costs and benefits of observing international law make observance a better option. For example, both Iran and Iraq have suffered greatly from being sanctioned by the international community when they flouted international laws. Iran was sanctioned when it violated the U.S. Embassy in 1979, and Iraq for its 1990 invasion of Kuwait.

Obedience to international law is obtained by the threat of coercion and negative world and/or domestic opinion. Finally, states obey international law because they have an interest in reciprocal action by others—action that would not be forthcoming if they were to scorn international rules of behavior (Deutsch 1978, 202-205; Bull 1977, 139). If a state were to ignore some treaty obligations, it might find its treaties with other states likewise spurned.

A second shortcoming of the legal methods of conflict management concerns judicial scope. Legal methods do not adequately address political questions. Inasmuch as few disputes relate purely to legal questions, litigation is suitable for very few international conflicts. It can even be argued that as states are political entities, that even strictly legal questions are never truly divorced from political considerations. Thus, most states are reluctant to use judicial methods where political interests are involved (Merrills 1991, 140, 150), which excludes nearly every armed conflict in modern times.

The third limitation is that law is a very conservative creature that does not adjust easily to change. The many changes in the nature and make-up of the international system have not been matched by appropriate changes in international law. For example, the main body of current international law originated in the European state system. As such, international law has little relevance for many new African and Asian states, which have no cultural affinity with it. Also, most international law sees only the state as a valid subject of law, whereas the contemporary international system contains a multitude of important nonstate actors, such as international organizations, ethnic groups, liberation movements, and powerful multinational companies. Yet many of the actors involved in internal conflicts do not qualify as states and, therefore, have no recourse to international law.

For example, the Kurdish minorities fighting for independence in both Iraq and Turkey have no legal standing in the international community, as they do not constitute a state. Therefore, even if they were to submit their dispute to an international court, the court would be unable to make a ruling because the Kurds are not a legally recognized member of the international community. The Iraqi Kurds have frequently appealed to the United Nations, alleging state-sanctioned genocide, but the world body has ignored them.

Political Methods of Conflict Management

Political methods of conflict management originate in the "functionalist" theory of international relations. More specifically,

> The theory of *functionalism* in international relations is based on the hope that more and more common tasks will be delegated to such specific functional organizations and that each of these organizations will become in time *supranational*; that is, superior to its member governments in power and authority. In this way, says the theory, the world's nations will gradually become integrated into a single community within which war will be impossible. (Deutsch 1978, 208)

These *international organizations,* or *intergovernmental organizations* (IGOs), usually have a dual task. They work to encourage intergovernmental cooperation in many areas, such as air traffic control, the international postal system, and global environmental controls. Also, they provide mechanisms and forums for the settlement of international disputes. Examples of such IGOs include the Universal Postal Union (UPU, founded in 1874), the International Telecommunication Union (ITU, 1932), the International Civil Aviation Organization (ICAO), the International Labor Organization (ILO, 1919), the Food and Agriculture Organization (FAO, 1945), and the World Health Organization (WHO, 1948).

The United Nations. The most important IGO today, however, is the United Nations, established in 1945 as a successor to the League of Nations. Both the League and the U.N. were born out of the chaos of a world war and reflected the hope that functionalism and collective security could provide a guarantee of peace and order in the international system. As such, they both had built-in mechanisms for conflict settlement. Currently, states in conflict can settle their differences through the United Nations by submitting their dispute to the U.N. Security Council, which then recommends a course of action. Actually, unlike other methods of conflict management, the Security Council does not need the disputing parties' consent to consider any conflict; under the U.N. Charter, the Security Council has the right to consider any conflict that might pose a threat to international peace and stability.

The U.N. Security Council can also appoint mediators or mediating committees, it can instruct the secretary-general to use his good offices, it can refer the dispute to regional organizations or other specialist agencies, or it can itself promote quiet negotiation between the disputants (Merrills 1991, 180–195). Furthermore, unlike other methods of conflict management, the Security Council can, theoretically at least, enforce its decisions "by any means." Usually, this includes imposing sanctions and military intervention. The United Nations has also employed peacekeeping operations in an attempt to keep disputant forces apart while a negotiated settlement is sought.

Typically, as with the first Kashmir war between India and Pakistan in 1947, the United Nations would appeal for a cease-fire when the fighting flared. Then it would send a mediator or mediation committee to gather information and bring the parties together. In 1948 the world body sent the U.N. Kashmir Commission to India and Pakistan on such a mission. Following this, and with the parties' permission, the United Nations might send peace-keeping troops to separate the warring factions and monitor a cease-fire.

Since the U.N.'s inception, states in conflict have used the world organization to manage their disputes. The United Nations has been involved to some extent in almost all armed conflicts since 1945, whether it be direct consideration in the Security Council, the sending of a fact-finding mission to the area of conflict, or mediation by U.N. personnel. Even the short-lived League of Nations (which was founded after World War I but collapsed at the outset World War II) considered sixty-six political disputes. Again, however, in comparison with negotiation and mediation, disputants have generally avoided conflict management by IGOs—realizing, perhaps, the limitations of IGOs in addressing international conflicts.

The Limitations of the United Nations. States will not submit their disputes to the United Nations unless they can foresee some advantage in doing so. Although the United Nations can consider a dispute without a state's permission, the world body has little hope of peacefully managing the conflict without it. In other words, the United Nations has scant power apart from that exercised by its members. This means it can do little, by itself, to enforce the process or outcome of peaceful conflict management (Claude 1964, 209–210). For example, the United Nations worked frantically to bring about a cease-fire and to separate the warring parties in the Balkans conflict (1989–1995), but the world body was for the most part simply ignored; it could do nothing to force the factions to the negotiating table.

Second, the United Nations is limited by the composition of its membership. Nonstate actors, such as liberation movements and rebel groups, cannot be members and are therefore unable to use U.N. machinery. Furthermore, the U.N. principle of noninterference in a country's internal affairs gives many states and nonstate actors a powerful tool—either to suppress internal unrest or to foment rebellion without fear of U.N. intervention. Internal conflicts, which are the most intractable kind to resolve, are overtaking interstate violence as the most common conflict in the international system since the end of the cold war. The failure of the United Nations to prevent the carnage in Rwanda is the most dramatic example of the organization's powerlessness in the face of civil conflicts.

Third, political factors severely constrain the United Nations, so much so that "the field of dispute settlement with which the United Nations has been concerned has been defined by the major political forces of the post-1945 period. . . . The tension between the United States and the Soviet Union has excluded a major group of disputes from the organization, while permitting or requiring its involvement in others" (Merrills 1991, 204). In other words, the world body could not tackle conflicts that involved superpower interests because the United States or the Soviet Union would simply veto any action it might want to take. The United Nations' involvement in the Korean War occurred only because the Soviet Union was not at the meeting to cast its veto when the vote was taken.

Fourth, conflict management is not the U.N.'s strong point. Saadia Touval argues that the world organization does not serve well as an authoritative channel of communication, it has little political leverage, its threats and promises lack credibility, and it is incapable of pursuing coherent, flexible, and dynamic negotiations guided by an effective strategy (1994, 45). For these and other reasons, states tend to turn to the United Nations as a last resort (Suter 1986, 94; Touval 1994). This further damages the United Nations' reputation, as conflicts that states have been unable to solve become associated instead with U.N. failure. For example, the United Nations was called in after regional actors failed to resolve the Somalian civil war (1988–). By this time, it was intractable and the world organization was forced to pull out in humiliating failure.

Regional Organizations. The U.N. encourages states to refer their conflicts to regional organizations before coming to the world body. Regional organizations are agencies created by treaty among states in a recognizable geographical area. There are two main kinds of regional organizations: collective defense organizations like the North Atlantic Treaty Organization (NATO) and regional arrangements or agencies like the Organization of African Unity (OAU).

The most important regional organizations include the OAU, the Organization of American States (OAS), the Arab League, the Association of South-East Asian Nations (ASEAN), the European Union (EU), and the Islamic

Country Organization (ICO). Most of these groups originated in the postwar period and, like the United Nations, all have built-in mechanisms of conflict management. In fact, for some like the OAU, conflict management among its members is its primary purpose. Most regional organizations effectively use mediation, conciliation, fact-finding, arbitration, and good offices in attempting to settle disputes. In other words, this represents conflict management *through* rather than *by* regional organizations (Merrills 1991, 217). Furthermore, regional agencies have addressed many conflicts since 1945—in several important cases, successfully.

The Limitations of Regional Organizations. Like the United Nations, however, regional organizations have several limitations. They are restricted to intraregional disputes and have little to offer the multitude of interregional conflicts (Merrills 1991, 219). For example, the OAS was of little use during the Falklands war (1982) between Argentina and Great Britain. Furthermore, like the United Nations, regional agencies are limited by problems of enforcement, political constraints, lack of resources, dependence on the political will of member states for action, and an inherent inability to interfere or involve themselves in internal disputes. Again, this usually means that states will attempt to resolve their conflicts bilaterally before submitting to a regional agency.

Patterns of Conflict Management, 1945–1995

In our study of international conflicts from 1945 to 1995, we paid close attention to the way each conflict was managed. When adversaries spurned outside help or refused to discuss their differences, we coded these conflicts as having no conflict management. Frequently, one side was much stronger than the other and simply overwhelmed the weaker party. Thus, they saw no need to negotiate an agreement. The United States' 1983 invasion of Grenada is a case in point.

If, on the other hand, the parties bargained with each other in some form or accepted outside assistance, we coded these conflicts as having undertaken negotiation, mediation, arbitration, referral to an international organization, or in a few cases, multilateral conference. Multilateral conferences occurred in complex conflicts involving several important disputants, such as the Trieste conflict (1952–1954), where Italy, Yugoslavia, and several Allied nations met in a conference in London in an effort to find a permanent solution.

Each case of conflict management was coded separately by determining the beginning and end dates of an effort and identifying the individuals involved. This way, for example, we could say that Lord Owen and Cyrus Vance undertook more than twenty mediations during the Balkans conflict (1989–1995), and China and Vietnam negotiated twelve times over the Spratly Islands (1988). A number of conflicts (76 out of 292) were not managed at all (see table 2). In other words, although less than a quarter of the disputants shunned peaceful solutions, more than three-quarters engaged in some form of peaceful

Table 2 Conflict-Management Type, by period

	1945–55	1956–65	1966–75	1976–85	1986–90	1991–95	TOTAL
No management	7	20	9	21	8	11	76
Mediation	119	183	363	532	170	428	1,795
Negotiation	70	85	128	222	71	146	722
Arbitration	0	0	0	2	0	0	2
Referral to int'l organizations	10	19	16	17	1	0	63
Multilateral conference	3	8	0	6	6	3	26

conflict management. Of the 76 unmanaged conflicts, most of these occurred during the cold war period (1956–1985), when many organizations, especially the United Nations, were prevented from intervening in certain conflicts because of competing superpower interests.

The data in table 2 highlight the states' preference for diplomatic methods of conflict management (mediation and negotiation), which maximize state control. States rarely allow international organizations or tribunals to settle a conflict, an unwillingness that reflects the perceived limitations of these methods.

When we turn to look at the effectiveness of each type of conflict management (see fig. 11), the states' reluctance to use international organizations is evinced once again, as they appear to be far less effective at settling conflicts. By way of contrast, mediation and negotiation seem to offer a relatively high chance of success, while allowing states to maintain control over the process. Arbitration's singular lack of success is explained by the small number of cases involved; it also reflects the fact that few conflicts that reach the stage of armed confrontation are amenable to a purely legal settlement. Arbitration is best suited to conflicts over points of law that have not been complicated by violence or other political considerations.

States, then, prefer diplomatic methods of managing their conflicts, and, indeed, as we see in figure 12, negotiation is a highly successful form of conflict management. Nearly half of all negotiations end in a settlement or cease-fire. This compares well with the other diplomatic method, mediation, where the rate of success is only around 35 percent. Nondiplomatic methods are even less successful.

When armed conflicts break out, however, the first response is often to expel the opposing country's diplomats and break off all contacts. This makes negotiation difficult, if not impossible. Mediation, then, becomes the preferred method of conflict management, as its flexibility allows the disputants to bargain without relinquishing control over the peace process and, if necessary, without having to face each other at a table. More than a third of all mediations are successful in achieving either a cease-fire, or a partial or full settlement (see fig. 13).

Figure 11   Conflict-management types and their effectiveness (%)

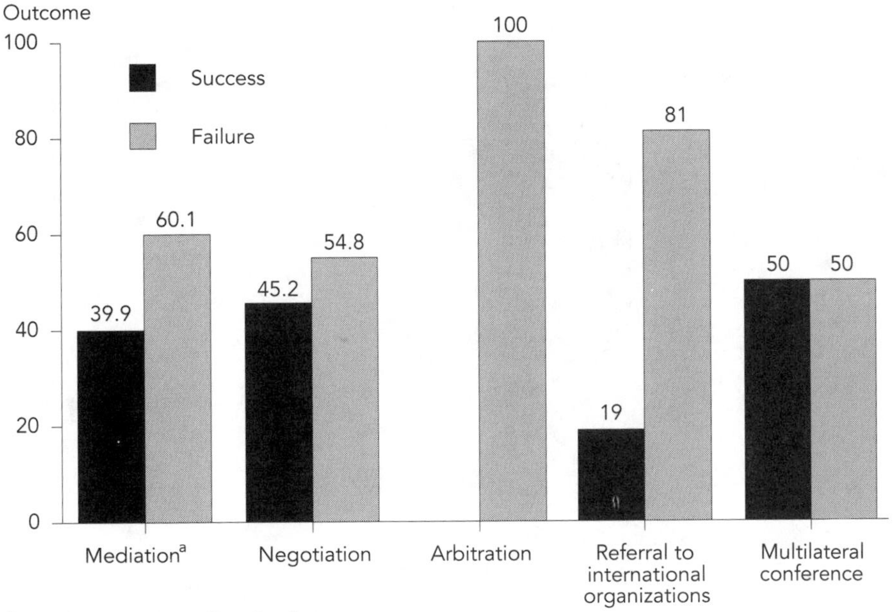

Outcome

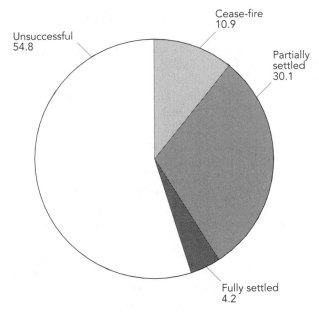

^aDoes not include "offered only."

Figure 12   Negotiation outcome (%)

Cease-fire
10.9

Unsuccessful
54.8

Partially
settled
30.1

Fully settled
4.2

Figure 13   Mediation outcome (%)

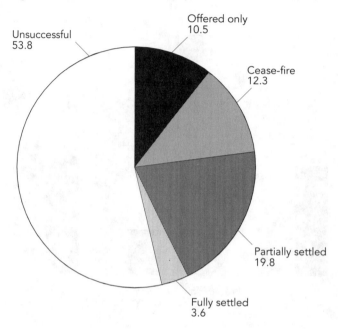

Most often, states themselves act as mediators (see fig. 14), as they may have interests in the conflict, or they may be closely aligned with one or both sides. This alignment gives them both an obligation and an opportunity for fruitful intervention. This is especially true for large states, who often have wide-ranging interests and a stake in the outcome of many conflicts. The United States, for example, has been actively mediating in the Middle East since the 1960s, not only because it has strategic interests in the region but also because it is closely aligned with Israel and is therefore in a stronger position to exert some leverage when pressing for concessions.

Comparatively speaking, international organizations do little mediating. This is partly because adversaries are encouraged to take their disputes to regional organizations first, and only if this fails to proceed to the United Nations. Regional organizations, furthermore, are especially equipped to deal with conflicts in their locale. The OAS has actively attempted to mediate in nearly every conflict involving its members, and the OAU has conflict management as one of its primary functions. The Economic Community of West African States (ECOWAS), a West African regional organization, has been the principal mediator in the Liberian civil war since it broke out in December 1989; it has even sent peace-keeping forces.

Most mediation efforts have focused on African and Middle Eastern conflicts (see fig. 15) because these regions have experienced the most postwar conflict overall. Interestingly, Europe has experienced relatively few conflicts compared with the Middle East, although it has received nearly as many mediation

Figure 14   Type of mediator (%)

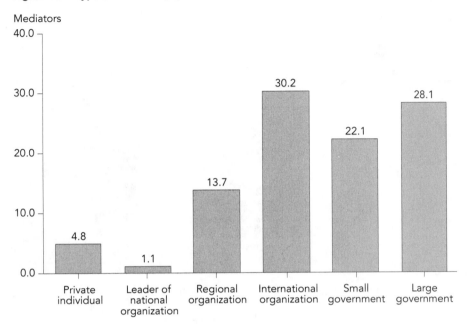

Figure 15   Mediations, by region (%)

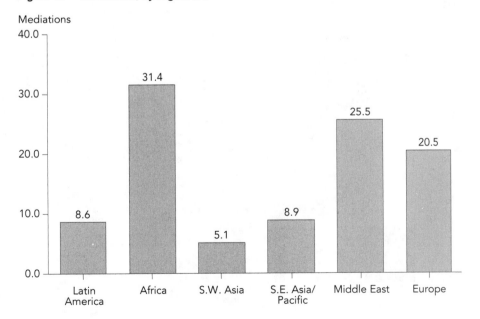

Figure 16   Functional mediation, by outcome

Number of mediations

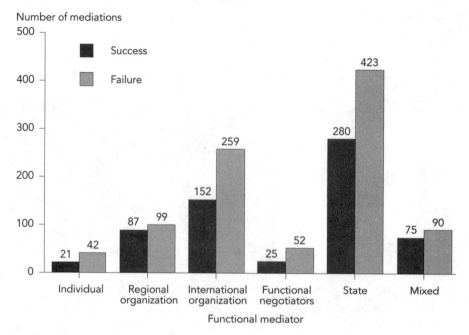

Functional mediator

Figure 17   U.N. involvement in disputes

Frequency of U.N. involvement

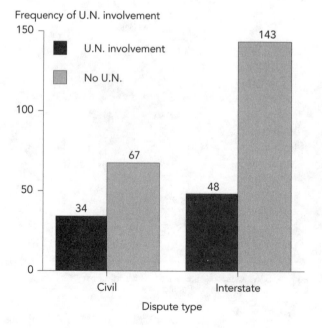

Dispute type

efforts (see fig. 3).This disparity is mostly explained by the war in the Balkans (1989–1995), which roused fears of a wider European war and thus garnered a great deal of diplomatic attention. More than 150 mediation attempts were made in the Balkans war before a settlement was reached in Dayton, Ohio, in November 1995.

Regional organizations appear to make the best, if not the most prolific, mediators (see fig. 16). Their success and failure rates are almost equal. States and international organizations are not always as successful as the regional bodies. Mixed groups of mediators, such as the Vance-Owen team in the Yugoslav war, also had respectable success rates. In cases mediated by mixed groups, separate members of the team can resort to different types of resources, and use their different relationships with the parties, to push for a settlement.

Although states have been the primary actors in managing international conflict, the United Nations has also played an important role. Its involvement in international conflict management has several interesting features (see fig. 17). First, on the whole, the U.N. has been more involved in interstate conflicts than in civil conflicts. This is not just because there have been more of the former than the latter, but also, as we discussed earlier, because the United Nations is designed primarily to deal with states and their affairs. Civil conflicts usually involve groups that do not belong to the United Nations, such as the Kurds in Iraq and Turkey, who cannot make use of the United Nations' conflict-management resources. The U.N. is also prevented in principle from interfering in the domestic affairs of member states.

U.N. involvement is fairly low, however, as a proportion of interventions in all interstate disputes (see fig. 17). This, again, reflects the states' preference for managing their own conflicts. Also interesting here is that quite a high proportion of all the civil disputes do end up at the United Nations' doorstep. This is because civil disputes are often the most intractable, and, as a result, states will eventually give up and ask the United Nations to intervene, even though the world organization is the least well equipped to do so. In recent years, the United Nations has become involved in civil conflicts in Angola, Western Sahara, Somalia, Cambodia, Afghanistan, Tajikistan, the former Yugoslavia, and, belatedly, Rwanda and Burundi. Each of these cases has defied attempts by interested states to manage the conflict peacefully.

As we have seen, U.N. mediations are less likely to succeed than mediation by states or regional organizations (see fig. 18). Although this discrepancy is partly explained by the United Nations' increasing involvement in protracted civil conflicts that are almost impossible to manage effectively, like the Western Saharan conflict (1974–), it is also a function of states' distrust of international organizations and their preference for managing conflicts bilaterally or with mediators of their own choosing.

Looking closer at U.N. involvement, we are able to observe a historical decline in U.N. involvement from 1956 onwards (see fig. 19). This is clearly the result of cold war inertia, when the U.N. became captive to the rivalry between the superpowers and their veto power in the Security Council. During these

Figure 18   U.N. mediation outcome (%)

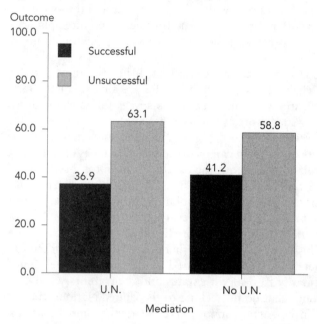

Figure 19   U.N. involvement in disputes, by period

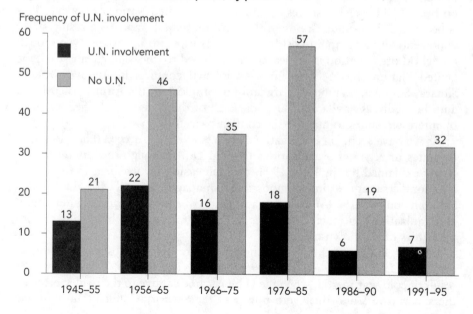

years, the United Nations was often confined to sending out fact-finding teams to the world's trouble spots and then withdrawing to let the major powers take over. After 1990, however, there was a slight rise in U.N. involvement in world conflicts following the liberation of Kuwait by the U.S.-led Coalition forces during the Gulf war (1990–1991), when hopes were high for an expanded and empowered U.N. role in managing world conflicts. Unfortunately, the rise of ethnic civil conflicts in the wake of the Soviet Union's collapse simply highlighted the United Nations' inability to deal effectively with civil conflicts, despite the new international environment.

Although international conflict is widespread and destructive, the situation is not totally hopeless. States in conflict have a wide range of mechanisms and opportunities for solving their differences without resorting to bloodshed. The three approaches discussed in this chapter can be distinguished by the degree to which states, or nonstate international actors, maintain control over the conflict-management process. Diplomatic approaches—negotiation, mediation, conciliation, and inquiry—give states the greatest control, and this accounts for their popularity. Negotiation and mediation especially are noted for their flexibility and creativity, and thus their level of success.

In contrast, legal approaches—arbitration and adjudication—provide states with the least degree of control and have limited applicability to complex, drawn-out political conflicts. Similarly, international organizations—universal and regional—lack the control, flexibility, and inventiveness of negotiation and mediation. For this reason, most states prefer to manage their conflicts bilaterally and usually refer to bodies like the United Nations only when their own efforts have failed or when they can see a definite advantage in submitting to the machinery of the organization.

As our survey has shown, international conflict-management methods can be effective and are used in most conflicts, often successfully. In most cases, the only element preventing a peaceful conclusion to the conflict was the lack of political will. What is clear is that without negotiation, mediation, and efforts by organizations like the OAS and the United Nations, many more international conflicts would spiral out of control and end in unprecedented levels of destruction.

The task of making peaceful conflict management more effective requires the careful study of international conflicts—its causes, patterns, outcomes, and management. The aim of this book is to aid in this task by providing a reference to international conflict from 1945 to 1995. The summary descriptions that follow in Part Two shed light on the causes, outcomes, and conflict-management efforts of each case.

Bibliography

Bailey, S. D. 1982. *How Wars End: The United Nations and the Termination of Armed Conflict, 1946-1964* (Oxford: Clarendon Press).

Bercovitch, J. 1984. *Social Conflicts and Third Parties: Strategies of Conflict Resolution* (Boulder, Colo.: Westview Press).

Bull, H. 1977. *The Anarchical Society: A Study of Order in World Politics* (London: MacMillan Press).

Claude, I. L. Jr. 1964. *Swords Into Ploughshares: The Problem and Progress of International Organization* (London: University of London Press).

Delbruck, J. 1987. "Peace Through Emerging Law." In *The Quest for Peace: Transcending Collective Violence and War Among Societies, Cultures, and States,* ed. R. Vayrynen (London: Sage Publications).

Deutsch, K. W. 1978. *The Analysis of International Relations,* second edition (Englewood Cliffs, N.J.: Prentice-Hall).

Fawcett, J. E. 1971. *The Law of Nations* (Harmondsworth: Penguin).

Frankel, J. 1969. *International Politics: Conflict and Harmony* (London: Allen Lane, Penguin Press).

Merrills, J. G. 1991. *International Dispute Settlement,* second edition (Cambridge: Grotius).

Northedge, F. S., and M. D. Donelan. 1971. *International Disputes: The Political Aspects* (London: Europa Publications).

Sawyer, J., and H. Guetzkow. 1965. "Bargaining and Negotiation in International Relations." In *International Behavior,* ed. H. Kelman (New York: Holt, Rinehart, and Winston).

Schuman, F. L. 1969. *International Politics: Anarchy and Order in the World Society,* seventh edition (New York: McGraw-Hill).

Suter, K. 1986. *Alternative to War: Conflict Resolution and the Peaceful Settlement of International Disputes* (Sydney: Women's International League for Peace and Freedom).

Touval, S. 1994. "Why the U.N. Fails." *Foreign Affairs* 73 (September–October): 44–57.

✦

Conflicts from 1945 to 1995

001. CHINA
Civil war, communist revolution; the Chinese civil war (1945–1949)

The roots of the Chinese civil war go back to 1927, when Chiang Kai-shek, leader of the Kuomintang (KMT, or Nationalists), finally ousted the Chinese warlords with the help of his Communist allies. Chiang then seized Shanghai in an effort to eliminate all Chinese Communist Party (CCP) members and their sympathizers. At least ten thousand people were slaughtered in the process.

The Communists fled to southern and central China, where they rebuilt the party among the peasantry. Constantly harassed by KMT troops and facing incredible barriers, the Red Army under Mao Zedong undertook the fabled Long March in 1934–1935, in which ninety thousand men and women marched west to Guizhou province and then to Shaanxi province in the north; more than half the marchers died during this one-year trek of some 9,660 kilometers (6,200 miles).

Believing the Red Army to be defeated, Chiang turned his attention to the Japanese, who had invaded China in 1937 prior to World War II. Mao's troops joined the Nationalists in the war against the Japanese, but following Japan's surrender in 1945, the CCP immediately began operations against Chiang's army for control of the country.

From about 1937 until the end of World War II, the United States sought to broker a political settlement between the two parties. In the months preceding the civil war, the Soviet Union also became involved in a minor way. U.S. special envoy George C. Marshall undertook to mediate between the parties from December 23, 1945, to January 10, 1946, managing to secure a cease-fire lasting until April 1946, but then fighting broke out again in Manchuria.

Throughout the course of the conflict, the United States gave extensive military aid to the Nationalists. Despite the U.S. aid, however, the Communists steadily gained battlefield dominance, culminating in victory over the Nationalists in January 1949. The CCP declared the mainland to be the People's Republic of China on October 1, 1949. The fighting was often intense, and an estimated one hundred thousand people died. Following their military defeat, the Nationalists fled to Formosa (Taiwan) in the Formosa Strait, where their presence continued to be the source of friction and armed conflict.

Although the Soviet Union immediately recognized Mao's new republic, the United States insisted that Chiang Kai-shek's regime was China's true government. This state of affairs lasted into the 1970s, when China was admitted to the United Nations. China remains committed to reuniting the Formosa islands, especially Taiwan, with the mainland. The rise of the People's Republic caused a major upheaval in Asia and armed conflict in the years that followed (see conflicts 021, 024, 025, 031, 036, 044, 058, 064, 066, 079, 084).

For further information and background reading, see reference item numbers 37, 46, 255, 698, 718, 729, 735, 771, 878 .

002. GREECE

Antimonarchist communist insurgency; the Greek civil war (1945–1949)

Civil war erupted in Greece after the Axis Powers were defeated in 1945. The communist resistance in Greece, composed of the National Liberation Front (EAM) and the National Popular Liberation Army (ELAS), declared a provisional government and attempted to violently prevent the return of the Greek government-in-exile led by King George II. With the aid of British troops, forces loyal to the government defeated the EAM and ELAS in Athens and restored the government under the Varkiya agreement. The agreement stipulated that a plebiscite would be used to determine whether the king should return.

The plebiscite was decided in the affirmative and the king returned on September 27, 1946. Days after the king returned, the communists resumed guerrilla warfare with the aid of the new communist governments of Albania, Yugoslavia, and Bulgaria. From 1947 the conflict expanded to include areas of Albania, Yugoslavia, and Bulgaria, as the Greek government launched attacks on rebel sanctuaries. Cross-border bombing raids and ground operations were common, and a number of foreign troops were killed.

Britain scaled down its military support for the government in 1947, with the United States immediately picking up the slack with large-scale military assistance—equipment, training, and military advisers.

Yugoslavia withdrew its support for the rebels in 1949 because of disagreements with the rest of the Soviet bloc. Without Yugoslav support, the rebels were unable to sustain operations, and the conflict ended in 1950 with their defeat.

More than 158,000 people lost their lives in this conflict, many of them civilian; foreign forces suffered no more than 200 fatalities. Although the U.N. attempted to mediate in November 1948, both sides showed an unwillingness to settle their differences peacefully. Even the Soviet Union could not use its influence to bring about a dialogue.

For further information and background reading, see reference item numbers 46, 255, 908, 950, 965, 1015.

003. INDIA

Civil war; partition and independence (1945–1948)

India's struggle for independence from Britain first escalated in 1942, when the Hindu-dominated National Congress Party launched its Quit India campaign of civil disobedience aimed at establishing an independent Indian state. India's Muslim population, represented by the Muslim League, laid claim to its own independent state. Although the campaign was interrupted by the outbreak of World War II, the demands for India's independence did not dissipate.

At the conclusion of the war, civil unrest, guerrilla warfare, and mutinies by Indian troops heightened in intensity. Police and British troops struggled to maintain order. Mahatma Mohandas Gandhi, who had been leading the

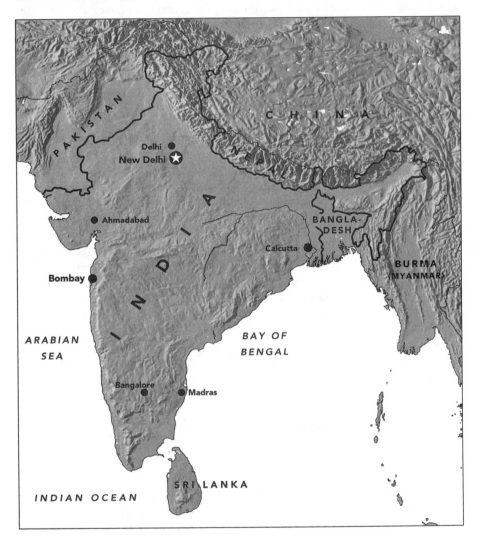

MAP 1. **Subcontinent of Asia**

Since the partition of the Subcontinent into Pakistan, India, and East Pakistan (now Bangladesh) in 1947, the nations of the region, especially predominantly Hindu India and Muslim Pakistan, have clashed repeatedly in boundary and territory disputes. Most recently, tensions erupted between Burma and Bangladesh (see conflicts 276 and 282).

nationalist movement since 1915, emerged as a major figure in the postwar negotiations leading to independence. Violence continued through 1946 and 1947 as leaders tried to create a political settlement that was amenable to both the Hindu and Muslim factions. A political solution was ultimately found, revolving around the partition of the Subcontinent into separate Muslim and Hindu states, Pakistan in the west, India in the center, and East Pakistan (later Bangladesh) in the east (see map 1). The India Independence Act of 1947 specified August 15 as the date of transfer of power from Britain to the newly independent states of India and Pakistan. Burma and Ceylon (later Sri Lanka) also became independent at this time.

No outside attempts at mediation were made, and the fighting and violence associated with the independence struggle were at times savage. Deeply opposed to partition, Gandhi himself was assassinated in 1948 by a Hindu fanatic who objected to his tolerance for Muslims. Although estimates of the death toll vary, as many as 1 million people are thought to have died during the conflict. Many of these deaths were the result of the partition, which caused perhaps one of the greatest forced migrations in history. Some 12 million people fled their homes—Muslims leaving India for Pakistan and Hindus and Sikhs flooding into India from Pakistan. Intercommunal massacres were widespread, as were the so-called trains of death, in which entire trainloads of refugees were slaughtered and sent on their way with only the train engineer alive. Britain was criticized for not intervening to prevent the bloodshed. The partition of the Subcontinent resulted in persistent boundary problems that have led to wars, border conflicts, and separatist violence (see conflicts 010, 015, 020, 023, 056, 066, 068, 076, 084, 098, 106, 107, 132, 162, 187, 195, 216, 219, 231, 233).

For further information and background reading, see reference item numbers 46, 255, 674, 679, 684, 700, 737, 765, 791, 819.

004. FRANCE-LEVANT (Syria and Lebanon)
Independence crisis (1945–December 1946)

Syria was once part of the Ottoman Empire's vast Arab lands, but World War I (1914–1918) brought about both the empire's collapse and Turkey's defeat alongside that of its allies, Germany and Austria. The Treaty of Versailles (1919) redrew the map of Europe and the Middle East, granting France a mandate to rule Turkey's former Levant holdings (Syria and Lebanon).

France subdivided the Levant to create Lebanon and Syria, continuing its presence in the territories until after World War II, at which point an independence movement had started. A campaign of civil disruption began and a formal protest was lodged with the United Nations against France. French troops were attacked.

Britain sought to persuade France in the strongest terms to grant independence to Syria and Lebanon. Indeed, British troops had been in Damascus since 1941—their mission to dispossess France's collaborationist Vichy regime. When the French shelled Damascus in May 1945 in an effort to quell rioting, the British responded by threatening to occupy Syria unless the French withdrew. The French finally acceded in December 1946.

There were no formal attempts at peaceful conflict management during the fighting, and overall, the fighting left more than two hundred dead. To this day, Syria does not fully recognize Lebanon as an independent state. It has intervened in Lebanese affairs on a number of occasions, and thousands of its troops are still stationed on Lebanese territory.

For further information and background reading, see reference item numbers 37, 255, 1050, 1083, 1111, 1175, 1254, 1264, 1299.

005. USSR-IRAN

Procommunist campaign of secession; the Azerbaijan crisis (August 1945–October 1947)

During World War II both Britain and the Soviet Union had stationed troops in Persia (Iran), later to be joined by U.S. troops. The United States withdrew its forces toward the end of 1945, as did Britain in February 1946, in compliance with the terms of the Tripartite Treaty signed on January 29, 1942. The Soviets remained in Azerbaijan and Iranian Kurdistan, however, actively fostering procommunist movements. These movements launched a violent campaign to secede from Iran. The Democratic Party of Azerbaijan declared independence from Iran in December 1945, while the Democratic Party of Kurdistan did the same in January 1946. Soviet troops actively supported the rebels, and the Soviet Union sent supplies to the rebelling communist parties.

Iran, with the assistance of the United States, placed the issue before the U.N. Security Council, which considered it in March 1946. With the Soviet Union absent, the Security Council ordered both Iran and the Soviet Union to report to it before April 3. They were to outline the status of bilateral negotiations that had commenced on February 19. On 4 April the Soviet Union announced it would withdraw its troops within five to six weeks in exchange for oil concessions. Accordingly, Soviet troops were withdrawn by May 9, 1946, and Iran quickly put down the procommunist rebellions in both Azerbaijan and Kurdistan. About two thousand people lost their lives in the disturbances, and apart from the intervention of the U.N. Security Council, there were no other outside attempts at peaceful conflict management.

For further information and background reading, see reference item numbers 76, 255, 1114, 1202.

006. THE NETHERLANDS–DUTCH EAST INDIES (Indonesia)

Indonesian nationalism; war of independence
(late 1945–November 1949)

The Netherlands acquired control over the Dutch East Indies between the seventeenth and early nineteenth centuries. Japan seized the islands in 1942. Two days after Japan's surrender at the end of World War II, on August 16, 1945, Indonesian nationalists led by Ahmed Sukarno declared independence. Armed with Japanese weapons, they resisted attempts by British and Australian troops to take control of the islands and to facilitate the Japanese surrender. The first Dutch troops arrived in October 1945 with the clear aim of regaining colonial control over their former possession; they were also forcefully resisted. At this stage the fighting was mainly confined to Java and Sumatra.

Early mediation efforts failed to forge a political solution to the war. British troops were withdrawn in late 1946, subsequent to which Britain exerted diplomatic pressure on both the nationalists and the Dutch to negotiate. The United States also threatened to cut off Marshall Plan aid if the Dutch did not grant independence. Negotiations and guerrilla warfare proceeded simultaneously for the next three years, and full-scale conflict was limited to two Dutch "police actions." Although the Dutch were fairly successful in reducing the territory under the nationalists' control, they had no allies and were under great pressure from the international community.

Britain, the United States, and the United Nations all attempted to mediate; overall there were seventeen different mediation attempts and numerous negotiation efforts. The breakthrough came when the U.N. Commission for Indonesia (UNCI) convened two conferences. The first ran from April 14 to August 1, 1948, and produced an agreement facilitating the withdrawal of Dutch troops and a cessation of hostilities on August 10. A second conference, held from August to November 1949, formalized Indonesian independence, which was duly declared on December 1949.

Throughout the course of the conflict, tens of thousands of Indonesians died; Dutch and British losses were put at four hundred and six hundred, respectively. Although the Dutch retained control of West New Guinea (later Irian Jaya), this was to produce protracted fighting in later years (see conflicts 078, 202).

For further information and background reading, see reference item numbers 255, 710, 746, 772, 856, 879.

007. FRANCE–FRENCH INDOCHINA
(Cambodia, Laos, Vietnam)
War of independence; the French-Indochina war
(December 1945–July 1954)

France acquired protectorates in Cambodia, Laos, and Vietnam (called French Indochina) in the nineteenth century, losing them to the Japanese in World War II. French Indochina's struggle for independence grew out of France's postwar attempts to reassert control over the region in the wake of Japan's capitulation and the subsequent supervision of the Japanese surrender by British and Chinese forces.

France regained control over Cambodia, Laos, and Vietnam by March 1946, despite violent resistance from local nationalist forces, which had declared independence with Japanese encouragement. France and Vietnam began negotiations, but these ceased with the eruption of more serious fighting after the French bombardment of Haiphong in November 1946 in retaliation for continued guerrilla attacks on French forces.

In the period up to 1949, Vietnamese guerrilla forces eroded French dominance throughout much of Vietnam. The position of the French worsened in the wake of the Chinese civil war, when Communist China began providing military support for the Vietnamese guerrillas.

Concurrent with the conflict in Vietnam, guerrilla action against the French was taking place in Laos and Cambodia. Thai forces were also drawn into the conflict in order to protect territories in Laos and Cambodia that were seized with Japanese acquiescence in 1941. Thai military involvement ended in December 1946 in the wake of repeated French incursions into Thai territory. Successful resistance from the Lao Issara (Free Lao) in Laos and the Khmer Issarak (Free Cambodia) in Cambodia resulted in their gaining independence in late 1953.

The end of French military involvement in Laos and Cambodia allowed France to devote its full attention to the worsening situation in Vietnam, where Vietminh forces controlled most of the country and parts of Cambodia and Laos. The Vietminh were communist forces led by Ho Chi Minh, who had begun a liberation movement in the 1920s, was driven underground, and returned to Vietnam during World War II to fight the Japanese. The army he raised upon his return, the Vietminh, attacked the French forces concentrated at Dienbienphu in March 1954. This was the climactic battle of the war, and it ended with the French surrendering on May 7, 1954. In July 1954 France accepted a negotiated settlement providing for full French withdrawal, the independence of Laos and Cambodia, and the partition of North and South Vietnam.

The war cost at least half a million lives, including approximately ninety thousand French fatalities and forty or so British troops. There were no outside attempts at peaceful conflict management, although there were numerous negotiations. This was not the end of conflict in Indochina, however, and a much more destructive conflict, the Vietnam War, began in 1960 (see conflict 069).

For further information and background reading, see reference item numbers 255, 689, 692, 711, 712, 713, 722, 749, 751, 755, 766, 802, 805.

008. UNITED STATES–YUGOSLAVIA
Cold war air incidents (August 1946)

This conflict was rooted in the growing postwar rift between the Allies, with the Soviet Union (and its new satellite regimes in Central and Eastern Europe) facing off against the Western powers—Britain, France, and the United States, all over Europe.

These cold war tensions boiled over on August 9, 1946, when an American C-47 transport plane on a flight from Vienna to Udine was shot down by Yugoslav fighters over Slovenia. On August 19 the United States alleged a second attack along the same route. The captured crew from the two aircraft were detained by Yugoslav authorities. Protests by the U.S. government over the incidents were countered by claims from Yugoslavia alleging unauthorized U.S. flights over Yugoslav territory. On August 21 the United States delivered an ultimatum to Yugoslavia requiring the release of all detained crew within forty-eight hours, or the matter would be placed before the U.N. Security Council.

Yugoslavia complied with the ultimatum on August 22 and gave assurances there would be no repeat of the air incidents. Although there was no fighting between U.S. and Yugoslav troops, the context of the conflict had made the potential for escalation very high. The United States was engaged in a number of similar incidents with the Soviet Union in following years (see conflicts 022, 034).

For further information and background reading, see reference item numbers 17, 57, 925, 971.

009. FRANCE-MADAGASCAR
Nationalist rebellion (March–August 1947)

France gained control over Madagascar and its associated islands between the seventeenth and nineteenth centuries. At the end of World War II Madagascan nationalists, represented by the Mouvement Democratique de la Renovation Malagalese (MDRM), demanded independence from France. Rebels claiming to represent the MDRM attacked French military strongholds on March 29, 1947, on the main island of Madagascar. The French authorities responded with violent repression. French troops crushed the main rebel bands by December 1947. Sporadic resistance continued after this date in the form of a guerrilla insurgency, but the rebellion was declared officially over on December 1, 1948. Additional French Senegalese and foreign legion were used to help crush the rebellion.

Approximately 350 French soldiers were killed, and official French figures put Madagascan deaths at 11,000. Many of these were civilians who died from starvation and disease after being driven from their homes. At no time did either side attempt to resolve the conflict peacefully. Madagascar eventually achieved independence in 1960.

For further information and background reading, see reference item numbers 255, 293, 314, 434, 456.

010. INDIA-PAKISTAN

Postpartition separatism; the first Kashmir war, the India-Pakistan wars (October 1947–January 1949)

After the 1947 partition of India (see conflict 003), the status of Kashmir and Jammu was particularly troublesome, and control over the territory has been contested by India and Pakistan in a series of wars (see conflicts 106, 195, 219, 231).

Although Kashmir and Jammu had been predominantly Muslim since the late fourteenth century, Britain had installed a Hindu prince there in the mid-1800s. The first Kashmir war had its roots in the territory's thorny postpartition decision of whether to cede to Pakistan or India. In early October 1947 Kashmir's Muslims sought to preempt a decision by staging a revolt in the city of Punch. The rebels were soon joined by deserters from the Kashmir state security force and by tribesmen invading from Pakistan.

By the end of the month the combined rebel force was nearing the state capital of Srinagar. In a transparent gambit to gain India's protection from the approaching rebels, the maharaja of Kashmir announced on October 27 that Kashmir would cede to India. Pakistan protested. The governor-general of India, Lord Mountbatten, responded by declaring that a plebiscite would be held on the territory's future status once the invaders had been repulsed and law and order restored

On December 22, 1947, Prime Minister Jawaharlal Nehru of India claimed Pakistan was actively aiding the rebels and demanded that such assistance cease. When Pakistan did not reply, the U.N. Security Council took up the matter on January 1, 1948, dispatching a U.N. investigating committee to the region. It recommended on August 13, 1948, that a cease-fire be implemented, that all invading forces be withdrawn, and that India and Pakistan begin negotiations on the fate of Kashmir.

Further U.N. mediation efforts secured a cease-fire on December 31, 1948. Neither side had gained any battlefield dominance, and the state was divided into two zones of control. In the subsequent years, protracted negotiations were held over the issue of a plebiscite in Kashmir. A series of U.N. negotiators sought to mediate the dispute, among them Sir Owen Simon, an Australian High Court judge; Frank P. Graham, an American university professor; and Gunnar Jarring of Sweden. They had little success.

For further information and background reading, see reference item numbers 255, 667, 679, 684, 700, 765.

011. COSTA RICA

Anticorruption military insurgency, civil war; the Costa Rican civil war (March–April 1948)

The roots of the Costa Rican civil war go back to 1942, when José Figueres Ferrer publicly denounced corruption within the government of Rafael Calderón Guardia. Forced into exile in Mexico, Figueres continued to agitate for reform and organize opposition, first against the Calderón government and then against its successor under Teodoro Picado Michalski, who assumed power in 1944.

In 1947, with the support of Guatemalan president Juan José Arevalo, Figueres and other revolutionary exiles signed the Caribbean Pact, which called for the overthrow of all dictatorial regimes in Central America and the Caribbean, including Costa Rica's. Following the presidential elections in Costa Rica in February 1948, won by opposition leader Otilio Ulate Blanco, President Picado delayed the transfer of power at the instigation of his predecessor, Calderón.

On March 11, 1948, Figueres, heading a national liberation army, invaded Costa Rica from bases in Guatemala. Full-scale civil war erupted. Figueres had reached the capital, San José, by April 13 and called for Picado's unconditional surrender. The national liberation army controlled most of the surrounding country. At this point, the papal nuncio and ambassadors from the United States, Panama, Mexico, and Argentina interceded in unsuccessful attempts to broker a peace agreement.

On April 17 the war escalated further with the movement of Nicaraguan troops into Costa Rica to support Picado. Nicaragua, also targeted by the Caribbean Pact, had been supporting Picado since the start of the conflict with arms and "volunteers." But Picado surrendered to Figueres on April 19. Nicaraguan forces withdrew on April 21, and Figueres established a new government on April 24, 1948. Total fatalities for the war were estimated at approximately one thousand, with no Nicaraguan troops killed.

For further information and background reading, see reference item numbers 255, 508, 510, 546.

012. ISRAEL
British decolonization, Arab-Israeli territorial dispute; war of independence (May 1948–January 1949)

Tensions in Palestine between Jews and Arabs became increasingly violent during the 1930s, following the massive influx of European Jews fleeing Nazi persecution. After World War II and disclosures of the Holocaust, Jews stepped up their campaign for an independent Jewish state in Palestine, using both political pressure and terrorist tactics. Britain, which had held a mandate over the territory since the collapse of the Ottoman Empire, found it increasingly difficult to control the escalation of violence and referred the problem to the United Nations in 1947. A U.N. Special Committee on Palestine (UNSCOP) recommended the partition of Palestine into Jewish and Arab states (see map 2). The Arab states rejected the plan totally, the Jews accepted it, and the British announced that they would evacuate regardless of whether the United Nations was ready to administer the territory.

Palestinians and Jews began preparing for war, and fighting broke out even before the end of the British mandate on May 15, 1948. As the British withdrew, Jews and Palestinians fought for control of the ports and cities the British had left behind. The unilateral proclamation of the state of Israel on May 14 led to the invasion of Israel from Egypt, Transjordan, Iraq, Syria, and Lebanon by Arab forces in support of Palestinian statehood. The war proceeded intermittently throughout the next eight months, punctuated by two truces. After initial Arab advances, Israeli forces took the initiative—reclaiming all Jewish areas lost, and then, at the cessation of hostilities, gaining control over all Palestine except the West Bank, the Golan Heights, and the Gaza Strip (see map 3). The Arab Legion also held parts of Jerusalem.

During the conflict, several mediation attempts were made by the U.N. mediator for Palestine, Count Bernadotte, and then by his successor, Ralph Bunche. These were often successful in attaining cease-fire agreements that lasted for varying periods. Hostilities ended on January 7, 1949. A series of armistice negotiations were held under U.N. auspices from January 6 to April 13, 1949, and agreements were signed with all the Arab nations involved in the war.

Fighting was very intense for most of the war, with Jewish fatalities estimated at six thousand, including two thousand civilians, while nearly eight thousand Arab troops lost their lives. The war displaced nearly 800,000 Arabs. They and their descendants, the Palestinians, became the center of much Arab-Israeli conflict in later years. The establishment of Israel in the region caused a major upheaval and led to numerous Arab-Israeli conflicts in the following years (see conflicts 026, 035, 042, 046, 051, 081, 096, 097, 108, 117, 128, 137, 141, 145, 170, 176, 186, 199, 213).

For further information and background reading, see reference item numbers 255, 1047, 1098, 1124, 1129, 1158, 1171, 1193, 1208, 1248.

MAP 2. **U.N. Partition of 1947**

MAP 3. **Israel After 1948-1949 War**

In November 1947 the U.N. General Assembly ratified a plan to divide Palestine
into separate Arab and Jewish states (top). As a result of the Arab-Israeli war of
1948-1949, Israel gained over thirty percent more territory (bottom) than it had
held under the 1947 agreement.

013. WESTERN POWERS–USSR; BERLIN
Cold war conflict; the Berlin airlift crisis (June 1948–May 1949)

In the wake of World War II, Berlin, which lay inside East German territory, was partitioned among the four World War II victors and allies—the USSR, the United States, Great Britain, and France. The three Western allies were accorded designated access corridors through East Germany to Berlin. With cold war strains mounting between the United States and Soviet Union, Berlin's status took on additional meaning, becoming the focus of the emerging East-West conflict. The Soviet Union began to limit Western access to Berlin.

The conflict escalated when the Western powers announced a currency reform on June 18, 1948, which applied to their respective sectors of occupation in Germany, including Berlin. On June 23 the Soviet Union announced its own currency reform, which it said would apply to the Soviet sector of Germany and the whole of Berlin. Then, on June 23–24, 1948, Soviet authorities imposed an air and land blockade of Berlin. The United States responded on June 28 with a daring airlift to break the blockade, sending U.S. supply planes into Berlin in the face of intense intimidation by Soviet jet fighters.

On July 1 the Soviet Union suspended its cooperation with the Western powers in the governance of Berlin. An offer from the U.N. secretary-general to mediate was declined, and an attempt to initiate multilateral negotiations failed. Berlin thus became divided into East and West sectors with completely separate administrations.

The blockade was eventually lifted following negotiations between Philip C. Jessup, the U.S. ambassador at large, and the Soviet's U.N. representative, M. Malik. Although there were no actual hostilities, the intimidating use of jet fighters by the Soviet Union, and the potential for escalation inherent in the strained superpower relations, made the Berlin crisis extremely serious. This crisis led to the formation in 1948 of the North Atlantic Treaty Organization (NATO), a Western military alliance devoted to safeguarding the Atlantic community against the Soviet bloc (see Soviet bloc nations in map 4). Berlin remained the focus of cold war conflict for a number of years.

For further information and background reading, see reference item numbers 255, 925, 935, 945, 960, 991, 1000.

014. UNITED KINGDOM–MALAYA
(Malaysia and Singapore)
*Anti-British communist insurgency; the Malayan emergency
(June 1948–July 1960)*

Britain gained control of the Malay Peninsula in the nineteenth century but lost it to the Japanese after the defeat of Singapore early in World War II. After the

Legend:

- Soviet gains in Western territory 1939–1947
- States under Soviet control by 1948
- Independent Communist State
- – – – – – Soviet border, 1939
- ———— Soviet border, 1947–1991

MAP 4. **Soviet Expansion in Europe, 1939–1991**

The Berlin airlift crisis of 1948-1949 was the first of several cold war incidents to chill the relationship between the Soviet Union and the United States following World War II. At the time of the crisis, the Soviet Union had already extended its control over much of East Central Europe.

war Britain resumed control over the peninsula and reformulated the prewar colonial arrangement to include Singapore. The new entity, called the Union of Malaya, signified a loss of some autonomy to local rulers, and opposition to British control grew as a consequence.

In 1948 the communist Malayan People's Anti-British Army (MPABA) was formed and undertook a campaign of guerrilla warfare and economic sabotage against the British-controlled government. Members were recruited almost entirely from the Chinese community in Malaya and represented the continuation of wartime resistance. The British initiated military actions in June 1948 following attacks on government posts and police and military patrols. Australian aircraft were deployed in August 1950 to provide air support for British troops, and in October 1955 Australian and New Zealand ground forces joined counterinsurgency operations.

The fighting involved small engagements in Malaya's vast jungles, which Britain's highly trained guerrilla warfare units almost always won. The insurgency gradually lost its momentum and virtually disappeared by mid-1960, owing in great part to the British army's tactic of creating "new villages" under government control. This approach to the insurgency cut the communists off from their popular base and dried up the "sea" in which they could, according to Maoist doctrine, "swim."

More than 10,000 fatalities were reported during the course of the conflict; of these, 525 British soldiers died and 50 New Zealand and Australian troops were killed. The last traces of the communist insurrection disappeared in December 1989, when the Communist Party of Malaya surrendered, although their actions had been inconsequential since the end of the emergency. There were only two minor attempts at conflict management in 1955, neither of which was successful.

For further information and background reading, see reference item numbers 46, 255, 664, 705, 803, 841, 862.

015. INDIA
Postpartition separatist violence (July–September 1948)

The 1947 partition of the Subcontinent allowed a number of states to choose the country, India or Pakistan, to which they wished to cede. Despite Indian pressure, the state of Hyderabad, in south-central India, chose to cede to neither India nor Pakistan. In 1948 Hyderabad, whose internal security forces possessed insufficient resources to retain control, was racked by communal violence resulting in thousands of deaths. India viewed the situation as a threat to its own internal security, especially after the unrest spilled into the neighboring Indian state of Madras.

Sir Mirza Ismail, a former dewan of Hyderabad, attempted to mediate the conflict in July and August, but failed, and India invaded on September 11,

1948. After intense fighting, India established control over the state on September 24. Hyderabad was formally incorporated into India in 1949. Approximately eight hundred Indian soldiers were killed during the two weeks of fighting, as were more than a thousand nonmilitary personnel.

For further information and background reading, see reference item numbers 255, 667, 769, 791.

016. BURMA; CHINA
KMT-PLA cross-border conflict (August 1948–1954)

Following its defeat in the Chinese civil war (see conflict 001), a 12,000-man Kuomintang (KMT) army known as the Yunnan Anti-Communist and National Salvation Army (YANSA), under Gen. Li Mi, fled into Burma. It occupied part of the Shan state on the eastern border, and from its base there launched attacks against the People's Liberation Army (PLA) of China. It was supported by both Taiwan and the United States.

The KMT army forcefully resisted Burmese troops, which tried to take control of the area, and actively supported guerrilla movements trying to overthrow the Burmese government. The Burmese government attempted to pacify the area through bombing raids, which often spilled into neighboring Thailand, sparking conflict between these two states.

After repeatedly asking Taiwan and the United States to facilitate the withdrawal of Li Mi's army, Burma took the issue to the United Nations in 1953. The U.S. military attaché in Siam, Col. R. V. Palmer, subsequently sought to mediate the dispute. At a conference held in Rangoon and attended by the United States, Burma, Thailand, and Taiwan, an agreement was reached under which the YANSA would be removed to Taiwan. An airlift of the KMT army was undertaken in late 1953 and 1954. More than one thousand people were estimated to have been killed during the conflict.

For further information and background reading, see reference item numbers 255, 688, 706, 774, 776, 778, 813, 843, 860.

017. COSTA RICA–NICARAGUA
Antigovernment rebel activity, border incidents
(December 1948–February 1949)

The conflict between Costa Rica and Nicaragua emerged directly out of the Costa Rican civil war (see conflict 011). Nicaragua had supported the regime of Teodoro Picado Michalski during the civil war by sending troops and supplies. Supporters of the now-deposed Picado fled to Nicaragua and set up bases there with the intention of overthrowing the new Figueres regime in Costa Rica. This led to a number of serious border incidents and a deterioration in relations between the two countries.

On December 10, 1948, armed rebels invaded Costa Rica from Nicaragua. Costa Rica charged Nicaragua with support for the rebels and protested to the Organization of American States (OAS). The OAS set up an investigating committee on December 14, which set about mediating the dispute. Costa Rican airplanes then attacked rebel bases within Nicaraguan territory on December 20, 1948.

OAS representatives met with the parties in Washington, and a cessation of hostilities was agreed to and signed on February 21, 1949. Approximately fifty people were killed during the course of the conflict. The issues were never fully resolved, and the two sides fought in 1955 (see conflict 039), 1977 (see conflict 174), 1978 (see conflict 178), and during the contra war (see conflict 190).

For further information and background reading, see reference item numbers 47, 255, 508, 510, 526, 546.

018. BURMA
Civil war, Karen separatist insurgency (January 1949–)

Britain annexed Burma in the nineteenth century as part of its conquest of the Indian Subcontinent. In light of the partition of India and Burmese agitation for independence, Britain signed a treaty in October 1947 granting independence to Burma. As with the other newly independent South Asian nations, Burma immediately fractured, with the revolt staged by the Karen tribal group leading to all-out civil war in the first six months of 1949. Complicating the conflict were remnants of Kuomintang armies, which had been driven out of China by CCP troops and had taken refuge in northern Burma (see conflict 016); various communist and tribal groups also opposed the Burmese government (see conflict 016).

The fighting was at first bitter, but no side ever achieved a decisive victory. Despite numerous campaigns, the war dragged on, eventually taking on the character of a guerrilla insurgency. There were periodic government campaigns to rid rebel areas of insurgents, while the rebels ambushed government posts and then disappeared into the dense jungle.

The war was internationalized when the Chinese supported tribal insurgents at various times. In November 1969 Chinese soldiers actually skirmished with Burmese troops within Burma. Also, Karen insurgents were especially active along the Thai border, and Burmese attempts to quell them often carried across the border. On March 12, 1984, 200 Burmese troops crossed the Thai border in pursuit of rebels. Fifteen Burmese troops were killed in this incident when they encountered Thai border police. There were very few serious attempts at conflict management during these years, especially by outside mediators.

Negotiations with some of the groups involved occasionally produced cease-fires, but the real political issues were never resolved.

From 1992 on there were a great deal more cross-border skirmishes, and in 1994 the Karens began to suffer some heavy defeats, culminating in the fall of Karen National Unity (KNU) headquarters at Manerplaw to government troops in early 1995. Also during this time, serious negotiations got under way between the Karen insurgents and the military government, but proved fruitless in the long run. By the end of 1995 the war continued unabated, with no sign of an end. Throughout the conflict, perhaps as many as 140,000 people have lost their lives, many of them civilians. It remains one of the longest-running guerrilla insurgencies in the world.

For further information and background reading, see reference item numbers 688, 706, 736, 774, 776, 777, 778, 843, 845, 859.

019. ERITREA-ETHIOPIA
Eritrean nationalism, agitation for independence
(July 1949–December 1950)

Italy acquired Eritrea in the nineteenth century and in 1936 added it to Italian East Africa, consisting of Italian Somaliland and Ethiopia. In the wake of World War II Italy was forced to give up its colonial territories in Africa, and British troops occupied the area. The status of Eritrea was disputed: the Eritreans requested independence, while both Sudan and Ethiopia claimed sovereignty over the territory. Eritrean nationalists agitated for independence, resorting to terrorism and attacks on foreign nationals, especially Italian residents. In January 1950 Britain used troops to quell the insurrection. Military activities were halted in July 1950. There were no reports of British fatalities.

In early 1950 a U.N. commission investigated the Eritrean case, and on the basis of its recommendations, Ethiopia was officially awarded a mandate to rule the region. Eritrea's union with Ethiopia was completed in 1962 when Haile Selassie annexed the territory. About 150 people lost their lives in the conflict, which foreshadowed a much graver conflict starting in 1965 and ending with Ethiopian defeat and Eritrean independence in 1993 (see conflict 099).

For further information and background reading, see reference item numbers 37, 76, 255, 341, 350, 352, 356, 363, 409.

020. PAKISTAN-AFGHANISTAN
Postindependence territorial dispute (August 1949)

The status of the territory between Afghanistan and what was to become Pakistan had been in dispute since the late nineteenth century, when Britain had imposed a boundary to include territory inhabited by a major Afghani tribe. Afghanistan intensified its claims on the region after Pakistan gained its independence, and then began to promote separatist sentiment in the area.

In June 1949 a Pakistani aircraft bombed an Afghan base, causing some casualties. In protesting the attack, Afghanistan also accused Pakistan of intervening in its internal affairs. A number of minor border incidents occurred during 1950, including an alleged crossing into Pakistan by Afghan tribesmen and regular troops on September 30, 1950 (see conflict 023). The Afghan government denied official involvement, claiming that the force consisted solely of tribesmen operating within Pakistan.

An offer to mediate the conflict from U.S. ambassador-at-large Philip C. Jessup was not taken up, and a similar attempt by the shah of Iran was also unsuccessful. The dispute intensified in 1955 when Afghanistan mobilized its forces along the disputed border. Turkish prime minister Adnan Menderes succeeded in restoring diplomatic relations between the two states when negotiations broke down in December 1956.

About seventy people were killed during the course of the conflict, and the dispute has strained relations between Afghanistan and Pakistan ever since.

For further information and background reading, see reference item numbers 76, 255.

021. CHINA-TAIWAN
KMT-CCP territorial dispute; amphibious assaults in the Taiwan Strait (October 1949–June 1953)

After Chiang Kai-shek's Kuomintang was defeated on the mainland in the Chinese civil war (see conflict 001), the KMT continued to fight on from bases on Taiwan (Formosa), other offshore islands (Quemoy and Matsu), Burma (see conflict 016), and pockets on the mainland. The victorious CCP was committed to a united China and therefore tried to eradicate the remaining Nationalist positions immediately after proclaiming the People's Republic, shelling islands in Amoy (Xiamen) harbor in October 1949.[1] Amphibious assaults on Nationalist-held islands followed, including an unsuccessful attempt on

---

1 China and Taiwan use different transliteration systems for romanizing Chinese ideographs. The Taiwanese employ the Wade-Giles system (hence, Kuomintang, Mao Tse-tung, Teng Hsiao-ping, Peking, Amoy, and so forth), while the Chinese use pinyin, resulting in much different spellings, e.g., Guomindang, Mao Zedong, Deng Xioaping, Beijing, and Xinmen.

Quemoy (Kinmen) in late October and the conquest of Hainan Island in May 1950. Small, retaliatory raids by the Nationalists and persistent bombings by the Communists continued until late 1952. A Chinese invasion of Taiwan was averted in June 1950 when the United States sent the Seventh Fleet to the Taiwan Strait.

The United States began training Taiwanese military units for large, amphibious operations in early 1952, and in October the Nationalists launched a successful amphibious attack against Communist-held Nanri island; other, smaller assaults were made on other positions until June 1953. The Communists continued to bomb Nationalist-held islands throughout this time. The conflict cost thousands of lives—mostly military—on both sides, and there was never any attempt at peaceful conflict management. Because the issues were never resolved, fighting broke out again in 1954–1955 (see conflict 036), 1958 (see conflict 058), and 1962 (see conflict 079). China remains committed to uniting Taiwan with the mainland and has not ruled out using force to achieve this end.

For further information and background reading, see reference item numbers 255, 698, 752, 852, 866, 878.

022. UNITED STATES–USSR
Cold war air incidents (April–October 1950)

Following the Berlin airlift crisis of 1948–1949 (see conflict 013), relations between the United States and the Soviet Union became exceedingly strained. All across Europe and the Far East, the armed forces of the two superpowers engaged in an increasingly uneasy standoff. On April 11, 1950, the Soviet Union alleged that two days previously, a U.S. plane flew over the Soviet republic of Latvia. Soviet aircraft opened fire after the U.S. plane failed to land on request and shot the plane down. The United States then announced that on the previous day it had lost an unarmed reconnaissance plane over the Baltic Sea. Further investigations revealed that the two incidents were related and that Soviet actions had violated international law. The United States demanded that the Soviet Union investigate the incident and issue instructions to the Soviet air force not to repeat its actions. The Soviets, in reply, reiterated their earlier allegations and did not address the U.S. demands. Relations continued to be tense.

On September 4, 1950, a Soviet aircraft was allegedly shot down by U.S. fighters off the west coast of Korea. On September 6 the Soviet Union asserted that the plane was within Soviet airspace and warned the United States of the consequences of such an attack. The incident was subsequently referred to the U.N. Security Council by the United States, but no action was taken. In the third air incident of 1950, the Soviet Union alleged that on October 8 two U.S. aircraft had strafed and bombed the Soviet airfield of Sukhaya Rechka, near the Korean border. The Soviet Union sought the strict punishment of those responsible. The United States admitted the incident on October 19 and offered to pay compensation.

Although there were few fatalities, the growing intensity of the cold war and the increasingly aggressive moves by each state to extend their areas of influence, such as in Korea, made these disputes very serious indeed. There were further incidents throughout the 1950s (see conflict 034).

For further information and background reading, see reference item numbers 17, 57, 925, 971.

023. AFGHANISTAN-PAKISTAN
Territorial dispute; the Pathan conflict (June–October 1950)

The Pathan conflict was the continuation of a previous dispute over territory that the British had given to Pakistan at Afghanistan's expense (see conflict 020). The territory contained Pushtun (Pathan) tribes people, a major Afghani tribe. Afghanistan began agitating for the establishment of an independent Pathanistan in the disputed territory, and a series of armed clashes resulted. There were incidents in June, and then on September 30, 1950, a large force of Afghan tribesmen supported by regular Afghan troops invaded the disputed territory. They were pushed back by October 5, 1950, after attacks by the Pakistan air force. Afghanistan withdrew its troops early on in the invasion.

The shah of Iran tried to mediate early on, without much success. Later mediations by Saudi Arabia in 1955 and prime minister Adnan Menderes of Turkey in 1956 also failed to resolve the issues. In all, more than a hundred people were killed during the fighting. Relations between the two countries were never friendly, and Pakistan allowed Afghan mujahedin rebels to operate from its territory during the Afghan civil war (see conflict 180).

For further information and background reading, see reference item numbers 76, 81, 255, 797.

024. UNITED STATES–NORTH KOREA
Cold war territorial dispute; the Korean War (June 1950–July 1953)

Korea had been taken over by Japan in 1905 following the Russo-Japanese war. After World War II the Soviet Union and the United States accepted Japan's surrender on either side of the 38th parallel, effectively partitioning Korea. In mid-1949 Soviet and U.S. forces were withdrawn from the demarcation line, and North Korea and South Korea were left to supervise their own borders. From this point there were frequent border incidents, as the two governments had become implacable enemies. North Korea was a communist state, while South Korea was pro-Western.

On June 24, 1950, North Korea invaded South Korea, quickly overwhelming the forces and surrounding the South Korean capital, Seoul. At South Korea's urgent request, the United States began military actions in aid of the South Korean forces on June 27. The U.N. Security Council, with the Soviet Union absent, passed a resolution requesting U.N. members to come to the aid of South Korea. Britain entered the war on June 28, and Australia on July 4. From September 1950 to June 1951 forces from Belgium, Canada, Colombia, Ethiopia, France, Greece, Luxembourg, the Netherlands, New Zealand, the Philippines, Thailand, Turkey, and South Africa joined the U.N. force.

After the loss of Seoul, U.N. forces landed behind the North Korean front line at Inchon and began to push from the south, quickly overwhelming the North Korean forces and regaining Seoul. In late September and early October the U.N. forces entered North Korean territory, thus fulfilling the original aims of the U.N. resolution. At the behest of Gen. Douglas MacArthur, its commander, the U.N. force continued to advance toward North Korea's border with China, provoking a large-scale deployment of Chinese forces. First contact with the Chinese troops was made in late October 1950. In November China launched a major invasion that eventually led to the recapture of Seoul. The U.N. force counterattacked, recapturing Seoul and reaching the 38th parallel in March 1951. From this point fighting stalemated and the front line changed little, despite continued efforts by both sides to break through.

In July 1951, after indications that both sides were amenable to a restoration of borders along the 38th parallel, negotiations were initiated in search of a cease-fire and peace settlement. After talks at Panmunjom, a neutral village in no-man's land, agreement was reached on a truce based on battle lines existing at the end of fighting, and a formal peace agreement was signed on July 27, 1953. An early agreement was delayed by the problems associated with the return of prisoners. India played a crucial role in these negotiations.

Total fatalities during the war amounted to approximately 3 million killed. China suffered 1 million deaths, North and South Korea each lost half a million people. The United States lost fifty thousand troops and the other members of the U.N. force suffered seven thousand fatalities. North and South Korea remained divided, and a number of smaller armed conflicts have continued to plague their relations.

For further information and background reading, see reference item numbers 255, 672, 675, 708, 709, 720, 784, 804, 816, 824, 848.

025. CHINA-TIBET
Military occupation and reincorporation (October 1950–May 1951)

Tibet enjoyed independence from the seventh century until the Manchu incorporated the area into China during the eighteenth century. China lost control over Tibet after the collapse of the Qing Dynasty in 1911. As a consequence, Britain and Tibet agreed on a new territorial boundary at the Simla Conference (1913–1914). This boundary remarcation, based on the McMahon Line, pushed Indian frontiers forward at Tibet's expense. Tibet successfully fought off a Chinese expedition in 1918, was left alone during World War II, and enjoyed an independent existence without widespread international recognition. With the victory of the Communists in the Chinese civil war in 1949 (see conflict 001), however, there were renewed fears within the Tibetan government that China would reassert its claims to the region. Tripartite talks were thus initiated between the Tibetan government, the Chinese ambassador to New Delhi, and Indian prime minister Jawaharlal Nehru.

While negotiations were under way, the People's Liberation Army (PLA) invaded Tibet on October 7, 1950. China occupied Lhasa in March 1951, but Tibetan tribesmen violently resisted Chinese attempts to establish control in outlying areas. India protested the invasion but stopped short of intervening militarily. Tibet requested international assistance and protested to the United Nations. The General Assembly deferred consideration of the issue pending a continuance of negotiations between Tibet and China.

Negotiations in Beijing resulted in the Agreement on Measures for the Peaceful Liberation of Tibet (Seventeen Articles Agreement), signed on May 23, 1951. The agreement provided for limited autonomy for Tibet, but for all intents and purposes it had been absorbed into China. Tibet was ruled as a military occupation until annexation in 1965 (see conflict 044). About two thousand people were killed in the invasion and subsequent crackdown, and the conflict poisoned relations between India and China for years to come (see conflicts 044, 066, 084, 107, 155).

For further information and background reading, see reference item numbers 255, 723, 827, 839, 877.

026. SYRIA-ISRAEL
Arab-Israeli territorial/resource dispute; Lake Tiberias
(April–May 1951)

The Israeli-Syrian armistice following Israel's war of independence (see conflict 012) left the opposing sides facing each other around Lake Tiberias. Various disputes over the use of the lake erupted into military confrontation in 1951 after Israel declared its intention to reclaim a marshy area near the lake, called the Hula swamp. In March 1951 Syrian and Israeli troops started exchanging fire. The conflict escalated, however, when Syria attacked the border town of El-Hammu on April 4, 1951. Israel retaliated the following day. Attacks and counterattacks continued throughout the month of April, and on May 2 Syria captured the Israeli outpost of Tel Mutillah. Israel responded with a series of attacks the same day, and serious fighting continued until May 5. The conflict abated quickly, though, and the fighting was over by May 9.

The United States and the United Nations both tried to mediate an end to the conflict. The U.N. Security Council managed to secure a cease-fire, and then at negotiations held at Lake Success, got Syria and Israel to settle many of the issues in dispute. There were approximately a hundred fatalities on both sides, and the conflict was the start of many more such encounters in the following decades.

For further information and background reading, see reference item numbers 1047, 1051, 1084, 1098, 1158, 1171, 1248, 1284.

027. OMAN–SAUDI ARABIA

Territorial/resource dispute; the Buraymī crisis (1952–October 1955)

When the Arabian Peninsula was divvied up among the World War I victors, some of the borders were a little indistinct, including those between Oman and Saudi Arabia. As a consequence, in the late 1940s, when Omani engineers began oil exploration around the Buraymī oasis. Saudi Arabia responded by claiming sovereignty over the region.

Negotiations between the Saudi government and Britain, which was representing Oman, proceeded from August 1949 to February 1952. When Saudi Arabia could not secure sovereignty through these negotiations, it sent a small force in August 1952 to occupy the oasis. Oman mobilized a force to take it back, but the intervention of the U.S. ambassador to Saudi Arabia led to a stand-still agreement between the parties on October 26, 1952.

On April 2, 1953, after unauthorized movements by Saudi forces, Britain notified Saudi Arabia that it reserved the right of complete freedom of action because it viewed Saudi actions as a nullification of the stand-still agreement. British and Omani forces subsequently blockaded the Buraymī oasis. In October 1955 they forcibly occupied the oasis, resulting in a number of fatalities.

Negotiations were resumed in October 1953 and continued intermittently until 1975, including a failed attempt at arbitration in 1954–1955. The U.N., too, made an unsuccessful attempt at mediation in 1960. In the spring of 1975 Saudi Arabia and Oman agreed to a settlement returning Buraymī to Oman in exchange for land with oil-producing potential that also provided Saudi Arabia with a sea corridor.

For further information and background reading, see reference item numbers 1022, 1023, 1100, 1142, 1195, 1252, 1255, 1258, 1323.

028. TUNISIA
African nationalism; war of independence
(January 1952–March 1956)

France obtained Tunisia as a protectorate in the late nineteenth century. Active resistance to French rule, organized around Habib Bourguiba's Neo-Déstour Party, began in 1934 and became more ferocious after World War II. Guerrilla activity began in January 1952, and French troops were quickly mobilized for a crackdown. The French authorities outlawed Neo-Déstour trade unions, and women and youth movements.

Preliminary bilateral negotiations between French and Tunisian representatives were unproductive, so the violence continued until December 1954, when France finally conceded independence to the territory in principle. The ban on the Neo-Déstour was lifted, and the party was included in independence negotiations, which led to internal autonomy in September 1955 and full independence in March 1956. About two thousand people were killed during this conflict, and France retained large military installations in Tunisia after independence, leading to a series of violent conflicts later on. A faction opposing the continuing French military presence had to be put down in late 1955 to mid-1956.

For further information and background reading, see reference item numbers 255, 293, 314, 401.

029. EGYPT–UNITED KINGDOM
Sovereignty dispute; the Canal Zone dispute
(January 1952–January 1956)

In 1869 the Suez Canal Company, owned by Britain and France, had been granted a ninety-nine-year concession to construct and operate the Canal. Great Britain gained control of the territory surrounding the Canal in a 1936 treaty with Egypt. Britain then stationed forces in the area. In an attempt to regain sovereignty the Egyptian parliament overturned the treaty in 1951 and sought to have British forces removed. Rioting broke out and British troops and installations were attacked.

The dispute intensified when the nationalistic Gamal Abdel Nasser became president of Egypt in July 1952 with the stated aim of removing all colonial influence from Egypt. Negotiations between Britain and Egypt ensued, and an agreement was reached on a partial British withdrawal from the Sudan and from around the Suez Canal. Britain refused to withdraw completely. Nasser's rhetoric heated up on February 24, 1953, when he threatened to attack the Canal Zone if any British troops remained after the withdrawal. Britain suspended further talks.

Between March and May 1953, the United States sought to mediate, but the parties were not amenable to American involvement. Incidents of violence and terrorist attacks became more prevalent and Egypt attempted to cut off the Canal Zone on May 15. Britain set in place a naval patrol of the Canal in response. Violence continued throughout 1953 and on February 14, 1954, Egypt refused to cooperate further at any level with Britain and the United States. Under U.S. diplomatic pressure, Britain finally agreed on July 28, 1954, to withdraw for the sake of Middle East stability but reserved the right to return within seven years in the advent of war. The withdrawal was completed on June 13, 1956. About twenty-five British soldiers and a thousand Egyptians were killed during the conflict. The issue was not entirely resolved, however, and a much more serious conflict, the Suez crisis, broke out in October 1956 (see conflict 047).

For further information and background reading, see reference item numbers 1052, 1066, 1076, 1107, 1110, 1122, 1192, 1194, 1201.

030. ITALY-YUGOSLAVIA
Cold war territorial dispute; the Trieste crisis
(March 1952–October 1954)

After World War I and the dissolution of the Austro-Hungarian Empire, Italy was awarded the port of Trieste at the head of the Adriatic Sea. During World War II an Allied force made up of U.S. and British troops and Yugoslav guerrillas took Trieste, and both Italy and Yugoslavia laid claim to the region after the war.

Beginning in 1947 the United Nations sought to resolve the conflicting claims to Trieste, and on March 20, 1948, the world organization produced the Tripartite Declaration. The declaration, signed by France, Britain, and the United States on March 20, 1948 recommended the return of the city and its surrounding territory to Italy. Yugoslavia rejected the declaration and proposed in February 1952 that Trieste be placed under a joint Italian-Yugoslav administration.

Italy reaffirmed its support of the Tripartite Declaration in 1953. In August of that year, in response to Yugoslavian hints of a forcible annexation of the region, Italy sent a naval force into the region and positioned troops on the Yugoslav border. These military movements greatly aggravated tensions, setting into motion intensive diplomatic efforts to avert a crisis.

On October 8 the Western allies announced their impending withdrawal from Trieste in keeping with the terms of the declaration. Yugoslavia responded that it would view any Italian movement into Trieste as an act of aggression and respond militarily. On November 4 riots broke out in Trieste; 6 died and 162 were injured. British troops were deployed to quell the disturbances.

A five-power conference was convened on November 13, 1953, with the purpose of resolving the territorial dispute; representatives were dispatched from Britain, France, Italy, the United States, and Yugoslavia. Eleven months later the conference participants issued a memorandum of understanding (October 6, 1954) to the effect that Italy and Yugoslavia would both govern Trieste on the basis of redrawn boundaries. Only intense U.S. and British efforts to mediate the dispute averted war.

For further information and background reading, see reference item numbers 76, 255, 906, 964, 971.

031. CHINA-PORTUGAL
Territorial dispute; the Macao conflict (July–August 1952)

Portugal had controlled Macao, a tiny peninsula on the coast of southeast China, since 1557; it was not recognized as Portuguese territory until the 1887 Treaty of Peking. Macao became an important port for Chinese international trade, even after the U.N. trade embargo against the communist country during the Korean War.

In 1952, however, Portugal sought to restrict Chinese access to the port in an attempt to halt smuggling. Both nations moved significant numbers of troops to the border, and a minor border conflict ensued. There were exchanges of fire on July 25–26. On July 29–30 a battle involving mortars and a gunboat ensued, for which Portugal later accepted responsibility and paid compensation. There were five Portuguese deaths and forty Chinese casualties. The two sides met in Hong Kong in August 1952, and a full settlement of the matter was reached.

For further information and background reading, see reference item numbers 76, 255, 821.

032. ARGENTINA-CHILE
Border conflict; the Beagle Channel dispute (July 1952–1968)

Border disputes between Chile and Argentina date back to the nineteenth century, when both countries achieved independence and borders were more or less set. A long-standing dispute over the Beagle Channel and its islands (which lie at the southernmost tip of the South American continent) flared in July 1952. Argentina simply ignored the International Court of Justice (ICJ) ruling that the area belonged to Chile.

Armed incidents involving force continued during this period. In 1958 Chile built a lighthouse on one of the disputed islands, but Argentine marines landed on the island and destroyed the lighthouse. Chile rebuilt it, and again Argentina destroyed it. Although there were no fatalities during this conflict, it was serious enough to cause international concern. Neither side attempted to settle the conflict peacefully, nor did any neighboring states offer to mediate. Eventually the conflict lapsed, but it flared again much more seriously in 1977 (see conflict 173).

For further information and background reading, see reference item numbers 46, 76, 255.

033. KENYA–UNITED KINGDOM

Anticolonial tribal uprising; the Mau Mau revolt
(August 1952–December 1963)

Kenya became a British protectorate in the late nineteenth century. British settlers established farms in areas formerly designated as tribal reserves. Land-ownership disputes after World War II led to the formation of opposition groups, some of which demanded independence. Known as the Mau Mau revolt, the tribal uprising by the Kikuyu tribe began in August 1952 as a campaign of guerrilla warfare against the colonial government in Kenya. British farms and police stations were attacked, and a state of emergency declared.

Heavy fighting continued for the next four years, during which 21,000 paramilitary police, thousands of Kenyan army units, and a division of the British army with support from the Royal Air Force, sought to contain the rebellion. The bulk of the Mau Mau forces were defeated by 1956, but sporadic fighting continued until 1960 when the state of emergency, imposed in 1952, was lifted. The Mau Mau were defeated by superior arms and a counterterrorist strategy that relied heavily on paramilitary units comprising locally recruited Kikuyu.

Only two attempts were made to engage the rebels in peaceful dialogue, both of which failed. The brutality of the uprising led to political pressure on the British government to grant Kenya independence, which was formally attained in 1963. In all, more than 45,000 people were killed during the course of the revolt, including 60 British soldiers.

For further information and background reading, see reference item numbers 255, 302, 326, 329, 343, 441, 477.

034. UNITED STATES–USSR
Cold war air incidents (October 1952–July 1956)

The increasing chill of the cold war, the aftermath of the Korean War, and previous air incidents (see conflict 022) led to an expanding disquiet between the superpowers. Matters were complicated in Europe, which was now partitioned into three blocs: Western, Communist, and neutral; Germany and Austria were divided into American, British, French, and Soviet occupation zones with their corresponding airspace. As the enmity between the superpowers grew, so did their need for intelligence. As a consequence, the United States and the Soviet Union undertook more air reconnaissance missions (and incurred more airspace violations) at the margins of the superpowers' spheres of influence.

On February 16, 1952, two Soviet aircraft were intercepted by U.S. jet fighters, which opened fire. One Soviet aircraft was damaged when the U.S. planes broke off the engagement. On October 7, 1952, an American B-29 Superfortress had, according to Soviet authorities, entered Soviet airspace in the vicinity of Yuri Island. After refusing to land at the Soviet's request, the bomber was shot down and the crew killed. The United States denied charges that the aircraft had been in Soviet airspace and demanded compensation for the loss of the bomber and crew. The Soviet Union refused to pay, and the matter lapsed.

On March 10, 1953, two Czechoslovak MiG-15 jets attacked two U.S. F-84 Thunderjets over Bavaria, shooting one down. Two days later, on March 12, Soviet jet fighters shot down a British bomber that had been flying over the British zone in Germany, killing seven airmen. Two days after this incident, on March 14, a Soviet fighter fired on a U.S. reconnaissance aircraft off the Kamchatka Peninsula. The American plane returned fire, but neither plane was damaged. Later, in July, the Soviet Union alleged that four U.S. jet fighters had downed a Soviet passenger aircraft, resulting in the loss of twenty-one passengers and crew. The Soviet Union demanded that the United States take action against those who orchestrated the attack and reserved the right to seek compensation.

On July 31, 1953, the United States accused the Soviet Union of shooting down a U.S. B-50 Superfortress over the Sea of Japan. One survivor of the attack was rescued by a U.S. vessel, and it was held that the remaining survivors had been picked up by Soviet vessels. The United States demanded information on the status of these crew members. The Soviet Union had earlier released a statement asserting that the U.S. bomber had entered Soviet territory near Vladivostok and had opened fire when two Soviet fighters had approached. On August 4 the Soviet Union denied holding the remaining crew members.

Although there was a hiatus over the next two years, this ended on June 23, 1955, when Soviet fighters downed a U.S. plane over the Bering Strait. Announcing its regret for the incident, the Soviet Union acknowledged the possibility that an error may have occurred and offered to pay 50 percent compensation for the loss of the plane. The United States accepted the offer on July 7. In all, fifty-four military personnel were killed in these air incidents, which eventually lapsed.

The cold war rendered these air incidents extremely dangerous, inasmuch as the superpowers were beginning to defy each other all over the world. Direct, armed confrontation could have spelled global catastrophe.

For further information and background reading, see reference item numbers 17, 57, 925, 971.

035. ISRAEL-JORDAN

Arab-Israeli hostilities, PLO incursions; West Bank border incidents (January 1953–December 1954)

Following Israel's war of independence (see conflict 012), Jordan annexed Palestinian land on the West Bank of the Jordan River; the area contained many Palestinian refugees. Despite the presence of U.N. peace-keepers, border incidents began almost immediately owing primarily to Arab infiltrators. Israel responded by ordering commando teams into Jordan.

The conflict escalated seriously in October 1953, when an Israeli commando raid on the Jordanian village of Qibya led to more than sixty civilian casualties. Thirteen months later, in November 1954, a Jordanian patrol exchanged fire with Israeli troops at Battir.

In all, 125 people were killed during the conflict. The United Nations made several largely unsuccessful attempts to mediate. These border difficulties presaged more serious conflicts (see conflicts 046, 097, 117).

For further information and background reading, see reference item numbers 255, 1031, 1047, 1098, 1158, 1171, 1248, 1284.

036. TAIWAN-CHINA

KMT-CCP territorial dispute; bombardment of Quemoy (April 1954–April 1955)

After the formation of the People's Republic of China in 1949 (see conflict 001), the Chinese Communist Party (CCP) laid claim to the offshore islands still controlled by the Nationalists (Kuomintang, or KMT) and tried to liberate them by force (see conflict 021). In 1954 China declared its intention to liberate these islands, including Taiwan. The United States expressed its support for the Kuomintang and warned that the Seventh Fleet would stand in the way of any invasion attempt. Nevertheless, on September 3, 1954, China began a massive bombardment of Quemoy island (called Kinmen by the Chinese), which continued intermittently for several weeks. During this period the United States refrained from any active intervention. In January 1955 Chinese forces began to move onto the Tachen islands. The United States promptly evacuated U.S. and KMT forces, leaving the islands to China.

Although the conflict deescalated when the Chinese halted its bombardment, a solution was not reached. U.S. forces remained in the region to supervise the situation. Both U Nu, the Burmese prime minister, and U.N. secretary-general Dag Hammarskjöld, attempted to mediate, but without success. There were few fatalities, but the conflict had brought two superpowers to the brink of war. Conflict in the same region broke out again in 1958 (see conflict 058).

For further information and background reading, see reference item numbers 255, 698, 718, 752, 852, 866, 878.

037. GUATEMALA
Left-wing insurgency; the Guatemalan civil war (June 1954–1995)

In June 1954 Guatemala's democratic regime was ousted in a coup d'état backed by the U.S. Central Intelligence Agency (CIA) and United Fruit (a U.S. multinational and the principal foreign interest in Guatemala). Carlos Castillo Armas was installed as the leader of Guatemala. This event inaugurated a period of political strife and civil war that was to endure for more than thirty years.

In July 1957 Armas was assassinated. Elections were held under the supervision of a military junta that resulted in victory for Gen. Miguel Ydigoras Fuentes. General Ydigoras acquiesced in the United States' disastrous Bay of Pigs invasion of Cuba (see conflict 072). His assent to the invasion (Ydigoras even allowed the invasion force to conduct training exercises in Guatemala) led to discontent in the army, and a military revolt broke out on November 13, 1960. It was rapidly crushed with U.S. assistance.

In the aftermath of the failed revolt, a left-wing guerrilla insurrection took shape. Made up of various opposition groups that formally united as the Rebel Armed Forces (FAR) in February 1962, this group of guerrillas was joined by the October 20 Front, led by the former defense minister in the democratic regime ousted in 1954. Massive rioting broke out in Guatemala City in March 1962, costing at least twenty lives and increasing the tensions between government and insurgency forces. In support of the government, the United States moved counterinsurgency forces into Guatemala, halting the insurrection.

In 1963 the army, with U.S. support, removed General Ydigoras from office and replaced him with the minister of defense, Enrique Peralta Azurdia, who continued the fight against the guerrillas. Elections held in 1966 installed Julio César Mendez Montenegro as a puppet president. Following the defeat of the FAR in 1970, army strongman Col. Manuel Arana Osorio replaced Mendez as president. His leadership was accompanied by brutal repression resulting in thousands of disappearances. The 1974 presidential elections changed little, as the results were annulled when a dissident army general won.

In the wake of the annulled election, a number of guerrilla groups reemerged. At first they operated independently, but in 1982 they formed an alliance called the Guatemalan National Revolutionary Unity (URNG). The civil war entered a new phase in that year, as the Reagan administration actively sought to promote democracy in Central America in order to resist the influence of communism. Another coup brought President Efrain Rios Montt to power in 1982. He intensified the fight against the URNG by organizing peasants into militias, and feeding and equipping them. The aim of the militias was to eradicate all opposition at the grassroots level. The campaign disabled the guerrillas but did not end their campaign.

With U.S. approval, a further coup in 1983 replaced Montt with Gen. Oscar Humberto Mejia, who set about a reconstruction plan with the help of renewed U.S. aid. It is estimated that in excess of 120,000 people died during the course of the civil war. Actions against suspected guerrilla targets continued throughout the 1980s, including a number of raids into neighboring Mexico (see conflicts 207, 222). In early 1995 there were numerous allegations of CIA involvement in the civil war, and an official inquiry was launched.

Conflict-management efforts began in earnest only in the late 1980s. Meeting in Mexico, Mgr. Roldolfo Toruno, a Roman Catholic bishop, and Jean Arnault, a U.N. mediator, engaged in more than twenty separate mediation attempts up to the end of 1994. Although the government did make some concessions and a number of minor agreements have been concluded, the major political issues remain unresolved and the bloodshed and civil unrest continue.

For further information and background reading, see reference item numbers 255, 547, 559, 577, 584, 607, 630.

038. ALGERIA

African nationalism; war of independence
(November 1954–March 1962)

France acquired Algeria from the Ottoman Empire in the nineteenth century, and large numbers of French citizens had settled there. Along with Tunisia and Morocco, Algeria began to seek independence from France in the period after World War II. At first, nationalists lobbied the French government. But, when independence appeared not to be forthcoming, the nationalists began a covert campaign to organize an armed force. The National Liberation Front (FLN) and the National Liberation Army (ALN) initiated a rebellion on November 1, 1954, which soon settled into a protracted guerrilla and terrorist war.

Violence broke out both in Algeria and in France itself, spreading across the border into Tunisia and Morocco (see conflicts 028, 052). With news of the terrible casualties suffered by French military units combined with revelations of the use of torture on suspected guerrillas, the French government collapsed in 1958. World War II hero Gen. Charles de Gaulle became president of France and in 1959 began to discuss Algerian independence. By the end of that year the French military had gained a greater degree of control over the country, and the nationalist guerrillas were on the defensive. The climate became more amenable to a political settlement, and negotiations got under way.

A series of referendums on the independence issue were held in both Algeria and France in 1961; they returned a positive response. Negotiations that had begun in 1960 were therefore continued, despite ongoing guerrilla activities. During this time, however, mutinous elements of the French army in Algeria formed a group known as the Secret Army Organization. It was committed to keeping Algeria in French hands, and made terrorist attacks on both French and Algerian targets. It even staged an unsuccessful coup in order to derail the peace process. The organization was suppressed, however, in March 1962 by loyal French forces.

On April 8, 1962, a final referendum in France produced an overwhelming vote for independence, which was subsequently granted on July 1, 1962. Fifteen thousand French troops died during the conflict, while tens of thousands of civilians, most of them Algerian, were killed in terrorist attacks and reprisals. Many French settlers returned to France.

For further information and background reading, see reference item numbers 255, 293, 294, 314, 325, 361, 373, 377, 422.

039. NICARAGUA–COSTA RICA
Attempted invasion by exiled rebels (January 1955)

In a reprise of the conflict between these Central American countries following the Costa Rican civil war (see conflicts 011 and 017), the two states traded accusations of harboring each other's exiled rebels with the aim of overthrowing their respective governments. In fact, on January 11, 1955, exiled opposition groups invaded Costa Rica with support from Nicaraguan troops. The fighting was intense, and Costa Rica's small army was unable to stem the rebels' advance.

Costa Rica immediately appealed for intervention by the Organization of American States (OAS), which formed an investigatory committee that recommended OAS air support for the beleaguered country. The United States was the only OAS country to respond, dispatching aircraft on January 16, 1955. The border conflict rapidly subsided after this.

The OAS asked both sides to reaffirm their commitment to the 1949 Amity Agreement, which they did on February 24, 1955. Approximately one thousand people were killed during the fighting. Relations between the two states improved only gradually after this time.

For further information and background reading, see reference item numbers 255, 508, 510, 526, 546.

040. TURKEY-SYRIA
Cold war tensions, border incidents (March 1955–1957)

Against the backdrop of the cold war, this dispute was precipitated by a Soviet-Egypt military pact and the conclusion of a Syrian-Soviet arms deal, which generated a crisis atmosphere in the region. Strains between Turkey and Syria increased when Syria became sympathetic to the pan-Arabist policies of Egyptian president Gamal Abdel Nasser and began obtaining arms from the Soviet Union. A close ally of the United States, Turkey viewed these developments with disquiet and suspicion, and, with U.S. support, moved troops to the Syrian border. Both sides viewed each other with increasing hostility, and there were a number of fatal border incidents.

The crisis escalated in September 1957, when the Soviet Union accused the United States of inciting Turkey to invade Syria. The United States responded by stating that any attack on Turkish territory would bring U.S. retaliation on Soviet territory. Rejecting an offer by Saudi Arabia's King Saud ibn Abdul Aziz to mediate, Syria made an appeal to the United Nations on October 15, citing Turkish border violations. In November the dispute deescalated, having amounted to little more than superpower saber-rattling, although about twenty people were killed in border incidents during the conflict.

For further information and background reading, see reference item numbers 255, 1050, 1175, 1200, 1254, 1275, 1295.

041. CYPRUS
Intercommunal violence; the enosis *movement*
(September 1955–February 1959)

Cyprus, populated by a Greek majority and Turkish minority, came under British control in the nineteenth century. It was subsequently annexed in 1914 and made a crown colony in 1925. After World War II, the Greek majority began to agitate for *enosis,* or union with Greece. Britain declared that it would never relinquish the island, despite its lack of economic or strategic value. In April 1955 the National Organization of Cypriot Fighters (EOKA) initiated a terror campaign aimed at both British and Turkish targets. Assassination and sabotage were the main tactics. Britain deployed 40,000 troops to quell the disturbances. There were frequent Turkish retaliatory attacks, and in the most serious fighting between the two ethnic communities in 1958, 115 people were killed.

Starting in 1957 a political solution was sought through negotiations and multilateral conferences among Britain, Greece, Turkey, and the United Nations. In February 1959 agreement was reached; Cyprus was granted independence in 1960. Approximately one hundred British soldiers and more than five hundred civilians died as a result of the violence. This conflict was the precursor to much more serious conflicts in 1963 and 1974, when Greece and Turkey went to war over events on the island (see conflicts 089, 143).

For further information and background reading, see reference item numbers 255, 887, 900, 907, 912, 916, 921, 924, 933, 934.

042. SYRIA-ISRAEL
Arab-Israeli hostilities, cross-border raids; Lake Tiberias (October–December 1955)

Lake Tiberias (the Sea of Galilee, or Lake Kinneret) was a continuing source of friction between Israel and Syria. Israel claimed it as a matter of right, while Syria had occupied positions near the eastern shore following Israel's war of independence (see conflict 012). There were various incidents throughout the 1950s, most involving fishing disputes. Occasionally, Syrian troops would shell Israeli positions.

These minor border incidents gave way, in October 1955, to an Israeli commando attack on Syrian border positions in order to silence the artillery. A larger raid followed in mid-December, also in an attempt to eliminate the artillery batteries. Six Israeli soldiers and fifty Syrian military personnel and civilians died in the conflict.

Maj. Gen. Arthur Burns of the U.N. Truce Supervisory Organization tried, unsuccessfully, to mediate a settlement. The conflict abated slowly after this, although the lack of progress on settling the underlying issues led to further armed disputes in following years.

For further information and background reading, see reference item numbers 255, 1047, 1051, 1084, 1098, 1158, 1171, 1248, 1284.

043. YEMEN–UNITED KINGDOM
Anti-British autonomy campaign; the Aden conflict (1956–1960)

The series of border clashes between British forces based in Aden and Yemeni troops occurring between 1956 and 1960 had its origins some years earlier in British efforts to influence tribal leaders in the region. The British had created a buffer zone around the port city of Aden. The local rulers retained autonomy but were subject to British control over their external relations, and relations among the rulers themselves.

In the period after 1948 Britain sought to withdraw from the area surrounding Aden, while maintaining indefinite control over the port itself. Yemen, to the north, set about to thwart British aspirations in Aden by turning sentiments against the British through a campaign of agitation among the local population. Yemeni raiding parties also crossed into southern Saudi Arabia, resulting in frequent border clashes in 1956 and 1957. British troops and the Royal Air Force (RAF) often pursued Yemeni attackers across the border into Yemen itself. The dispute became part of wider regional and global politics following alliances formed by Yemen with Egypt and Saudi Arabia in 1956 and with the Soviet Union in 1957. Britain cut back its military and air operations starting in February 1959.

In January 1958 U.S.-brokered negotiations between Britain and Yemen failed to produce any definite solution to the conflict. Military clashes lapsed in 1958, and Yemen extended its claim to the entire region, including the port of Aden. Approximately one thousand people were killed in the conflict, including about forty British soldiers and airmen. Aden was again dragged into war in 1962, when civil war engulfed Yemen and dragged Egypt and Saudi Arabia in with it (see conflict 083).

For further information and background reading, see reference item numbers 255, 1126, 1255, 1270, 1323, 1333.

044. TIBET-CHINA
Anti-Chinese guerrilla warfare; incorporation struggle
(March 1956–September 1965)

After the Chinese invasion of Tibet in 1950–1951 (see conflict 025), Tibetans continued to agitate for autonomy. In May 1956 a guerrilla movement began in eastern Tibet, resulting in brutal repression by Chinese forces. Revolts continued to surface periodically, until virtually the whole country was involved in a full-fledged guerrilla war by 1959. The Chinese moved in more than 200,000 troops. The Dalai Lama, whom Tibetans regard as both a king and a god, failed to reach a concessional agreement with Chinese authorities, and the full-scale conflict that broke out in March 1959 forced him and 100,000 Tibetans to flee to India. China soon crushed the revolt and killed thousands in reprisals and repressive measures; persistent Tibetan resistance continued until 1965.

The attempt to put down the revolt led indirectly to armed conflict with India in 1959 (see conflict 066), and provoked incidents on the unmarked Tibetan-Nepali border when Chinese troops pursued rebel Tibetan tribesmen into Nepal territory. There were no attempts at peaceful conflict management, and the conflict cost approximately 100,000 lives. As many as 40,000 Chinese soldiers were killed in the fighting.

Chinese authorities have sought to suppress Tibetan culture and religion since the time of the revolt; they also instituted a campaign of Chinese resettlement in Tibet in order to dilute resistance to the authorities. The Dalai Lama is still campaigning for Tibetan independence.

For further information and background reading, see reference item numbers 255, 723, 827, 839, 877.

045. TAIWAN–SOUTH VIETNAM
Territorial dispute; Paracel Islands (June–August 1956)

The Paracel Islands in the South China Sea have been claimed by the Philippines, South Vietnam, China, Brunei, and Taiwan. It was thought the area had valuable mineral deposits. South Vietnam had a small garrison on one of the islands for some time. In June 1956 Taiwan sent a naval force to the area that hoisted the Taiwan flag with the intent of taking possession of the islands.

A month later, on July 11, Taiwan then sent armed forces to the Spratly Islands, some 600 miles south of the Paracels, and raised its flag there too. South Vietnam responded by sending its own force to the area and raising its flag on one of the islands in August 1956. The conflict gradually abated, although it proved to set the stage for a much more serious conflict in 1974 (see conflict 142), 1988 (see conflict 243), and 1995 (see conflicts 288, 289). Although there were no armed clashes, the tensions caused by the incidents, and subsequent armed clashes, made it a very serious dispute. None of the parties involved attempted to settle the conflict peacefully, and none of the issues involved were ever resolved.

For further information and background reading, see reference item numbers 76, 255, 870.

046. ISRAEL-JORDAN
Arab-Israeli territorial dispute; the Mt. Scopus conflict (July 1956–January 1958)

The series of armed clashes between Israel and Jordan from 1956 to 1958 were part of the wider Arab-Israeli conflict concerning the area of Mt. Scopus, which is near Jerusalem on the Jordanian West Bank. The West Bank had been occupied by Jordanian troops during Israel's war of independence (see conflict 012), and Jordan's toleration of Arab infiltrators into the new Jewish state had been the source of armed conflict in 1953 (see conflict 035).

The first armed clash was initiated on July 24, 1956, when Jordanian forces occupied a house on Mt. Scopus and began firing on Israeli border positions.

On July 27 Israel launched retaliatory artillery strikes at various points along the border and launched ground operations on August 2. Further fighting on September 10 resulted in a number of Israeli fatalities. A series of retaliatory raids were launched, culminating in a major battle at Qalgulya in Jordan on October 10, 1956.

A second conflict occurred on Mt. Scopus in July 1957 when Israeli farmers began moving onto land in the disputed area. Jordanian forces attacked the farmers and the Israeli soldiers guarding them on August 22, 1957, provoking further fighting. A third incident occurred on Mt. Scopus on May 26, 1958, when an Israeli border patrol crossed over into Jordan, where it engaged a Jordanian army unit. There were fatalities on both sides. Approximately two hundred people died during the conflict, and throughout, the United Nations' peace-keepers under Maj. Gen. Arthur Burns and U.N. secretary-general Dag Hammarskjöld attempted to mediate. There were some successes in this, and the referral of the conflict to the U.N. Security Council also resulted in some short-term agreements.

For further information and background reading, see reference item numbers 1031, 1047, 1098, 1158, 1171, 1248, 1284.

047. EGYPT–UNITED KINGDOM, FRANCE
Sovereignty dispute; the Suez crisis (October–November 1956)

The war over the Suez Canal was precipitated by Egyptian president Gamal Abdel Nasser's nationalization of the Suez Canal, thus appropriating it from its Anglo-French owners (see conflict 029). Also, Israel was concerned about the Arab states' failure to pursue a long-term peace treaty, an increasing spate of terrorist attacks, and Nasser's aggressive foreign policy in the region.

Britain and France formed a secret agreement with Israel under which British and French forces would occupy the Canal Zone following an Israeli invasion of the Sinai. The Israeli invasion began on October 29, 1956, and the Israeli Defense Forces (IDF) quickly seized the whole peninsula, destroying most of Egypt's tanks and heavy weaponry in the process. On October 30 the British and French governments called for a halt to the fighting and requested permission from Egypt to station troops in the Canal Zone, ostensibly to safeguard shipping. Egypt refused, and on October 31 Britain and France began an air offensive against Egyptian bases, virtually wiping out the Egyptian air force. British and French troops landed in the Canal Zone on November 5.

The United States and Soviet Union opposed the military actions against Egypt from the outset. The United States threatened economic reprisals, and the Soviet Union offered to send troops to Egypt and Syria if the British and French forces did not withdraw. The military plan was a fiasco. British and French forces declared a cease-fire on November 6 and started to withdraw.

Under great pressure from the United States, Israel also started a to pull out from the Sinai. The United Nations sent a peace-keeping force to separate the Israelis and the Egyptians, which began to move into the Sinai on November 15. By March 1957 Israel had relinquished most of the territory it had gained in the invasion.

More than six thousand military personnel were killed during the conflict, including twenty British and ten French soldiers. Although the U.N. Security Council moved quickly to resolve the conflict, it met with little success. Only the heavy-handed approach of the superpowers had any effect. Relations between Israel and Egypt remained tense, and the two states went to war again in 1967 (see conflict 117) and 1973 (see conflict 141).

For further information and background reading, see reference item numbers 1052, 1066, 1068, 1076, 1107, 1110, 1118, 1120, 1122, 1188, 1192, 1201, 1209.

048. HUNGARY-USSR

Anticommunist revolt, Soviet invasion; the Hungarian uprising of 1956 (October–December 1956)

Hungary had been incorporated into the Soviet sphere of influence after World War II and belonged to the Warsaw Pact, the Soviet-led military alliance of Communist states set up as a countermeasure to NATO. Following the death of Joseph Stalin in 1953, the Hungarian leadership split into two factions: those under Premier Imre Nagy, who favored a program of liberalization; and those who favored a continuation of authoritarian communist policies led by Mutyas Rakosi.

Nagy was forced to relinquish the premiership in a leadership struggle in 1955. In October 1956 riots broke out all over Hungary calling for the return of Nagy. When central intelligence forces loyal to the Stalinist premier Erno Gero fired on protesters, the crisis escalated and Gero was forced to resign from office. Nagy was returned to power on a wave of popular support. Anticommunist protests developed into open revolt.

The Soviet Union feared the effect of such open dissent on other Warsaw Pact countries (Albania, Bulgaria, Czechoslovakia, East Germany, Poland, and Romania). Nagy negotiated a cease-fire on October 28 and the Soviets withdrew from Budapest. Unrest continued, however, and on November 1 Nagy announced Hungary's withdrawal from the Warsaw Pact. On November 4 Soviet forces launched a massive attack on Budapest with 200,000 troops, 2,500 tanks, and armored cars.

The Hungarian revolt ended on November 14 when it became clear that no outside help was likely. Nagy was executed, and approximately three thousand civilians died during the course of the uprising and hundreds of thousands of

Hungarians fled the country. At no time did either side attempt to settle the conflict peacefully. A similar conflict occurred in Czechoslovakia in 1968, in which Hungarian troops were involved as part of the Warsaw Pact invasion force (see conflict 120), and in Poland in 1981 (see conflict 197).

For *further information and background reading, see reference item numbers* 255, 896, 897, 936, 948, 951, 953, 955, 961, 963.

049. CUBA
Civil war, communist revolution; the Cuban civil war
(December 1956–January 1959)

In 1954 Fulgencio Batista sought a democratic mandate for his control of Cuba, which he had seized in a March 1952 coup. The election saw Batista victorious, but opposition groups contested the result. In May 1955 political prisoners were released from prison; among them was Fidel Castro, who promptly left Cuba for Mexico City in order to organize a revolutionary force to oust Batista. Opposition groups began a terrorist campaign against the government in late 1955.

In the autumn of 1956 the Dominican Republic began to support Castro's force, training and equipping it in preparation for an invasion of Cuba. The revolutionary force launched their invasion in November 1956, but the Cuban army quickly defeated it in early December. Severely weakened, the revolutionary force had to hide out in the jungle and limit its activities to small-scale terrorist attacks against government outposts. Throughout 1957–1958, popular support for the Batista regime evaporated, guerrilla activities intensified, and the United States moved to restore confidence in the regime.

Batista called elections in November 1958, but army support for his regime diminished and he was forced into exile in the Dominican Republic on January 1, 1959. A power vacuum ensued and civil war continued. Castro's forces eventually prevailed, and Castro entered Havana on January 8, 1959, to assume power.

At least five thousand people were killed during the war, and neither side sought to resolve the conflict peacefully. Upon his accession to power, Castro set about to establish a communist state and export the revolution. In this latter respect particularly, Cuba became the locus of international conflict for a number of years. Cuba mounted invasion attempts and insurgency operations against Panama in April 1959 (see conflict 053), Dominican Republic in June 1959 (see conflict 063), Haiti in August 1959 (see conflict 065), Bolivia in November 1966 (see conflict 113), and Venezuela in April 1967 (see conflict 116).

For *further information and background reading, see reference item numbers* 46, 255, 507, 509, 513, 514, 515, 533, 563, 569.

050. HONDURAS-NICARAGUA
Boundary dispute; Mocoran seizure (April–June 1957)

Honduras and Nicaragua had disputed a section of the border between the two countries since the nineteenth century. Honduras was awarded the area in a 1906 arbitration decision rendered by the king of Spain. Nicaragua rejected this decision, however, and kept a small military force stationed in the disputed region. Honduras reasserted its claim in 1947.

On April 18, 1957, Nicaraguan forces moved to take control of the disputed border region, including the town of Mocoran. The Honduran army counterattacked with air and ground forces, and there was sustained fighting until May. The OAS brokered a cease-fire by mediation, and a month later Honduras and Nicaragua agreed to submit their dispute to the International Court of Justice. In November 1960 the ICJ ruled in favor of Honduras, and in 1961 the boundary was redrawn and residents relocated. An estimated one thousand people were killed during this conflict, and a much graver conflict broke out again in 1980 following the Sandinist revolution in Nicaragua (see conflict 190).

For further information and background reading, see reference item numbers 46, 76, 526, 615.

051. ISRAEL-SYRIA
Arab-Israeli territorial dispute; Golan Heights conflict (June 1957–February 1958)

Following the Israeli war of independence (see conflict 012), Israeli and Syrian forces faced off periodically over the Golan Heights (see conflicts 026 and 048). In July 1957 Syrian troops launched an assault on Israeli border positions on the Golan Heights. Israeli troops responded in kind, and an intense firefight ensued.

Intermittent skirmishes continued into 1958, when the conflict subsided somewhat. U.N. mediation efforts failed. Although there were only three deaths, the potential for escalation was always high given the strategic importance of the Golan Heights. Other conflicts over the Golan Heights occurred in 1964–1966 (see conflict 096) and again in 1972–1973 (see conflict 137).

For further information and background reading, see reference item numbers 1047, 1051, 1084, 1098, 1158, 1171, 1248, 1284.

052. SPAIN-MOROCCO

Postindependence autonomy dispute; the Sahara conflict
(November 1957–April 1958)

After Moroccan independence in 1956, Spain maintained military bases and a protectorate in southern Morocco. This rankled the newly independent Morocco, which greatly desired sovereignty over the entire territory. An army of twelve thousand guerrillas, fighting under the name "the Army of Liberation for the Sahara" (AOL), began harassing French forces, which were then fighting Algerian nationalists, and Spanish forces stationed in the southern protectorate.

Serious guerrilla attacks on the Spanish forces began in November 1957. Morocco moved its regular troops into the area and surrounded the Spanish enclave, ostensibly for the purposes of containing the fighting and preventing Spanish incursions.

The fighting died down in 1958 following large-scale Spanish operations and Spanish threats to take the war into Agadir, an important Moroccan port. In February 1958 a joint French-Spanish military operation pushed the AOL back into Moroccan territory. Morocco deescalated the conflict from this point and sought negotiations. U.S. mediation helped to push the negotiations toward agreement.

Approximately one thousand fatalities were recorded during this conflict. Spain ceded its southern protectorate to Morocco on April 7, 1958, but remained in possession of other Saharan territories. Morocco continued to press for all of Spain's territories in North Africa.

For further information and background reading, see reference item numbers 76, 255, 471.

053. PANAMA

Cuban-backed invasion; the Panama revolutionaries conflict
(1958–May 1959)

The immediate cause of this conflict was a political feud between Panamanian president Ernesto de la Guardia and the wealthy Arias family in 1950. After Arias-owned newspapers criticized President Guardia, Finance Minister Gilberto Arias and diplomat Roberto Arias were dismissed from their posts. After returning to Panama from his diplomatic post in London, Roberto Arias began plotting to overthrow Guardia's regime. Cuba was supporting destabilization efforts in the entire region at the time, so the Ariases recruited an invasion force in Cuba, and in late April 1959 the force landed in Panama.

Panama immediately appealed to the OAS for support, and Ecuador, Peru, and Guatemala sent planes, gunships, and troops. An OAS committee persuaded the rebels to surrender, and Roberto Arias fled into exile in Brazil. Cuba was exonerated, even though the invaders had been recruited there. Approximately twenty fatalities were reported during the fighting.

For further information and background reading, see reference item numbers 46, 255, 541, 551, 582, 591.

054. EGYPT-SUDAN
Postindependence territorial dispute (February 1958)

Egypt had a long-standing claim to parts of northern Sudan based on an 1899 agreement under which the 22d parallel was to form the Egypt-Sudan border. This issue came to a head shortly after Sudan became independent from Britain in 1956.

On February 9, 1958, Sudanese army units were stationed in the border area after reports of Egyptian troop movements in the region. Against Sudanese wishes, Egyptian officials then sought to move into the area in an attempt to hold a plebiscite. Sudan registered a protest with the U.N. Security Council.

Following negotiations between President Gamal Abdel Nasser of Egypt and the Sudanese foreign minister and mediation by the U.N. Security Council, the conflict was largely settled. Egypt moved its forces back to the existing frontier and did not press its claim. The dispute erupted into armed conflict again in 1992 (see conflict 274), when Egypt reasserted its claim to the territory.

For further information and background reading, see reference item numbers 76, 1106, 1147, 1207, 1221.

055. FRANCE-TUNISIA
Postindependence autonomy dispute; the military bases conflict (February–May 1958)

After Tunisian independence in 1956 (see conflict 028), France retained substantial military installations within Tunisia. Rebels opposed to the French presence began attacks on the French military, and France alleged Tunisian government complicity. A counterinsurgency operation was launched, and on February 8, 1958, Sakiet-Sidi-Youssef, a town on the Tunisian border, was bombed by French military aircraft. The Tunisian army responded by surrounding the French military installations and on February 13 lodged a complaint about French activities to the United Nations.

Negotiations arranged by the U.N. secretary-general Dag Hammarskjöld succeeded, and the siege was partially lifted. An Anglo-American good offices committee then began to mediate a more permanent solution to the crisis. Although the French created a buffer zone on the Algerian border, this did not prevent incidents. Tensions flared with the arrest on February 20 of a number of Tunisians in retaliation for a mine explosion that killed two French soldiers. The situation appeared to ease somewhat until May 1958, when serious fighting broke out at Remada and Gabes, causing more than three hundred casualties. Negotiations continued despite the fighting, and in June an agreement was reached under which all French troops, excepting a force of 12,000 stationed at Bizerte, would be withdrawn. This was not the end of the conflict, however, and fighting broke out again in 1959 (see conflict 061) and 1961 (see conflict 075).

For further information and background reading, see reference item numbers 255, 293, 314, 401, 434.

056. INDIA–EAST PAKISTAN
Postpartition border tensions; Surma River incidents
(March 1958–September 1959)

Tremendous strains were produced by the 1947 partition of the Subcontinent (see conflict 003) and the ensuing secession of a primarily Muslim Pakistan from Hindu-dominated India. The period of open conflict from March 1958 to September 1959 grew out of these postpartition tensions.

Border smuggling across the Surma River, which separates India from what was then East Pakistan (and now Bangladesh), precipitated a number of skirmishes involving small-arms fire between Pakistani and Indian patrols. The conflict escalated in early June when India began a series of cross-border raids. Pakistani troops began attacking Indian positions across the border in August.

Cross-border raids continued until a cease-fire was declared on August 26, 1958. At least twenty Indian and Pakistani military personnel were killed during the conflict. Senior officials from both countries, including Prime Minister Jawaharlal Nehru of India and President Muhammad Ayub Khan of Pakistan, met nine times before the issue was settled in January 1960. Ongoing tensions between the two states, however, led to conflict again in 1965 (see conflict 098).

For further information and background reading, see reference item numbers 255, 667, 679, 684, 700.

057. LEBANON
Internal strife; the first Lebanese civil war (May 1958–June 1959)

Lebanon was originally part of the Levant—territory given to France by the League of Nations following the breakup of the Ottoman Empire at the end of World War I. The French partitioned this territory into Syria and Lebanon in 1947. Lebanon was populated primarily by Maronite Christians in addition to three Muslim sects—Druze, Sunni, and Shiite. Large numbers of Palestinian refugees also came to live in Lebanon following Israel's war of independence (see conflict 012).

Lebanon operated under a confessional political system, designed to ensure fair political representation of the country's diverse range of religious groups. This was achieved through a national pact that left power largely with each religious community. In June 1957 the president, Maronite Christian Camille Chamoun, attempted to preserve his position by manipulating elections. Opponents organized demonstrations, and after the assassination of the editor of an opposition newspaper in May 1958, full-scale civil war broke out between several heavily armed religious and political factions.

The Lebanese army avoided taking a direct part in the war, but Syria (which had claimed Lebanon as its own territory ever since the French partition) was accused of supporting opposition violence, and Lebanon's border with Syria was closed on May 13, 1958. The United States intervened on President Chamoun's request on July 15, when a battalion of marines landed at Beirut. The conflict subsided as U.S. Marines took up strategic positions; the U.S. forces were able to withdraw in October. More than 1,300 people were killed during the conflict, which heralded a much deadlier civil war in 1975 (see conflict 151), when the national pact broke down completely. The conflict was referred to the Arab League and the United Nations, with no success.

For further information and background reading, see reference item numbers 1027, 1083, 1103, 1111, 1133, 1181, 1215, 1224, 1245, 1263, 1299.

058. UNITED STATES–CHINA; TAIWAN
KMT-CCP territorial dispute; bombardment of Quemoy
(July–December 1958)

Nationalist (KMT) control over Taiwan and other offshore islands continued to rankle the CCP leadership a decade after the Communists had taken power on mainland China (see conflict 001). The persistent dispute had produced a number of assaults and bombardments of the Nationalist-held islands (see conflicts 021 and 036), and in an effort to protect Taiwan from invasion, the United States had stationed part of the Seventh Fleet in the Taiwan Strait. Sino-

U.S. negotiations were held throughout this period in an attempt to reach an understanding about the Taiwan issue.

On August 23, 1958, however, the Chinese resumed their bombardment of Quemoy. On September 4 China announced it was extending its territorial limit from 3 to 12 miles, thus bringing Quemoy within its jurisdiction. On September 7 U.S. warships were deployed to escort Taiwanese supply convoys into Quemoy. On October 6 the Chinese halted the bombardment on the condition that U.S. ships refrain from conducting escort duties, but the bombardment resumed on October 20 amid allegations that the United States had infringed these conditions. Bombardments were restricted to alternate days after October 25, thus allowing supply convoys safe passage. In December 1958 the shelling stopped altogether. About 1,500 people were killed during the intense bombardment.

The United States and China conducted ambassadorial-level talks in Warsaw, but these ended inconclusively. Once again, the United States had narrowly avoided being dragged into a direct military confrontation with China.

For further information and background reading, see reference item numbers 255, 698, 718, 752, 852, 866, 878.

059. CAMBODIA-SIAM (Thailand)

Regional rivalry, communist insurgency fears; border conflict (November 1958–February 1959)

Siam (Thailand) and Cambodia had been traditional enemies for centuries, and relations between the two states deteriorated following Cambodia's recognition of the People's Republic of China at the end of the Chinese civil war in 1949 (see conflict 001).

Cambodia obtained independence from France in 1956. As security against a possible communist insurgency, the Siamese government moved troops to the frontier. On November 24, 1958, Cambodia severed diplomatic relations with Siam, and Siam retaliated the following day by sealing off the border area. It was feared the conflict could escalate into war.

Cambodia referred the dispute to the United Nations on December 3, 1958, and both countries subsequently asked for a mediator to be appointed. U.N. mediator Baron Johan Beck-Friis managed to ease tensions along the border, secure the release of thirty-two Siamese prisoners arrested by Cambodia for border violations, and create conditions allowing for the return of the respective ambassadors to their posts by February 1959.

For further information and background reading, see reference item numbers 255, 689, 692, 755, 869.

060. LAOS
*Political anarchy, civil war; the first Laotian civil war
(December 1958–1962)*

The 1954 Geneva Conventions signed at the end of the French-Indochina War
(see conflict 007) attempted to unite Laos under a single government. By 1958
the coalition government of national reconciliation had overcome numerous
obstacles and integrated the country's various factions. The International
Control Commission overseeing the transition to Laotian rule was adjourned.
The United States wanted a friendly government in Laos and began to undermine the government of unity while supporting right-wing factions.

Fighting broke out in December 1958, and by 1959 Laos was in the midst
of full-blown civil war. The government had split into left- and right-wing factions. The United States alleged North Vietnamese involvement, and a French
investigation revealed that North Vietnam was training and equipping left-
wing Pathet Lao forces. The United States began stepping up its support for the
conservatives , and the conflict became embroiled in cold war politics. By 1961
the Soviet Union was airlifting supplies to the Pathet Lao, and the United States
was sending troops to support the government. North Vietnamese forces also
became actively involved, fighting for the Pathet Lao.

After the United Nations failed to solve the conflict, another Geneva conference was convened in June 1961. After months of talks, agreements were
reached that led to the withdrawal of all foreign troops from Laos and the
establishment of a new coalition government. By late 1962 Laos was again
neutral. The Geneva agreements did not last, however, and civil war again
broke out in 1964 (see conflict 095). The number of casualties is not known
for this conflict but is thought to be in the thousands.

*For further information and background reading, see reference item numbers
46, 255, 714, 728, 757, 854, 865.*

061. FRANCE-TUNISIA
French-Algerian war; border incidents (February–August 1959)

From 1954 to 1962 French troops were engaged in a brutal war against
Algerian nationalists (see conflict 038). The fighting often spilled over into bordering countries, including Tunisia, one of France's former colonies. Tunisia
itself had engaged in a number of armed conflicts with France from 1952 to
1956 (see conflict 028) and in 1958 (see conflict 055).

On February 14, 1959, Tunisia alleged that French fighter aircraft had
crossed the border and attacked a group of Tunisians, causing three deaths and
several casualties. Further sorties by French troops across the Tunisian border
were reported on February 9 and again in April. France alleged a Tunisian

incursion on May 26 in which six French troops were killed. Incidents were reported in July and August, but the conflict gradually abated. Neither side attempted to settle the conflict by peaceful means, and the continued French presence in the region led to armed conflict in 1961 (see conflict 075).

For further information and background reading, see reference item numbers 255, 293, 314, 325, 401, 434.

062. SYRIA-IRAQ

Syrian-backed putsch, government suppression; the Mosul revolt (March–April 1959)

Having come to power in 1958 through a military coup that ousted King Faisal II, Abdel Karim Kassem served as Iraq's prime minister and head until 1963, when he himself was deposed and killed in a military coup. His opposition to the pan-Arabist movement did not endear him to neighboring Syria, then part of Egyptian president Nasser's United Arab Republic.

Syria had been fomenting opposition to Kassem's regime for some time, supplying large amounts of military hardware to units of the Iraqi army stationed in the Mosul region and led by Colonel Shawaf, an Arab nationalist. Colonel Shawaf's forces seized control of Mosul in March 1959 but failed to link with the colonel's supporters in Baghdad; Kassem was able to remain in command. He ordered the Iraqi air force to attack the rebel units in and around Mosul; Colonel Shawaf was killed.

Once Mosul was recaptured, Kassem allowed communist forces to go on a rampage of revenge killings. Some of the rebels sought refuge in Syria, which led to a number of border clashes between Iraqi and Syrian forces. The Iraqi air force bombed Syrian villages thought to be rebel sanctuaries. Eventually, the dispute lapsed. In all, two thousand people were killed in the fighting. An Arab League attempt to mediate a peaceful settlement ended in failure.

For further information and background reading, see reference item numbers 255, 1050, 1175, 1183, 1254, 1295, 1303.

063. DOMINICAN REPUBLIC

Cuban-sponsored military invasion; the exiles conflict (June–July 1959)

During the brutal dictatorship of Rafael Trujillo Molina, Dominican opposition leaders found refuge in Cuba. Cuban involvement in Dominican affairs emerged out of the activities of this group of exiles, who were using Cuba as a base from which to engineer the overthrow of Trujillo. In June and July 1959, the exiles launched a series of invasions against the Dominican Republic with the support of Cuba.

The invasions were small-scale affairs and easily repulsed by the Dominican army. They did, however, expose the problems of the Trujillo regime, as some regular army units defected to the exiles during the invasions. At least eighty people were killed during the conflict, and no real attempts were made to settle the conflict peacefully. Trujillo did appeal to the OAS for aid, but his brutal regime was so unpopular that no action was taken.

For further information and background reading, see reference item numbers 46, 255, 507, 513, 562, 569.

064. CHINA-NEPAL
Boundary dispute (June 1959–July 1960)

The Chinese-Nepal border had never been officially demarcated; the dispute was precipitated by this fact. Following China's invasion of Tibet (see conflict 044), Chinese forces made numerous sorties into Nepalese territory in pursuit of Tibetan rebels. A number of serious border incidents were reported from April to October 1959. On October 29, 1959, China and Nepal began negotiations on the border issue, and agreement was reached on March 22, 1960.

Chinese border violations continued, however, and Nepal began massing troops in the area, as did China. A major clash occurred on June 30, 1960; there were some casualties. Nepal protested, and China agreed to pull back its troops. In October 1960 both sides agreed to officially demarcate the border, and a border pact was signed in October 1961. Although there were only a few fatalities, a major border war had only narrowly been avoided.

For further information and background reading, see reference item numbers 76, 255.

065. HAITI
Cuban-sponsored military invasion; the Haitian exiles conflict (August 1959)

In February 1959 a revolutionary force of Haitian exiles was formed in Cuba. Its aim was to invade Haiti and depose Haiti's hated dictator, François (Papa Doc) Duvalier. Cuba's official policy at the time was to refrain from supporting revolutionary groups based in Cuba. In April the Cuban coast guard blocked the exiles' attempt to invade Haiti from Cuba.

The continued presence of Haitian exiles in Cuba strained relations between the two countries. Haiti appealed for international aid to prevent invasion. The

United States sent large amounts of military and economic aid to the Haitian military, while the Dominican Republic mobilized its coastal forces as a joint defense exercise with Haiti.

On August 15, 1959, a small invasion was once again launched from Cuba. The invading rebels were quickly repulsed, and most were killed. Haiti protested vigorously about Cuban complicity. Cuba denied any official involvement in the invasion and eventually the dispute lapsed. In this case, only twenty-six people were killed during the conflict, and no efforts were made to settle the conflict peacefully.

For further information and background reading, see reference item numbers 46, 255, 507, 513, 562, 569, 573.

066. CHINA-INDIA

McMahon Line boundary dispute; Sino-Indian wars (August 1959–February 1960)

China lost control of Tibet after the collapse of the Qing dynasty in 1911. As a consequence, Britain and Tibet agreed on a new territorial boundary at the Simla Conference (1913–1914). This boundary remarcation, based on the McMahon Line, pushed Indian frontiers forward at Tibet's expense. The Communists disputed the validity of the boundary when they came to power in China in 1949.

Following China's invasion of Tibet in 1950–1951 and the exile of the Dalai Lama to India (see conflicts 025 and 044), the issue became a source of real contention. China claimed India was interfering in Tibet's internal affairs by giving Tibetan nationalist rebels bases from which to launch attacks against occupying Chinese forces. China began moving large numbers of troops to the border areas.

On August 25, 1959, a Chinese force attacked Indian positions and captured the border post of Lonju. On October 21 a Chinese force took an Indian patrol hostage. In an attempt to ease tensions, Chinese premier Zhou Enlai and Indian prime minister Jawaharlal Nehru met in New Delhi for a series of negotiations about the disputed territory. The talks were soon abandoned. The dispute abated somewhat in the months that followed, only to reemerge in 1962 in a much more serious confrontation (see conflict 084). At least twenty-five soldiers were killed during this conflict.

For further information and background reading, see reference item numbers 76, 255, 691, 738, 788, 831, 873.

067. THE BELGIAN CONGO (Congo; Zaire)
Secession, anarchy, civil war; the Congo crisis (July 1960–mid-1964)

Nationalists in the Belgian Congo, most notably Patrice Lumumba and Joseph Kasavubu, began agitating for independence from Belgium in the 1950s. Although plagued by intertribal fighting and civil disorder, the country was granted independence on June 30, 1960, with Lumumba as prime minister and Kasavubu as president. But on July 5, 1960, about a week after the country was granted independence, Congolese troops mutinied and began attacking Belgian nationals. Belgium sent in troops to quell the rebellion without Congolese permission.

Six days later a second crisis developed when the mineral-rich province of Katanga (now called Shaba) was declared independent by Moïse Tshombe, who worked closely with foreign mining interests. Tshombe bolstered his army with large numbers of foreign mercenaries. Alarmed about the possibility that Belgium would regain control over Katanga, Lumumba appealed for U.N. assistance to quell the rebellion and reestablish civil order. The United Nations formed a special operation, the U.N. Operation in the Congo (UNOC), and called for the withdrawal of Belgian troops. By August 1960 U.N. troops had replaced Belgian troops but refused to take Katanga by force. In September the government split into three factions, one under Prime Minister Lumumba, one under President Kasavubu, and still another under army chief of staff Lt. Gen. Joseph Désiré Mobutu (later Mobutu Sésé Séko, president of Zaire from 1965 to 1997).

These three factions and the secessionist regime in Katanga then engaged in a year of unlimited civil war. The UNOC supported the Kasavubu faction, while the Soviet Union began supplying the Lumumba faction. Mobutu was backed by the United States. Throughout this period, the United Nations tried desperately to mediate a peaceful solution, but without success. Lumumba was taken to Katanga and murdered in January 1961 and his faction defeated in early 1962. A government of national unity was gradually established. Following inconclusive talks with the Katangan separatists, the breakaway province was invaded in December 1962. By January 1963 the rebels had been defeated and Katanga reincorporated into the country. But Katanga (Shaba) separatism would continue to plague Congo (see conflicts 169, 177, 226, 229).

With the war winding down, the UNOC began to disband in February 1963. The fighting had always been intense, and more than 110,000 people were killed, including 50 Belgian soldiers and 126 U.N. peacekeepers. U.N. efforts at mediation were largely ineffective in the many-sided conflict, and the U.N. secretary-general himself was killed in a plane crash during one of the peace missions. Mobutu took power from Kasavubu in a 1965 military coup.

The civil war caused massive upheaval in Congo (which Mobutu renamed Zaire in 1971), and military pacification efforts continued for several decades. The Mobutu regime recruited mercenaries in its initial drive to establish control over a country the size of the United States east of the Mississippi, and these initial pacification efforts led to conflict with Uganda, Congo's northern neighbor (see conflict 103). A surge in rebel activity in 1996 eventually saw the complete collapse of the Mobutu regime in 1997, leading to instability throughout Central Africa (see map 5). Soon after Mobutu's ouster, the country was renamed Democratic Republic of the Congo.

For further information and background reading, see reference item numbers 255, 285, 305, 349, 387.

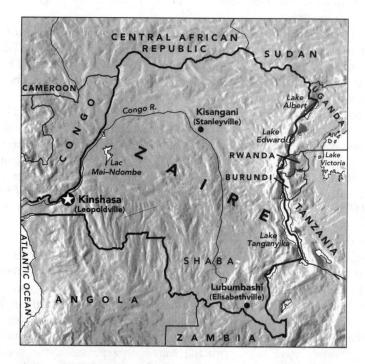

MAP 5. **Central Africa**

Congo's civil war of 1960 to 1964 witnessed the rise of Mobutu Sésé Séko, whose U.S.-backed forces battled two other factions and a secessionist regime based in mineral-rich Katanga (now Shaba) for control of the government. Mobutu became president in 1965 and six years later renamed the country Zaire. Following his ouster in 1997, the name was changed again to Democratic Republic of the Congo.

068. PAKISTAN-AFGHANISTAN
Boundary dispute; the Pathan conflict (September 1960–May 1963)

Pakistan and Afghanistan had already fought twice over this disputed boundary (see conflicts 020, 023) on the eastern side of their common border. Because it was inhabited by an Afghan tribe, the Pathan (or Pushtu), Afghanistan refused to accept the internationally recognized border, demanding that the area either be integrated into Afghanistan or established as an autonomous Pathanistan.

Tensions rose dramatically in March 1960, when the Soviet Union openly declared support for the Afghanistan position. Starting in September, both Pakistan and Afghanistan made mutual allegations of border transgressions, with Pakistan protesting to Afghanistan about the country's mistreatment of Pakistani nationals living there.

In March 1961 military actions increased, and intermittent fighting continued for two years. Pakistan used the air force to bomb supposed arms distribution points, and cross-border raids became more serious. The Soviet Union began sending arms to Afghanistan, while the Afghan government stepped up its program of fomenting rebellion among the Pathan tribes people. The situation was extremely tense.

With the shah of Iran mediating and a change of government in Afghanistan, a settlement was reached on May 30, 1963. The border between the two countries reopened on July 20. In all, approximately thirty fatalities were recorded, but the two countries had narrowly avoided all-out war.

For further information and background reading, see reference item numbers 76, 81, 255, 797.

069. UNITED STATES–VIETNAM
Civil war, anticommunist U.S. military intervention; the Vietnam War (December 1960–May 1975)

After the French-Indochina war ended in 1954 with the defeat of France (see conflict 007), Vietnam was divided into the Socialist Republic of Vietnam (North Vietnam) and the Republic of Vietnam (South Vietnam). Acting with the support of North Vietnam, communist rebels, called the Vietcong, began a terrorist campaign in South Vietnam in 1957. They were opposed to the U.S.-backed military regime in the South and wanted to see the establishment of a communist state.

In its early years, the war was largely restricted to insurgent attacks on South Vietnam from rebel camps in North Vietnam, Laos, and Cambodia. South Vietnamese army units conducted counterinsurgency operations in these countries in an effort to stamp out the rebels.

U.S. military involvement began in 1961 when large numbers of advisers and aircraft were sent to South Vietnam to aid in the fighting. Despite frequent allegations of North Vietnamese battle support for the Vietcong, full-scale hostilities between the United States and North Vietnam did not begin until August 2, 1964, after the Gulf of Tonkin incident. Here, North Vietnamese torpedo boats attacked a U.S. destroyer, allegedly in retaliation for U.S. support of South Vietnamese attacks against North Vietnamese targets in the Gulf area. On August 4, after allegations of a North Vietnamese attack against a U.S. naval vessel, the U.S. initiated bombing raids of North Vietnamese military facilities along the Gulf. Attempts by U.N. secretary-general U Thant to bring the two sides together to seek a peaceful settlement failed, as did similar efforts by Soviet foreign minister Aleksei Kosygin.

The United States initiated repeated bombing raids against North Vietnamese and Vietcong bases in Laos following the Gulf of Tonkin incident. These raids were expanded in 1966 to include Cambodia. U.S. ground troops were engaged in a combat role in March 1965 after a U.S. military base at Pleiku was attacked by the Vietcong. International involvement in the war expanded in mid-1965 when Australia, New Zealand, and South Korea contributed forces to the conflict. In subsequent years, Thailand and the Philippines also entered the war.

The Tet offensive of 1968 changed the course of the war. Backed by North Vietnamese troops, the Vietcong won a series of battles that brought serious fighting close to Saigon (now Ho Chi Minh City), the South Vietnamese capital. Although the United States quickly regained the lost territory, it sought to scale down its involvement and step up negotiations. The United States ended its bombings of North Vietnam on November 1, 1968. At the same time, representatives of the Vietcong were admitted to the peace talks.

U.S. troop withdrawals began in 1969, and negotiations continued until a peace agreement was signed in January 1973, providing for a cease-fire, a withdrawal of all U.S. troops, a joint military commission, and an international commission for control and supervision to oversee the implementation of the peace agreement. Australia, New Zealand, and Thailand withdrew their forces in 1972. South Vietnam and the Vietcong continued to fight alone until the government in South Vietnam was toppled in April 1975.

The war was particularly brutal and cost the lives of an estimated 1.8 million people, including almost sixty thousand U.S. troops and four thousand South Korean troops. Thailand and Australia each lost five hundred troops, but by far most of the fatalities were civilian. Hundreds of thousands of civilians were killed in indiscriminate bombing raids. The war polarized U.S. public opinion and had a profound effect on subsequent U.S. foreign policy. The now-united Vietnam began to flex its powers in the region (see conflicts 181, 182, 211, 218, 243).

For further information and background reading, see reference item numbers 686, 690, 711, 712, 717, 719, 733, 739, 741, 749.

070. AFRICAN TERRITORIES–PORTUGAL
African nationalism; struggle for independence (1961–July 1975)

Portugal's colonial holdings in Africa go back to the sixteenth century. By the middle of the twentieth century its African territories included Angola, Guinea-Bissau, Cape Verde Islands, Mozambique, and São Tome and Principe. Portuguese rule was generally harsh, and the colonial administration did little to prepare the territories for independence.

Beginning with armed revolt in Angola in 1961, these territories began to press for independence. In February 1961 the Union of Angolan People (UPA) began to make terrorist attacks against European settlers. The conflict expanded significantly in March when the Marxist Movimento Popular de Libertação de Angola (MPLA) merged with the UPA and precipitated total guerrilla warfare. Protracted, bloody conflict went on for thirteen years; it was then immediately followed by civil war (see conflict 148).

Similar armed struggles for independence began in Guinea-Bissau in 1963 and in Mozambique in 1964. Nationalist parties took up arms in a guerrilla war to liberate their countries from the oppressive Portuguese rule. Throughout the conflict, rebels received aid from independent front-line states such as Zambia, from where they also launched attacks. On the other side, Portugal received significant aid from South Africa and what was then Southern Rhodesia (now Zambia) in its attempts to contain the fighting. Portugal also employed mercenaries, most notably in an effort to destabilize Zaire (Congo), which was actively supporting the Frente Nacional de Libertação de Angola (FNLA) guerrilla movement. Typically, small guerrilla bands would attack Portuguese targets and then vanish into the bushland. Portuguese troops and mercenary forces would take repressive measures and periodically mount operations to flush out the rebels.

Neither side was able to get the upper hand, but Portuguese casualties were mounting and the costs becoming unbearably high. The intransigence of the Portuguese government and the unwinnable nature of the war led to a military coup in Lisbon on April 25, 1974. The new military government implemented a unilateral cease-fire and offered independence to all the territories on July 27, 1974. Guinea-Bissau formally gained independence on September 10, 1974. Mozambique completed the transition to independence on June 25, 1975, and Angola on November 11, 1975. More than a hundred thousand people were killed during the struggle for independence, including large numbers of civilians and Portuguese troops. As many as five thousand Portuguese troops died in the war, and the only negotiations undertaken were those that led to independence at the end of the conflict. As with Angola, Mozambique splintered and plunged into civil war upon gaining independence (see conflict 160).

For further information and background reading, see reference item numbers 255, 306, 311, 312, 367, 370, 379.

071. THE KURDS–IRAQ
Attempted secession (March 1961–1966)

A Sunni Muslim tribe of non-Arab stock, the Kurds live in a mountainous plateau region comprising parts of Turkey, Iran, and Iraq (see map 6). Never united under one government, the Kurds have nevertheless agitated for secession from the three countries they inhabit.

In 1946 the Kurds staged an uprising in northern Iraq with Soviet support, but the revolt failed (1945–1947; see conflict 005). The Kurdish leader Mullah Mustafa Barazani had survived, however, and was living in exile in the Soviet Union, waiting for another opportunity to lead a secessionist revolt. When a pardon from the new government of Abdel Karim Kassem allowed him to return to Iraq in 1958, Barazani immediately took up control of the Kurdish Democratic Party (KDP).

Following years of indirect conflict with the government, open warfare broke out between Kurdish rebels under Barazani and the Iraqi army in March 1961. By October the rebels controlled one-third of the country. Iraqi troops immediately counterattacked; intermittent guerrilla warfare continued for much of the next decade.

At the war's outset, Turkey frequently alleged Iraqi violations of its sovereignty because of Iraqi operations along its border. Turkey was temporarily

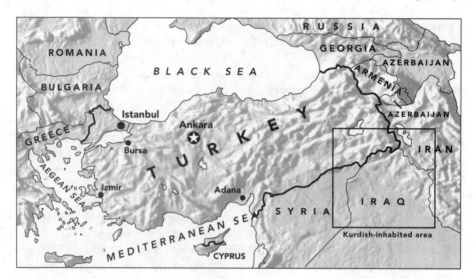

MAP 6. **Kurdish Areas in Turkey, Iran, and Iraq**

The Kurds have tried since 1920 to secede from the countries they inhabit—Turkey, Iran, and Iraq. The attempted secession of 1961 to 1966 ended with a 12-point plan designed to improve conditions for Kurds, but their struggle for independence continues to the present day (see conflict 224).

drawn into the war in August 1962 when the Iraqi air force attacked Turkish border positions and a village. An Iraqi plane was subsequently shot down over Turkey, and Iraq quickly backed down to avoid stepped-up Turkish involvement. During a major Iraqi offensive against the Kurds in June 1963, Syria contributed a force of five thousand combat troops and aircraft to the Iraqis. Heavy bombing raids, however, failed to suppress the Kurdish guerrilla movement.

In the period 1965–1966 Iraq reintensified its efforts to defeat the Kurds, and its operations once again involved sorties into Turkey and Iran. In June 1966 the Kurds and the Iraqi government agreed on a 12-point plan aimed at improving conditions for Kurds. Fighting continued for the next four years, and it was only after a reaffirmation of the 12-point plan by the Iraqi government in January 1970 that the negotiations leading to an armistice agreement made any progress. The armistice was signed on March 11, 1970. Approximately ten thousand people were killed during the conflict.

For further information and background reading, see reference item numbers 1038, 1078, 1109, 1128, 1170, 1190, 1240, 1250, 1300.

072. UNITED STATES–CUBA
Anti-Castro military invasion; the Bay of Pigs (April–May 1961)

Following the fall in 1959 of the U.S.-backed Batista regime at the end of the Cuban civil war (see conflict 049), the United States began to investigate the possibilities for effecting an overthrow of Fidel Castro's new communist state. It was the height of the cold war, and the United States was worried about Cuba's role in fomenting communist insurgencies in the region.

With CIA encouragement, the new administration of John F. Kennedy adopted a plan to equip and train anti-Castro Cuban exiles as an invasion force. Having recently installed a friendly regime in Guatemala, the CIA used that country to train Cuban exiles it had recruited in the United States (see conflict 037).

The invasion was launched by 1,500 exiles on April 17, 1961, landing at the Bay of Pigs in Cuba. Covert U.S. air strikes failed to knock out Cuban air superiority, and the invasion force was quickly pinned down on the beaches. The exiles were forced to surrender on April 20. Those who escaped were to establish guerrilla bases in the Cuban highlands. However, all remaining invaders were hunted down and caught by early May.

The Bay of Pigs operation was a humiliating embarrassment for the new administration and to U.S. foreign policy. In the ensuing months tensions between Cuba and the United States remained extremely high. There were hijackings of planes and boats by both sides, and numerous other such incidents. In all, approximately three hundred people were killed in the failed invasion. This conflict was the precursor to a far more serious confrontation in

1962, the Cuban Missile Crisis, when the Soviet Union attempted to station nuclear missiles on the island nation (see conflict 082).

For further information and background reading, see reference item numbers 46, 255, 506, 513, 515, 562, 569, 574.

073. IRAQ-KUWAIT
Territorial dispute; the Kuwaiti independence crisis
(June 1961–February 1962)

Kuwait had been a part of the Ottoman Empire's massive Arab land holdings during the nineteenth century. When Kuwait declared its independence in 1899, it sought and gained British protection in exchange for British control over its foreign affairs. Kuwait gained full independence from Britain on June 19, 1961.

On June 25, 1961, Iraqi prime minister Abdel Karim Kassem declared that all Kuwait was in fact part of Iraq's Basra province of (a claim Saddam Hussein would repeat in 1990—see conflict 261). He also expressed Iraq's intention to incorporate Kuwait. Britain, which under the independence agreement with Kuwait promised to defend the small state, positioned troops close to the Iraqi border. Tensions were extremely high.

In July 1961 Kuwait was elected into the Arab League, which passed a resolution requiring that the British force in Kuwait be replaced by Arab League troops. The Arab League force began to arrive on September 10, and by October 19 the British forces had been withdrawn.

Kassem failed to reassert his claims to Kuwait, the threat dissipated, and the Arab League force was disbanded by February 1962. This conflict was later to prove an ominous precursor to much deadlier disputes from 1973 to 1975 (see conflict 140) and again in 1990–1991 (see conflict 261). Although there were no actual fatalities, the strains and subsequent armed disputes made this a potentially serious conflict.

For further information and background reading, see reference item numbers 46, 76, 255, 1041, 1095, 1219, 1220.

074. UNITED STATES–USSR
Cold war dispute; the Berlin Wall (July–November 1961)

The events of July to November 1961 have their roots in the postwar division of Germany (and the city of Berlin itself) into four sectors, with the Eastern sector dominated by the Soviet Union. The airlift crisis of 1948–1949 (see conflict 013) served as a precursor to this conflict. Berlin's exceptional status, hundreds of miles into the Soviet zone of occupation, was the source of some friction between the Soviet Union and the Western powers (Britain, France, and the United States). The friction escalated into an all-out crisis when the Soviet government sought to incorporate Berlin's Western sectors into a demilitarized "free city." When a summit between President John F. Kennedy and Soviet premier Nikita S. Khrushchev in June 1961 failed to guarantee Western access to West Berlin, the East Germans responded by constructing the Berlin Wall—perhaps the most powerful symbol of the cold war.

On June 28, 1961, East Germany announced restrictions on Western air traffic. These were ultimately not enforced, but they did worsen East-West strains. The NATO allies warned of dire consequences if their access to West Berlin were impeded. On July 7 and again on August 4, restrictions were placed on East Germans working in West Berlin in an attempt to stem the flow of refugees to the West. The Western powers protested these restrictions.

On August 13, 1961, the border between East and West Berlin was closed and the Berlin Wall more fully erected on August 17–18. In the ensuing days massive U.S. troop reinforcements arrived in Berlin and patrols were set up in the no-man's land around the wall. The saber-rattling continued over the next few weeks and included a resumption of nuclear weapons testing by both superpowers in November 1961. Neither side attempted to settle the conflict by dialogue; though there was no actual fighting, the conflict fueled tensions that eventually produced the 1962 Cuban Missile Crisis (see conflict 082).

For further information and background reading, see reference item numbers 255, 925, 935, 945, 960, 991, 1000.

075. FRANCE-TUNISIA

Postindependence autonomy dispute; the Bizerte conflict (July–September 1961)

Fighting between France and Tunisia had occurred from 1952 to 1956 (see conflict 028), in 1958 (see conflict 055), and again in 1959 (see conflict 061). This latter conflict emerged out of France's continued military presence at a base at Bizerte, despite protracted negotiations aimed at a complete French withdrawal from Tunisia.

When France sought to extend the runway at Bizerte to accommodate more modern aircraft, Tunisia intensified its efforts to gain an immediate withdrawal of French units. It issued political demands to France, and on July 19, 1961, instituted a military blockade of the base. Tunisia announced it would open fire on any French aircraft attempting to land at the base. A French helicopter and some reconnaissance aircraft were shot at, and the French responded by strafing Tunisian troops.

On July 20, 1961, French troops opened fire on Tunisian demonstrators surrounding the base. French troops then tried to take the town of Bizerte, and over the ensuing two days, hundreds of Tunisians and several French soldiers were killed. Tunisia protested to the United Nations and broke off all diplomatic ties with France. U.N. secretary-general Dag Hammarskjöld sought to mediate the conflict, but his efforts were unsuccessful, although a cease-fire was arranged. A stand-off ensued for the next several weeks, but in September tensions eased somewhat when both sides expressed interest in negotiating an eventual French withdrawal. Withdrawal was finally completed on October 15, 1963. About one thousand people were killed during the conflict.

For further information and background reading, see reference item numbers 255, 293, 314, 401, 434.

076. INDIA-PORTUGAL

Anti-Portuguese territorial dispute; the Goa conflict
(December 1961)

Portugal had occupied a number of ports on the Indian coast since 1505. Many had been relinquished, but at the time of Indian independence in 1948, Portugal still had control over Goa, an economically valuable colony, and a few other smaller territories. India sought to take possession of the protectorates, but Portugal refused. India responded by smuggling in agitators to begin a passive resistance campaign in 1955, but Portuguese authorities brutally suppressed this movement.

In 1961 the Indian government passed legislation annexing the territories. Both sides strengthened their military forces in the region during a stand-off period. On December 11, 1961, Indian prime minister Jawaharlal Nehru formally demanded that Portugal withdraw from Goa, and on December 15 the first minor border incidents between Portuguese and Indian troops occurred. Portugal appealed to the United Nations, but the Security Council was unable to deal with the conflict.

India launched a full-scale invasion of Goa on December 17, and after brief fighting, Portugal surrendered the territory the following day. All the territories were subsequently incorporated into India. About seventy people were killed in the fighting, including two Indian and two Portuguese soldiers. Bitterness between the two states over the conflict continued until the 1974 coup in Lisbon, when Portugal dropped all its claims to the territories.

For further information and background reading, see reference item numbers 76, 255, 821, 832.

077. INDONESIA-MALAYSIA
Separatist civil disturbances; the Borneo conflict
(1962–November 1965)

Before World War II the island of Borneo was divided between Britain and the Netherlands. Britain controlled Sabah, Brunei, and Sarawak, while the rest of the island was a Dutch colonial territory, which Indonesia incorporated at its independence in 1949. In 1961 Britain declared its wish to federate the British protectorates on Borneo with Malaya. Both the Philippines and Indonesia protested, as it infringed on their own territorial claims to Borneo.

In the period immediately before the granting of independence to Sabah and Sarawak, Indonesia actively supported opposition groups in the British territories, including the Sarawak United People's Party (SUPP), the Sarawak Advanced Youth's Association (SAYA), and the National Army of North Borneo (TMKU). These organizations sometimes engaged in guerrilla activities against colonial targets, forcing British troops to be deployed.

Both Sabah and Sarawak were granted independence on September 16, 1963, and they subsequently joined the Federation of Malaysia. Indonesia refused to recognize the incorporation of Sabah and Sarawak into Malaysia and, starting in January 1964, began military operations on the border with Malaysia Borneo. British troops were brought in to contain Indonesian activities in the border area. The conflict escalated dangerously from August 1964, when Indonesia began initiating attacks from the air and from the sea. New Zealand and Australian troops subsequently assisted British and Malaysian forces in repelling the attacks.

Several states in the region attempted to mediate, including Cambodia, the Philippines, and Thailand. The United Nations and the Commonwealth also tried to facilitate dialogue, with varying degrees of success. As it was, the conflict deescalated rapidly after October 1965, when civil unrest in Indonesia undermined President Ahmed Sukarno's powers. Britain scaled down its deployment from November 1965, and the conflict evaporated completely in March 1966 when Sukarno was forced to resign. Perhaps as many as one thousand people were killed during the conflict, including seventy-five British soldiers and six hundred Indonesian military personnel.

For further information and background reading, see reference item numbers 255, 664, 710, 746, 782, 856.

078. THE NETHERLANDS–INDONESIA; WEST IRIAN (Irian Jaya)

Separatist insurgency; the West Irian conflict (January–August 1962)

The status of the western part of the island of New Guinea, known as West Irian, remained unresolved after Indonesia was granted independence in 1949 (see conflict 006). The Netherlands retained control over the region, despite talks aimed at incorporating the territory into Indonesia. In an effort to remove the Netherlands from West Irian, Indonesia initiated a full mobilization of its armed forces and began a series of small raids into the region (see map 7).

Following a number of serious troop and naval clashes, the United Nations intervened in a desperate attempt to restrict the spread of the conflict. U.N. secretary-general U Thant arranged talks in January 1962. U.S. ambassador Ellsworth Bunker, U Thant's representative, took over in March, and on July 31, 1962, he secured an agreement. Both sides agreed to withdraw their troops, and U.N. troops would then administer the territory until May 1, 1963, at which time Indonesia would take possession. This all took place according to the agreement, and the last violence associated with this conflict occurred in

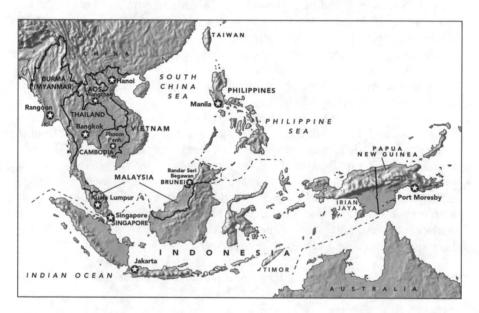

MAP 7. **Southeast Asia**

Under the terms of a U.N.-brokered agreement between Indonesia and the Netherlands, Indonesia took possession of West Irian (now Irian Jaya) in May 1963. Indonesia's failure to implement a key provision of the agreement—a program of West Irian self-determination— sparked a secessionist movement on West Irian, then a war with Papua New Guinea. The secessionist movement remains active today.

August 1962 when the Netherlands transferred the territory to Indonesia under U.N. supervision. A condition of the agreement, however, was that Indonesia implement a program leading to West Irian self-determination by 1969. But Indonesia never carried out this program, and a guerrilla movement emerged in 1965 aimed at Irian independence; this movement still plagues Indonesia (see conflicts 100, 202).

Much of the fighting involved guerrilla warfare and fomenting violence among the local population. It is possible that as many as thirty thousand people were killed in the disturbances, including one hundred Indonesian military personnel, mostly at the hands of the police.

For further information and background reading, see reference item numbers 255, 710, 732, 746, 764, 772, 834, 856.

079. CHINA-TAIWAN
KMT-CCP territorial dispute; invasion threat
(March–December 1962)

Following the Nationalists' defeat on mainland China in 1949 (see conflict 001), conflict between China and Taiwan broke out into warfare from 1949 to 1953 (see conflict 021), in 1954 to 1955 (see conflict 036), and in 1958 (see conflict 058). China remained committed to reuniting all the territories that had once been part of mainland China, and this caused a constant state of alarm in Taiwan. Since December 1958, however, tensions had eased somewhat, but conflict broke out again from March to December 1962 when China moved major army units near Nationalist-controlled islands in the Taiwan Strait. The troop concentrations were thought to be greater than at any other time, and Taiwan went on alert, anticipating an invasion.

At the same time, Nationalist leaders in Taiwan made bellicose statements about a "return to the mainland" (that is, a military invasion of China), indicating the United States would back any invasion attempt. Conscription was increased and new taxes added. Following U.S. statements indicating the United States would not back a Taiwanese invasion of mainland China but would defend Taiwan against invasion, the conflict abated, although tensions remained extremely high because no conflict-management attempts had been made. China gradually reduced troop concentrations near the islands but did not renounce its aim to unite all of China.

For further information and background reading, see reference item numbers 255, 698, 718, 752, 852, 866, 878.

080. NEPAL-INDIA
Prodemocratic rebellion; border incidents (April–November 1962)

In December 1960 the king of Nepal dissolved the country's first democratically elected government. Nepalese rebels led by General Subarna began a
guerrilla campaign in an effort to restore democratic government. The rebellion spread to areas bordering with India, and Nepal accused India of organizing the rebellion. In fact, a number of Nepalese opposition groups were in
exile in India, from where they had mounted a vicious propaganda campaign.

The conflict escalated after Nepal made several agreements with China,
including the building of a road from Nepal to Tibet. This threatened India, as
Chinese troops could be supplied all the way to the Indian border. By June
1962 the rebellion had become a full-scale uprising, and there were a number
of border incidents as Nepalese troops pursued rebels into Indian territory.
China then announced it would defend Nepal if India invaded.

Events in Nepal were overtaken by the Sino-Indian war (see conflict 084),
and the conflict lapsed completely in 1963. The rebellion diminished and was
over by April 1963. Approximately thirty-five people were killed during the
fighting, and there were no serious attempts at peaceful conflict management.

*For further information and background reading, see reference item numbers
255, 691.*

081. SYRIA-ISRAEL
*Arab-Israeli territorial dispute; Lake Tiberias
(June 1962–August 1963)*

Since the Israeli war of independence in 1948–1949 (see conflict 012), Syrian
and Israeli troops had frequently clashed along their common border (see conflicts 026, 042, 051). In 1962 the strains were especially severe at Lake Tiberias
(Kinneret), controlled by Israel. Israel claimed the area on the basis of British
maps, but Syria controlled strategic positions on the eastern shore. There were
frequent incidents involving Syrian fishermen who did not get Israeli permission for their activities.

Syrian artillery pieces on the eastern shore shelled Israeli positions and
patrol boats in February and March 1962, leading to a retaliatory Israeli attack
on Syrian gun positions on March 16–17. There were four reported fatalities.
Later, in August 1963, Gen. Odd Bull of the U.N. Truce Supervisory
Organization tried to settle the issue through mediation but was only partially
successful.

*For further information and background reading, see reference item numbers
255, 1047, 1051, 1084, 1098, 1158, 1171, 1248, 1284.*

082. UNITED STATES–USSR
Cold war confrontation; the Cuban Missile Crisis
(September–November 1962)

As a result of its poor relationship with the United States following the failed Bay of Pigs invasion attempt in 1961 (see conflict 072), Cuba had allied itself closely with the Soviet Union and received substantial military support from the communist superpower. In mid-1962 the Soviet Union began to station nuclear-capable missiles on Cuba. The United States became aware of this through spy satellite photos in mid-October 1962. On October 22 President John F. Kennedy demanded their removal and declared that a naval blockade of Cuba would begin on October 24. The United States stated that any attacks by Cuba would result in retaliation against the Soviet Union. The Soviet Union refused to acknowledge the stationing of the missiles on Cuba but offered to reach an understanding with the United States over the issue on October 26.

Meanwhile, Soviet ships carrying nuclear weapons continued to steam toward Cuba, heightening the possibility of nuclear confrontation. U.N. efforts to resolve the crisis were unsuccessful. Tensions were extremely high, especially when a U.S. spy plane was shot down over Cuba on October 27. It was thought that the United States might even invade Cuba to prevent the stationing of missiles there, thus provoking direct confrontation between the superpowers.

Despite the downing of the spy plane, a U.S.-Soviet agreement was reached on that day whereby the Soviet Union agreed to remove the missiles in exchange for U.S. assurances that it would not invade Cuba. This was the superpowers' first game of nuclear brinkmanship, and although there were no fatalities, the world had come to the very threshold of catastrophe. Relations between the superpowers remained extremely strained, as did those between Cuba and the United States.

For further information and background reading, see reference item numbers 46, 255, 501, 507, 513, 515, 563, 565.

083. NORTH YEMEN
Civil war; the royalist rebellion (September 1962–October 1967)

At the end of the nineteenth century, the British divided Yemen into North Yemen and South Yemen (the Aden Protectorate) for administrative purposes. Britain retained Aden as a protectorate, but North Yemen was ruled by a series of imams. Following the death of Imam Saif al-Islam Ahmad on September 18, 1962, who had held power in North Yemen since 1948, his son Muhammad al-Badr claimed to be his legitimate successor. He was deposed in a military coup staged on September 26, 1962 (see conflict 133).

The deposed al-Badr sought to regain power through arms, and civil war ensued between the deposed royalists and the newly established republican government. The war was internationalized from October 1962, when Egyptian troops moved into North Yemen in support of the republicans. Jordan and Saudi Arabia entered on the side of the royalists, and Egyptian air force units stationed in North Yemen intermittently raided Saudi Arabia between November 1962 and May 1967.

A U.N. observer unit arrived in July 1963. Britain was also involved from October 1962 when the civil war spilled into Britain's protectorates around Aden (South Yemen). The National Front for the Liberation of South Yemen and occasional cross-border sorties by republican Yemeni troops resulted in the British Royal Air Force (RAF) undertaking containment actions in order to secure Aden's borders. An RAF raid into North Yemen in March 1964 was the sole action involving British forces north of the border. Ground forces saw action in Aden from April 1964 following a rebellion against British rule.

The U.N. observer unit withdrew from North Yemen in September 1964, and by the end of that year the royalists were restricted to a small region adjoining the border with Saudi Arabia. From this point, Egyptian forces began to be withdrawn. The withdrawal was completed by October 1967, when the royalists had been weakened to the point where they no longer posed a threat to the republican government. It is estimated that more than one hundred thousand people were killed in the war, most of them civilian. Egypt and Saudi Arabia lost one thousand troops each.

Both the U.N. and the Arab League tried to solve the conflict peacefully in the early stages of the war but were ineffective, leading to a long, drawn-out conflict. The Arab League was inhibited by internal rifts, and direct negotiations proved unsuccessful. The end of the war did not end the civil strife in the region, which fell into war in 1969 (see conflict 125), 1972 (see conflict 135), 1979 (see conflict 183), and 1993 (see conflict 278).

For further information and background reading, see reference item numbers 1045, 1060, 1167, 1188, 1238, 1253, 1316, 1333.

084. INDIA-CHINA

McMahon Line border dispute; Sino-Indian wars
(October–November 1962)

The armed incidents of October and November 1962 were a continuation of the ongoing border dispute between India and China (see conflict 066) over the McMahon Line. Negotiations had proved fruitless, largely owing to Indian intransigence. India reinforced outposts in the area in early 1962, hoping to cut off Chinese supply lines. There were numerous incidents, and China also moved to reinforce its troops in the area. Determined to force a settlement,

China attacked in full force on October 20, 1962. The intense fighting compelled Indian forces to retreat. The United States extended military aid to India, while China used its position of strength to make proposals for a settlement. China declared a cease-fire on November 21 and withdrew across the border. India still refused Chinese offers.

Negotiations were held in Colombo under the auspices of the prime minister of Ceylon, Sirima Bandaranaike (widow of Solomon Bandaranaike, the Ceylonese premier assassinated in 1959), and involving representatives from Burma, Ceylon, Ghana, Indonesia, Cambodia, and Egypt. The Colombo conference led to a package aimed at resolving the dispute, which was accepted by both China and India on January 28, 1963. It was not implemented owing to differing interpretations of each party's obligations under the package. China lost more than a thousand troops during the fighting, while India lost two thousand. The issues involved were not fully settled until the 1990s and thus remained a source of contention between the two states for many years.

For further information and background reading, see reference item numbers 76, 255, 691, 738, 788, 831, 873.

085. SOMALIA-KENYA; ETHIOPIA

Somali expansionism; separatist insurgency
(November 1962–September 1967)

Somalia gained independence in 1960 and immediately announced its intention of uniting all the Somali tribes under a single state. Such an aim involved making territorial claims on Ethiopia and Kenya, which both had significant numbers of Somalis living within their borders. In 1962 Somali tribes living in northern Kenya declared their wish to join the new Somali republic and initiated guerrilla attacks on Kenyan government targets to reinforce their claims. There were a few border incidents between Kenyan and Somali troops. The violence was halted in March 1964, when the Somali tribes declared their acceptance of Kenyan rule. Somali tribes in the Ogaden region of Ethiopia also began a campaign during this period, and Kenya and Ethiopia allied themselves against Somalia.

In the autumn of 1965 relations between Kenya and Somalia degenerated once again when serious fighting resumed in the border areas. The Organization of African Unity made several unsuccessful attempts to settle the conflict peacefully. The conflict began to deescalate in late 1967 when Somalia began to adopt a policy of disengagement in favor of negotiations over its territorial claims. Negotiations from 1967 led to an understanding in 1969, and relations between Somalia and Kenya were normalized. The issues were never fully resolved, however, so a number of similar conflicts reemerged in later years. The fighting cost at least 4,200 lives.

For further information and background reading, see reference item numbers 253, 341, 352, 356, 363, 378, 421.

086. CHINA-USSR
Territorial dispute; the Ussuri River conflict
(March 1963–September 1969)

A series of treaties concluded between Chinese and Russian governments between 1600 and 1900 ceded vast tracts of land on both sides of Mongolia to Russia. Following the deterioration in Sino-Soviet relations beginning in 1960 over ideological differences, China reopened the issue of sovereignty over land ceded under the treaties. In March 1963 an official Chinese statement defined them as "Chinese territories taken by imperialism." In September 1964 both countries issued statements alleging border violations and involvement in their counterpart's internal affairs in the Idi region of Xinjiang. Bilateral negotiations over the boundary problems commenced in February 1964, but these were not fruitful and were therefore suspended in May

A number of diplomatic exchanges were made in the ensuing years, but tensions did not increase until the advent of the Cultural Revolution in China in 1966. In January and February 1967, the Soviet embassy in Beijing was besieged for more than two weeks by protesters inflamed by the Cultural Revolution and the developing conflict. These unruly demonstrations were followed by a massive buildup of Chinese and Soviet forces along the border. The threat eased on February 21, 1967, when Chinese forces withdrew.

In the late 1960s a major point of tension was Damansky island in the Ussuri River. Armed clashes occurred on the island in March 1969, after a Chinese patrol ambushed a Soviet patrol. An initial engagement took place on March 1–2, and intense fighting recurred on March 15, when both sides returned with reinforcements. Intermittent clashes continued on the island for the next few months.

On March 29 the Soviet Union issued a note reaffirming its claim to Damansky island and called for the Chinese government to resume negotiations. Eventually, tensions eased and the dispute lapsed. It was thought that as many as three thousand Soviet and Chinese troops were killed during the fighting, which was at times intense. The issues remained unresolved until 1991, when the Soviet Union as such disintegrated. The new Russian government has taken steps to begin talks over the disputed territories.

For further information and background reading, see reference item numbers 76, 255, 666, 680.

087. SUDAN
Southern separatism; Anya-Nya terrorism; the first Sudan civil war (September 1963–March 1972)

Egypt and Britain had ruled Sudan since the nineteenth century. The protracted Sudanese civil war had its roots in the British decision, prior to Sudanese independence in 1955, to combine northern and southern Sudan instead of implementing the favored alternative, which had southern Sudan joining Uganda. Uganda and southern Sudan shared a similar ethnic and religious composition of black African animists, whereas northern Sudan was largely Arabic and Muslim.

Following independence, the more economically and socially advanced north ruled from Khartoum with an iron fist. It sought to expand missionary activity in the south and began a program of imposing Islamic culture and Arabic language. Those who resisted were harshly repressed, and many southern Sudanese were driven into neighboring Uganda, Ethiopia, Kenya, and the Central African Republic. From here, rebel organizations emerged with the express aim of attaining independence for southern Sudan. Attacks were often launched from bases in these countries.

Resistance emerged from within southern Sudan in 1963, with the Anya-Nya terrorists. Terrorist attacks began in September 1963 and continued until 1972. Most of the rebels operated under the umbrella of the Sudan Africa National Union (SANU) organization. Although SANU and the government met for talks on more than one occasion, they were unable to resolve their differences.

The conflict was internationalized from 1966, when the Sudanese government of Sadiq al-Mahdi was aided by Milton Obote's Ugandan army operating in Uganda to crush rebel activities in the border areas. Ugandan involvement continued until an Ethiopian-mediated cease-fire ended military hostilities on March 12, 1972. As many as 700,000 people were killed during the course of the war, many of them civilians killed by government troops in reprisals. Others died from starvation and disease. The issue of race and religion was never fully resolved, however, and this conflict presaged another civil war (1983–; see conflict 209).

For further information and background reading, see reference item numbers, 255, 288, 289, 295, 303, 304, 348, 386, 423, 478, 479.

088. ALGERIA-MOROCCO
Territorial dispute; the Tindouf war (October 1963–February 1964)

Morocco and Algeria had both been ruled by France, which in 1952 assigned a mineral-rich zone including Bechar and Tindouf to Algeria. Morocco tried to reclaim the area after it gained independence in 1956. Following Algerian independence in 1962, Morocco made a number of hostile moves in the disputed territory, raising tensions between the two states considerably.

In September 1963 Morocco sent troops into the area and attempted to occupy it forcibly. Algeria launched a counterattack in October and repulsed the invading troops. War then broke out, and Morocco recaptured the towns on October 14, 1963. The intense fighting spread to other border areas. Algeria gained military support from Cuba on October 27, including tanks and troops.

A mediation attempt by Haile Selassie of Ethiopia succeeded in securing a cease-fire on November 4, 1963, however, and a demilitarized zone was established in the disputed area in February 1964. There were thought to be as many as a thousand fatalities during the conflict. Relations between the two states remained strained, and they came into indirect conflict during the Western Sahara war (see conflict 146) and direct confrontation in 1979 (see conflict 185).

For further information and background reading, see reference item numbers 76, 255, 325, 361, 373, 377, 422.

089. CYPRUS
*Intercommunal violence; the Cypriot civil war
(December 1963–November 1967)*

Cyprus gained independence in 1960 following a violent campaign against British rule (see conflict 041). The island state was composed of a Greek majority and a Turkish minority, both of which looked to their homelands for support. Following independence, the parties began negotiations on drafting a constitution that addressed the island's intercommunal difficulties. These problems were not resolved, and the strains produced frequent intercommunal violence. The violence erupted into civil war in December 1963 following an incident between Greek Cypriot police and Turkish Cypriot citizens. Despite British efforts to broker a cease-fire, the fighting continued to escalate throughout 1964.

Units of the Turkish navy took up positions off the coast of Cyprus in December 1963, and the Greek government alleged that a Turkish invasion was imminent. NATO proposed that a peace-keeping force be sent to the island, but this was rejected by both parties, and on March 4, 1964, the U.N.

authorized that a U.N. Peace-keeping Force in Cyprus (UNFICYP) move onto the island. This force continues to the present day.

The U.N. force failed to halt the violence, and major incidents continued throughout 1964, including the bombing of Greek Cypriot targets by the Turkish air force on August 9, 1964. A cease-fire was declared on the following day, and although there were frequent outbreaks of violence, moves were made toward finding a peaceful settlement to the dispute.

In a series of bilateral talks between the two communities over the subsequent six years, little progress was made. Foreign military involvement (apart from the U.N. peace-keeping forces) in the Cypriot war ended in December 1967, when the United States was able to secure the withdrawal of Greek and Turkish forces stationed on Cyprus. The withdrawal was completed in mid-February 1968. In all, about a thousand people were killed during the course of the conflict, many of them civilians. The issue of the relationship of the two communities was never resolved, and in 1974 violence once again overtook the island, in this case, leading to a Turkish invasion (see conflict 143).

For further information and background reading, see reference item numbers 255, 887, 900, 912, 916, 921, 924, 933, 934.

090. SOMALIA-ETHIOPIA

Somali expansionism, separatist guerrilla fighting; the first Ogaden war (January–March 1964)

When Somalia became independent from Britain in 1960, the new government began to lay claim to territory in surrounding states. This practice had already brought Somalia into armed conflict with Kenya from 1962 to 1967 (see conflict 085). Somalia's strongest claim, however, was to the Ogaden region of Ethiopia, which was inhabited by Somali tribes people. Somalia asserted that the region should be united with Somalia or allowed to pursue self-determination. Ethiopia was totally opposed to this notion, and relations between the two states became strained.

With some Somali agitation, an insurrection by the Somali tribes in the Ogaden in 1960 and 1961 led to serious fighting with the Ethiopian army. When Somali soldiers began supporting Ogaden tribes in their guerrilla activities in November 1963, both states moved major units to the border. Ethiopia launched air attacks against Somalia in mid-January 1964, followed by an invasion of Somali territory in February. Fighting ended in March, following Sudanese mediation, but guerrilla attacks continued until April. As many as seven hundred people were killed in the fighting, which foreshadowed a much graver conflict in the 1970s and 1980s (see conflict 139).

For further information and background reading, see reference item numbers 255, 341, 352, 356, 363, 396, 421.

091. UNITED STATES–PANAMA
Sovereignty dispute; the flag riots (January–April 1964)

The Panama Canal was vital to U.S. shipping interests. After a sovereignty dispute in 1959, the United States reached a compromise with Panamanian authorities in 1963 that provided for the flying of both U.S. and Panamanian flags within the Canal Zone. On January 9, 1964, riots broke out in the Zone after hundreds of Panamanians attempted to raise a Panamanian flag over a school at which American students had raised a U.S. flag on January 7, 1964.

In an effort to quell the riots, U.S. troops took control of the Canal Zone, but disturbances along the border with Panama continued for several days. There were a number of serious cross-border sniping incidents, and tensions were high. The situation eased on January 16, when Panamanian civil authorities cleared the border area. The dispute was later settled without further violence. There were twenty-four fatalities during the conflict, four of them U.S. servicemen.

For further information and background reading, see reference item numbers 46, 255, 541, 551, 582, 591.

092. RWANDA-BURUNDI
Postindependence ethnic violence (January 1964–January 1965)

Rwanda and Burundi had been ruled by Belgium as a single territory, but obtained independence as separate states in July 1962. The two states both contained a mix of Hutu and Tutsi tribes people. The Belgian colonial policy of promoting Hutu to positions of prominence in Rwanda and Tutsi to positions of prominence in Burundi had already led to serious ethnic violence (1959–1962). This violence had caused large numbers of Tutsi to flee from Rwanda into Burundi and other surrounding states.

An organization known as the Union Nationale Rwandaise (UNAR) sought to promote the interests of the Tutsi within Rwanda, but began military operations against the Hutu-dominated Rwandan government on November 25, 1963. The UNAR launched guerrilla operations from Burundi and other surrounding states. A second attack was launched on December 21, 1963. The Rwandan authorities countered with severe repression of Tutsi within Rwanda, killing thousands in massacres. Most of the invading force was also killed, but some attacks continued.

Relations between Rwanda and Burundi deteriorated rapidly as Rwanda accused Burundi of supporting the Tutsi guerrillas. The conflict escalated even further when Rwandan troops raided Tutsi refugee camps located inside Burundi territory. The fighting eventually abated, but not before approximately fifteen thousand people, mainly Tutsi, had been killed. This ethnic conflict was the beginning of a cycle of violence that thirty years later ultimately produced the genocidal wars in Burundi (1988–; see conflict 245) and Rwanda (1990–; see conflict 263).

For further information and background reading, see reference item numbers 255, 397, 407, 440, 463.

093. FRANCE-GABON
Military putsch, French military intervention; Aubame's coup (February 1964)

After Gabon gained independence from France in 1960, a coalition government under the leadership of Leon M'Ba of the Democratic Bloc Party took control of the nation's affairs. Beginning in February 1963, M'Ba undertook to form a one-party state—moves opposed by the opposition Democratic and Social Union Party, which was led by Jean-Hilaire Aubaume.

On February 17, 1964, Gabonese armed forces officers staged a bloodless coup, detained M'Ba, and installed Aubaume as president. M'Ba loyalists immediately requested assistance from France under existing security arrangements, and French troops entered Gabon and reinstated M'Ba as president on February 20. French troops remained at large for the next two months, and were slowly withdrawn during April 1967. The dispute lapsed after this point. An estimated thirty people were killed during the restoration moves, including two French soldiers.

For further information and background reading, see reference item numbers 255, 293, 314, 327, 434.

094. SOUTH VIETNAM–CAMBODIA
Anti-Vietminh cross-border raids (March–December 1964)

Beginning in 1957 North Vietnamese sympathizers known as the Vietcong conducted terrorist operations in South Vietnam with the aim of destabilizing the government (see conflict 069). North Vietnam was a communist state supported by the Soviet Union, while South Vietnam was supported by the United States. Beginning in 1960 South Vietnamese forces began to conduct intermittent cross-border operations into Cambodia on the pretext of pursuing the Vietminh. The raids intensified in March 1964, after Cambodia continued to resist U.S. and South Vietnamese pressure to take action against the insurgents.

In April 1964 Cambodia lodged a complaint with the U.N. Security Council, which passed a resolution calling for a halt to the border violations. A U.N. fact-finding mission recommended a remarcation of the border between Cambodia and South Vietnam. This was rejected by Cambodia, however, as it feared it would lose territory to South Vietnam. The dispute remained unresolved and gradually abated. About one hundred fatalities resulted from the conflict. Beginning in 1965, with the North's large-scale troop infiltrations into South Vietnam, the conflict grew into all-out war involving the United States and North Vietnam. At various times during the Vietnam War, fighting would spill over into Cambodia (see conflict 069).

For further information and background reading, see reference item numbers 686, 689, 692, 711, 712, 730, 731, 741, 749, 755.

095. LAOS–NORTH VIETNAM
*Political anarchy; the second Laotian civil war
(April 1964–May 1975)*

Although the 1962 Geneva agreements had brought the first Laotian civil war to an end (1958–1962; see conflict 060), the second civil war grew directly out of the failure of these agreements to provide a basis for lasting peace. The Geneva-prescribed coalition government was headed by neutralist Prince Souvanna Phouma and had representatives fron neutralist, communist, and conservative factions.

But the political struggle among the factions led to the Pathet Lao's withdrawal from the coalition, a military coup in April 1964, and the almost immediate resumption of the civil war between the U.S.-supported conservative forces and the Pathet Lao, a communist organization supported by North Vietnam. South Vietnam and Thailand also sent troops and equipment to the rightists. From 1964 to 1970 the war followed a consistent pattern, with the Pathet Lao and Vietminh forces launching offensives between October and May and the rightists countering in the middle months of the year, supported by U.S. air strikes.

Discussions between Prince Souvanna Phouma and Prince Souphanouvong, leader of the Pathet Lao, began in 1970 in an attempt to end the conflict, but these were unsuccessful and the fighting continued. By 1972 the Pathet Lao had made some gains and controlled two-thirds of Laos.

Concessions by both sides led to a peace conference in Paris in February 1973. These talks led to the formation of a provisional government that equally represented both parties. By 1975 the Pathet Lao had de facto control over the government and large numbers of right-wing supporters began to flee the country. Thousands are thought to have been killed during this war.

For further information and background reading, see reference item numbers 46, 255, 714, 728, 757, 854, 865.

096. SYRIA-ISRAEL
Arab-Israeli dispute; border incidents (June 1964–July 1966)

Following the Israeli war of independence in 1948 (see conflict 012), relations between Israel and Syria remained hostile and their forces were frequently embroiled in firefights. Armed conflicts had already taken place in 1951 (see conflict 026), 1955 (see conflict 042), 1957–1958 (see conflict 051), and 1962–1963 (see conflict 081)—all of which had the potential to escalate into war.

Beginning in June 1963, Syria began to shell Israeli positions in northern Israel from its strategically valuable position on the Golan Heights. Israel responded by launching an air strike on Syrian territory. Syrian shelling continued throughout 1964, with Israel responding in kind. It was reported that twenty-five people were killed during this conflict, and Syria and Israel were soon at war again in 1967 during the Six-Day War, when Israel captured the Golan Heights (see conflict 117).

For further information and background reading, see reference item numbers 255, 1047, 1051, 1084, 1098, 1158, 1171, 1284.

097. ISRAEL-JORDAN
Arab-Israeli dispute; border incidents (December 1964–April 1966)

Following the Israeli war of independence in 1948–1949 (see conflict 012), relations between Israel and Jordan were strained. Armed conflicts had already broken out in 1953–1954 (see conflict 035) and 1956–1958 (see conflict 046). Matters between the two countries were worsened by the large numbers of Palestinian refugees encamped in Jordan; Palestinian guerrillas also launched attacks into Israel from Jordanian territory.

In December 1964 Israeli and Jordanian troops clashed in Jerusalem. This was followed by a number of artillery duels and guerrilla attacks by Palestinian nationalists, which continued throughout 1965. Occasionally, both sides would engage in cross-border raids. Dozens of people were killed in the conflict, and there was only one relatively minor attempt at conflict management. The incidents made the volatile region even more unstable, and fueled the possibility of another war in the region. About fifty people were killed in the incidents. Eventually, the fighting ended, and Israel and Jordan did not battle each other directly until the Six-Day War in 1967 (see conflict 117).

For further information and background reading, see reference item numbers 1031, 1047, 1098, 1158, 1171, 1284.

098. INDIA-PAKISTAN

Regional rivalry, territorial dispute; the India-Pakistan wars (1965–1970)

Following the partition of the Subcontinent in 1947 (see conflict 003), India and Pakistan immediately went to war over the disputed territory of Kashmir and Jammu (see conflict 010). Relations had been hostile since then, and armed conflict erupted again in 1958–1959 (see conflict 056) and yet again in August 1965 (see conflict 106).

The period from late 1965 to 1970 saw an intensification of the India-Pakistan conflicts, with frequent border incidents. Clashes occurred regularly in Kashmir, the Rann of Kutch, and along the West Pakistan border. Although there were a number of attempts to mediate between the two sides, relations did not improve. In all, it is estimated that three hundred Indian and Pakistani military personnel were killed during these incidents. Four more wars broke out after this: 1971–1974 (see conflict 132), 1981–1982 (see conflict 195), 1984–1985 (see conflict 219), and 1986– (see conflict 231).

For further information and background reading, see reference item numbers 255, 667, 679, 684, 700.

099. ERITREA-ETHIOPIA

Eritrean nationalism; war of secession (1965–May 1993)

Part of ancient Ethiopia, Eritrea was taken over by the Italian government in 1882 and, in 1936, made part of Italian East Africa along with Italian Somaliland and Ethiopia. Following a short-lived war of independence (1949–1950; see conflict 019), Eritrea became federated with Ethiopia until 1962, when Ethiopia annexed the territory and made it an Ethiopian province. Eritrean nationalists, however, had not given up hope, and since 1956 the Eritrean Democratic Front (EDF) had been agitating for full independence. The EDF initiated armed resistance under the banner of the Eritrean Liberation Front (ELF) soon after Ethiopia's annexation of Eritrea.

The conflict then entered a stage of steady escalation, culminating in an unrestricted guerrilla war in 1967. The ELF expanded its operations with large-scale military support from Egypt, Cuba, and the People's Republic of China. The conflict often spilled into Sudan, as Ethiopian troops pursued Eritrean rebels across the border between the two countries. Following the 1974 ouster of Emperor Haile Selassie in Ethiopia, Sudan offered increased support for the rebels, resulting in repeated clashes between the two countries in the border area.

The war continued throughout the 1980s, with neither side able to win complete victory. At various times, the Eritrean rebels held vast areas under their control. A severe drought combined with the effects of the war to create a massive famine in 1985, which was partly relieved by worldwide humanitarian aid. In the 1990s, under pressure from several devastating famines and a similar rebellion in the Tigre province, the Ethiopian government was unable to maintain effective control and finally fell in May 1991, after a concerted offensive by several rebel groups.

After a period of instability and, at times, factional violence, a referendum in the province overwhelmingly voted for independence. With a relatively stable government in place, Ethiopia was beginning to recover at the end of 1995, while Eritrea was rebuilding and establishing its independence. The fighting throughout the conflict was often intense and brutal, and 200,000 people are estimated to have been killed as a result. Many of these were civilians killed in reprisal attacks, and many more died as a result of war-induced famine.

For further information and background reading, see reference item numbers 37, 76, 255, 341, 350, 352, 356, 363, 409.

100. IRIAN JAYA–INDONESIA
Territorial dispute; secessionist insurgency (1965–)

The Netherlands had granted independence to Indonesia in 1949 following a bloody war (see conflict 006) but had retained control over West Irian (Irian Jaya), which occupies the western half of the island of New Guinea. Following another war between Indonesia and the Netherlands in 1962 (see conflict 078), the Netherlands ceded the territory to Indonesia on the condition that it would implement a program leading to Irian independence. West Irian was inhabited by Papuans, who were ethnically closer to Papua New Guineans.

Once Indonesia gained control of the area, it reneged on its promise to grant independence and instead tried to pacify West Irian beginning in 1965. Ethnic Papuans in particular resisted these efforts forcefully. The separatist Organisasi Papua Mendeka (OPM) fomented violence in the region, particularly along the ill-defined Indonesian–Papua New Guinean border. The conflict grew more serious in the 1970s when Indonesia was forced to commit a regular army battalion to the area and engaged in repression and reprisals against villagers. A pattern of attacks by the OPM, followed by reprisals by Indonesian troops continued into the 1990s.

The conflict was internationalized when Indonesian troops began crossing the Papua New Guinea border in pursuit of rebels, who had a natural sanctuary among Papuans. Tensions associated with the OPM insurgency became a feature of Papua New Guinea–Indonesian relations throughout the 1980s and 1990s. No attempts at conflict management have been made, and the war continues at the end of 1995 without any sign of ending, although the rebel army appears to be shrinking. As a result, the OPM have offered talks with the government, but without response. Perhaps as many as ten thousand people have been killed in this conflict, and in 1995 foreign governments began to raise questions about Indonesia's human rights record in the territory. Also, the OPM gained international attention when it kidnapped a number of foreign nationals.

For further information and background reading, see reference item numbers 255, 710, 746, 764, 856.

101. COLOMBIA
Banditry, leftist guerrilla insurgency (1965–)

Colombia had a problem with banditry for many years, but in 1965 some bandits linked up with left-wing political movements in an attempt to overthrow the government. The left-wing guerrillas consisted originally of two groups, the Ejército de Liberación Nacional (ELN), and the Fuerzas Armadas Revolucionarias de Colombia (FARC). They were motivated by a desire for greater social justice and supported by many priests, peasants, students, and workers. Ambushes, assassinations, kidnapping, bombings, and attacks on villages began to claim hundreds of lives every year from this time. A move by the government to undermine peasant support for the guerrillas through a program of land reform failed to make any headway. In 1976 a new guerrilla group called M19 emerged, and in 1978 the Workers' Self-Defense Movement also joined the guerrilla groups in their war against the government.

In 1980 Colombia accused Cuba of aiding the guerrillas and broke off diplomatic relations. By 1984 it was thought that between six thousand and fifteen thousand guerrillas were operating in Colombia, and the government seriously pursued efforts to find a negotiated settlement with the guerrillas. The ELN also began operating closely with Venezuelan, Peruvian, Ecuadoran, and Salvadoran guerrilla groups in this period.

Despite various truces and agreements with the guerrilla groups, including the surrender and incorporation of the M19 group into government, the peace process never took hold, and the fighting continued. By the end of 1995, the conflict still had no end in sight, and relations with Venezuela had deteriorated seriously as a result of cross-border raids in pursuit of rebels. There were also allegations of Venezuelan aid to the rebels. Evidence has also emerged that FARC was collaborating with the Calí drug cartel, complicating the conflict even further. An estimated thirty thousand people have been killed in the conflict so far, many of them civilians, and peace efforts continue intermittently.

For further information and background reading, see reference item numbers 571, 584, 588, 589.

102. GHANA-TOGO
Ghanaian expansionism; border incidents (January–May 1965)

Relations between Ghana and Togo were strained because colonial boundaries had split the Ewe tribe between the two states, and Ewe organizations were campaigning for reunification. Togo was also suspicious of Ghana's president, Kwame Nkrumah, who was committed to expansionist policies and regularly sought to undermine his neighbors by supporting dissident movements and military subversion.

From January to May 1965 a number of border incidents between Ghana and Togo were reported, in which Ghanaian police crossed the border into Togo. During one such sortie, a member of the Togolese security forces was killed. Similar allegations and complaints of interference were made against Ghana by Ivory Coast, Niger, and Upper Volta, and these three states brought Ghana's actions to the attention of the OAU.

Togo did not formally take part in this action for fear of further intimidation by Ghana. The OAU passed a broad resolution condemning involvement in neighboring states' internal affairs, although it did not mention Ghana directly. This state of relations led to further armed conflicts in 1982 (see conflict 206), 1986 (see conflict 237), and 1994 (see conflict 280).

For further information and background reading, see reference item numbers 46, 255, 297, 313.

103. CONGO (Zaire)-UGANDA
Rebel activity; border incidents (February–March 1965)

Bands of rebels still roamed Congo's frontiers following years of bloody civil war and secessionist warfare in Katanga province (see conflict 067).[2] Government efforts to pacify the country were initially aided by foreign mercenaries and involved the pursuit of rebels along Zaire's northern border with Uganda. Some evidence suggests that Uganda may have been supporting the northern rebels. In any event, the military activity strained relations between these two Central African nations.

In February 1965 Uganda accused Zaire of bombing Ugandan villages while in pursuit of the rebels; Zairean and Ugandan troops also engaged in a number of clashes. The conflict began to intensify when the countries closed their mutual border and sent troop reinforcements to the area. The conflict quickly died down, however. Although no formal attempts were made at peaceful con-

---

[2] Following its independence in 1960, the Belgian Congo was renamed the Democratic Republic of the Congo. President Mobutu Sésé Séko, who ruled the Central African nation from 1965 to 1997, changed the country's name to Zaire in 1971. The name reverted to the Democratic Republic of the Congo when Laurent Kabila came to power in May 1997.

flict management as such, the border was soon reopened and relations resumed later that year.

For further information and background reading, see reference item numbers 296, 376, 453.

104. UNITED STATES–DOMINICAN REPUBLIC
Civil war, U.S. military intervention; the constitutionalist rebellion (April 1965-September 1966)

After the brutal Trujillo regime was toppled in 1961, the Dominican Republic had been beset by civil unrest and political violence. The constitutionalist rebellion began on April 24, 1965, when a group of rebels ousted the civilian regime. Calling themselves the constitutionalists, the rebels were mostly supporters of Juan Bosch, who had been president until his ouster in a 1963 military coup.

The pro- and anti-Bosch forces engaged in heavy fighting in Santo Domingo over control of strategic positions. U.S. forces intervened on April 28, 1965, on the side of Col. Pedro Bartolene Benoit, who wanted to form a new government with the anti-Bosch faction. Fearing a constitutionalist victory would lead to a procommunist government, the United States was eager to support Benoit. U.S. troops quickly seized the constitutionalist-controlled areas of Santo Domingo, although there was heavy fighting.

The Organization of American States (OAS) deployed a peace-keeping force to the country, and domestic opinion in the United States turned against the intervention. Negotiations led to the formation of an interim government led by Hector Garcia Godoy. There were some isolated acts of political violence. In OAS-supervised elections held in June 1966, Joaquín Balaguer defeated Bosch and served as the country's president until 1978 and again from 1986 to 1996, bringing a new measure of economic security to the nation. U.S. troops pulled out on September 21, 1966. As many as 3,500 people were killed in the fighting, including 30 American soldiers.

For further information and background reading, see reference item numbers 46, 255, 527, 559, 566, 594, 600, 601, 619, 622.

105. NORTH KOREA–SOUTH KOREA
Cold war border incidents (mid-1965–March 1968)

Following the Korean War (1950–1953; see conflict 024), relations between the two Koreas were extremely volatile. The 38th parallel was heavily reinforced with troops, and each side waged a virulent propaganda war against the other. The tensions erupted into a serious border conflict in October 1965, when North Korea began cross-border commando raids. In November 1965 U.S. troops clashed with North Korean troops; these skirmishes continued periodically until September 1971. South Korean artillery and other small ground forces also retaliated.

In January 1968 North Korea captured a U.S. naval vessel off its coast. The crew was returned only after a ten-month period of negotiations in Panmunjom, which consisted of twenty-eight meetings between U.S. and North Korean negotiators; North Korea refused to return the vessel itself. As many as 550 soldiers were killed during these clashes, including 40 U.S. troops. Eventually, the conflict abated. Fighting broke out again, however, in 1975 (see conflict 150), 1984 (see conflict 227), and 1992 (see conflict 270).

For further information and background reading, see reference item numbers 255, 672, 675, 720, 804, 816, 848.

106. INDIA-PAKISTAN
Territorial dispute; the second Kashmir war, the India-Pakistan wars (August–September 1965)

India and Pakistan had been bitter rivals since the 1947 partition of the Subcontinent (see conflict 003), with war breaking out almost immediately over the status of Jammu and Kashmir (see conflict 010); after intense fighting, the territory was finally divided between the two countries in 1949 and a cease-fire line drawn.

The second Kashmir war began in August 1965, when large numbers of Pakistani irregulars began infiltrating India-controlled Kashmir. India responded by invading and capturing areas of Pakistan-controlled Kashmir. War broke out when Pakistan counterattacked across the 1949 cease-fire line.

The war took a major turn when India attacked West Pakistan across a wide front. The fighting was fierce, and India made significant territorial gains in the early stages. Intense U.N. mediation efforts secured a cease-fire in late September 1965, and the world organization then supervised troop withdrawals. More than seven thousand Indian and Pakistani troops were killed in this conflict, and the issues in the dispute remained unresolved—since 1990 more than 20,000 people have been killed in Kashmir. Fighting between the two states recurred in 1971–1974 (see conflict 132), 1981–1982 (see conflict 195), 1984–1985 (see conflict 219), and 1986 (see conflict 231).

For further information and background reading, see reference item numbers 255, 667, 679, 684, 700, 765.

107. CHINA-INDIA

McMahon Line border incidents; the Sino-Indian wars
(September 1965)

Sino-Indian relations had been hostile since China's invasion of Tibet in 1950
(see conflict 025), just a year after the Communists had come to power in
Beijing. China disputed the McMahon Line, which had demarcated the
Tibetan-India border since 1914. From 1956 to 1958 India was seen to be supporting Tibetan rebels during Tibet's guerrilla war against the Chinese (see conflict 044); furthermore, the Dalai Lama, whom the Tibetans revere as a god and
king, chose exile in India, which did little to soothe Sino-Indian relations.
Fighting erupted again in 1959–1960 (see conflict 066) and once more in 1962
(see conflict 084), resulting in a humiliating military defeat for India.

Embroiled in a war with Pakistan (see conflict 106), India was irked by
China's support for Pakistan's territorial ambitions. Mutual recriminations
ensued about border violations and intimidating troop maneuvers. India
asserted that on September 19, 1965, Chinese border guards had abducted and
killed three Indian policemen, also accusing China of having kidnapped three-
man border patrols in Ladakh and Sikkim on September 26.

At the same time, China began to shell Indian positions on the border of
Sikkim; India responded in kind. Neither side made any serious attempts to settle the conflict peacefully, but the fighting did ease after this time. About ten
people were killed in the incidents. Armed conflict broke out again between the
two states in 1975 (see conflict 155).

For further information and background reading, see reference item numbers
76, 255, 691, 738, 788, 831, 873.

108. LEBANON-ISRAEL

Arab-Israeli dispute (PLO sorties, IDF counterattacks); the Hoûla
raids (October 1965)

Lebanon had joined other Arab states in fighting Israel in the 1948 war of independence (see conflict 012). Many Palestinian refugees had fled to Lebanon
after the war, providing a fertile recruitment ground for Palestinian nationalist
organizations like the PLO (the Palestinian Liberation Organization).
Although Israeli Defense Forces (IDF) had frequently skirmished with Syria
and Jordan during the 1950s and early 1960s, the Israeli-Lebanese border was
generally quiet.

In the mid-1960s, however, relations between the two states became
strained when the PLO set up guerrilla bases in southern Lebanon with the
tacit compliance of the Lebanese government. IDF border guards detected frequent Palestinian sorties into Israeli territory, and on October 29, 1965, an

Israeli force staged a retaliatory raid on Hoûla and Meiss ej Jabal in southern Lebanon. There was one fatality, and the dispute eventually lapsed. This pattern of PLO infiltration and Israeli retaliation was to characterize Israeli-Lebanese relations for the next two decades, with armed incidents in 1974–1975 (see conflict 145), 1977 (see conflict 170), 1978 (see conflict 176), 1982–1983 (see conflict 199), and 1983 (see conflict 213).

For further information and background reading, see reference item numbers 255, 1047, 1069, 1098, 1123, 1145, 1158, 1171, 1284.

109. CHAD-SUDAN

Internal strife, Sudanese intervention; the first Chad civil war (November 1965–1972)

Chad had been riven by dissension between the politically dominant black south and the largely Muslim north since its independence from France in 1960. Ngarta Tombolbaye, a southerner, had been Chad's president since independence from France in 1960. Controlled by Christians from the south, his regime was deeply resented by Muslims in the east and north. Matters worsened in 1963, when Tombolbaye sought to establish a one-party state.

Opposition groups responded by organizing the Front de liberation nationale du Tchad (Frolinat) with the aim of deposing Tombolbaye and instituting an Islamic state. A new military regime in neighboring Sudan permitted various exile groups to operate in the country, and Frolinat set up headquarters in the Sudanese capital, Khartoum. This led to serious tensions between Chad and Sudan.

A rebellion was instigated in the eastern province of Ouadai, and fighting began on the border between Chad and Sudan in November 1965. Chadian armed forces pursued the rebels throughout 1966, undertaking frequent cross-border incursions. For the next two years, however, the war was largely confined to Chadian territory.

In August 1968 French troops were sent to help the government forces. By April 1969 two thousand French troops were in Chad, and by May 1970 most of the rebel-held territory had been recaptured and returned to government hands. Sporadic fighting continued until late 1972, when the rebellion collapsed. The conflict cost as many as 3,500 lives, including 50 French soldiers. Chad again fell into civil war in 1978, when Libya became involved in the conflict (see conflicts 175, 203).

For further information and background reading, see reference item numbers 255, 336, 386, 466, 481.

110. SOUTH WEST AFRICA (Namibia)
Violent insurrection, war; independence (1966–March 1990)

From the 1880s until World War I, South West Africa (Namibia) had been a German colony. German rule had been particularly brutal. In 1908 German forces suppressed a Namibian revolt, and nearly 85,000 black Africans lost their lives. South Africa took over the administration of the territory during World War I and then governed it under a League of Nations mandate.

Asked to surrender its mandate in 1945 and place the country under a U.N. trusteeship, South Africa refused. Namibians had begun to agitate for independence in the meantime. The South West Africa People's Organization (SWAPO), working primarily out of neighboring Angola, lobbied the United Nations for Namibian independence.

In 1966 and the world body complied, passing a resolution condemning continued South African administration of the territory. SWAPO began a simultaneous campaign of violent insurrection, sabotage, and low-level guerrilla warfare. Despite an International Court of Justice ruling in 1971 that South Africa withdraw from Namibia, South Africa continued to govern the territory. During this period, police actions were sufficient to contain SWAPO-inspired violence. More serious violence erupted after a general strike in December 1971, and Portuguese troops from Angola joined South African units in suppressing rebel activities. Starting in February 1972, an intense guerrilla war between SWAPO and South African Defence Forces persisted continuously until the late 1980s.

Between 1978 and 1980 the war expanded into Zambia, where SWAPO had set up training bases, later spreading to Botswana and Angola as well. By the 1980s Angola (independent since 1975) and its Cuban allies became much more heavily involved in SWAPO's struggle, providing significant support. The United States and the Soviet Union initiated peace overtures in the Angolan civil war (see conflict 148), linking any progress to Angolan support for SWAPO. A series of U.N.-sponsored mediations by U.S. negotiator Chester Crocker led to a settlement signed on December 22, 1988, providing for the withdrawal of South African troops from Namibia The withdrawal was completed by November 23, 1989, and U.N.-supervised elections were held in 1990. The elections brought SWAPO's guerrilla leader, Sam Nujoma, to power with 57 percent of the vote; he was reelected in 1994

More than thirteen thousand people were killed during the course of the conflict, many of them civilians. Large numbers of South African troops were killed in the fighting, as well as a number of Portuguese and Zairean soldiers. Namibia made a successful transition to independence and has been rebuilding its economy.

For further information and background reading, see reference item numbers 255, 312, 328, 355, 374, 382, 385, 389, 393.

111. GUINEA–IVORY COAST
Coup plot (March–April 1966)

Guinea was declared independent from France in 1958, and Sékou Touré had ruled the country from its independence until his death in 1984. Because his regime became progressively more Marxist over time, this created some domestic turmoil. As a consequence, a number of the regime's opponents fled to Senegal, the Ivory Coast, and France. In addition, Touré's radical stance isolated the country and created friction with its more moderate neighbors.

In late 1965 Guinea announced it had foiled a plot to overthrow Touré's regime and accused the Ivory Coast of aiding the rebels. Relations between Guinea and the Ivory Coast became exceedingly strained, as there was some evidence of Ivory Coast's complicity in the plot. Guinea broke off all relations with Ivory Coast. There were no fatalities and no attempts at peaceful conflict management. Eventually, the dispute lapsed altogether, although a much more serious conflict emerged in February 1967 (see conflict 115).

For further information and background reading, see reference item numbers 46, 286, 287, 319.

112. GHANA-GUINEA
Postcoup tensions (October–November 1966)

Relations between Ghana and Guinea had been good since the countries gained their independence in the late 1950s. Kwame Nkrumah had ruled Ghana since its independence in 1957. But following his ouster in a 1966 military coup, Nkrumah sought refuge in the neighboring West African state. This led to a rapid deterioration in relations between Guinea and the new Ghanaian regime.

On October 30, 1966, 19 Guineans were removed from a Pan Am flight while on stopover in Ghana. Ghana announced that the detainees were being held in retaliation for Guinea's aggressive stance. Furthermore, they would not be released until Guinea freed Ghanaians who, the government claimed, were being held in Guinea. Guinea denounced Ghana's actions and accused the United States of complicity, detaining the U.S. ambassador and Pan Am representatives There were fears that the conflict could escalate.

Ethiopia sent its minister of justice to mediate the dispute, and on October 31, 1966, an OAU mediation team was appointed. Guinea freed the U.S. ambassador that same day; then nineteen Guineans were subsequently released by Ghana on November 5. The Ghanaians who were alleged to have been detained in Guinea said they wished to remain where they were. A last-minute crisis was averted when Ghana dropped its demands for their return.

For further information and background reading, see reference item numbers 46, 286, 287.

113. BOLIVIA
Cuban-assisted guerrilla insurgency (November 1966–July 1970)

This conflict was precipitated by the woeful state of Bolivian society and by Cuba's wish to export the revolution to other Latin American countries. In late 1966 Cuban revolutionary leader Che Guevara entered Bolivia with the aim of establishing a rural guerrilla movement that would oust the government in a Cuban-style revolution. At least ten other high-ranking Cuban officers were involved with the operation, and Fidel Castro maintained contact with them by radio and courier. The insurgents received supplies smuggled in from Brazil, Argentina, and Paraguay.

The revolutionaries failed to win popular support, however, and the guerrilla training camp was soon pinpointed by the Bolivian authorities. A counterinsurgency operation was soon mounted with U.S. assistance. Skirmishes continued for months, and the guerrillas had to go on the defensive. On October 7, 1967, Guevara was captured and subsequently killed. By the end of the year the guerrilla movement had been completely eradicated. Some guerrillas escaped to Chile, and attempts by Bolivia to extradite them led to strains on Bolivian-Chile relations. Fatalities caused by the conflict were reported at 138, and there were a number of unsuccessful conflict-management attempts.

For further information and background reading, see reference item numbers 46, 255, 507, 513, 542, 562, 569, 596, 597, 598.

114. RHODESIA (Zimbabwe)
African nationalism, guerrilla warfare; war of independence (1967–January 1980)

Rhodesia had been a self-ruling British Crown colony since 1923. In November 1965 the Rhodesian government, under staunch conservative Ian Smith, declared unilateral independence from Britain, an act the British denounced as a rebellion. Although Rhodesia's white-ruled government developed the country, the benefits of prosperity were not shared with the majority black population. Denied the franchise by the new republic, black African nationalists initiated a two-pronged uprising through the Zimbabwe African People's Organization (ZAPO) and the Zimbabwe African National Union (ZANU).

South Africa came to the aid of Rhodesian security forces in 1967, sending large quantities of both arms and advisers. At this stage, the fighting was confined to small-scale terrorist attacks, sabotage, and guerrilla warfare that targeted isolated, white-owned farms.

The liberation of Angola and Mozambique from Portuguese rule in 1975 (see conflict 070) greatly aided the guerrillas, for the new African regimes gave them sanctuary. The rebels gained formal support from neighboring black African states in August 1977, when Botswana, Mozambique, Tanzania, and Zambia formed the front-line states.

On May 3, 1979, Abel Muzorewa became prime minister in an ill-fated internal settlement proposed by Smith. This solved none of the issues, as the white minority still wielded the real power, and the fighting intensified. In September Lord Harrington undertook a mediation effort at Lancaster House in London. It produced a cease-fire to begin on December 5, 1979, and a plan for elections and independence, which came into effect in January 1980.

More than thirty thousand people were killed during the conflict, and there were numerous mediation attempts by Britain and the United States. The transition to independence was smooth, and Zimbabwe began to rebuild in the following years.

For further information and background reading, see reference item numbers 312, 321, 323, 357, 372, 380, 383, 402, 439.

115. GUINEA–IVORY COAST
Regional rivalry; hostage crisis (February–September 1967)

Regional rivalry between the Guinea and the Ivory Coast had created simmering tensions between the two West African states since 1965 (see conflict 111). Opponents of Sékou Touré's one-party socialist regime in Guinea conducted a campaign against their government from Ivory Coast and were therefore a source of antagonism between the two states.

A crisis erupted on February 19, 1967, when Guinea captured a fishing vessel from the Ivory Coast, claiming the boat had violated Guinean territorial waters and was conducting covert operations. The Guinean action followed an earlier incident in January, when the Ivory Coast exiled students who were participating in antigovernment demonstrations. The students were subsequently invited to reside in Guinea in what amounted to a diplomatic snub of the Ivory Coast. The worsening diplomatic situation elicited an attempted mediation by Liberian vice president William Richard Tolbert Jr. in March, but nothing came of his efforts.

The crisis escalated alarmingly on June 26, when the Ivory Coast removed the Guinean foreign minister and the country's U.N. ambassador from an international flight on stopover in Abidjan. The Ivory Coast announced the officials would be released only when the crew of the fishing vessel was returned. The conflict threatened to escalate into war at this point.

Diplomatic representations to the United Nations and OAU by both sides led to peaceful intervention by the U.N. secretary-general U Thant and President William V. S. Tubman of Liberia. Continued mediation by the Liberian president led to the freeing of the fishing vessel crew by Guinea on September 21 and the release of the diplomats four days later.

For further information and background reading, see reference item numbers 46, 286, 287, 330.

116. CUBA-VENEZUELA
Cuban-assisted invasion (April–May 1967)

Following the Cuban revolution in 1959 (see conflict 049) and the establishment of Castro's communist regime, Cuba attempted to export communist revolution to other Latin American states. This often led to conflict. Cuba had already interfered in the Dominican Republic (1959; see conflict 063), in Haiti (1959; see conflict 065), and in Bolivia (1966–1970; see conflict 113).

In the early months of 1967, unrest and political upheaval in Venezuela resulted in an attempted communist coup d'état. Relations between Venezuela and Cuba became inordinately strained because of Castro's support for the Venezuelan communists. In May 1967 the Venezuelan government announced that its troops had repulsed a guerrilla force that had landed 90 miles from Caracas. The invasion force had originated in Cuba and was led by Cuban army officers. Although the fighting resulted in only two reported fatalities, tensions between the two countries remained high for some time. Neither side attempted to settle the conflict peacefully, and it eventually lapsed.

For further information and background reading, see reference item numbers 46, 255, 507, 513, 562, 569.

117. ISRAEL–ARAB STATES
The Six-Day War, the Arab-Israeli wars (June 1967)

Relations between Israel and its Arab neighbors had been strained since Israel gained its independence in 1948. But matters were especially difficult in 1967. From its militarily advantageous position on the Golan Heights, Syria would often shell Israeli villages in northern Galilee. Furthermore, the PLO had begun raiding Israel from its camps in Jordan, Lebanon, and Syria, and all three states had announced plans to divert the Jordan River and thus deprive Israel of two-thirds of its water. Tensions escalated dramatically when Egypt closed the Straits of Tiran to Israeli shipping, cutting off Israel's access to the Red Sea. Egypt then demanded that U.N. peace-keeping forces be withdrawn from the Sinai, announcing the time had come to destroy Israel. All sides mobilized their forces.

Attempts were made to settle the conflict peacefully, but these failed. Israel was dismayed when both the United States and France declined to supply military aid. On June 5, 1967, the Israeli air force attacked Egyptian, Iraqi, Jordanian, and Syrian air bases in a surprise attack; Arab air forces were almost entirely destroyed. With complete air superiority, Israeli ground forces invaded the Sinai, reaching the Suez Canal in four days. Although Jordan had attacked the Jewish state, Israeli ground forces had occupied the West Bank, Gaza, and the Old City of Jerusalem by June 7. Two days later, on June 9, Israel stormed the Golan Heights, capturing it in two days.

The fighting was intense throughout the war: Israel lost seven hundred troops, while Arab casualties approached twenty-five thousand. U.N. mediation efforts were totally unsuccessful. Egypt and Syria attempted to regain lost territory in the 1973 Yom Kippur war (see conflict 141).

For further information and background reading, see reference item numbers 255, 1031, 1047, 1098, 1129, 1158, 1163, 1171, 1189, 1199, 1284.

118. NIGERIA-BIAFRA

Ethnic and regional rivalries, attempted secession; the Biafran civil war (July 1967–January 1970)

A period of civil instability followed Nigerian independence in 1960, caused in the main by regional differences and resistance to northern domination. Ethnic rivalries ultimately led to a military coup in January 1966, through which a Biafran military commander, Maj. Gen. Aguiyi Ironsi, gained power. Ironsi was toppled by another coup in July 1966, led by Lt. Gen. Yakubu Gowon. The new regime then took revenge on Biafrans in a program of violent repression. Numerous massacres caused Biafrans to flee to their tribal lands in eastern Nigeria. This provoked Biafran leader Col. Chukwuemeka Odumegwu Ojukwa into declaring Biafran secession and independence on May 30, 1967.

Initially, Gowon sought a peaceful solution to the crisis, but in the face of Biafran refusals to negotiate on the issue of sovereignty, Nigeria launched an invasion on July 6, 1967, beginning a protracted and bloody war. Although a number of African states recognized Biafran independence, a complete blockade of the territory prevented any outside assistance from reaching the beleaguered Biafrans. Several mediation efforts by the OAU, the papal nuncio, and the Commonwealth secretary-general, among others, were unsuccessful, and apart from short Biafran offensives, Nigeria slowly took control of Biafra in heavy fighting. Biafran forces finally surrendered on January 15, 1970, and Ojukwa went into exile. The war and the Nigerian blockade of Biafra caused a famine that killed hundreds of thousands of people. In all, more than 1 million people, many of them civilians, died as result of the conflict.

For further information and background reading, see reference item numbers 255, 345, 416, 418, 428, 461.

119. CONGO (Zaire)-RWANDA
Regional instability; the mercenaries dispute (August 1967–April 1968)

Since its independence in 1960 Congo (renamed Zaire in 1971) had experienced massive civil unrest. The separatist fighting in the copper-rich southern province of Katanga (see conflict 067) involved numerous foreign mercenaries. In fact, their numbers in Central Africa were now so great that they became the source of some instability. Mercenaries were employed not only by the Congolese government in its intensive pacification efforts (see conflict 103) but also by Portugal to destabilize the Mobutu regime, which was actively supporting Angolan rebels (see conflict 070).

In August 1967 a large contingent of Portuguese-backed mercenaries took refuge in Rwanda after being defeated by Congolese troops at the town of Bukavu. President Mobutu Sésé Séko demanded their immediate extradition, while Rwanda intended to repatriate them. In January 1968 Congo closed its border with Rwanda and broke off all relations. A tense war of words followed, and there were fears of an escalation. After mediation, however, the conflict was settled and the mercenaries were all repatriated. In the initial fighting, nearly two thousand people were killed.

For further information and background reading, see reference item numbers 255, 286, 287, 326, 464.

120. USSR-CZECHOSLOVAKIA
Liberalization movement (the "Prague Spring"); Soviet military invasion (August 1968)

Liberated by Soviet forces during World War II, Czechoslovakia was ruled by a communist regime from 1948 to 1989. In January 1968, however, a democratic reform movement spread explosively through the country. The country's longtime Stalinist leader, Antonin Novotny, was deposed as Communist Party leader and replaced by Alexander Dubcek. Dubcek immediately announced a reform program aimed at lifting restrictions imposed by the Party on Czechoslovakia's economic and public life, including censorship.

The Soviet Union and its Warsaw Pact allies, Bulgaria, Hungary, Poland, and East Germany, demanded an end to Czechoslovakia's liberalization efforts. When the Dubcek regime pressed on with the reform program, Soviet, Bulgarian, Hungarian, Polish, and East German armies invaded on August 18, 1968, detaining Dubcek and his closest aides. Protesters—mostly students and workers—clashed with Warsaw Pact troops; many were killed. Although Czechoslovak citizens called for and expected Western intervention, none was forthcoming. Foreign troops withdrew in September and October after a new government had been installed and the protest movement crushed.

Soviet military forces left a permanent military presence in Czechoslovakia. The initial clashes and the following crackdown left nearly a thousand dead. The Soviet Union intervened again in Poland in 1980 (see conflict 197).

For further information and background reading, see reference item numbers 255, 913, 939, 942, 954, 976, 977, 978, 986, 990.

121. IRAQ–THE KURDS
Struggle for autonomy (October 1968–March 1970)

The Kurds, a non-Arab tribes people inhabiting a mountainous plateau region comprising parts of Iran, Iraq, and Turkey, have been fighting for an independent Kurdistan since the end of World War I, when the Treaty of Sèvres granted them autonomous status. The terms were never implemented. Kurdish rebels under Mullah Mustafa Barazani had been fighting a guerrilla war against Iraq for an independent Kurdistan since the early 1960s (see conflict 071). The 12-point program signed in 1966 had led to a cessation of fighting, but in 1968 strenuous government efforts to quell Kurdish rebel activity again led to serious fighting. There were massive human rights violations by the Iraqi government, and Barazani sent communications to the United Nations alleging Iraqi genocide against the Kurdish population. Given the Kurds' lack of international standing, however, the United Nations did not take up their cause.

Fighting continued until January 1970, when the Iraqi government reaffirmed the 12-point program. Following further negotiations, an armistice agreement was signed and the war proclaimed over. The Kurds were given almost complete autonomy in a new peace agreement, but Iraqi failures to fully implement the agreement led to continuing resentment among the Kurds. Fighting broke out again in 1974 (see conflict 144). More than two thousand people were killed between 1968 and 1970, most of them Kurdish villagers slaughtered by Iraqi troops.

For further information and background reading, see reference item numbers 1038, 1073, 1109, 1128, 1170, 1190, 1240, 1250, 1300.

122. CHINA–BURMA
Tribal conflict, border incidents (January–November 1969)

China and Burma had signed a friendship treaty in 1960 that resolved some lingering territorial disputes. In spite of this, the two countries continued to vie for control over tribal groups—the Kachins and the Shans—that lived along their mutual border and had long resisted government efforts to absorb them. In fact, these tribes did not intrinsically identify with either China or Burma.

A conflict erupted in 1969 when Burma launched a military campaign to assert control over these tribes. At the time, Chinese road construction near the border was straining relations and causing security concerns, which China compounded by providing military assistance to some of the tribes. Between May and October 1969, Burmese units occasionally clashed with Chinese troops operating within Burma; as many as three hundred fatalities resulted from these skirmishes. Only one negotiation attempt was made, which failed. The dispute eventually lapsed altogether, as Burma refocused on its ongoing guerrilla insurgency (see conflict 018).

For further information and background reading, see reference item numbers 688, 706, 736, 776, 778, 813, 843, 864.

123. EL SALVADOR–HONDURAS

Border dispute; the football war (July 1969)

El Salvador and Honduras had disputed territory on their common border since the early 1800s. Several agreements had failed to resolve the issue, which had become a major source of contention. Relations had also been complicated by the migration of thousands of Salvadorans to Honduras, where they cultivated land. The Honduran government began an agrarian reform program in early 1969, which left thousands of Salvadorans without land and facing deportation. Relations between the two states became extremely strained (see map 8).

In June 1969 the two countries' teams were in qualifying matches for the World Cup. The games ended in serious rioting that led to a diplomatic crisis. Relations were severed on June 27, and on July 8 Salvadoran troops began cross-border raids. On July 14 El Salvador invaded Honduras and heavy fighting continued. Honduras engaged in retaliatory air attacks on Salvadoran cities until a cease-fire was finally brokered by the OAS on July 18.

Further mediations ultimately led to a full settlement on July 30 under which Salvadoran troops were to withdraw from Honduran territory. Also called "the football war," this conflict resulted in the deaths of five thousand people, mainly civilians. Continuing contacts in following years led to a treaty in 1976, but fighting again broke out before the treaty could be implemented (see conflict 165).

For further information and background reading, see reference item numbers 255, 503, 506, 535, 537, 545, 615.

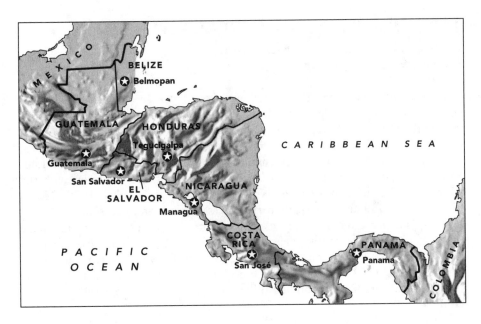

MAP 8. **Central America**

Central America has been a hotbed of political unrest in the postwar period. The 1969 dispute between El Salvador and Honduras is just one of the many conflicts that have plagued the region since 1945.

124. GUYANA-SURINAME
New River Triangle border dispute (August 1969–November 1970)

Neighbors on the northeastern coast of South America, Guyana and Suriname (then under Dutch colonial control) had contested sovereignty over the New River triangle of the Corantijn River since its discovery in the late 1800s. The disputed area was then part of the territory administered by Guyana and had been the source of some tension. Following Guyana's independence from Britain in 1966, Suriname reasserted its claim to the region. Talks in London failed to resolve the issue.

In December 1967 Suriname sent a survey party into the triangle to conduct a survey for a hydroelectric power plant. Guyana claimed the men were armed and sought to expel them. Suriname then claimed that Guyana had occupied a Surinamese airstrip in retaliation. There were a few other minor incidents, but no reported fatalities. Tensions remained high, but then negotiations were resumed in an attempt to find a peaceful solution to the conflict. Talks continued intermittently for decades, and relations remained cordial.

For further information and background reading, see reference item numbers 76, 579, 599.

125. NORTH YEMEN–SAUDI ARABIA
Post–civil war tensions; border conflict
(November 1969–January 1970)

Following the civil war in North Yemen (1962–1967; see conflict 083), Saudi Arabia continued to support the defeated royalists in the hope that the imamate would be restored. As a consequence, its relations with the republican government in North Yemen were quite strained.

In September 1969 North Yemeni troops captured the royalist stronghold of Sada. Two months later, royalists attempted to recapture the town with the support of Saudi troops. From November 1969 to October 1970, North Yemeni aircraft launched retaliatory strikes against Saudi positions. North Yemen also alleged Saudi air strikes on its territory. Although no attempts were made to manage the conflict peacefully, the dispute abated. Saudi Arabia did become involved, however, in subsequent wars between North and South Yemen (1971–1972, see conflict 133; and 1979–1980, see conflict 183). The two Yemens were finally reunified following a civil war in the early 1990s (see conflict 278).

For further information and background reading, see reference item numbers 1045, 1060, 1167, 1188, 1238, 1253, 1316, 1333.

126. CAMBODIA–SOUTH VIETNAM;
UNITED STATES
U.S. bombing campaign; the Vietnam War
(January 1970–April 1975)

Cambodia was a major battlefield during the Vietnam War (see conflict 069). Vietcong and North Vietnamese troops used the country as a transit area and supply line to the fighting in South Vietnam, and the United States responded to the traffic with punishing air strikes.

Cambodia's ruler at the time was Prince Norodom Sihanouk, who was ousted in a 1970 military coup led by South Vietnamese army general Lon Nol, who then took control of the country, hoping this would curb North Vietnam's military onslaughts. But the North Vietnamese simply stepped up their incursions into the south. By April 1970, U.S. ground troops were fighting in Cambodia.

Although the bulk of U.S. troops were withdrawn in June 1970, three months later, the United States continued to provide logistical support to South Vietnamese troops there and made heavy bombing runs until 1973. Causing thousands of fatalities, this U.S. bombing campaign turned many rural Cambodians into ardent supporters of the communist Khmer Rouge rebellion, which deposed the Lon Nol regime in 1975.

Aside from a U.S. commando raid into Cambodia in 1975, all U.S. involvement in Cambodia ended with the signing of the Paris Peace Accords in
January 1973. North Vietnamese and South Vietnamese troops continued
operations in Cambodia until the fall of South Vietnam in 1975. Only two
attempts were made at negotiation, and both failed. It is estimated that perhaps
as many as 300,000 people lost their lives in Cambodia during this period of
fighting.

*For further information and background reading, see reference item numbers
686, 689, 692, 711, 712, 730, 731, 734, 741, 749, 755.*

127. MINDANAO–THE PHILIPPINES
*Communal violence, land disputes; Muslim secessionist insurgency
(January 1970–1995)*

An archipelago nation of more than seven thousand islands, the Philippines
was administered for four hundred years by the Spanish, who in 1898 lost control of the nation to the United States during the Spanish-American War.
Mindanao, the country's southernmost and second-largest island, is home to a
sizable Muslim minority population, a disenfranchised and oppressed group.

This conflict began when a militant movement known as the Blackshirts
staged acts of violence against new Christian settlers arriving from the northern islands. The Blackshirts were made up of Moros (as members of the
Muslim minority were known), many of whom had never recognized the legitimacy of the Manila government. Fearing secession, the government immediately sent in troops.

In the first year of the conflict more than one thousand people lost their lives
in violent clashes. In 1971 the conflict took on the aspect of a religious war
when Christians began attacking Muslims, and Muslims attempted to drive
Christians off land that they considered their own. In 1973 the conflict became
a much more organized and intense struggle for secession by the Moros.

The insurgents organized themselves into the Moro National Liberation
Front (MNLF) in the mid-1970s and the conflict began to be much more
intense, and thousands were being killed every year. The conflict was internationalized when Muslim countries such as Libya, Egypt, Pakistan, Afghanistan,
and Saudi Arabia began to aid the Moros, including sending arms through
Malaysia. A strain was put on Malaysian-Philippine relations when it was
alleged that Malaysia was arming and training the Muslim insurgents.

By the early 1980s as many as ten thousand government troops alone had
been killed in the conflict. The conflict was further complicated in the mid-
1980s by a split in the MNLF. Despite numerous negotiations between the government and the MNLF, and mediation attempts by the Islamic Conference
Organization (ICO) and other Muslim nations, no solution to the conflict

could be found. The Moro Islamic Liberation Front (MILF), the MNLF's main rival, remained outside the peace talks and continued to fight without respite.

There were a number of agreements and cease-fires with the MNLF, however, plus government efforts to improve the lives of the Muslims, but these led to only temporary lulls in the fighting. In early 1995 large-scale fighting broke out when a Christian town was attacked by the rebels and more than fifty civilians killed. Approximately sixty thousand people have lost their lives in the conflict so far, and the violence continues at the end of 1994 with no sign of an end.

For further information and background reading, see reference item numbers 37, 857, 868.

128. PLO-JORDAN; SYRIA
Attempted coup (February 1970–August 1971)

Following the Six-Day War of 1967 (see conflict 117), the Palestinian Liberation Organization (PLO) began to use Jordan as a base for operations against Israel. Israel regularly responded with retaliatory raids into that country. Seeking to deescalate its conflict with Israel, Jordan began to suppress PLO activities in mid-1970. This led to strains between PLO and Jordanian troops.

In a bold move, the PLO attempted to depose King Hussein of Jordan in September 1970. A fierce battle was fought between the PLO and Jordanian troops near Amman on September 17, escalating when Syrian troops intervened on the side of the PLO. Jordan launched retaliatory raids against Syria on September 20; Syrian troops were expelled from Jordan by September 23. On September 27 the PLO moved its forces out of Jordanian cities.

Lingering PLO activities in the towns brought continuing government actions against PLO bases throughout 1971, and the PLO was finally driven out of Jordan by July 1971. More than two thousand people were killed in the conflict, including one hundred Syrian troops. There were numerous attempts at conflict management during the fighting, but they achieved only temporary solutions. The PLO later established itself in southern Lebanon and continued to launch attacks against Israel. This changed with the 1982 Israeli invasion, which among other things secured the PLO's deportation from Lebanon (see conflict 199). Relations between Israel and Jordan continued to be volatile.

For further information and background reading, see reference item numbers 1046, 1053, 1069, 1082, 1088, 1228, 1234.

129. GUINEA-PORTUGAL
PAIGC guerrilla warfare; the Conakry raids (November 1970)

The Partido Africano da Independência da Guinée Cabo Verde (PAIGC) in Guinea-Bissau had been fighting the Portuguese in a guerrilla war of independence (see conflict 070). Along with a number of other neighboring states, Guinea had granted diplomatic recognition to PAIGC, which strained border relations with Portugal. Furthermore, Guinea had allowed PAIGC to operate from within its frontiers.

From the beginning of the 1961 uprising in Guinea-Bissau, Portuguese counterinsurgency operations were concentrated along the borders of both Guinea and Senegal, both of which frequently charged that Portuguese forces were making unauthorized incursions into their territory. In November 1970 a group of mercenaries invaded Guinea from Guinea-Bissau, and fighting broke out in Conakry, Guinea's capital. The fighting lasted for several days, causing several hundred fatalities, and Guinean forces eventually repulsed the invaders.

A U.N. fact-finding mission later revealed that Portugal had sponsored the invasion, which had been aimed at ousting President Sékou Touré's regime. The conflict lapsed in 1975, when Portugal withdrew altogether from its African territories following the Lisbon coup (see conflict 070).

For further information and background reading, see reference item numbers 255, 306, 311, 312, 367, 370.

130. IRAQ-IRAN
Territorial dispute, border tensions (1971)

Iran and Iraq have had a long-standing border dispute over the Shatt al Arab Waterway, which runs into the Persian Gulf and serves both the Iraqi port of Basra and the Iranian port of Abadan. Numerous negotiations have failed to resolve their conflicting claims.

In 1970–1971 this long-running dispute began to heat up because of two Iranian gambits: first, Iran lent covert support to a Kurdish rebellion in Iraq (see conflict 121). Second, it occupied the Tunb islands in the Gulf, claimed by Iraq and the United Arab Emirates (see conflict 134). Iraq broke off diplomatic relations with Iran over the incident and, in October 1971, forcibly expelled eleven thousand Iranians. War appeared imminent, but by the end of the year the strains had eased somewhat, although the issues remained unresolved. Armed conflict broke out again in early 1972 (see conflict 136).

For further information and background reading, see reference item numbers 255, 1020, 1091, 1096, 1139, 1159, 1180, 1185.

131. UGANDA-TANZANIA
Postcoup tensions; border clashes (1971–October 1972)

In January 1971 Maj. Gen. Idi Amin ousted A. Milton Obote in a military coup. Obote had been Uganda's leader since its independence from Britain in 1962. During Amin's reign of terror, about 250,000 Ugandans were killed and the country's 80,000-strong community of Asians was expelled. Obote and his supporters fled to Tanzania and with that country's compliance conducted cross-border raids in an effort to destabilize Amin's new government. Tanzania refused to recognize the Amin regime altogether. Starting in August 1971, Tanzanian regulars participated in these cross-border raids, and Uganda retaliated. Both states closed their borders and conducted a number of air strikes on each other's territory.

Intensive Kenyan mediation efforts led to a resumption in diplomatic communications between the two countries in November 1971, and the conflict was considered settled. As many as two hundred Ugandan and Tanzanian military personnel are reported to have died in the fighting. This conflict was a precursor to much more grievous wars later on (see conflicts 179 and 198).

For further information and background reading, see reference item numbers 255, 296, 376, 410, 419, 453.

132. PAKISTAN-BANGLADESH
Secessionist warfare; the Bangladesh war of independence (March 1971–February 1974)

In addition to creating two new nations, the partition of the Indian Subcontinent in 1947–1948 (see conflict 003) led to the creation of two separate provinces for Pakistan, one northwest of India (West Pakistan) and one east (East Pakistan). Over time, East Pakistan grew to begrudge West Pakistan's control of the central government. This resentment was fueled by the eastern province's geographical isolation in addition to its powerful feelings of Bengali separatism.

Accordingly, in the late 1960s the Awami League, formed by Sheikh Mujibar Rahman, began to agitate for separation. The Awami League overwhelmingly won the 1970 elections to the national assembly. But on March 1 West Pakistani authorities postponed the inaugural sitting of the assembly. Large demonstrations and riots followed, bringing cruelly repressive action from the Pakistani military. More than 10 million refugees flooded into India, where some received arms and training and returned to East Pakistan (Bangladesh) to fight government forces.

Starting in April 1971, Pakistani troops conducted raids against Bengali sanctuaries in India, bringing some Indian retaliation. In November 1971 a large Indian force occupied border areas of East Pakistan, provoking a Pakistani mobilization on the West Pakistani border with the Punjab. India subsequently invaded West Pakistan on November 21, and East Pakistan on December 3, 1971. Pakistani forces in East Pakistan surrendered on December 17, and Bengali nationalists proclaimed the Republic of Bangladesh.

A cease-fire was announced in the west on the following day, although skirmishes continued in some areas until 1974. Perhaps as many as 1 million Bengalis were killed in the fighting and associated violence and dislocation. Civilians were often the target of attacks, and reprisals and ethnic violence were rife. Nearly eight thousand West Pakistan troops are thought to have been killed during the conflict, along with two thousand to three thousand Indian troops.

For further information and background reading, see reference item numbers 255, 661, 667, 701, 743, 744, 810, 828, 844.

133. NORTH YEMEN–SOUTH YEMEN
Anticommunist insurgency; border conflict
(October 1971–October 1972)

When Britain withdrew from Aden in 1967, the protectorate renamed itself the People's Democratic Republic of Yemen (South Yemen) and allied itself with the Soviet Union. North Yemen had been an independent imamate since 1918, and after civil strife from 1962 to 1967 (see conflict 083) and conflict with Saudi Arabia in 1969 (see conflict 125), the country allied itself to Saudi Arabia.

The rebel organization, the Front for the Liberation of South Yemen, had been actively seeking the overthrow of the South Yemeni government for a number of years. It was supported in this aim by Saudi Arabia and North Yemen, both of which were hostile to the communist state. Starting in October 1971 South Yemen sought to repress opposition to the government by pursuing insurgents across the border into North Yemen. Rebel activities continued throughout 1972, however, and North Yemeni troops actively aided South Yemen rebels.

In October 1972 South Yemeni troops invaded North Yemen border areas. The Arab League immediately sought to mediate between the parties, and a cease-fire was agreed to on October 19. It was reported that two hundred people were killed during the fighting, including forty to fifty North and South Yemeni regular troops. Tensions remained high between the two states, and a war broke out again in 1979 (see conflict 183). North and South Yemen were finally reunified following a civil war in the early 1990s (see conflict 278).

For further information and background reading, see reference item numbers 255, 1060, 1143, 1167, 1188, 1238, 1253, 1316, 1317, 1333.

134. IRAN–UNITED ARAB EMIRATES
Territorial dispute; the Tunb islands dispute (November 1971)

Britain granted independence to Bahrain and the United Arab Emirates (U.A.E.) in 1971. Bahrain passed the transition to independence without incident, but on the day before the U.A.E. was to become independent, Iran forcibly seized the islands of Abu Musa and the Tunbs, which are strategically situated at the entrance to the Persian Gulf in the Strait of Hormuz. The islands were originally ruled by individual emirates, which had been controlled by Great Britain since the nineteenth century; Iran and Iraq also laid claim to the islands.

A number of policemen and Iranian soldiers were killed in the fighting. Britain did not press the point, however, and the conflict eventually lapsed, although Iraq and other countries did consider Iran's move as a threat to regional security. The islands became the focus of further conflict in 1992 (see conflict 269).

For further information and background reading, see reference item numbers 76, 1021, 1022, 1023, 1028, 1034, 1154.

135. OMAN–SOUTH YEMEN
*Antigovernment insurgency; the Dhofar rebellion
(1972–August 1974)*

The rebel province of Dhofar in the south of Oman had long been a problem for the Omani government. With the aid of British forces, Oman launched numerous counterinsurgency operations against the Dhofari rebels in the years preceding this conflict. In 1970 Sultan Said bin Timur was deposed by his son, Sultan Qabus bin Said. The new sultan subsequently invited Dhofari rebels to work with the government in a national development program. The rebels refused and continued to agitate against the government.

In February 1972 the rebels formed the Popular Front for the Liberation of Oman and the Arab Gulf (PFLOAG) and, with the support of South Yemen, launched a leftist guerrilla campaign against the Omani government.

In early May 1972 the Omani government began attacking PFLOAG camps and positions within South Yemen. South Yemen retaliated with artillery strikes on Omani positions. At Oman's request, Iran sent large numbers of troops in December 1973 to help drive out the rebels, By late 1974 the Dhofari had largely been defeated, and the conflict with South Yemen gradually abated. In January 1975, after the main rebellion was over, Jordanian troops arrived to help keep the peace. About two thousand people were killed in the rebellion, including five hundred Iranian troops, twenty British troops, and six or more South Yemeni regulars. Saudi Arabia made some efforts to mediate, but these were largely unsuccessful.

For further information and background reading, see reference item numbers 255, 1060, 1143, 1167, 1188, 1238, 1253, 1316, 1317, 1333.

136. IRAN-IRAQ
Territorial dispute; border war (January 1972–February 1975)

Relations between Iran and Iraq were quite strained following Iran's 1970 seizure of the Tunb islands in the Strait of Hormuz (see conflict 134). Matters worsened after Iraq forcibly expelled eleven thousand Iranians in 1971 (see conflict 130). Iran and Iraq also had a long-standing dispute over the ownership of the Shatt al Arab Waterway, which was crucial for shipping for both states. These tensions finally erupted into armed conflict in early 1972.

Iran commenced artillery attacks and cross-border raids on Iraq in January 1972. Numerous border incidents and low-intensity fighting continued until February 1974, when Iraq launched a ground offensive in an attempt to seize full control of various disputed areas. Iran launched a counteroffensive in March. Sporadic artillery exchanges and raids persisted until February 1975 despite a U.N.-arranged cease-fire.

Iraq formally acceded to Iranian claims in March 1975, in return for Iran's pledge to halt support for Kurdish rebels within Iraq. The 1975 border agreement remarcated the boundary so that it went down the middle of the Shatt al Arab Waterway, giving both sides joint access. About one thousand Iraqi and Iranian military personnel died in the sometimes intense fighting. Peaceful conflict management was not pursued, and a bloody and protracted war broke out in 1980 (see conflict 191).

For further information and background reading, see reference item numbers 255, 1020, 1091, 1096, 1139, 1159, 1180, 1185.

137. SYRIA-ISRAEL; PLO
PLO raids, retaliatory air strikes; the Golan Heights conflict (March 1972–January 1973)

Since its war of independence in 1948, Israel's relations with its Arab neighbors were tense. In 1972 Israel's relations with Syria were particularly strained (see conflicts 026, 042, 051, 081, 096) because several years earlier Israel had wrested the strategically valuable Golan Heights from Syria during the Six-Day War (see conflict 117). For its part, Syria began lending heavy support to the PLO, especially following the PLO's expulsion from Jordan in 1971 (see conflict 128).

In early 1972 Palestinian guerrillas began to launch attacks on Israeli positions on the Golan Heights from within Syrian territory and with Syrian support. In March Israel responded with retaliatory air attacks, drawing reprisals from the Syrian air force. Intermittent attacks continued in the ensuing months, finally diminishing in January 1973. About two hundred people are thought to have been killed during the fighting, and this conflict proved to be the precursor to the 1973 Yom Kippur war, when Syria and Egypt attacked Israel during the High Holy Day of Yom Kippur (see conflict 141).

For further information and background reading, see reference item numbers 255, 1047, 1084, 1098, 1158, 1180.

138. EQUATORIAL GUINEA–GABON

Territorial dispute; the Corisco Bay islands dispute
(June–November 1972)

In 1900 France and Spain, the colonial powers, respectively, of Gabon and Equatorial Guinea, signed a treaty assigning the small islands in Corisco Bay to Equatorial Guinea. Neither country had established an official presence on the islands, however, nor had they ever worried over issues of sovereignty. Following Gabon's independence in 1960, Gabonese fishermen frequently used the islands for shelter.

This changed in 1972, however, when traces of oil were found in the area. In an effort to preempt Gabonese actions, Equatorial Guinea, then on the eve of achieving full independence from Spain, asserted its claims to the islands. Its military units began attacking Gabonese fishing camps on the islands in September 1972. Gabon referred the issue to the United Nations. Equatorial Guinea responded that Gabon had invaded the islands.

A propaganda war began, as did a number of serious firing incidents. President Mobutu Sésé Séko of Zaire and President Marien Ngouabi of Congo sought to mediate the dispute in September, finally gaining agreement between the two sides on November 13, 1972. The two sides agreed to "neutralize" the disputed islands, but tensions only gradually decreased. Approximately twenty fatalities were reported during the conflict.

For further information and background reading, see reference item numbers 76, 286, 287.

139. ETHIOPIA-SOMALIA

Somali expansionism, territorial dispute; the second Ogaden war
(June 1972–March 1978)

Successive Somali regimes claimed territory that was occupied by Somali tribes but belonged to other states—a practice that had already led to a war with

Ethiopia over the Ogaden region in 1964 (see conflict 090) and armed conflict with Kenya in 1966–1967 (see conflict 085).

The second Ogaden war began in mid-1972, when Somali tribesmen in the region resumed their revolt. Somali regulars again began to fight alongside the rebels starting in mid-1972, and a low-intensity conflict began. The war escalated in June 1972 when Somalia launched combat operations, a precursor to invasion the following month. The fighting was fierce, but Somalia began to make headway. Five years later, by October 1977, it had occupied the entire Ogaden area.

With the aid of Soviet military hardware and troop support from both Cuba and South Yemen, Ethiopia launched a massive counterattack and retook the region by March 1978. There were intermittent border clashes in the ensuing years, but the conflict did not escalate again to the level seen in 1977 and 1978. Upwards of thirty thousand people died in the conflict, and when fighting did die down in 1985 the issue had still not been fully addressed. Tensions between the two states remained high, and armed conflict over the Ogaden broke out again in 1987–1988 (see conflict 239).

For further information and background reading, see reference item numbers 255, 341, 352, 356, 363, 396, 421.

140. IRAQ-KUWAIT
Territorial dispute, border incidents (March 1973–July 1975)

Kuwait, long a part of the Ottoman Empire's massive Arab land holdings, had nevertheless declared itself independent in 1899. In 1914 the British agreed to protect Kuwait in exchange for control over its foreign policy. When the protectorate expired in June 1961, Kuwait became fully independent, whereupon Iraq announced its claim to the territory. A serious conflict ensued (see conflict 073). An Arab League force was deployed in Kuwait to deter Iraqi attack following the conflict.

On March 20, 1973, Iraqi forces captured Kuwaiti border posts at Sametah. Saudi troops were once again deployed but did not engage Iraqi forces. With the acquiescence of both parties, PLO leader Yasser Arafat mediated the dispute, managing to secure an Iraqi withdrawal in early April. There were two Iraqi fatalities at Sametah, and the conflict was partially settled. Iraqi claims to Kuwait never completely lapsed, however, and in 1990, Iraq launched a full invasion of Kuwait, starting the Gulf war (see conflict 261).

For further information and background reading, see reference item numbers 46, 76, 255, 1041, 1219, 1220.

141. ISRAEL-EGYPT

Arab-Israeli territorial dispute; the Yom Kippur war, the Arab-Israeli wars (October 1973)

Israel's relations with its Arab neighbors had been strained since its 1948 war of independence (see conflict 012). These strains burst into armed conflict on a number of occasions, the most serious being the Six-Day War in 1967, when Israel attacked Egypt, Jordan, and Syria (see conflict 117). During this campaign Israel gained control of the Sinai Peninsula from Egypt and wrested the Golan Heights from Syria. In 1973 President Anwar al-Sadat of Egypt had indicated his intentions of winning back the Sinai by war, but Israel considered this to be mere bluff.

On October 6, 1973, Egypt and Syria launched simultaneous offensives into Israeli-occupied Sinai and the Golan Heights on the Jewish High Holy Day of Yom Kippur. Israel responded with air attacks against Syrian and Egyptian positions. By October 11 Israeli troops had regained the Golan Heights in fierce fighting and advanced into Syrian territory, drawing Morocco, Kuwait, Saudi Arabia, and Jordan into the conflict in defense of Syria. On October 14, Israel launched an offensive on the Sinai, crossing the Suez Canal. Kuwaiti, Tunisian, and Algerian forces came to the aid of Egypt. The Israeli offensive continued, and by October 20 Israel had consolidated its position around the Suez Canal and had a large part of the Egyptian army completely surrounded.

After frantic efforts by the United Nations and the United States to stop the fighting, a cease-fire was declared on October 22, but fighting continued for a number of days and a military stand-off between the belligerents continued until February 1979. Israel unilaterally withdrew from Syrian territory, back to its former positions on the Golan Heights in June 1974.

More than ten thousand soldiers lost their lives in this conflict, including five thousand Egyptians, three thousand Israelis, three thousand Syrians, and two hundred Iraqis. After the fighting stopped, there were strenuous attempts at conflict management, which in 1979, under the good offices of U.S. president Jimmy Carter, produced the Camp David Accords between Egypt and Israel. Relations with Israel's other neighbors continued to be tense, however, and there were numerous subsequent cases of militarized hostilities.

For further information and background reading, see reference item numbers 1029, 1031, 1046, 1098, 1129, 1134, 1157, 1158, 1164.

142. SOUTH VIETNAM–CHINA

Territorial dispute; the Paracel Islands (January 1974–June 1978)

At the end of World War II Japan renounced its claims to the Paracel Islands in the South China Sea. Since then, these islands, along with the Spratlys, had been disputed by China, South Vietnam, the Philippines, Malaysia, and Brunei. The islands were thought to contain oil deposits, although there had been no independent evidence to date.

In January 1974 South Vietnam formally incorporated the Paracel Islands into its Phuoc Tuy province and began granting contracts for oil exploration. China rigorously objected to this de facto assertion of ownership. South Vietnam then sent naval patrols to the area to bolster its claims, and there were a number of naval clashes. The conflict escalated when both sides sent in troops and land fighting broke out. The Chinese held the Paracels, taking the Vietnamese inhabitants prisoner, while South Vietnam reinforced its garrisons on the Spratlys. There were twenty to thirty fatalities, and although the dispute lapsed after this, China took the Spratlys in an armed encounter in 1988 (see conflict 243; see also conflicts 288, 289). There were no serious attempts at peaceful conflict management during the conflict.

For further information and background reading, see reference item numbers 76, 255, 870.

143. CYPRUS
Communal violence, Turkish-Greek invasions; partition
(January 1974–June 1978)

Cyprus had gained independence from Britain in 1960 following a violent campaign (see conflict 041). The issue of the relationship between the majority Greek-Cypriot population and the minority Turkish-Cypriot population was never resolved, however, and led to massive communal violence in 1963 (see conflict 089). Although U.N. troops had been stationed on the island to keep the peace between the two communities, tensions remained high.

After disputes with the national guard, dominated by Greek army officers, Cypriot president Makarios was overthrown in a military coup on July 15, 1974. Installed in his place was Nikoi Giorgiades Sampson, a former terrorist who had fought against the British for the Greek National Organization of Cypriot Fighters (EOKA). This provoked alarm among the Turkish Cypriot community, some of whom began fleeing the country; British soldiers aided in the evacuation of Turkish civilians. Others began arming themselves, and Turkey and Greece quickly mobilized as the conflict escalated.

Five days after the coup, on July 20, 1974, a Turkish invasion force landed on the island and after fierce fighting gained control of northern Cyprus by the end of August. Almost simultaneously, a Greek force had landed, assisting the local Greek militia in halting the Turkish advance. When a cease-fire mediated by the United States failed, a British-mediated cease-fire was signed on July 30, 1974. Cyprus had effectively been partitioned by this point. President Makarios returned to head the official Cypriot government in the southern part of the island. A Turkish Cypriot federated state was established in northern third of the island.

A period of protracted negotiations sponsored by the United Nations was initiated in an effort to find a political solution that would reunify the island, but without much success. More than five thousand people lost their lives in the conflict, including a thousand Turkish troops. Despite the presence of U.N. troops, tensions between the two countries remain high, and incidents are not uncommon (see conflict 277). The civil war also heightened the rivalry between Greece and Turkey, leading to a clash in 1984 (see conflict 221).

For further information and background reading, see reference item numbers 255, 887, 900, 912, 916, 921, 924, 933, 934.

144. THE KURDS–IRAQ
Attempted secession; the Kurdish rebellion (March 1974–July 1975)

The Kurds are a non-Arab tribes people inhabiting an extensive mountainous plateau region that includes parts of Iran, Turkey, and Iraq. They have been fighting unsuccessfully for an independent state since the end of World War I, when the Kurds were granted an autonomous state by the Treaty of Sèvres (1920). The terms were never carried out.

Like Turkey and Iran, Iraq has suppressed the Kurds' many secessionist revolts, and this led to clashes in 1961–1966 (see conflict 071) and again in 1968–1970 (see conflict 121). In the period leading up to March 1974, the Kurds were particularly dissatisfied with the implementation of the 1970 agreement (which had ended the most recent revolt).

The Kurdish rebellion resumed under the leadership of Mullah Mustafa Barazani. Fighting broke out on March 12, 1974, and Iran provided the rebels with arms and assistance. In the face of cruel Iraqi repression, Kurdish leaders appealed to the United Nations and accused Iraq of genocide. As in the past, the United Nations pointed to the Kurds' status as a stateless people and took no action. The Kurds were driven close to the Iranian border, resulting in frequent border violations by Iraqi forces. Iran began to shell Iraqi positions in retaliation.

A March 1975 agreement resolved a territorial dispute between Iraq and Iran (see conflicts 130, 136) on the condition that Iran cease its support for the Kurds. Without Iranian support, the Kurds could not withstand Iraq's advances. Iraq quickly quelled the rebellion, proclaiming an amnesty for Kurds who surrendered by April 1. More than three thousand people were killed during the rebellion, many of them civilians. Barazani fled into exile in Iran. The Kurds returned to armed conflict the following year (see conflict 163).

For further information and background reading, see reference item numbers 1038, 1078, 1109, 1128, 1170, 1190, 1240, 1250, 1300.

145. ISRAEL-LEBANON
Arab-Israeli dispute; cross-border attacks (April 1974–July 1975)

Following the Israeli war of independence in 1948 (see conflict 012), many Palestinian refugees settled in southern Lebanon. Also, after being ejected from Jordan in 1971 (see conflict 128), the Palestine Liberation Organization (PLO) began to move its headquarters to Lebanon. From there, infiltrators were sent across the border into Israel to attack civilian and military targets. This led to border tensions.

This conflict started in April 1974 when Arab terrorists based in southern Lebanon crossed into Israel and massacred eighteen Israelis in the northern town of Qiryat Shemona. The Israelis responded by raiding several villages in southern Lebanon and by threatening Lebanon with massive retaliation if it allowed terrorists to operate from its territory. Similar terrorist attacks in May and June led to massive bombing raids on Palestinian camps in Lebanon, and to naval attacks on Lebanese ports from where infiltrators launched amphibious assaults.

This pattern of conflict continued until July 1975, when Israel became involved in the Lebanese civil war (see conflict 151) on the side of Christian militias. In December 1974 relations between Israel and Lebanon deteriorated further when Israeli planes attacked Palestinian targets on the outskirts of Beirut. Several hundred people were killed during the conflict, and the only two conflict-management attempts failed. This conflict was a precursor to armed conflict involving both states in 1977 (see conflict 170), 1978 (see conflict 176), 1979 (see conflict 186), 1982 (see conflict 199) and 1983 (see conflict 213).

For further information and background reading, see reference item numbers 1047, 1058, 1069, 1098, 1123, 1145, 1158.

146. MOROCCO-MAURITANIA; WESTERN SAHARA
Saharan nationalism, territorial dispute; the Western Saharan conflict (October 1974–)

Since independence in 1956, Morocco had pressed a claim to the large expanse of desert to its south. Spain had controlled the territory, known as Western Sahara, since the nineteenth century, and when it decided to withdraw in 1975, it conceded the area to Morocco and Mauritania for partition in spite of an International Court of Justice ruling that neither state possessed an enforceable claim to the area. While Spanish troops withdrew, both states occupied the area militarily.

The indigenous Saharan nationalist organization, Polisario (Frente Popular para la Liberatión de Saguia el-Hamra y Rio de Oro), which was initially formed to resist Spanish rule, promptly began attacking Moroccan and

Mauritanian forces. Polisario was backed by Algeria, and Algerian troops intervened in the conflict in January 1976, clashing with Moroccan troops. Morocco had to deploy thousands of troops to Mauritania in July 1977, when Polisario began attacking targets within Mauritanian territory. France increased its military aid to Morocco and even engaged in air attacks against Polisario bases in Mauritania in December 1977.

In 1979 Mauritania abandoned the territory it held in Western Sahara due to the heavy costs involved in maintaining a presence there, and Morocco attempted to occupy the entire area. Serious fighting continued in the region throughout the 1980s. Despite Moroccan attempts to prevent infiltration across the Algerian frontier, the conflict often spilled into neighboring states because Moroccan forces pursued the rebels into Mauritania and Algeria. Polisario also began attacking targets in Moroccan territory.

Neither side has been able to achieve a significant advantage, and tens of thousands of deaths have occurred throughout the conflict; by 1989 Morocco had sustained nearly ten thousand military fatalities. Although the conflict had dozens of mediation attempts and numerous negotiations, no lasting solution has been found. An agreement to hold a referendum on the status of the area in 1992 under U.N. auspices was postponed several times because of disagreements between Morocco and Polisario and problems with the United Nation's voter identification operation. By the end of 1995 these problems were still unresolved. The conflict remains unresolved at the end of 1995, although the level of fighting is not quite at the level of previous years owing to an agreement signed in 1991.

For further information and background reading, see reference item numbers 76, 255, 361, 471.

147. MALI–UPPER VOLTA (Burkina Faso)
Territorial/resource dispute (December 1974–June 1975)

Mali and Upper Volta (Burkina Faso, or "Land of the Upright People," after 1984) had both gained independence in 1960. France's 1919 demarcation of the colony of Upper Volta was overturned in 1932, and then reinstated in 1947. This led to a dispute over the border area with Mali, which contained a chain of pools through which the flowed the Belí River—the region's only source of fresh water. Regular talks on the disputed territory since 1961 had failed to resolve the issue, leading to tensions between the two states.

A crisis in relations occurred in December 1974, when armed clashes occurred. A Malian patrol attacked Upper Voltan troops on December 14, 1974, near the village of Gasselago in Upper Volta. This incident was followed by further clashes and arrests, and military operations intensified from December 1974 to June 1975. There were few fatalities from these encounters, but tensions were extremely high.

Ivory Coast, Senegal, and Guinea attempted to mediate the conflict. This failed, but an appeal to the OAU president resulted in the establishment of a mediation commission consisting of Guinea, Niger, Senegal, and Togo to guarantee safety in the disputed territory and supervise troop withdrawal. A final agreement to the border dispute was achieved in Lomé on June 18, 1975, mediated by the presidents of Togo, Niger, Senegal, and Guinea, and the OAU. The agreement recommended an independent demarcation of the common frontier. This ultimately did not solve the issue, and a much more serious armed conflict broke out in 1985–1986 (see conflict 230).

For further information and background reading, see reference item numbers 76, 310, 354, 399, 442, 463.

148. ANGOLA–SOUTH AFRICA
Guerrilla warfare in Namibia; intervention and civil war (1975–1995)

The conflict between Angola and South Africa, provoked in the main by Angolan government support for Namibian independence (see conflict 110), represented an extension of the conflict that had engulfed region since the early 1960s. During Portugal's withdrawal from Angola in 1975, civil war erupted among the three rival nationalist organizations that had earlier been fighting for Angolan independence. These were the Union for the Total Independence of Angola (UNITA), which was supported by South Africa and the United States and in control of most of southern Angola; the Soviet-backed Movimento Popular de Libertação de Angola (MPLA), which held Luanda and parts of the south; and the Frente Nacional de Libertacão de Angola (FNLA), backed by Zaire (Congo) and in control of the north.

The FNLA and UNITA both launched offensives in 1975 in an attempt to gain control of Luanda, the capital of Angola. By October of that year, the pressure on the MPLA brought Cuban troops into the war at the instigation of the Soviet Union. The MPLA soon gained enough of an advantage to declare itself the sole government of Angola. While the FNLA was defeated, the UNITA forces retreated and began a long-term guerrilla war against the MPLA government.

Angola came into direct fighting with South Africa in 1976 after it joined Zambia in declaring support for the South West African People's Organization (SWAPO), which was fighting a guerrilla war of independence in Namibia. For the next decade Angola and South Africa clashed regularly when the apartheid government lent support to UNITA, or pursued SWAPO guerrillas into their bases in Angola.

In 1987 and 1988 the war escalated when South African invaded Angola, and Angola counterattacked with Cuban troop support. In June 1987 MPLA and Cuban forces surrounded a large South African force within Angola. South

Africa was subsequently forced to agree to a withdrawal of its forces from Angola by mid-1988, and U.N. mediation efforts, which had punctuated the entire conflict, finally secured a cease-fire on August 22, 1988. Subsequent negotiations led to an agreement providing for Namibian independence and South Africa's withdrawal from Angola.

The civil war in Angola continued until the 1990s, however, when mediation finally secured an agreement to hold multiparty elections and to lay down arms. Having narrowly lost the 1992 elections, UNITA immediately went back to war. The fighting was so intense and vicious that the United Nations declared it the worst war then being waged, estimating that a thousand people were dying per day as a direct result of the conflict.

The fighting continued throughout 1994, despite desperate diplomatic efforts by the United Nations and states in the region. In November 1994 government forces took Huambo, UNITA's headquarters and center of support. At the same time, both sides signed a peace accord in Lusaka, Zambia. The United Nations made intense efforts throughout 1995 to consolidate the Lusaka Agreement. Although meetings between UNITA leader Jonas Savimbi and President José Eduardo dos Santos suggested the war was finally over, the peace was still extremely fragile.

In all, more than 360,000 people were killed during the course of the war, many of them civilians. Two thousand Cuban troops died in the fighting; South Africa lost about one thousand personnel and Zaire a few hundred.

For further information and background reading, see reference item numbers 255, 301, 306, 311, 312, 370, 379, 392.

149. BANGLADESH

Postindependence territorial dispute; the Chittagong Hill Tracts conflict (1975–)

Inhabited by 600,000 Buddhist tribal people, the Chittagong Hill Tracts in eastern Bangladesh was originally administered separately from the rest of India by the British, and strict laws prevented outsiders from settling there. Having just emerged from a war of independence (see conflict 132), however, the new Bangladesh government abolished the area's special status and encouraged Bengalis to settle there. Tribal leaders set up an association to fight the moves, called the Chittagong Hill Tracts People's Solidarity Association (JSS).

The JSS formed a military wing known as the Shanti Bahini, which began attacking army outposts and Bengali villagers from the mid-1970s. Hundreds of people died in these notoriously brutal attacks. A ruthless campaign of repression ensued. India began supporting the insurgents from an early stage, and there were frequent cross-border incidents. Despite British counterinsurgency training for Bangladeshi forces, the fighting continued into the 1990s, by which time at least 300,000 Bengalis had settled in the Hill Tracts.

Limited autonomy was granted to the Tracts in 1992, and regular peace talks were held, but these failed to resolve the conflict, and low-level fighting continued intermittently through to the end of 1995. In 1995, there were two thousand tribal insurgents operating in the Hill Tracts, and Bangladesh as a whole was in a state of civil unrest and political instability. More than 3,500 people are estimated to have died in the fighting, and fifty thousand refugees, having fled the conflict, are encamped in the Indian state of Tripura.

For further information and background reading, see reference item numbers 37, 76, 661, 838, 844.

150. NORTH KOREA–SOUTH KOREA
Cold war border crisis (February–July 1975)

North and South Korea had been implacable enemies since the Korean War (1950–1953, see conflict 024). The constant strain produced border incidents in 1965 (see conflict 105) and a continuous state of alert. Talks aimed normalizing relations had been going on since 1972 without success, and tensions escalated again in early 1972 following the discovery of tunnels under the demilitarized zone (DMZ). The recent communist victories in Cambodia and Vietnam combined with stepped-up contacts between Pyongyang and Beijing served only to heighten tensions, prompting South Korean allegations of an imminent invasion by North Korea. U.S. warnings against such an invasion included the threat of using tactical nuclear weapons.

During May and June 1975, North Korean leader Kim Il Sung railed against the United Nations' North-South ("two Koreas") plan. Both sides alleged military buildups in the border areas, published propaganda, and staged hostile incidents in the DMZ. No attempts at peaceful conflict management were made, and the dispute gradually abated. Armed conflict broke out again in 1984 (see conflict 227) and 1992 (see conflict 270).

For further information and background reading, see reference item numbers 255, 672, 675, 720, 804, 816, 848.

151. LEBANON
Internal strife, communal violence; the second Lebanese civil war (February 1975–1976)

Lebanon was originally part of Syria, and together they formed the Levant states, long a part of the Ottoman Empire. After World War I France was awarded the territory, and it immediately partitioned the area into two independent states, which were administered under the French mandate until 1941.

Under the 1943 national pact, all Lebanese political positions were divided among the country's many religious communities (among them the Christian Maronites and the Muslim Sunni and Druze sects), with Christians holding the majority. Lebanon's delicately balanced civil society began to change in 1948, however, when Israel's war of independence sent droves of Palestinians northward (see conflict 012).

In 1958 Lebanon was plunged into its first civil war when the national pact broke down with the help of a Syrian-aided revolt against the government's policies; U.S. Marines briefly intervened (see conflict 057). Following the first civil war, an uneasy peace existed among Lebanon's confessional communities. By the 1970s, however, Muslims had become the majority and were agitating for a greater share of political power. Fighting broke out once again when twenty-five Palestinians were massacred by members of the conservative Christian Phalange militia. Heavily armed leftist Muslim factions retaliated, and by the end of the year full-scale civil war was under way, as each side tried to gain control of Beirut.

By May 1975 the government had collapsed, and in March 1976 the Lebanese army split into Christian and Muslim units. In June 1976 up to fifteen thousand Syrian troops intervened on the side of the Maronites to fight the Palestinians, and a cease-fire was declared. Syria then occupied much of southern Lebanon and the Bekaa Valley, acting as a buffer between the combatants.

Approximately sixty thousand people lost their lives in the 1975–1976 civil war. Sporadic fighting continued in Lebanon until 1992, with several serious outbreaks of violence (see conflicts 176, 199, 213). Although there were more than a hundred attempts at peaceful conflict management, few succeeded and none has produced a lasting solution to the conflict.

In 1992 a number of limited peace agreements among various factions brought the major fighting to an end, although small outbreaks of violence erupted periodically. In 1992 Hezbollah (Party of God) was still attacking Israel from southern Lebanon, while Israel attempted to maintain the area as a security zone (see conflict 213). Israel also continued to support Christian militias in the area. The new government of Lebanon was attempting to rebuild its shattered country, and relative calm was still in evidence at the end of 1995—though this was to be shattered in early 1996.

For further information and background reading, see reference item numbers 255, 1027, 1083, 1103, 1111, 1133, 1181, 1215, 1264, 1299.

152. SYRIA-IRAQ
Resource dispute; the Euphrates dispute (April–late 1975)

Syria and Iraq often clashed, and in 1959 fighting erupted when Syria backed the Mosul revolt in an effort to unseat the Iraqi government (see conflict 062). In the months leading up to April 1975, both sides were waging a propaganda war against each other. Their relations began to worsen in early April 1975 in a dispute over the use of water from the Euphrates.

Requesting an emergency meeting of the Arab League foreign ministers, Iraq claimed Syria was diverting excessive amounts of water from the dam, thus endangering the livelihoods of Iraqi farmers. The dispute intensified when Syria closed its airspace to Iraq, broke off diplomatic relations, and threatened to bomb the Tabqa Dam. An Arab League meeting on April 22, 1975, established a technical committee to mediate the dispute, but the mediation failed when Syria withdrew. A further mediation by Saudi Arabia on May 3 also ended inconclusively, but another attempt in June produced a limited agreement over water allocation, without solving the basic conflict. Relations did not improve, and there were minor border clashes. The propaganda war continued, but eventually the conflict lapsed.

For further information and background reading, see reference item numbers 76, 255, 1059, 1179, 1183, 1219, 1295.

153. UNITED STATES–CAMBODIA
Post–Vietnam War tensions; the Mayaguez *incident (May 1975)*

Cambodia had served as a major battlefield and transit area (see conflict 069) during the Vietnam War and had been subjected to a massive aerial bombardment by the United States. As a consequence, U.S.-Cambodian relations were quite strained in 1975. This particular incident began when a United States merchant ship, the *Mayaguez,* was stopped and boarded by Cambodian forces near the island of Poulowai, which was claimed by both Cambodia and South Vietnam. The ship was seized in international waters, and, on charges of spying and carrying military cargo, the crew was detained and interrogated. The United States called it an act of "piracy" and responded with aerial actions against the boat carrying the U.S. crew. The conflict escalated when the United States landed marines near the Cambodian coast and began bombing raids on the Cambodian mainland, using Thailand as a military base for these operations, without Thai permission.

The United States used a Chinese liaison to demand the release of the crew members, without success, and on May 14, 1975, appealed to U.N. secretary-general Kurt Waldheim to secure their release. On May 15, 1975, the Cambodian authorities released the ship and crew, but the United States continued its air assaults on Cambodian targets with numerous Cambodian casualties. Offensive U.S. operations stopped on May 20, 1975, and the dispute eventually lapsed. About fifty people were killed during the conflict, and tensions remained high for some time.

For further information and background reading, see reference item numbers 689, 692, 696, 730, 731, 755, 840.

154. LAOS-THAILAND
Postrevolution exodus; border incidents (June 1975–January 1976)

When the leftist Pathet Lao came to power in 1975 following years of civil war (see conflict 095), Laotians, most of them from the professional and commercial classes, began flooding into neighboring Thailand (see map 9). The presence of these exiles, plus a number of unresolved border disputes, greatly strained relations between Laos and Thailand in the period leading up to June 1975. The conflict escalated when both sides broke off diplomatic relations and closed their common borders.

Beginning in June 1975, daily skirmishes on the frontier led to casualties, and on August 5 Laos arrested two Thai military attachés. Relations improved slightly after the attachés were released on August 15, and, in a conciliatory gesture, Thailand expelled leaders of the Meo tribes people (54,000 Meo refugees were encamped in Thailand, and their leaders were engaging in anti–Pathet Lao activities). Unsuccessful negotiations and border clashes continued until early 1976, when the conflict abated. The unresolved issues led to a recurrence of fighting in 1982 (see conflict 204), and a war in 1984–1988 (see conflict 223).

For further information and background reading, see reference item numbers 663, 714, 728, 757, 778, 854, 865, 869.

155. CHINA-INDIA
McMahon Line territorial dispute; border incidents (October 1975)

Sino-Indian relations had been hostile since China's invasion of Tibet in 1950 (see conflict 025), just a year after the Communists had come to power in Beijing. Chinese Communists disputed the McMahon Line, which had demarcated the Tibetan-India frontier since 1914. Relations between China and India deteriorated in 1956, when India supported Tibetan guerrillas in their war against the Chinese (see conflict 044). Matters worsened when India gave sanctuary to the Dalai Lama, whom the Tibetans revere as a god and king. By the time this particular conflict erupted, China and India had already clashed three

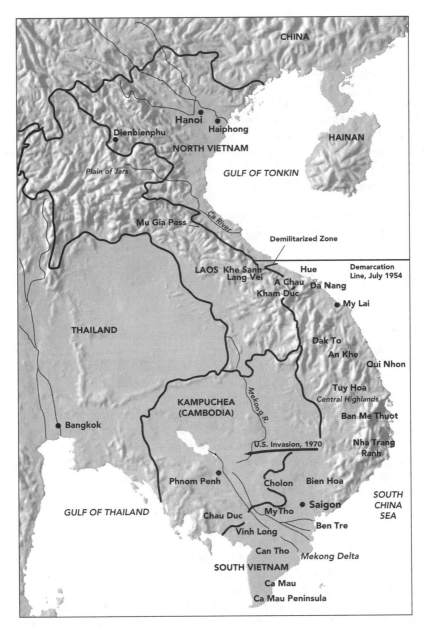

MAP 9. **Indochina**

The number of conflicts initiated by Southeast Asian nations since World War II (56) is third highest overall, after 79 for Africa and 70 for the Middle East (see tab. 1, p. 10). The United States–Vietnam war (see conflict 69) is perhaps the best known conflict to grip the region, but disputes involving Laos, Thailand, and Cambodia (now Kampuchea), among other nations, have been similarly devastating.

times over this disputed area (called the Arunachal Pradesh): in 1959–1960 (see conflict 066), in 1962 (see conflict 084), and in 1965 (see conflict 107).

On October 20, 1975, a serious border skirmish occurred when four Indian soldiers were killed in what the Indians described as an ambush by Chinese troops thirty-five miles east of Bhutan. China denied these allegations on October 22, stating that the Indian troops had intruded into Tibet and when told to withdraw had opened fire on a Chinese civilian border post. The bodies of the Indian soldiers were returned on October 28 and no further hostilities in relation to the incident occurred. Eventually the dispute simply lapsed altogether. There were no attempts at peaceful conflict management, and relations returned to their normal state of antagonism.

For further information and background reading, see reference item numbers 76, 255, 691, 738, 788, 831, 873.

156. EAST TIMOR–INDONESIA
Independence struggle (October 1975–)

Portugal had ruled the eastern half of Timor (an island in the Lesser Sundas, which form the southeastern portion of the Malay archipelago) since the sixteenth century. Japan took over the island during World War II, but Portugal regained control of the territory following Japan's defeat. In 1949 Indonesia assumed control over West Timor, which had been ruled by the Dutch.

In 1959 an East Timor revolt against Portuguese rule was put down. But following the 1974 Lisbon coup and the loss of its African territories (see conflict 070), Portugal allowed political organizations to form on the island. East Timorans obliged, quickly forming the proindependence Frente Revolutionario de Este Timor Independente (Fretilin), along with Partido Democratico (PDU), which favored federation with Portugal. Another party, the Associacão da Populaca Democratica de Timor (Apodeti) was supported by Indonesia and advocated union with Indonesia.

Fighting among these factions broke out in October 1974 but ended in January 1975. In mid-September 1975 small-scale Indonesian military units began operating in East Timor on behalf of Apodeti; by October civil war had broken out. Fretilin proclaimed independence from Portugal at the end of November, and on December 7, 1975, Indonesia began a full invasion of the island. Fighting was intense, and it is thought that as many as 100,000 people were killed during this period. In July 1976 Indonesia formally annexed East Timor and sent more than 20,000 Indonesian troops to East Timor. Fretilin supporters continued to fight on.

Hostilities have continued in East Timor since 1976, and casualties have been heavy. An Australian fact-finding team in April 1977 found that Indonesia's incorporation of East Timor had become an irreversible fact. Despite this, during the late 1970s and into the 1980s the United Nations repeatedly reaffirmed East Timor's right to self-determination and continues to regard it as a Portuguese-administered colony. Along with the Red Cross, the United Nations has continually called for an end to human rights violations committed by Indonesian troops.

Guerrilla activity continued in the early 1980s, despite Indonesian military offensives, a program of "Jawanization" and resettlement, development funds, and amnesties for Fretilin guerrillas who surrendered. The first half of 1983 was relatively peaceful, but fighting broke out in August 1983 with an Indonesian offensive that lasted well into 1984. International pressure on Indonesia by the United Nations, United States, and Australia to find a solution to the conflict continued.

By December 1988 Fretilin was no longer perceived as a security threat in East Timor, and Indonesia lifted a thirteen-year closed-territory status that had limited information on the situation in the territory. In 1990 reports emerged, however, of violent suppressions of student-led demonstrations, continued unrest, and government refusals to negotiate with Fretilin. The year 1991 was characterized by persistent reports of human rights abuses against proindependence activists.

On November 12, 1991, Indonesian troops opened fire on demonstrators in Dili, killing perhaps as many as 180 people, but blaming provocation on the demonstrators. The protest was to coincide with a visit from a Portuguese parliamentary delegation, subsequently canceled by Indonesia. As a result of international pressure over the incident, senior army officers were punished for their role in the massacre. This event marked an upsurge in proindependence activities in the area, and hostilities persisted. In 1995 there were a number of U.N.-sponsored high-level talks between Indonesia and Portugal, but these failed to resolve any of the substantive issues, and human rights abuses, riots, and proindependence activities continued in the area. Also significant was the capture of Xanana, Fretilin's leader in December 1992, and his subsequent trial and imprisonment.

There have been few attempts by the Indonesian authorities to negotiate with Fretilin, and it is thought that as many as 200,000 people have been killed in the conflict. Many of these have been civilians who died in reprisals, disease, and starvation.

For further information and background reading, see reference item numbers 255, 665, 685, 710, 745, 746, 856.

157. ZAIRE-ANGOLA
Rebel activity; border war (November 1975–February 1976)

This particular conflict grew out of Angola's civil war, which broke out on the eve of that country's independence from Portugal in November 1975 (see conflict 148). The fighting was primarily between the Soviet-backed Movimento Popular de Libertação de Angola (MPLA) government and right-wing rebel factions, including the Union for the Total Independence of Angola (UNITA) and the Frente Nacional de Libertação Liberation de Angola (FNLA). Zairean president Mobutu Sésé Séko had been supporting the right-wing factions for some time—mostly in a cold war gambit to secure Western aid.

Once civil war erupted, Zaire openly sided with FNLA-UNITA forces, and substantial U.S. aid began flowing into FNLA coffers through Zaire, and by November 6, 1975, at least two battalions of regular Zairean troops were supporting FNLA forces advancing on Luanda.

Fighting was also fierce near Angola's oil-rich coastal enclave of Cabinda, near the mouth of the Congo River. Zairean troops began massing on the border. As a result of the continuing hostilities and foreign aid (especially through Zaire), a meeting was held in Bangui on January 1, 1976, between Emperor Jean-Bédel Bokassa of Central African Republic, Ugandan president Idi Amin, and Mobutu. This meeting called for the formation of a government of national unity in Angola to prevent foreign troops from passing through their countries to Angola, and to end the international intervention in the civil war.

By mid-January 1976 Zaire threatened to declare open war on the MPLA after claiming that it had attacked Zairean border positions. It lodged a protest with the United Nations, alleging that Cuban troops had been involved in the MPLA bombing of the Zairean border town of Dilolo. The United States and the OAU both made mediation attempts, but they ended in deadlock, as Zaire continued to refuse to recognize the MPLA government in Angola. Also, calls for a cease-fire were rejected because the MPLA claimed its aim was to drive the FNLA back into Zaire.

By February Zaire still refused to recognize the MPLA government, despite OAU recognition. Eventually, mediation by Congo produced a settlement. The fighting subsided, and relations were soon normalized. An estimated five hundred fatalities occurred during the fighting. Further armed conflict broke out again in 1977 (see conflict 169) as a result of Zairean support for Angolan rebels and ongoing tensions between the two states.

For further information and background reading, see reference item numbers 255, 305, 306, 349, 370, 387.

158. CAMBODIA-THAILAND

Refugee influx, regional tensions; border skirmishes (December 1975–February 1976)

Cambodia fell in 1975 to the communist Khmer Rouge, whose brutal collectivization drives and massive purges caused many Cambodians to flee to surrounding states, primarily Thailand. The new regime, which renamed the country Democratic Kampuchea, was hostile to foreigners, and relations with surrounding states were tense. During December 1975 a number of incidents took place along the Thai-Cambodian border and in the Gulf of Thailand.

On December 12–15, 1975, Thai border police clashed with Khmer Rouge troops in the Ta Phraya district east of Bangkok, resulting in several fatalities. There were also reports of Khmer troops crossing the border into Thailand and of activities by Cambodian guerrillas opposed to the Khmer regime, commanded by former prime minister In Tam. The Thai government responded by expelling In Tam from Thailand on December 22, 1975, after which he fled to France. Other incidents included two sinkings in the Gulf of Thailand on February 20, 1976—an armed Cambodian fishing vessel and a Thai fishing boat.

On January 22, 1976, the foreign ministers of Thailand and Cambodia agreed to meet for talks on February 27, but these were postponed on February 22 at the request of the Cambodian government, which gave no reason. On February 26, 1976, the Khmer government alleged that a U.S. aircraft had dropped bombs on Siem Reap, causing heavy damage and fatalities, and that these aircraft were based in Thailand. Thai premier Kukrit Pramoj denied these allegations, stating that there were no U.S. combat troops stationed in Thailand. There were no other attempts at peaceful conflict management, and the dispute eventually lapsed. This was not the end of hostilities between the two regimes, however, and there were further armed incidents in 1976 (see conflict 166), 1977 (see conflict 168), and 1979 (see conflict 189).

For further information and background reading, see reference item numbers 689, 692, 730, 731, 754, 840.

159. IRAN

Internal strife, orthodox Muslim backlash; the Iranian civil war and Islamic revolution (1976–1980)

In 1954 strong monarchist factions in Iran, with powerful Western backing, ousted Muhammad Mossadeq, a militant nationalist who had forced the shah to flee Iran a year earlier. Muhammad Reza Shah Pahlevi was returned to power and quickly instituted a pro-Western modernization program. But the regime became increasingly repressive, alienating both progressive and traditional factions in the country, so that by the mid-1970s Iran was beset with intense civil and political unrest. There were frequent allegations of human rights abuses—including torture and politically motivated killings. Members of the Tudeh Party, the banned communist party, were especially targeted for state repression.

In March 1975 the shah decreed Iran to be a one-party state. By 1976 the country was in a state of widespread civil disorder, as opposition groups and government forces resorted to increasingly violent methods. It was alleged that extremist outside regimes and groups—among them the PLO and Libya's Muammar Qaddafi—were providing support and military aid for some of the opposition groups.

The unrest was caused mainly by Shiite Muslim clerics opposed to the shah's reform program and the emancipation of women. But the civil disturbances could also be traced to the actions of "Islamic Marxists." By the end of 1977, the Union of National Front Forces was formed to fight the shah's dictatorship and to work for its replacement by a constitutional monarchy. The violence continued throughout 1978, escalating in August with the declaration of martial law and the imposition of curfews.

Although the shah appointed a so-called government of reconciliation, Iran's internal situation worsened. Powerful opposition was being voiced by the militantly conservative followers of Ayatollah Ruhollah Khomeini, then in exile in Paris. Despite the continuing violence, the United States continued to back the shah, and on September 14, 1979, sent military aid in the form of aircraft and missiles. On December 29, 1979, the U.S. government was reported to have issued contingency orders for an aircraft carrier task force to move into waters near Iran in the event of anarchy—and to discourage Soviet involvement in the conflict. Allegations continued in 1979 of Libyan and PLO military aid to Iranian Muslim groups.

On January 16, 1979, popular opposition finally forced the shah into exile, as his regime had become untenable. On February 1, the Ayatollah Khomeini returned to Iran after sixteen years in exile, denouncing foreign involvement in Iran and establishing an Islamic republic. Recognition of the new regime came soon afterward, Iran broke off relations with Israel, and the Ayatollah began to agitate for worldwide Islamic revolution.

Unrest continued in the wake of reforms of the armed forces, imprisonment and execution of the shah's supporters, and the strict enforcement of Islamic law. In November 1979 militant Islamic revolutionaries seized the U.S. embassy in Tehran and held more than eighty embassy personnel hostage, demanding the return of the shah (see conflict 188). Following the shah's death from cancer in 1980, negotiations finally succeeded in gaining the release of the Americans.

After the revolution, which together with the civil war caused the deaths of nearly four thousand people, Iran took up a devastating and costly war with Iraq over the Shatt al Arab Waterway. Lasting nine years, the Iran-Iraq War nearly depleted the country's oil reserves and cost more than 1.5 million lives all together (see conflict 191). Iranian civil society in the meantime was wracked with political violence and unrest.

For further information and background reading, see reference item numbers 1034, 1074, 1150, 1267, 1276, 1304, 1318, 1338, 1340, 1341.

160. MOZAMBIQUE–SOUTH AFRICA
African nationalism; intervention and civil war (1976–October 1992)

Mozambique, on the southeastern coast of Africa, had originally been one of Portugal's overseas territories. Rebels launched a war of independence in 1964, and by the 1970s guerrilla forces controlled much of the country. Following the 1974 Lisbon coup, Mozambique was finally granted independence (see conflict 070). By this time Mozambican nationalists had been split into two main groups—the Soviet-backed Mozambique Liberation Front (Frelimo), operating in the north, and the right-wing Mozambique National Resistance Movement (Renamo), controlling the south. Samora Moïses Machel, Frelimo's leader, assumed control of the country as president of the Marxist regime, nationalized the land, and supervised the departure of the country's 220,000 whites. Frelimo's efforts to integrate Renamo into the new government failed.

In 1976 full-scale civil war broke out between the new regime and the Renamo rebels. South Africa assisted the rebels, and the Frelimo government returned the favor by joining forces with its newly independent neighbors—Botswana, Tanzania, and Zambia—to form the so-called front-line states, devoted to overturning white rule in the region. Mozambique therefore served as a base of operations for rebels from the ANC (African National Congress) and ZANU (Zimbabwe African People's Organization) fighting white rule in South Africa and Rhodesia (see conflict 114).

Although South Africa provided only covert support for Renamo in the early years of the war, open warfare between the two countries became more common in the 1980s. In the early 1980s Zimbabwe committed thousands of troops to fight the South African–backed Renamo rebels, as did Tanzania and Malawi. South Africa invaded and bombed ANC camps in Mozambique on a number of occasions, and there were numerous border incidents. Despite a 1984 nonaggression pact (the Nkomati accord) between South Africa and Mozambique, Mozambique continued to allege South African support for Renamo, and fighting flared periodically into the late 1980s.

The fighting was intense throughout the war, and beginning in the early 1980s Renamo began to target Mozambique's economic infrastructure. This led directly to a number of serious famines from 1985 onwards. The collapse of the Soviet Union and the subsequent loss of aid to the Frelimo government created pressure for a settlement. From 1989 to the end of 1991 numerous mediation attempts led to some short-lived cease-fires and various settlements. In March 1991 a protocol was signed paving the way for multiparty elections.

By the end of 1992 the fighting had ended and tentative moves were being made to end the war and hold elections. But the situation remained tense. Further talks into 1994 saw a peaceful, though strained, transition, and successful elections in which Frelimo won a majority. It is thought that the war cost almost 1 million lives, many of them civilians who fell to hunger and disease because of Renamo's deliberate policies of economic and infrastructural destruction. In the 1990s Mozambique was ranked as one of the poorest countries in the world by the United Nations.

For further information and background reading, see reference item numbers 255, 306, 311, 312, 367, 379, 392.

161. UGANDA-KENYA
Amin provocations; border incidents (February–August 1976)

In 1971 Maj. Gen. Idi Amin led a military coup that ousted Ugandan president A. Milton Obote, setting the stage for a brutal and unpredictable regime that by 1977 had led to the deaths of 300,000 Ugandans and the deportation of the country's entire Asian community. In addition to plunging his own nation into chaos, Amin destabilized the entire region.

This particular conflict began in February 1976, when Amin claimed that part of Kenya (and Sudan) was historically Ugandan territory. He demanded an explanation from the British government about areas of Uganda "illegally" transferred to Kenya from 1894 to 1902, further stating he did not want to go to war with Kenya, but would fight if Uganda's access to the sea were threatened.

Incidents over the next few months included Ugandan raids on Kenyan villages in border areas. An increase in anti-Kenyan propaganda broadcasts, expulsions, and political killings led to a rapid deterioration in relations between the two states. The situation worsened with word that the United States and Britain were providing Kenya with military aid; Libya was said to be assisting Uganda. There were also reports of the massing of troops on the borders.

The dispute intensified on July 8, 1976, when it was announced that Uganda would have to use Kenyan currency at the port of Mombasa, the principal gateway for Ugandan trade. Calling this action a deliberate economic blockade, Amin cut off supplies of electricity to Kenya. Tensions were high, and there were fears that Amin might do something desperate.

The dispute was finally settled through negotiations between government ministers of Kenya and Uganda in the presence of the OAU secretary-general Eteki Mboumosa. A statement was issued on August 6, 1976, in Nairobi, later approved by Amin and Kenyan president Jomo Kenyatta on August 7, 1976. Just over forty people were killed during the incidents. Fighting recurred between Uganda and Kenya in 1987 (see conflict 243) and 1989 (see conflict 249).

For further information and background reading, see reference item numbers 296, 376, 410, 453.

162. BANGLADESH-INDIA
Postcoup tensions; border incidents (April 1976)

Relations between India and Bangladesh had been cool ever since Bangladesh gained its independence from Pakistan in an extremely bloody war (1971–1974; see conflict 132). The strains can be partly explained by the border itself, which had been hastily and arbitrarily drawn during the 1947 partition (see conflict 003). In addition, the terrain allowed easy passage for guerrillas, bandits, and refugees intent on crossing the border, and this often led to incidents. India had already been accused of supporting Chittagong Hill Tracts rebels in their insurgency against the Bangladeshi government (see conflict 149).

Tensions between India and Bangladesh were especially high in 1976 over allegations of Indian involvement in a 1975 military coup in which Sheik Mujibar Rahman, president and founder of Bangladesh, was assassinated and nine members of his family were killed, including his wife, three sons, and a brother. Border incidents involving Bangladesh guerrillas and police had already been reported in Meghalaya, an Indian state on Bangladesh's northeastern border. The guerrillas had apparently attacked from the Indian side of the border. Negotiations on the incidents failed to produce any solution, and during April Indian and Bangladeshi forces clashed four times, resulting in a number of casualties. Captured Bangladeshi guerrillas admitted to having been trained in India. There were no other peaceful conflict-management activities, and the conflict quickly abated. Relations remained cool, however, and fighting broke out again in 1979 (see conflict 187), 1983–1984 (see conflict 216), and again in 1986 (see conflict 233).

For further information and background reading, see reference item numbers 76, 661, 701, 743, 744, 844.

163. IRAQ–THE KURDS
Kurdish separatist insurgency (May 1976–)

The Kurds are a non-Arab tribes people inhabiting a mountainous plateau region comprising parts of Iran, Iraq, and Turkey. They have been fighting unsuccessfully for an independent Kurdistan since just after World War I, when the Treaty of Sèvres (1920) granted them autonomous status. Its terms were never implemented. A number of conflicts have arisen from their struggle, most notably from 1961 to 1966 (see conflict 071), 1968 to 1970 (see conflict 121), and 1974 to 1975 (see conflict 144).

In this particular conflict, Kurds attacked Iraqi forces in May 1976. The fighting was precipitated by government plans to forcibly move Kurds from their mountainous home in northern Iraq—replacing them with Arabs—and relocate them in southern Iraq. Despite a 1975 agreement giving Kurdistan limited autonomy, Iraqi implementation of the accord was not marked by speed, and persistent government atrocities further fueled Kurdish separatism and intensified the fighting. The Democratic Party of Kurdistan (DPK) and the Patriotic Union of Kurdistan (PUK) were the two main Kurdish resistance organizations.

The conflict was internationalized from an early stage. It was revealed in April 1978 that the Soviet Union was providing arms and aid to the Kurds; in the 1980s the Kurds received arms from Syria and Libya via Iran. In June 1978 fighting spread to Turkey, and in 1979 Turkey and Iraq agreed to join forces to quash Kurdish separatism. The collapse of the Iranian army following the Islamic revolution in Iran (see conflict 159) allowed the Kurds to cross into that country for supplies, arms, and refuge. In June 1979 Iraq bombed Kurdish villages in Iran, prompting a formal protest from Iran.

The outbreak of the Iran-Iraq War in 1980 (see conflict 191) took some pressure off the Kurds, and when Iran invaded northern Iraq in 1983, Kurds linked up with dissident Shia groups to assist Iranian revolutionary guards in consolidating their hold on captured territory. This forced Iraq to come to an agreement with the PUK, but the agreement broke down in late 1984. From 1987, the Kurds made large gains with Iran's help and controlled enough territory to be able to threaten important Iraqi economic and strategic targets. Immediately following the July 1988 cease-fire with Iran, however, Iraq went on a brutal offensive against the Kurds, often using poison gas in attacks on their villages.

The 1990 Gulf war (see conflict 261) was also advantageous to the Kurds. After Iraq's defeat in 1991 by the Coalition forces, the Kurds mounted a massive rebellion in the north, but without allied support, it soon faltered. The fighting was brutal, forcing the Coalition to establish "safe havens" for the Kurds. A number of negotiations between Iraq and the Kurds at this time were largely unsuccessful. In mid-1992 the Kurds held elections, and by the end of that year Kurdistan had achieved some degree of autonomy, although the conflict was far from resolved.

In 1993–1994 the Kurds were riven by infighting, which continued into 1995 despite intense diplomatic efforts to mediate a cease-fire. There were hundreds of fatalities in the internecine warfare, which greatly hampered efforts to build a viable Kurdish administration in Iraqi Kurdistan. The Kurds continued to face attacks by the Iraqi military, and the situation was complicated by regular Turkish incursions into northern Iraq pursuing PKK rebels fighting an insurgency in Turkey (see conflict 224).

The fighting was often intense throughout the conflict; more than sixty thousand people were killed, many of them civilians. The Kurds resorted to terrorism, while the Iraqis employed torture, deportations, executions, and poison gas.

For further information and background reading, see reference item numbers 1038, 1078, 1109, 1128, 1170, 1190, 1240, 1250, 1300.

164. CHAD-LIBYA
Guerrilla warfare, factional fighting; Libyan annexation of the Aozou strip (June 1976–November 1979)

Tensions between Chad and Libya along their common border had existed for a number of years. Libya's active support for the Muslim factions in northern Chad greatly exacerbated friction between the Muslim Arab north and the politically dominant black south. On October 10, 1976, Chad closed its border with Libya, citing Libya's "equivocal attitude" toward the Front de libération nationale du Tchad (Frolinat), a rebel group operating in northern Chad.

In fact, Libya had been actively supporting Frolinat (see conflict 175), and its September 1976 annexation of the uranium-rich Aozou strip in northern Chad further fueled the conflict. President Félix Malloum of Chad declared there would be no cooperation with Libya until it had withdrawn from the Aozou strip.

Hostilities were reported in June 1977 between Libyan and Chadian forces in northern Chad; it was also alleged that Libya had armed and aided rebels in the region with the intention of setting up a puppet state. Chad appealed to the OAU to use its authority to restore Chad's rights in the Aozou strip. An early 1978 cease-fire between Chad troops and the rebels was unsuccessful, and Chad and Libya suspended diplomatic relations in February 1978.

Relations between the two countries improved in February 1978 as a result of Sudanese mediation, when a cease-fire was reached and diplomatic relations resumed. In March 1978 France sent in one thousand troops to Chad, allegedly on training exercises but in reality to prevent a Libyan invasion. In June 1978 Chad stated that Libya had invaded in the north, advancing all the way down to the central provinces of Kanem, Batha, and Ouadai. Other Libyan offensives were reported in April and June 1979, but the Libyan troops were repulsed and they retreated after heavy fighting. At this time, the Chadian rebel groups initially supported by Muammar Qaddafi turned against Libya and demanded the return of the Aozou strip.

Libya continued to intervene periodically on the side of various Chadian rebels groups in the civil war, but from late 1979, the new Chadian government and Libya had friendly relations, and the conflict abated. Approximately 250 people were killed in the fighting. Libya took a close interest in Chadian affairs, however, and once again intervened after a change of government and a renewed outbreak of fighting in 1982 (see conflict 203).

For further information and background reading, see reference item numbers 76, 255, 336, 391, 466, 481.

165. EL SALVADOR–HONDURAS
Territorial dispute; border incidents (July 1976–October 1980)

Relations between El Salvador and Honduras were strained because of an ongoing territorial dispute and the large numbers of Salvadorans living in Honduras. On June 14, 1976, following years of negotiations, the presidents of El Salvador and Honduras signed a document resolving the 1969 football war (see conflict 123). The treaty provisions included the conditions of withdrawal of military forces from a demilitarized zone along their common frontier (the San José plan). Despite this, fighting broke out again on July 13, when Honduran troops clashed with Salvadoran soldiers on the frontier.

A cease-fire agreement was reached on July 25, placing the frontier zones under direct military control to prevent further incidents. The OAS also sent an investigation team to the border, while Costa Rica, Nicaragua, and Guatemala (guarantors of the San José agreement) held talks with the presidents of Honduras and El Salvador in late July 1976. Despite an improvement in relations between the two presidents, border hostilities continued. By October 6, 1976, an agreement was signed placing the long-standing border dispute in the hands of a mediator.

Finally, after four years of negotiations mediated by a former president of Peru, José Luis Bustamente y Rivero, and the International Court of Justice in the Hague, a peace treaty was signed on October 30, 1980. The treaty reopened a newly demarcated border, provided for OAS supervision of the border area and arranged for future discussions on disputed areas. The state of war that had existed since the 1969 conflict had finally ended. Approximately 150 fatalities had resulted from the border clashes.

For further information and background reading, see reference item numbers 255, 503, 506, 535, 537, 545, 615.

166. THAILAND-CAMBODIA

Refugee influx, regional instability; Khmer Rouge border incidents (November–December 1976)

The Khmer Rouge took control of Cambodia in 1975. Renaming it Democratic Kampuchea, the Khmer Rouge launched a vicious collectivization drive that sent Cambodians fleeing to Thailand. By 1978 perhaps as many as 1 million Cambodians had been killed or died from the enforced hardships. The massive numbers of refugees strained border relations between Thailand and Cambodia, and armed conflict erupted almost immediately (see conflict 158).

Relations had been improving between the two countries during 1976, however, with increasing diplomatic contacts, agreement on border markings in June, the reopening of their mutual frontier for trade (which had been closed since April 1975), and notably few incidents along the disputed frontier areas.

But tensions rose again when on November 22, 1976, fighting broke out in the Thai coastal province of Trat. Cambodian troops and Thai border police exchanged fire, and both sides sustained fatalities. The hostilities increased when gunboats from both sides joined in the fighting; one of them sank. On December 24, 1976, more fighting occurred between the two countries' navies. There was no attempt at peaceful conflict management, and the dispute eventually lapsed. There were only three reported fatalities, but the tensions caused by this conflict and the general instability in the region owing to the brutality of Pol Pot's regime led to armed conflict again in 1977 (see conflict 168) and 1979 (see conflict 189).

For further information and background reading, see reference item numbers 692, 694, 730, 731, 742, 754, 840.

167. EL SALVADOR

Civil conflict; the Salvadoran civil war (January 1977–end of 1992)

The El Salvador civil war is rooted in the country's vast number of landless peasants, the dominance of a small, landed oligarchy, and a succession of authoritarian military dictatorships. In the 1970s numerous small guerrilla groups representing various leftist tendencies emerged; they began mounting serious armed challenges in 1977. Right-wing terrorist squads, commonly known as death squads, were developed as counterpoise. Often the death squads involved members of the military establishment in El Salvador.

Fighting in eastern and western areas led to large numbers of refugees attempting to flee into Honduras. In 1980 Honduran soldiers forced six hundred refugees back across the border river, where they were immediately massacred by the Salvadoran army. In 1981 several left-wing guerrilla groups combined to form the Farabundo Martí National Liberation Front (FMLN), the most important group from this time. The FMLN made serious inroads in a number of offensives, but the Salvadoran army's counteroffensives always succeeded in winning back lost territory.

Beginning in the 1970s the United States provided heavy weapons and logistical support to the Salvadoran army—without such aid the government may not have been able to control the situation. Committed to fighting communist forces in Latin America, especially under the Reagan administration, the United States was also actively helping the contras in their war against the socialist government in neighboring Nicaragua (see conflict 190) and was aiding the Guatemalan army in its fight against communist guerrillas (see conflict 037).

The Salvadoran army often engaged in cross-border raids into Honduras in pursuit of rebel forces, sometimes provoking formal Honduran protests. Nevertheless, the two countries cooperated in a ten-day joint operation against the rebels in 1982, involving more than two thousand Honduran troops operating on both Salvadoran and Honduran territory.

The Salvadoran conflict is estimated to have cost more than 75,000 lives, most of them civilian. Numerous mediation attempts, especially by the United Nations, ended the fighting in late 1992, following decades of low-level guerrilla warfare and civil terror. There followed an uneasy period of demobilization by the FMLN, the FMLN's transition to a political party, a purge of the military, and the resettlement of the former guerrillas. The United Nations oversaw the whole operation, which was considered one of its most successful peacemaking efforts.

For further information and background reading, see reference item numbers 506, 535, 537, 542, 568, 584, 603, 612.

168. CAMBODIA-THAILAND

Refugee influx, regional instability; Khmer Rouge border incidents (January 1977–October 1978)

The enforced hardships and brutality of Pol Pot's rural collectivization program in Cambodia (renamed Democratic Kampuchea by the Khmer Rouge) had caused the deaths of approximately 1 million Cambodians by 1978, a massive influx of refugees into Thailand, and regional instability, which particularly affected Thai-Cambodian border relations. Renewed strains between Thailand and Cambodia in 1976 were marked by several border incidents (see conflict 166).

These strains worsened in late January 1977, when three hundred Khmer Rouge soldiers crossed the border and raided three villages in the Prachin Buri province (east of Bangkok), resulting in severe damage, a number of fatalities, and more refugees. This was followed by a clash with border police in the disputed border area. A major source of friction was attributed to the "Free Khmers," supporters of the former Lon Nol regime in Cambodia (see conflict 126) whose border raids were aimed at discrediting Pol Pot's regime. As a result of the January 1977 incursion, the border at Ban Aranya prathet was closed on January 29.

Border incidents continued throughout 1977 between Thai, Khmer Rouge, and Cambodian rebel forces. On February 25 the Cambodian government alleged that Thai forces were responsible for several serious incidents over the past months and were aiding the Cambodian rebels. Interestingly, the 1977 incidents are believed to have been caused by maps: The Khmer Rouge used maps based on a 1909 Thai-French border agreement, whereas the Thai authorities were using at U.S. military map prepared in 1954. Furthermore, the 420-mile boundary was designated by only seventy-three markers, and some of the disputed areas were claimed by Thailand when in fact the majority of the inhabitants were ethnic Khmers (Cambodians).

As clashes and incidents continued throughout the year, it was feared that Thailand would take full-scale military action. By January 1978 Cambodian troops were being reinforced along the Thai border because of fears that Thailand would use the border fighting as an excuse to launch retaliatory attacks.

Despite an agreement in February by the new Thai government to normalize relations with Cambodia, raids by Pol Pot's troops and small groups of Thai communist guerrillas continued into 1978, including frequent attacks on Thai villages causing numerous fatalities and damage. Thai military officials indicated that 111 border incidents had occurred in the first half of 1978 and that strong retaliatory action had been taken after each one.

Incidents continued until October 1978, when Cambodian troops were redeployed to the Vietnamese border. There were no attempts at peaceful conflict management, and the dispute eventually lapsed. About 120 fatalities resulted from this conflict, a number of them civilian. Further armed conflict broke out in 1979 (see conflict 189).

For further information and background reading, see reference item numbers 692, 694, 730, 731, 742, 754, 840.

169. ZAIRE-ANGOLA

Internal dissension, regional instability; the first invasion of Shaba (March–May 1977)

Civil war had broken out in Angola immediately upon independence in 1975 (see conflict 148) as rival factions vied for control of the government. The Soviet-backed Movimento Popular de Libertação de Angola (MPLA), supported by Cuban troops, emerged victorious after a year of fighting. Zaire's right-wing regime immediately started to support factions fighting Angola's communist government, straining relations between the two countries. Fighting had already broken out in 1975–1976 (see conflict 157).

Relations between Zaire and Angola were normalized in January 1977 when Zaire offered formal recognition of President António Agostinho Neto's government. They agreed that no military activities would be permitted against the other in their territories. Angola repeated allegations, however, that FNLA (Frente Nacional de Libertacão de Angola) rebels were training in Zaire for war against the government. Zaire claimed these people were only refugees.

Tensions came to a head on March 8, 1977, when a rebel army led by Lt. Gen. Nathanael Mbumba invaded Shaba (formerly Katanga) from Angolan territory. Mbumba, a Katangan rebel, claimed the aim of the invasion was not to sabotage Zaire's mineral production (the southern province was rich in cobalt and copper mines) but to depose President Mobutu Sésé Séko and form a government of national unity. Zaire accused Angola of being a Cuban-Soviet pawn by aiding the invasion force, but Angola denied any involvement. On March 11, 1977, the Congolese National Liberation Front (FLNC)—an opposition group made up of the remnants of Katangan (Shaba) rebels who fled Zaire after the civil war (see conflict 067)—claimed responsibility for the invasion, saying it was a popular national uprising.

Exercising his penchant for using outside forces to put down revolts (see conflict 119), Mobutu immediately called for assistance from other African states and the United States and Belgium, resulting in the stationing of 1,500 Moroccan troops in Zaire. In March and April Nigeria attempted to reconcile differences between the two countries and end the invasion. Meanwhile, suspicions of Cuban and Soviet involvement in the invasion continued. As a result of rebel advances into Zaire, Mobutu appealed to the OAU for help in driving the socialist invaders out of Zaire. A joint Zairean-Moroccan force was approved and, with the diplomatic backing of other countries (Egypt, Sudan, Uganda, Saudi Arabia, Togo), gradually advanced in the face of the retreating rebels, with few fatalities.

In May 1977 the rebel forces retreated farther into Angola, and Zairean and Moroccan troops recaptured lost territory and ended the invasion. In early June all foreign forces, having completed their mission, returned to their countries. About a thousand people were killed during the invasion. Identical invasions by Zairean rebels operating from foreign territory recurred in 1978 (see conflict 177), 1984 (see conflict 226), and 1985 (see conflict 229).

For further information and background reading, see reference item numbers 255, 306, 370.

170. ISRAEL-LEBANON

Arab-Israeli tensions, Christian-Muslim factional fighting; border incidents (mid–late 1977)

Israel had been attacked on numerous occasions by Palestinian guerrillas operating from southern Lebanon. These attacks had provoked armed conflict between Israel and Lebanon in 1965 (see conflict 108) and 1974–1975 (see conflict 145). The situation was complicated by Lebanon's 1975–1976 civil war (see conflict 151). Although a cease-fire had been declared and Syrian forces occupied southern Lebanon, the situation was still volatile. Israel was closely aligned with Christian militias based in the south.

Israel objected both to the proximity of thirty thousand Syrian troops and to the failure to implement the third stage of the July 1977 peace agreement. This was supposed to include the withdrawal of Palestinian guerrillas from the southern border areas and their replacement by Lebanese troops. Israel demanded a wider-scale withdrawal of Palestinians than previously agreed to and demanded that its border gates, "the good fence," be kept open so that Lebanese civilians had access to medical treatment, employment, and free movement into Israel.

In October and November 1977 Lebanese Muslim factions and Israeli-backed Christian militias clashed several times. On November 6 the PLO's Yasser Arafat rejected Israeli demands, stating there would be no Palestinian withdrawal, particularly if Christian forces remained. Further cross-border incidents occurred in November, including air strikes by Lebanon. Israeli forces retaliated, attacking villages and refugee camps.

Talks in Beirut between the U.S. ambassador and the Lebanese and Syrian presidents took place on November 1977, creating some pressure for a reactivation of the cease-fire, and Lebanon released a statement that it was doing all it could to deal with Israeli aggression. No other peaceful conflict-management attempts were made during the conflict, and it gradually abated. Approximately fifty people were killed in the fighting, and there were further armed conflicts in 1978 (see conflict 176), 1979–1980 (see conflict 186), 1982–1983 (see conflict 199), and 1983–1995 (see conflict 213).

For further information and background reading, see reference item numbers 1047, 1058, 1069, 1098, 1123, 1145, 1158.

171. ECUADOR-PERU

Regional rivalry, territorial dispute; border incidents (June 1977–January 1978)

Ecuador has claimed the Loreto area in northern Peru for more than 150 years—ever since a territorial reorganization under Spanish colonial rule had assigned it to Peru. This disputed area left Ecuador without access to the Amazon or the Marañón River. Negotiations in 1942 had settled the issue in Peru's favor.

In the 1970s, however, Ecuador began to claim that the 1942 border peace treaty, the protocol of Río de Janeiro, had been forced on Ecuador. Both sides raised this issue at the United Nations during 1976, but no action was taken. Between June 1977 and January 1978, tensions were heightened when the Peruvian government claimed Ecuador had on several occasions attacked Peruvian posts in the disputed area. Ecuador blamed Peru for the incidents.

The tension was defused after talks between the countries' top military commanders on January 19–20, 1978. No other peaceful conflict-management efforts were undertaken, and the matter appeared settled. This conflict was merely a precursor, however, to much graver conflict in 1981 (see conflict 193) and 1984 (see conflict 217). In this case, there were about ten fatalities during the actual fighting.

For further information and background reading, see reference item numbers 46, 76, 255, 552, 633.

172. EGYPT-LIBYA

Regional tensions; border war (July 1977–September 1977)

Relations between Egypt and Libya had been strained since 1973, when in the wake of the Yom Kippur war Egypt sought closer ties with the West, alienating its hard-line Arab allies. The enmity between Col. Muammar Qaddafi and President Anwar el-Sadat was characterized by unceasing accusations of sabotage and propaganda along with periodic troop buildups along their common border. Finally, on July 12–17, 1977, they accused each other of initiating hostilities along the border area. Exchanges of fire escalated into heavy fighting involving tanks and aircraft, after Egyptian troops crossed the border to clash with Libyan troops on July 21.

Hostilities continued despite Yasser Arafat's mediation efforts on July 21, which he initiated after heavy attacks on Libyan targets. On July 22 Egyptian troops were recalled from the border area, having "taught Libya a lesson," although the following day Egyptian aircraft based in Sudan continued to attack Libyan targets. Arafat's mediation efforts, aided by the Arab League, secured a cease-fire on July 24, ending the heavy Egyptian air strikes. But troops remained mobilized on both sides of the border, and the propaganda war between the two leaders continued.

The Arab League, Arafat, and Sheikh al-Sabah of Kuwait proposed a peace formula on July 27, 1977, which Egypt immediately accepted. Arab efforts to consolidate the cease-fire through talks with Qaddafi continued into August, and, finally, talks mediated by Arafat on August 28, 1977, achieved a settlement ending the conflict. By September 1977 all troops had withdrawn from the border area. By October 1977 bilateral relations between Libya and Egypt had improved significantly. Approximately three hundred fatalities resulted from the fighting.

For further information and background reading, see reference item numbers 255, 286, 287, 310, 333.

173. ARGENTINA-CHILE
Regional rivalry, territorial dispute; the Beagle Channel dispute (July 1977–November 1984)

Argentina and Chile had been rivals for decades. A dispute over ownership of the islands in the Beagle Channel, located at the tip of Tierra del Fuego, had led to armed conflict in 1952–1968 (see conflict 032). Argentina had ignored an ICJ ruling that gave the islands to Chile and had continued to press its claims. In July 1977 conflict once again broke out when the Chilean and Argentine navies clashed. A serious escalation occurred, and both sides mobilized large numbers of troops in border areas and sent naval reinforcements.

There followed four rounds of negotiations, which failed, and persistent conflict—and both sides continued to mass troops, expel each other's citizens, provoke naval confrontations, drop bombs near each other, and engage in other brinkmanship.

Starting in 1979, the Vatican made it its mission to solve the dispute before it resulted in all-out war. Cardinal Samore mediated for more than four years, until November 1984, when a full agreement was signed. Incidents had continued throughout this period, the most serious involving an Argentine shelling of Chilean positions in October 1984, although Argentina claimed it was the work of a dissident officer.

For further information and background reading, see reference item numbers 46, 76, 255.

174. NICARAGUA–COSTA RICA
Regional rivalry, border incidents (October 1977)

Relations between Nicaragua and Costa Rica had been cool since the 1948 Costa Rican revolution (see conflict 017), and there had been armed conflict in 1955 (see conflict 039). Matters worsened in 1977 over accusations that Costa Rica was harboring Sandinista guerrillas then fighting the Nicaraguan regime. Relations were further strained on October 14, 1977, when a Nicaraguan aircraft strafed three boats on Costa Rica's side of the border on the Frio River.

One of the boats was carrying the Costa Rican minister of public security, and he was detained on the Nicaraguan side for several hours.

After his release, Costa Rican president Daniel Oduber Quiros ordered units to avoid any confrontations with the Nicaraguan army. It was suggested that the incident was a case of mistaken identity, as the presence of the boats in the area had not been announced, and they could have held Sandinista guerrillas. But Costa Rican foreign minister Gauzalo Facio protested the incident on October 15, 1977, requesting that Nicaraguan aircraft refrain from flying into Costa Rican airspace without permission. This request was ignored by Nicaragua, which continued to violate Costa Rican airspace in its search for Sandinista guerrillas.

The same day, an OAS team was sent to investigate Nicaraguan complaints that Costa Rica and Honduras were harboring Sandinistas and allowing them to operate from their territory. Nicaragua also accused Cuba of funding the Sandinistas. At Costa Rica's request, the OAS stationed observers along the border as a security measure. There were forty fatalities because of the conflict, and the OAS action settled it for the time being. In 1978 similar fighting broke out again (see conflict 178).

For further information and background reading, see reference item numbers 255, 510, 526, 546.

175. CHAD

Internal strife, foreign intervention; the second Chad civil war (January 1978–June 1982)

Following Chad's independence from France in 1960, fighting broke out between the Muslim north and the politically dominant south, which was primarily black Christian. Tensions grew throughout the 1960s and 1970s, and foreign elements, supporting different factions, began to involve themselves. On January 28–29, 1978, armed conflict finally erupted when Frolinat (Front de libération nationale du Tchad), a Libyan-backed rebel group, attacked government troops in the town of Faya-Largeau. Hostilities continued through February, and all sides ignored calls for a cease-fire. Mediation efforts were hampered by renewed tensions between Libya and Chad, while a number of negotiations between some of the warring parties failed.

March and April 1978 brought French military involvement in support of the Chadian government. This was partly a response to fears of a Libyan invasion. Government troops and rebels engaged in sporadic fighting, and France stepped up its intervention in central and east Chad, while Libya increased its support for the northern rebels. Talks on national unity broke down in early July 1978, and despite the formation in August of an interim government, hostilities continued with increasing severity.

The remainder of 1978 and early 1979 saw a deterioration in relations between President Félix Malloum and Prime Minister Hissène Habré, a former rebel leader, and dissent among different rebel factions. Fighting in the north was predominantly between Muslim Arab guerrilla forces and troops of the national army, the Forces armées tchadiennes (FAT), loyal to President Malloum, who represented black Christian or animist southerners.

In February 1979 renewed hostilities between the president's troops and rebel groups engulfed Ndjamena, the capital of Chad. Neighboring countries attempted to reconcile the opposing sides in a series of meetings in Nigeria. Finally, by late August 1979 the Lagos accord was signed, establishing a transitional government of national unity comprising all eleven factions under the leadership of Goukouni Oueddei, a former rebel from the north; Malloum and Habré had resigned their posts in March 1979. The 1979 accord broke down in March 1980, with the onset of fierce fighting in Ndjamena.

Previous conflict in the civil war had been along religious and regional lines, but it now involved rival northern groups struggling for supremacy in the new government. The main protagonists were Oueddei's rebel group, Forces armées populaires (FAP), and Habré's faction, Forces armées du nord (FAN). Fighting continued throughout 1980 with five thousand to six thousand deaths and severe infrastructural damage. The OAU made many unsuccessful attempts to reconcile the rival factions. The situation changed in late 1980 with large-scale Libyan intervention. Together with Libyan and OAU support, President Oueddei's FAP forced FAN to retreat. By this stage France was withdrawing its troops from the country.

Early in 1981 Chad and Libya announced their intention to merge the two countries, but mounting internal opposition to Libyan troops in Chad resulted in their withdrawal by November 1981. In an attempt to contain internal strife and encourage stability, the OAU sent in a peace-keeping force in November and December 1981, but it was completely ineffectual. The coalition government was too fragile. Habré's FAN took the capital in June 1982. Despite this defeat, hostilities continued and further OAU proposals for a cease-fire, draft constitution, and elections were disrupted by continuing fighting between government and FAN forces.

After Libya withdrew from areas in Chad, FAN progressively gained control of regions in eastern and northern Chad. Habré eventually became head of state on June 19, 1982, and formed a new government. For the time, the opposition was defeated. As many as nine thousand people were killed during the conflict, including more than three hundred Libyan troops and nine French military personnel. Peace did not last long, however, and war broke out again almost immediately (see conflict 203).

For further information and background reading, see reference item numbers 255, 336, 391, 456, 466, 481.

176. ISRAEL-LEBANON; PLO

Arab-Israeli tensions, PLO incursions; Israeli invasion of southern Lebanon (March–June 1978)

Following Israel's war of independence in 1948 (see conflict 012), Palestinian refugees flooded into Lebanon. From here, Palestinian guerrillas could regularly launch attacks on northern Israeli settlements. Israel's efforts to halt these attacks had resulted in numerous conflicts with Lebanon—in 1965 (see conflict 108), 1974–1975 (see conflict 145), and 1977 (see conflict 170). Meanwhile, peace efforts continued to be made, although the PLO was apparently determined to demonstrate that any settlement would have to include and accommodate the Palestinians.

A serious deterioration in Middle East relations occurred in March 1978, when a major Palestinian guerrilla raid provoked an Israeli invasion of southern Lebanon. On March 11 members of the Al Fatah faction of the PLO attacked northern Israel; there were many civilian fatalities. On March 12 the Lebanese prime minister declared his country was not responsible for the incident.

Hostilities escalated on March 14–15 when Israel launched a major invasion of southern Lebanon by land, sea, and air, despite warnings of the consequences to Middle East peace. Israel stated that the operation was a preventive action in that eliminating Palestinian bases in southern Lebanon would help to establish security against further PLO attacks. Although Israel had overwhelmed Palestinian positions, the PLO was able to withstand the attack and saved many of its forces by evacuating the border area before the invasion.

Although Israel had achieved its military objective by March 15, it stressed that it required guarantees that south Lebanon remain free from Palestinian guerrillas before it could withdraw. Within days it was claimed that Israel had cleared a six-mile security belt along the border that was free of guerrillas. PLO counterattacks were continuing, however, and there still loomed the threat of Arab support for Lebanon against Israel and the Christian militia.

On March 18 Israel pushed farther north, past the security zone and well into Lebanon—its aim the complete eradication of the PLO from Lebanon. The U.N. Security Council immediately called for Israel's withdrawal from Lebanon and the deployment of U.N. forces in the area. Israel's action was widely condemned in the international community. After separate requests by Israel and Lebanon to the U.N. Security Council in March, a resolution was passed to carry out a two-stage operation for a cease-fire, Israeli withdrawal, and U.N. monitoring of the area. The cease-fire was accepted by Israel, but not by the PLO, which demanded unconditional Israeli withdrawal.

The U.N. Interim Force in Lebanon (UNIFIL) began arriving on March 22, but fighting continued and U.N. troops came under fire. Israel began withdrawing soon after, but radical Arab guerrillas infiltrated UNIFIL areas and began low-level attacks against Israel. The conflict abated somewhat after this time. As many as 1,500 people were killed in the conflict, many of them civilians. This conflict was the precursor to a more serious invasion of Lebanon in 1982 (see conflict 199).

For *further information and background reading, see reference item numbers 1047, 1058, 1069, 1098, 1123, 1145, 1158.*

177. ZAIRE-ANGOLA
Regional instability, Congolese dissension; the second invasion of Shaba (May 1978)

Relations between Zaire and Angola had been hostile for some time. Zairean president Mobutu Sésé Séko was opposed to Angola's communist MPLA (Movimento Popular de Libertação de Angola) government and therefore permitted Angolan rebels to operate from his territory. In 1977 Angola returned the favor by supporting dissident Zairean forces in their invasion of Shaba province (see conflict 169); this copper-rich southern province then accounted for two-thirds of Zaire's foreign earnings. Shaba had also figured prominently in the Congo crisis (see conflict 067), when for several years powerful secessionist forces waged war against the central government.

In May 1978 an invasion force of four thousand rebels again entered the Shaba from Angolan territory, this time in an attempt to gain control of the strategic copper- and cobalt-mining area and bring down the Mobutu government. The rebels, which included many members of the local Lunda tribe, were again led by Gen. Nathanael Mbumba and directed by the Congolese National Liberation Front (FLNC).

The invasion force reached the town of Kolwezi on May 11–12, 1978. As a consequence, two hundred French and Belgian nationals were killed over the next ten days by the rebels and uncontrolled Zairean army troops; five hundred troops and civilians also died in the fighting. It was alleged that the Soviet Union, Cuba, Libya, and Algeria had planned in meetings in Havana and Algiers and supported the rebel operation, code-named "Operation Dove." These allegations were later denied by the parties involved, although Cuban troops did participate in the fighting in the town of Mutshatsha on May 14, 1978, against the Zairean army.

On May 14, 1978, the Zairean foreign minister asked the ambassadors of the United States, France, Belgium, China, and Morocco for assistance. Foreign nationals were then evacuated from Zaire, while the United States provided the country with fuel, equipment, and financial aid, but no personnel. On May 19 the French government sent a paratroop regiment of eight hundred foreign legionnaires, along with Belgium paratroopers, to rescue trapped Europeans, and alongside the Zairean army, they took back the town of Kolwezi from the rebels.

The evacuation of foreign nationals was completed by May 22 and was followed by the withdrawal of the foreign troops, but rebel fighting continued. On May 27, 1978, the rebels were reported to have recaptured the town of Mutshatsha. In June, the Angolan government ordered the disarming of the rebels, and the pulling back of the FLNC rebels from the border area. The rebellion dissipated after this.

In late May, Mobutu, the European Community's Tindemans, and French president Valéry Giscard d'Estaing proposed the formation of an "African corps," composed entirely of African troops, to keep peace in African countries. Mobutu, with Morocco's King Hassan II, set up the provision of troops to keep the peace in Shaba starting in June 1978. There were no attempts at peaceful conflict management during the conflict. As many as one thousand people were killed in the fighting, many of them civilians. This conflict led to other invasions in 1984 (see conflict 226) and 1985 (see conflict 229).

For further information and background reading, see reference item numbers 255, 305, 306, 369, 387.

178. NICARAGUA–COSTA RICA
Regional rivalry, cross-border raids; border incidents
(September–December 1978)

Mutual hostility and armed conflict had marked Nicaraguan–Costa Rican relations since 1948 (see conflicts 017, 039, 174), mostly over exiled opposition groups forming rebel armies and staging cross-border attacks. The dictatorial Somoza regime had ruled Nicaragua since 1937, and Gen. Anastasio Somoza Debayle had been president off and on since 1967. In December 1974 he imposed martial law after Sandinista guerrillas kidnapped some government officials, an action that sparked intense opposition culminating in nationwide antigovernment strikes in 1978 and a virtual civil war. Of particular concern to the regime was the Sandinistas' burgeoning Marxist guerrilla insurgency.

This particular conflict began on September 12, 1978, when the Costa Rican government, which had no military forces of its own, accused Nicaragua of bombarding its territory near the frontier and pursuing Sandinista rebels across the border. Nicaragua defended its actions, claiming that many rebel attacks had been launched from Costa Rican soil. The Somoza regime became increasingly beleaguered when on September 14 Venezuela sent military aircraft, along with support from the government of Panama, to the Sandinista rebels. The Nicaraguan government reacted by recalling its ambassadors from Costa Rica, Panama, and Venezuela.

An OAS foreign ministers meeting was held on September 21–23 in Washington, D.C., to discuss events in Central America; they agreed only to provide humanitarian aid and to abstain from direct intervention in Nicaragua.

Although the foreign ministers' negotiations with General Somoza and the Nicaraguan Broad Opposition Front (FAO) failed, the OAS did send an investigation team to examine the alleged border violations. On November 21, following further clashes between Nicaraguan troops and the Costa Rican civil guard, Costa Rica severed diplomatic relations with Nicaragua and called for its expulsion from the OAS.

On December 15, 1978, a U.N. General Assembly resolution (33/76) demanded a halt to the military hostilities between Nicaragua and Costa Rica. Nicaragua closed its mutual border with Costa Rica on December 27 and threatened invasion if Sandinista guerrillas continued their attacks from Costa Rica. About ten fatalities resulted from the fighting, and eventually the dispute abated. When Somoza regime fell to the Sandinistas on July 19, 1979, this kindled further conflict in the region (see conflict 190).

For further information and background reading, see reference item numbers 255, 510, 522, 523, 526, 546.

179. TANZANIA-UGANDA
Cross-border raids, invasion; Amin ouster
(October 1978–May 1979)

Relations between Tanzania and Uganda had been strained since Gen. Idi Amin seized power from President A. Milton Obote in a 1971 military coup. Amin had repeatedly accused Tanzania of planning to invade the country in order to reinstate the former president. Indeed, after his ouster, Obote fled to Tanzania, where he had started a destabilization campaign against the Amin regime (see conflict 131). Furthermore, Tanzania had initially refused to recognize the Amin government.

This particular conflict began in early October 1978 with small Ugandan cross-border raids. In late October Ugandan troops occupied the "Kagera salient," an area between the Ugandan-Tanzanian border and the Kagera River. Tanzania viewed this move as tantamount to a declaration of war and staged a massive counterattack involving both Tanzanian troops and exiled Ugandans opposed to Amin's regime. The cross-border fighting and bombing went on until late January 1979, when Tanzania launched a full-scale invasion deep into Uganda. By the end of March fighting was focused on the capital, Entebbe, and even the dispatch of several hundred Libyan troops to the side of Amin could not prevent the fall of the capital in April 1979.

The Amin regime and some surrounding states appealed to the OAU, the United Nations, and the Arab League to no avail; in November 1978 Kenya, Libya, and the OAU all extended offers of mediation, but these were rejected. Attempts at negotiations and offers of withdrawals were similarly unsuccessful during December 1978 and January 1979. An OAU ad hoc committee on interstate conflict met on February 22, 1979, and suggested a cease-fire, but no agreement was reached. The OAU was subsequently asked to refrain from interfering in Ugandan affairs.

The anti-Amin Ugandan National Liberation Front (UNLF), an umbrella organization of Ugandan exiles, took control of Uganda following the collapse of Entebbe and the flight of Amin. Tanzania officially recognized the new Ugandan government on April 12, and other African countries extended recognition on April 15. An estimated 3,500 people were killed during the conflict, including 1,000 Tanzanian military fatalities and at least 200 Libyan soldiers. Amin fled to Saudi Arabia, and Uganda fell into total civil war in late 1981 (see conflict 198).

For further information and background reading, see reference item numbers 255, 296, 376, 410, 419, 453.

180. USSR-AFGHANISTAN
Civil war, Soviet invasion; the Afghanistan civil war (1979–)

A low-level civil war broke out in Afghanistan in 1973, after Lt. Gen. Sardar Mohammad Daoud Khan deposed the last Afghan king, Mohammad Zahir Shah, in a military coup and proclaimed a republic. The new regime quickly aligned itself with the Soviet Union, provoking violent resistance from traditional tribal and other elements (see conflict 184). Daoud was assassinated in a 1978 coup, and President Hafizullah Amin was killed in a Soviet-backed 1979 coup and replaced by the pro-Soviet Babrak Karmal.

The new regime proved unable to contain the growing civil war, despite massive Soviet aid. In an attempt to halt the fighting and rebuild the Kabul government, the Soviets immediately began to move massive numbers of troops and heavy weaponry into Afghanistan. Mujahedin rebel factions continued to resist the Soviet and Afghan armies for the next ten years in a particularly brutal war that often singled out civilians for reprisal attacks. The rebels received substantial aid from the United States and Pakistan. Cross-border raids into Pakistan and Iran by Afghan and Soviet forces continued throughout the 1980s, and Pakistani troops occasionally entered Afghanistan in support of mujahedin units.

Rebel groups controlling large sections of the Afghan countryside formed the Islamic Alliance of Afghan Holy Warriors in May 1985. The alliance elicited financial support and volunteer fighters from other Islamic states. By the mid-1980s Soviet forces were taking huge losses, and the war was becomingly increasingly unpopular at home. In 1986 the United Nations began negotiating a Soviet withdrawal from Afghanistan. In 1988 the Soviets began withdrawing their forces in stages—with the last contingents pulling out in 1989. The Soviets continued to support the Kabul regime, however, even attacking rebel bases by air from the USSR.

Beginning in 1990, the Kabul regime was less and less able to resist the rebel advance, and it collapsed completely in 1992. The rebel alliance had by this time, however, split into various factions, which then engaged in a bloody battle for control of Kabul. By 1993 Afghanistan was engaged in warfare far more intense than any previous fighting, with hundreds being killed every day in Kabul. At least three main factions were involved—the most important being the radically fundamentalist Talaban movement and the forces led by Gulbuddin Hekmatyar (the latter were a coalition of local mujahedin warlords centered around Jalabad). But no side was able to defeat any other, so the fighting surged back and forth across Afghanistan into late 1995. By December intense fighting was once again centered on Kabul. With the end of the cold war, however, no major powers seemed interested in intervening in the conflict. Although the Islamic Conference Organization (ICO), Pakistan, the United Nations, and Iran all made intense mediation efforts beginning in 1992, peace was elusive and no breakthroughs were reported.

The Afghanistan conflict cost 1.5 million lives—most of them civilian. The Soviets lost approximately fifteen thousand military personnel, while Afghan troop losses were two to three times greater. Numerous peace initiatives failed to find any lasting solution to the conflict.

For further information and background reading, see reference item numbers 255, 894, 895, 899, 903, 926, 932.

181. CAMBODIA-VIETNAM

Border fighting, Vietnamese invasion, civil war; the Cambodian civil war (January 1979–)

Pol Pot's Khmer Rouge guerrillas had taken control of Cambodia in 1975. Renaming the country Democratic Kampuchea, the Khmer Rouge launched a program of violent domestic repression in which an estimated 1 million Cambodians lost their lives. Violently xenophobic, Khmer Rouge troops also targeted the many ethnic Vietnamese residing in Cambodia. In the late 1970s Pol Pot's forces began a brutal purge of eastern Cambodia, which led to cross-border attacks on Vietnam in pursuit of refugees.

The many Vietnamese fatalities and border violations led to the formation of a Vietnamese-backed army of dissident Cambodians. In 1978 this army staged a full-scale invasion of Cambodia that succeeded in capturing Phnom Penh by January 8, 1979. The Vietnamese then installed a puppet government under Heng Samrin. The new Vietnamese-backed regime then set about driving the Khmer Rouge out of Cambodia.

Although the rebel communist regime staged major offensives throughout the 1980s against the Khmer Rouge forces, it was never totally successful. The Khmer Rouge were given sanctuary and aid in Thailand and China, and they also received aid from the United States and other Western states, despite their appalling human rights record. Prince Norodom Sihanouk, the former Cambodian premier, and the noncommunist leader Son Sann joined with the Khmer Rouge in an anti-Vietnamese alliance, but they were unable to drive out the Vietnamese army. The war ebbed and flowed with many fatalities throughout the 1980s.

In the late 1980s the Soviet Union pressured Vietnam to begin negotiating a withdrawal. A period of intense diplomatic activity ensued, producing a Vietnamese withdrawal in 1989 and U.N.-sponsored elections in 1993. The Khmer Rouge refused to disarm, however, and threatened to boycott the elections and resume full-scale civil war. They engaged in many provocative incidents throughout 1992.

True to their word, the Khmer Rouge boycotted the 1993 elections and resumed a limited, though at times intense, guerrilla war against the coalition government. Despite massive defections in 1994–1995, Khmer Rouge strength was estimated to be 5,000–10,000 dedicated guerrillas who fought regular battles with government troops in Khmer-controlled areas. The government was unable to defeat the rebel army, and attacks were continuing at the end of 1995. Many attempts at finding a formula for including the Khmer Rouge in the Cambodian government and halting the fighting were made without success at this time. In other areas of the country, a slow rebuilding process got under way.

Most peaceful conflict-management attempts failed to solve the basic problems presented by the presence of several well-armed and ideologically opposed factions. This was a particularly brutal war—half a million people are thought to have died, many of them civilian. The Vietnamese army is estimated to have lost more than fifty thousand personnel.

For further information and background reading, see reference item numbers 689, 692, 694, 697, 717, 730, 731, 734, 742, 755, 840.

182. CHINA-VIETNAM
Regional rivalry; border war (February 1979–June 1982)

Chinese-Vietnamese relations had been troubled since the unification of Vietnam at the end of the Vietnam War (see conflict 069). Chinese support for the Khmer Rouge in Cambodia, who were slaughtering ethnic Vietnamese people and violating Vietnam's borders, and the ongoing dispute over the Spratly and Paracel Islands (see conflicts 045, 142, 243) led to a high level of tension between these two nations. Vietnam was also closely allied to the Soviet Union, now China's bitter enemy.

Tensions were raised to the breaking point in 1978 after a number of incidents in poorly demarcated border areas. China suspended all technical and economic aid to Vietnam, and Vietnam responded by persecuting and expelling thousands of Chinese. Vietnam's invasion of Cambodia (see conflict 181) proved to be the final straw for China, and it began to prepare for war.

In January 1979 a number of very serious border incidents occurred, and in February 75,000 Chinese troops invaded Vietnam along the entire length of their mutual border. After capturing five provincial capitals by sheer weight of numbers, China was forced to pull back after a fierce Vietnamese counterattack. China announced its withdrawal from Vietnam in March 1979 following heavy defeats, but fighting continued in some border areas. It was a total defeat for China, and the initial fighting was thought to have cost China and Vietnam more than fifty thousand troops. Fighting along the border, which was at times serious, continued until 1982, when both sides agreed to repatriate prisoners. Although there were a number of bilateral negotiations, these failed to fully resolve the issues in dispute, and this conflict was a precursor to more fighting in 1983 (see conflict 211), 1984–1987 (see conflict 218), and 1988 (see conflict 243).

For further information and background reading, see reference item numbers 255, 695, 696, 715, 735, 830, 878.

183. NORTH YEMEN–SOUTH YEMEN
Border war (February 1979–February 1980)

South Yemen gained its independence from Britain in 1967 and in 1970 became the Arab world's only Marxist state. More than 300,000 South Yemenis fled north after independence, provoking two decades of strains and hostilities between the Marxist state and its more moderate northern neighbor, North Yemen (see conflict 133).

In February 1979 North Yemeni troops invaded South Yemen, while a North Yemeni dissident group called the National Democratic Front (NDF) staged a simultaneous invasion of North Yemen with the help of South Yemeni regulars. The fighting was intense, and Saudi Arabia placed its troops on full alert. Concern over the possible spread of the conflict to other Arab states led to intense mediation efforts in March 1979. Combined with other conflict-management activities, these efforts led to the cessation of hostilities and the withdrawal of troops. By February 1980 many of the issues were resolved, and some progress was made toward unifying the two countries. About 150 fatalities resulted from the fighting. Eventually, after lengthy negotiations, complete unification was achieved in 1990, although a bloody civil war erupted in 1993 (see conflict 278).

For further information and background reading, see reference item numbers 1060, 1143, 1167, 1188, 1253, 1316, 1317, 1333.

184. AFGHANISTAN-PAKISTAN
Promonarchist revolt; the Peshawar rebellion (March–July 1979)

Afghanistan and Pakistan had been rivals since the 1940s, skirmishing a number of times over territorial issues (see conflicts 020, 023, 068). Afghanistan's
last king, Muhammad Zahir Shah, was deposed in a 1973 military coup that
led to the establishment of a pro-Soviet regime. In early 1979 rebel Muslim
organizations based in Peshawar, the northwest frontier province of Pakistan,
proclaimed war on the Kabul government. Their intent was to restore the
monarchy, and they immediately began cross-border raids. The conflict was
complicated by an internal rebellion that broke out in the Afghan city of Herat,
near the border with Iran. Government forces quashed the Herat rebellion at
the cost of five thousand lives. The border with Iran was closed as a result.

Using Pakistan territory as sanctuary from April to July 1979, rebels continued their cross-border raids in an attempt to restore the monarchy.
Government troops responded with their own regular cross-border attacks on
Pakistan. There were allegations of Soviet aid to the Afghan government, while
Pakistan was accused of actively aiding the rebels. Pakistan stated its desire to
restore normal relations with Afghanistan, and on June 25 Indian prime minister Morarji Ranchhodji Desai offered to mediate. On July 1–3 talks between
the president of Pakistan and the Afghan deputy foreign minister resulted in an
agreement on refugees and the need for further high-level talks. The dispute
abated, but later in 1979 Afghanistan itself plunged into civil war and the
Soviet Union invaded (see conflict 180).

*For further information and background reading, see reference item numbers
255, 797, 899.*

185. ALGERIA-MOROCCO; WESTERN SAHARA
Western Saharan nationalism; border conflict (June–October 1979)

In 1979 Algeria and Morocco came into direct conflict over the issue of
Western Sahara, which Morocco had claimed since 1974. Algerian-backed
Western Saharan nationalists, calling themselves the Polisario Front (Frente
Popular para la Liberatión de Saguia el-Hamra y Rio de Oro), had started a
guerrilla war to gain independence for the territory (see conflict 146).
Beginning in June 1979, Polisario began attacking Moroccan territory itself,
and Morocco threatened to attack Algeria in retaliation. Algeria warned
against any violations of its border, and there were fears of war.

Border incidents continued, and following a massive attack by Polisario in
which 792 Moroccan troops were killed, Morocco began attacking Algerian
territory. In September 1979 the conflict threatened to escalate when Egypt
began shipping arms to Morocco and offered its full support. Although the

conflict was referred to the OAU, the organization could do little to resolve the fighting. Algeria rejected Tunisia's offer to hold a summit on the issue. After October 1979 the fighting waned, and the conflict eventually subsided. Fighting in the Western Sahara continued without respite, however, into the 1990s. The status of Western Sahara has yet to be resolved.

For further information and background reading, see reference item numbers 76, 255, 361, 377, 471.

186. ISRAEL-SYRIA
Arab-Israeli tensions; air incidents (June 1979–February 1980)

Israel and Lebanon had had numerous armed conflicts since 1947, when Israel declared its independence. Israel constantly raided Lebanese territory, attacking the Palestinian camps that harbored PLO guerrillas responsible for attacks on northern Israel. Because of Syria's significant military presence in Lebanon, especially in the Bekaa Valley, it came under mounting pressure to protect Muslim civilians—both Palestinian and Lebanese. At the same time, Syrian president Hafez al-Assad was under pressure from a number of serious domestic challenges to his authority.

The Syrian air force therefore engaged Israeli jet fighters over southern Lebanese air space on June 27, 1979. The following day, Israel described its raids as "legitimate national self-defense" and said that the clash with Syria would not alter its policy of preemptive strikes on Palestinian targets in Lebanon. Israeli raids continued throughout July and August, intensifying in their effect and damage. A U.N. cease-fire on August 26 was immediately violated by both sides.

After a period of little Israeli activity in the first three weeks of September 1979, Israeli warplanes again clashed with Syrian planes on September 24, south of Beirut. Tension was also heightened by border clashes in southern Lebanon on September 21. Later that month, the United States announced a major diplomatic initiative to find a peaceful solution to the crisis in Lebanon. This was to be through consultations with Middle East and European countries and the eight nations contributing to the U.N. Interim Forces in Lebanon (UNIFIL).

On October 4, 1979, the PLO announced a unilateral cease-fire in Lebanon, but Israel ignored it. Hostilities continued through to the end of 1979 and early 1980, and by February 8, 1980, Israel had put its forces on the Lebanese border on full alert. Approximately forty fatalities resulted from the clashes. The U.S. diplomatic initiative was largely ineffectual, and a major war in Lebanon broke out in 1982 after Israel invaded the country (see conflict 199).

For further information and background reading, see reference item numbers 255, 1046, 1084, 1098, 1145, 1158.

187. INDIA-BANGLADESH
Boundary dispute; border incidents (November 1979)

The borders between India, Pakistan, and Bangladesh had been the source of disputes ever since the Subcontinent was partitioned in 1947 (see conflicts 003, 132, 149). These border disputes erupted into conflict once again in November 1979, and there were almost daily firefights between border troops. Border strains were aggravated by the constantly shifting course of the Muhuri River, which formed the border between the two states. India placed spurs on the riverbank in an effort to prevent flooding. Bangladesh protested that this caused erosion on its side. Combined with other questions of border demarcation, the dispute might have escalated into more serious confrontation. As it was, the question was resolved in negotiations in late October and November, and the firefights abated. Relations remained cool, however, and armed conflict broke out again in 1983 (see conflict 216).

For further information and background reading, see reference item numbers 76, 661, 701, 743, 744, 844.

188. UNITED STATES–IRAN
Anti-U.S. sentiment, Islamic revolution; the hostage crisis (November 1979–January 1981)

After the Ayatollah Khomeini's Islamic revolution of February 1979 (see conflict 159), anti-Western (especially anti-U.S.) sentiment grew in Iran. The United States had been closely aligned with the recently ousted Muhammad Reza Shah Pahlevi, who had headed a brutally repressive regime. Wanted in Iran for trial as a criminal, the shah lived in exile until his death from cancer in July 1980. Despite Iran's repeated threats and appeals to the United States to deny asylum to the former shah, the United States admitted him on humanitarian grounds on October 22, 1979, for medical treatment. The Iranian government officially protested to the United States in October, and demanded the shah's extradition.

On November 4, 1979, with anti-American fervor at a fever pitch, the U.S. embassy in Tehran was occupied by armed Iranian "students" who held all embassy personnel hostage and demanded the extradition of the shah. On November 6 the U.S. government stated that it would not accede to the demands, despite Iranian government support for the students.

Despite repeated U.S. and U.N. demands for the unconditional release of the hostages, Iran did not comply and instead accused the embassy staff of espionage. Iran also warned against any attempts to rescue them. Some hostages were released in November 1979, and there were many unsuccessful mediation attempts during this time. The United States retaliated with economic and financial pressure, as well as the expulsion of Iranian students. U.S. and British warships began maneuvers in the Arabian Sea, south of Iran, in a provocative display of force; diplomatic relations were sundered. Attempts at negotiation were hampered by factional struggles within the Iran government.

On April 24, 1980, the United States launched an abortive military operation to free the hostages, which failed when the rescue helicopters crashed in the desert. Iran interpreted this as a hostile action, and tensions were high. The death of the shah in July 1980 did nothing to defuse the crisis. After intense and secret mediation by Algeria, an agreement providing for the hostages' release was reached in January 1981. Relations with the United States remained tense, however, and the United States stepped up its support for Iraq, a bitter enemy of Iran.

For further information and background reading, see reference item numbers 1033, 1074, 1080, 1150, 1267, 1276, 1304, 1318.

189. CAMBODIA-THAILAND

Khmer Rouge insurgency; border conflict
(December 1979–October 1980)

Although the Vietnamese had deposed Pol Pot's brutal regime in 1979 (see conflict 181), fighting continued between the newly installed Heng Samrin regime and insurgent Khmer Rouge forces. The new regime in Phnom Penh renamed the country the People's Republic of Kampuchea (PRK). Beginning in December 1979 Thai-Cambodian relations deteriorated because of PRK military offensives against Khmer Rouge strongholds on the Thai border. The PRK accused Thailand of harboring the Khmer Rouge and Cambodian noncommunist resistance forces, allowing them to train and rest. During this period rival groups fought over black-market food supplies along the Thai border, resulting in more than two hundred casualties.

In June 1980 the repatriation of refugees from Thailand prompted fears in the Vietnamese-backed PRK regime that Khmer Rouge forces would be strengthened; the act was said to demonstrate Thailand's hostile attitude to the PRK. On June 23–24 serious fighting once again broke out along the Thai border between Thai units and PRK forces. The Thai government protested the incident to the Vietnamese government and the U.N. secretary-general, appealing for the restoration of peace and security. Meetings of the Association of Southeast Asian Nations (ASEAN) in late June reinforced ASEAN and U.N. support for peace and backed recognition of the new PRK government. The United States also strengthened its military support for Thailand. From July to December 1980, there were repeated accusations of border violations and more fighting between border troops.

ASEAN countries offered peace proposals that brought a partial settlement and cessation of hostilities in early August 1980, largely through the mediation of U.N. secretary-general Kurt Waldheim. The two states then had further discussions in September and October at the United Nations that led to the resolution of further issues. The fighting between Thai and PRK troops resulted in approximately three hundred fatalities.

For further information and background reading, see reference item numbers 692, 694, 730, 731, 742, 754, 840.

190. HONDURAS-NICARAGUA
Right-wing insurgency; the contra war
(January 1980–February 1994)

The right-wing, U.S.-backed Somoza regime had ruled Nicaragua from 1937 to 1979, until it was overthrown by the leftist guerrillas belonging to the Sandinist National Liberation Front (FSLN, named for Augusto César Sandino, an early Nicaraguan patriot). Somoza supporters and national guardsmen fled to Honduras. Beginning in January 1980, these exiled antigovernment forces began an insurgency from bases in Honduras, and they became even more active after 1981, when the United States began to give them massive military and economic support with Honduran cooperation. The recently elected Reagan administration in the United States was violently opposed to the new FSLN government, as they saw it as a communist threat. In one operation, the United States mined Nicaraguan harbors, sinking many ships. Commonly known as *contras,* the right-wing insurgents were formed into an army that frequently invaded Nicaragua from Honduras with the aim of ousting the socialist FSLN regime.

The contras' activities led to numerous armed clashes on the Honduras-Nicaraguan border throughout the 1980s. Also, heavy U.S. support for the contras through the CIA led to a number of domestic scandals for the U.S. administration. In August 1987 the Arias peace plan led to direct negotiations between the FSLN and the contras, and a number of cease-fires were arranged. Over the next few years the FSLN government made many concessions, including the holding of free elections, which the government lost. At the end of 1992 the war as such was over, but the defeated Sandinistas underwent a serious division in and the contras were proving difficult to demobilize. These tensions threatened to escalate into serious civil conflict. In 1993 some fighting broke out between disgruntled right-wing and left-wing rebel factions and the government, but after OAS mediation, their grievances were settled and the fighting ended. Nicaragua was continuing to rebuild at the end of 1995.

More than 25,000 lives were lost because of the war, most them civilian fatalities. The war also devastated the Nicaraguan economy, as the contras and the CIA targeted many of the country's economic facilities.

For further information and background reading, see reference item numbers 255, 511, 522, 523, 526, 567, 584, 615.

191. IRAN-IRAQ
Regional rivalry, territorial dispute; the Iran-Iraq War
(February 1980–1989)

Iran and Iraq had been rivals following years of conflict over the Shatt al Arab Waterway, which flowed into the Gulf in the southern border area between the two states. It served ports from both countries and was crucial to shipping. Armed conflict had broken out in 1971 (see conflict 130) and 1972–1975 (see conflict 136), although an agreement in 1975 had seemed to resolve the issue. Iranian support for Kurdish rebels in Iraq, and the overthrow of the shah in Iran (see conflict 159) had raised tensions in 1979. Iraq was highly suspicious of the Ayatollah Khomeini and still had designs on the Shatt al Arab.

In February 1980 Iraq repudiated the 1975 border agreement and invaded the Shatt al Arab region in force. At first it seemed Iraq would win easily, but Iran held on and launched its own counteroffensive in 1981. A lengthy war of attrition followed, with Iran using lightly trained Revolutionary Guards and Iraq resorting to chemical weapons, prompting worldwide condemnation. Although neither side was able to gain an advantage, both still believed they could win. The fighting spread to the Gulf waters in 1984, and there were frequent attacks on oil facilities and shipping. The United States sent a naval task force to the region to protect Western oil interests, but owing to Soviet interest in the region did not get actively involved in the conflict, despite numerous attacks and incidents.

In the late 1980s Iran appeared to be getting the upper hand, largely because it was prepared to sacrifice greater numbers of troops. Various breakthroughs occurred, but in the end, the Iraqis could not be dislodged. Both sides attacked civilians, firing Scud missiles randomly into each other's cities in an attempt to demoralize the other. The war took such a toll on both countries that conflict-management efforts, largely by the United Nations, produced a cease-fire and partial settlement by 1989, although the underlying issues were never fully resolved.

It is estimated that more than 1 million people lost their lives in this war, and both economies sustained billions of dollars of damage. Iran lost approximately 400,000 troops in the war, while Iraq lost nearly 200,000. It was the most violent war since Vietnam and by far the most costly conventional war since Korea.

For further information and background reading, see reference item numbers 1020, 1091, 1096, 1108, 1159, 1180, 1185, 1242.

192. VANUATU–ESPIRITU SANTO
Secessionist fighting (May–September 1980)

The New Hebrides Islands in the South Pacific had been a jointly administered British and French condominium since 1906. During the late 1970s, as the islands moved toward independence, there was a great deal of political turbulence from various groups, including some who wanted to secede. The islands became independent as the Republic of Vanuatu on July 30, 1980. Secessionist movements immediately erupted—primarily on the island of Espiritu Santo, but also on Aoba, Malakula, and Tanna—and were supported by numbers of local French-speaking residents.

On May 28, 1980, members of the Nagriamel movement, which was led by Jimmy Stevens, took control of Santo town and proclaimed a provisional government. In June and July negotiations between the secessionists and Vanuatu, French, and British officials failed, leading to the armed intervention involving 200 British and French troops, who took control of Santo on July 24 with only light resistance. There were similar events on the island of Aoba. The Anglo-French joint force was replaced on August 18 by 150 Papua New Guinean (PNG) troops. Approximately three people were killed in clashes between the PNG troops and secessionists, but by September 24, 1980, most of the rebels had been arrested and imprisoned.

For further information and background reading, see reference item numbers 255, 676.

193. ECUADOR-PERU
Territorial dispute; border war (January–April 1981)

In early January 1981 fighting erupted over disputed territory in the Loreto area of northern Peru—a remote jungle region in the Condor mountain range that had been the scene of previous Ecuador-Peruvian clashes in 1977 (see conflict 171). This area has been claimed by Ecuador for more than 150 years, following a territorial reorganization under Spanish colonial rule that left Ecuador without access to the Amazon River or the Marañón waterway. Although Peru regarded the dispute settled under the 1942 protocol of Río de Janeiro, Ecuador claimed the treaty was imposed, and challenged its validity.

Fighting erupted on January 28, 1981 (the eve of the thirty-ninth anniversary of the protocol), following Ecuadoran accusations that Peru had violated its airspace and fired on a military outpost. The president of Ecuador, Jaime Roldós Aguilera, declared a state of emergency and imposed a press blackout on news from the border. The border was immediately closed and troops mobilized on both sides. Peru rejected offers of mediation from the OAS, Colombia, and Venezuela. Fighting continued, and Peru retook its military posts. On

January 31, 1981, the guarantor nations of the protocol (Argentina, Brazil, Chile, the United States) mediated discussions between the warring states in Brasília, resulting in a cease-fire and acceptance of observers to supervise the disputed area.

In early February 1981 the OAS adopted a resolution calling for peace in the border area, which was supported by the four guarantor nations. In late February, however, hostilities recurred in the border area, and Peru declared that any further infiltration of the region by Ecuador would be regarded as "an act of war." The two countries sealed their mutual border on February 23 but then agreed to proposals by the guarantor nations to withdraw their troops from either side of the border. A series of meetings of OAS countries and the guarantor nations from February to March 1981 resulted in a firm commitment on the withdrawal of troops by both parties. On April 2, 1981, the border was reopened. About ten fatalities were reported during the fighting. Tense relations led to renewed fighting in 1984 (see conflict 217) and 1995 (see conflict 287).

For further information and background reading, see reference item numbers 46, 76, 255, 552, 635.

194. CAMEROON-NIGERIA
Territorial dispute; border incident (May–July 1981)

A plebiscite in 1961 had resulted in the transfer of parts of Cameroon's northern territories to Nigeria, although Cameroon had never pressed any claim on the area. Another plebiscite had seen territory with Nigerian tribes living in it given to western Cameroon, despite some opposition from the tribes. These issues were a source of tension between the two states and led to some incidents.

Relations between Cameroon and Nigeria steadily deteriorated in early 1981 over these territorial issues, culminating in a border incident on May 15, when five Nigerian soldiers were killed and three wounded after a Cameroon patrol boat attacked the border area of the Akpa Yafi River. Nigeria called for effective military action against Cameroon and rejected the Cameroon government's apology and peace proposal. Nigeria demanded full reparations and spurned the suggestion of a joint commission of inquiry, preferring instead to seek international arbitration.

Over this period, Nigeria continued to call for military action against Cameroon, and there were accusations of troop buildups. In mid-July 1981 the sitting OAU president, Kenyan president Daniel arap Moi, successfully mediated an agreement between the parties. The agreement called for full compensation to the families of the Nigerian soldiers killed in the fighting and for the establishment of an international arbitration panel to examine the border question so as to avoid further disputes. The panel failed to resolve the outstanding issues, however, and minor incidents and tensions continued to plague Nigerian-Cameroon relations in following years.

For further information and background reading, see reference item numbers 76, 310, 469.

195. PAKISTAN-INDIA

Regional rivalry; border incidents, the India-Pakistan wars (July 1981–August 1982)

Pakistan and India had been rivals since the 1947 partition and the first Kashmir war (see conflicts 003, 010). Relations were typically hostile, and many unresolved disputes led to armed conflict in 1958–1959 (see conflict 056) and again in 1965 (see conflicts 098, 106). Both sides distrusted the other, and both were committed to maintaining strong military positions.

After the Soviet invasion of Afghanistan in 1979, however, relations between Pakistan and India temporarily improved, but they deteriorated again in 1980 after each had taken steps to strengthen its armed forces. Tensions increased after India expressed concern that Pakistan was planning to develop nuclear weapons capability. This was denied by Pakistan. The United States was also renewing its military aid to Pakistan in 1981. During June 1981 each country agreed it had a right to acquire arms for its own security and reiterated its commitment to the principles of nonalignment. However, India and Pakistan continued their mutual allegations of military buildups, including the acquisition of nuclear weapons.

On July 7–14, 1981, India alleged that ten Pakistani and four Indian soldiers had been killed in an exchange of fire near the Punch sector of the cease-fire line in Kashmir, and that Pakistan had deployed 350,000 troops along the Indian border. The troop movements were denied by the Pakistan Foreign Ministry. Hostilities in the disputed area of Jammu and Kashmir were very intense in November 1981, and there were numerous armed incidents. Both sides began expelling each other's diplomats and repatriating each other's nationals. Tensions were high, and there were fears of an outbreak of war.

On December 24, 1981, India formally invited Pakistani representatives to preliminary discussions, which resulted in a proposal for a permanent joint commission and a possible friendship treaty After further negotiations in May and June 1982, both sides declared that an understanding had been reached and bilateral discussions would continue on August 11, 1982, in Islamabad. The incidents stopped after this period, and relations were normalized for the time being. About fifteen fatalities resulted from the actual fighting. The issues in dispute remained unresolved, however, and there were further armed conflicts in 1984 (see conflict 219) and 1986 (see conflict 231).

For *further information and background reading, see reference item numbers*
255, 667, 679, 684.

196. UNITED STATES–LIBYA
Regional instability; air incidents (August 1981)

U.S. attitudes toward Libya hardened following the accession of Ronald
Reagan to the presidency in 1980. The Reagan administration claimed Col.
Muammar Qaddafi's regime was not only destabilizing the region but also promoting international terrorism. Libya, for its part, also engaged in hostile anti-
U.S. propaganda. U.S.-Libyan relations deteriorated rapidly in mid-1981 amid
hostile diplomatic moves and mutual recriminations. Provocative U.S. naval
maneuvers in the Gulf of Sirte (or Sidra), which Libya claimed as territorial
waters, produced a number of incidents, the most serious of which was a jet
fighter clash on August 19, 1981, in which two Libyan Su-22 jet fighters were
shot down. Incidents and recriminations continued after this point, but the dispute gradually abated. There were no attempts at peaceful conflict management, and fighting broke out again in 1986 (see conflict 232) and yet again in
1989 (see conflict 248).

For *further information and background reading, see reference item numbers*
1097, 1141, 1220, 1305, 1307, 1315.

197. POLAND
Labor turmoil, martial law (December 1981–February 1982)

Poland had been part of the Soviet sphere of influence since the end of World
War II. By the early 1980s, however, internal demands for economic liberal-
ization and greater political freedom were creating fissures in the monolithic
Soviet bloc. This was particularly evident in Poland, where Lech Walesa, a
Gdansk shipyard worker, had founded the Solidarity labor union. The Soviet
Union had amply demonstrated its views on internal dissension with its mili-
tary invasions of Hungary in 1956 (see conflict 048) and Czechoslovakia in
1968 (see conflict 120).

This particular conflict began in December 1981, when Gen. Wojciech
Jaruzelski, apparently fearing a Soviet invasion, ordered a preemptive military
crackdown. Claiming that Solidarity had plans to overthrow the government,
Jaruzelski declared martial law and ordered the arrests of thousands of Poles
(including Walesa and other Solidarity leaders). Strikes and demonstrations
were brutally suppressed in the ensuing crackdown.

Although there was little indication at the time of Soviet collusion in the crisis, subsequent evidence reveals the Soviet Union's deep involvement in prepar-

ing for and implementing the crackdown. Once discovered, this complicity provoked a crisis in NATO-Soviet relations and heightened tensions in Europe. Eventually, however, the crisis dissipated. Martial law was lifted in December 1982, a month after Walesa was released from prison. No attempts at peaceful conflict management were made during the conflict. Walesa was awarded the 1983 Nobel Peace Prize and in 1990 elected president of Poland.

For further information and background reading, see reference item numbers 17, 57, 904, 943, 989.

198. UGANDA
Post-Amin civil war (December 1981–1995)

In 1971 Maj. Gen. Idi Amin led a military coup that ousted Ugandan president A. Milton Obote, setting the stage for a brutal and unpredictable regime that by 1977 had led to the deaths of 300,000 Ugandans and the expulsion of the country's entire Asian population. In addition to plunging his own nation into chaos, Amin had also managed to destabilize most of Central Africa.

Exiled opposition groups united under the banner of Obote's Ugandan National Liberation Front (UNLF). Backed by the Tanzanian army, the Obote's group invaded Uganda in 1979 and deposed Amin (see conflict 179), who then fled to Saudi Arabia to live in exile. As the Tanzanian army withdrew and the new Obote government began to establish itself, a number of disaffected groups undertook an antigovernment insurgency. Especially important was Yoweri Museveni's Uganda Patriotic Movement (UPM), later called the National Resistance Army (NRA). Many of these groups had been defeated in the national elections held after Amin's ouster; there were also claims of extensive human rights violations by the Obote government.

Within a few months, the country was engulfed in civil war. The fighting was intense, with rebel attacks on the military, police, government patrols, and industrial installations, in addition to assassinations and bombings. After mid-1983 the war reverted to an insurgency, although at various times the rebels maintained effective control over portions of the countryside and claimed to have established "administrations." This was especially true for Museveni's NRA, which by this time had become the strongest and most significant rebel group.

Throughout the fighting, there were persistent reports that Libya was providing aid to the rebels. Meanwhile, the Ugandan government was remaining in power with the help of Tanzanian and North Korean troops. The conflict was further complicated by the intervention of Amin loyalists backed by Zairean troops.

On July 27, 1985, Obote was deposed in a coup led by Bazilio Okello, the commander of the army's northern region. The new military government, headed by Okello, initiated negotiations in August 1985, and in December a power-sharing agreement was signed in Nairobi, Kenya. The agreement provided for an end to the civil war and the holding of elections.

The agreement was never implemented, however, and within weeks fighting broke out again. Kampala fell on January 26, 1986, to the NRA; Museveni was sworn in as president on January 29. The National Resistance Council (NRC) was then established to govern the country. By the end of March 1986 Museveni claimed to have established control over the whole country through an intensive military campaign.

By August 1986 a guerrilla war once again flared, fueled by a whole gamut of rebel groups and factions, including supporters of deposed presidents Amin, Obote, and Okello, in addition to alienated members of the NRAs. The most important rebel group was the Ugandan People's Democratic Army (UPDA). Throughout 1986 and 1987, however, the rebels sustained several major setbacks, including the defeat of Alice Lekwana's "Holy Spirit" in November 1987. Over the next few years, the government gradually established greater control over the countryside and, through negotiations and amnesties, obtained the surrender and absorption of numerous rebel groups.

Although rebel activities continue on a relatively small scale, they do not appear to directly threaten Museveni's government. Throughout the course of the civil war, it is thought that more than half a million people lost their lives as a direct result of the conflict.

For further information and background reading, see reference item numbers 255, 296, 376, 410, 453.

199. ISRAEL-LEBANON
Arab-Israeli conflict; Israeli military invasion (early 1982–mid-1983)

Following Israel's war of independence in 1948 (see conflict 012), Palestinian refugees flooded into southern Lebanon. From there, Palestinian guerrillas, mainly from the PLO, continued to launch attacks into northern Israel. Lebanon's intractable civil strife appeared to add to Israel's disquiet about its northern borders (see conflict 151). In any event, the PLO's presence in Lebanon and persistent cross-border attacks led to armed border conflicts in 1965 (see conflict 108), 1974–1975 (see conflict 145), 1977 (see conflict 170), and 1978 (see conflict 176), and air incidents in 1979–1980 (see conflict 186).

The escalation of cross-border Israeli-PLO and Israeli-Syrian engagements in the north from late 1980 to July 1981 led to increasing strains in the area. The Syrian deployment of antiaircraft missile batteries in the Bekaa Valley also caused a potentially explosive situation. This was defused only by intense diplomatic efforts, which procured a cease-fire and a period of relative stability in southern Lebanon from July 1981 to April 1982. But cease-fire violations led to Israeli air strikes in April 1982, an increase in tensions during May, and Israeli troop concentrations in the area.

In an operation code-named "Peace for Galilee," Israel launched an invasion of Lebanon on June 6, 1982, with the stated intention of eliminating the military threat posed by the PLO to Israel's northern borders. Israeli forces stormed through Lebanon, reaching the outskirts of Beirut four days later. By June 14 Israeli forces had completely encircled the Lebanese capital, in which were trapped large numbers of PLO and Syrian troops. During its advance, Israel had destroyed Syrian surface-to-air missile batteries in the Bekaa Valley and engaged in aerial battle with the Syrian air force, in which hundreds of Syrian planes are thought to have been shot down. Diplomatic efforts failed to stop the fighting, although they did succeed in averting a wider Israeli-Syrian war.

Israeli forces gradually tightened their grip on Beirut, laying siege to PLO and Syrian forces trapped there. On June 13 Israel announced its demands for a peace plan, saying it would invade West Beirut, where the PLO was cornered, unless the PLO left Lebanon along with the Syrian troops. Owing to intense U.S. diplomatic efforts and continued Israeli pressure, the plan was accepted in late June. The evacuation of PLO and Syrian forces from Beirut began on August 21 and was completed by September 1. Playing a peace-keeping role, U.S., French, and Italian forces moved into Beirut as part of the security plan.

Israeli troops entered West Beirut following the September 14 assassination of Lebanese president-elect Bashir Gemayel. Two days later, Lebanese Christian troops entered the Sabra and Shatila refugee camps, massacring hundreds of Palestinian refugees. Israel troops were accused of complicity in the massacres, and the resulting uproar eventually led to the resignation of the Israeli defense minister Ariel Sharon. Intense U.S. diplomatic activity eventually led to direct Israeli-Lebanese negotiations, and Israel began troop withdrawals in September 1983 despite continued violence, attacks on the peace-keeping forces, deadlocks in negotiations, breakdowns in cease-fires, and at times, escalations in hostilities.

Lebanon fell into heavy factional fighting after the Israeli withdrawal. Tensions remained high in southern Lebanon, with recurring cross-border incidents as Israel attempted to establish a security zone (see conflict 213). The fighting was intense throughout the conflict, and as many as 100,000 people were killed in the fighting, many of them civilians. Israel lost nearly 800 troops.

For further information and background reading, see reference item numbers 1027, 1047, 1058, 1069, 1098, 1123, 1129, 1145, 1158, 1293.

200. ZAIRE-ZAMBIA
Lake Mweru border dispute (February–September 1982)

Beginning in 1979, Zaire and Zambia maintained a running border dispute concerning the Lake Mweru region on Zambia's northern border. Zambia claimed that Zaire had set up border posts in the Kaputa district, nearly 30 km inside its territory. On February 28, 1982, an exchange of fire and the seizure of Zambian troops led to large numbers of refugees and the closure of the border.

Following talks by a joint commission in April 1982, both sides agreed to exchange prisoners. Zaire continued to establish border posts within Zambian territory, however, and there were further abductions of Zambian citizens. Zaire agreed to withdraw its troops only after talks between Zambian president Kenneth Kaunda and President Mobutu Sésé Séko of Zaire and further sessions of the joint commission in September 1982. The conflict lapsed after this and tensions were eased. The dispute was not fully resolved, however, and more fighting broke out in September 1983 (see conflict 214).

For further information and background reading, see reference item numbers 290, 319, 383, 435, 469.

201. UNITED KINGDOM–ARGENTINA
Sovereignty dispute; the Falklands war (April–June 1982)

The Falkland Islands (together with its dependencies, the South Georgia and South Sandwich islands), have been a British crown colony since the 1830s. Calling them the Islas Malvinas, Argentina had disputed British sovereignty ever since British forces took control of the islands in 1833 and continued to pursue a long-term policy of establishing sovereignty over the islands. As a consequence, there have been a number of incidents related to the islands, which lie 600 km off the Argentine coast in the South Atlantic Ocean. Inconclusive negotiations over the issue had been going on for years.

The conflict began to escalate after bilateral negotiations broke down in February 1982. On March 21, after the hard-line Argentine government issued some particularly bellicose statements, a group of about sixty Argentines, said to be scrap merchants, landed illegally at Leth Harbor, on the island of South Georgia. Tensions escalated steadily amid repeated Argentine claims to the islands and the buildup of naval and military hardware. Intense diplomatic activity and repeated warnings from Britain and the United Nations did nothing to defuse the situation.

On April 2, 1982, Argentine troops invaded and took control of the Falkland Islands, overwhelming the seventy Royal Marines stationed there. By April 12 there were reported to be ten thousand Argentine troops on the islands. The invasion was widely condemned by the United States, the European Community (now the European Union), and the United Nations. Great Britain quickly dispatched a naval task force to deal with the invasion. It was composed of nearly six thousand troops, almost seventy destroyers, carriers, frigates, and submarines, in addition to air support. Both nations then declared maritime exclusion zones around the islands and off the Argentine coast.

Despite a Peruvian truce proposal and diplomatic initiatives by U.S. secretary of state Alexander Haig and the United Nations, tensions heightened. On April 24 Great Britain announced its readiness to retake the islands, and the following day British marines, landing by helicopter, recaptured South Georgia. On April 30 Britain announced a Total Exclusion Zone of 200 nautical miles around the islands, which further escalated the conflict.

War began on May 1, 1982, with British air attacks on Port Stanley, and major naval engagements, bombardments, and attacks on installations. Major diplomatic initiatives by the United States, Peru, and the United Nations failed to stop the fighting, and on May 21, 1982, five thousand British troops landed on East Falkland and around Port San Carlos, establishing a bridgehead. Heavy ground, air, and sea fighting ensued, but British forces made steady advances, and on June 14–15 Argentina surrendered the islands to Britain. Prisoners were returned and British troops and naval ships began to be returned in the following months.

Throughout the conflict more than 1,200 troops and civilians were killed, hundreds of planes destroyed, and many ships sunk. Despite the British victory, the dispute over sovereignty of the islands continued. British forces remain on the island, at great cost, while negotiations continue on resolving the sovereignty debate.

For further information and background reading, see reference item numbers 76, 255, 516, 519, 525, 528, 529, 536, 547, 555, 556.

202. INDONESIA–PAPUA NEW GUINEA; IRIAN JAYA
Secessionist warfare; border incidents (May 1982–October 1985)

The status of Irian Jaya (formerly West Irian) has long vexed Indonesia. In 1962 it went to war with the Netherlands in an effort to oust the former colonial power from the region—which comprises the western half of the island of New Guinea—and gain control over its abundant natural resources (see conflict 078). A U.N. intervention in 1962 secured an end to the fighting and granted Indonesia possession of the territory. There was one condition: Indonesia would have to effect a program leading Irian Jayan self-determination by 1969. This was never implemented.

An armed secessionist movement took shape in Irian Jaya by 1965 (see conflict 100) after it became clear to the ethnically Papuan inhabitants that Indonesia had no intention of granting them independence. The rebels often operated from Papua New Guinean (PNG) territory, on the eastern half of the island, where the local population provided them with sympathy and support.

Relations between Indonesia and PNG deteriorated in early 1982. By May 1992 Indonesian troops had begun crossing into PNG in pursuit of insurgents, provoking protest and troop buildups in the border area. Relations between the two countries were further strained by the alleged infringement of PNG's airspace by Indonesian military aircraft and some border incidents. The dispute was resolved after a new five-year border agreement was signed in October 1984, replacing a similar agreement signed in 1979. There were five reported fatalities related to these incidents. The agreement did not prevent the Irian Jayan rebels from continuing their activities.

For further information and background reading, see reference item numbers 76, 255, 710, 817, 856.

203. CHAD-LIBYA
Political instability, rebel fighting, foreign intervention; the third Chad civil war (mid-1982–)

Chad had been riven by civil conflict and foreign interventions since its independence from France in 1960 (see conflicts 109, 164, 175). In the previous round of violence, Hissène Habré's Forces armées du nord (FAN) finally ousted President Goukouni Oueddei. After Habré was named president, he attempted to effect reconciliation with the other Chadian factions while consolidating his position. He was unsuccessful, however, and low-level fighting continued.

In October 1982 former president Oueddei established a rival "national peace government" in the northern town of Bardaï with Libyan support. In mid-1983 Oueddei's forces advanced southward with Libyan troop support, but they were then driven back in a successful government counterattack. With the aid of Libyan air power, the rebels recaptured the town of Faya-Largeau in early August and again marched south. The fighting subsided only after French and Zairean forces, invited in by President Habré, assisted government forces in establishing a series of strong points across the country.

Fighting and famine continued into 1984, with increased French and Libyan involvement and the arrival of more Zairean troops. Growing numbers of French fatalities fueled diplomatic efforts to end the war, but these were unsuccessful. Despite a September 1984 agreement providing for the withdrawal of all foreign troops from Chad, Libyan troops remained and continued to clash with government forces. The government consolidated its position in central and southern Chad in 1985, often resorting to repressive tactics, but the north remained under rebel control. Drought and famine continued to wrack the country.

Fighting continued without letup throughout 1986 and 1987, with U.S. support and renewed French involvement on the side of the Habré regime and Libyan defeats in the north. Neither side managed to defeat the other, and fortunes fluctuated. In 1988 the Chadian government signed agreements with both Libya and the Forces armées tchadiennes (FAT) rebels, but other factions, including Oueddei's forces (GUNT, or Transitional Government of National Unity), continued to fight. The government survived a coup attempt in April 1989, but on December 1, 1990, the Habré regime fell to the rebel Patriotic Salvation Movement (MPS) under the leadership of Col. Idriss Déby, who had been in exile since the 1989 coup attempt. Based in Sudan, the MPS had launched a series of offensives from the northern Darfur province.

In late 1991 forces loyal to former president Habré began actions in the Tibesti region of northern Chad. Rebel attacks began in earnest in December 1991 and included an invasion from the Lake Chad region, which was repulsed only with the aid of French paratroopers. Despite peace agreements signed throughout the 1992–1995 period with various rebel factions, the Chadian government remained vulnerable and rebel activities continued. Starting in 1994, Déby's regime committed itself to national reconciliation and a timetable for democratic elections. Agreements were signed with several main rebel factions, but low-level fighting continued into late 1995. Also, in 1995 the ICJ ruled in favor of Chad's sovereignty over the Aozou strip, a disputed territory on the Chad-Libyan border that Libya had seized in 1973 (see conflict 164). Approximately 25,000 people have died during this conflict, including 2,000 Libyan fatalities and 9 French deaths.

For further information and background reading, see reference item numbers 255, 335, 336, 391, 466, 481.

204. LAOS-THAILAND
Territorial dispute; border incidents (June 1982)

Relations between Laos and Thailand were complicated by an ill-defined and dense jungle border and a number of unresolved disputes over territorial boundaries. Relations had also been strained after the Pathet Lao came to power in 1975, following years of civil war (see conflict 095). Large numbers of Laotians, most of them from the professional and commercial classes, flooded into Thailand seeking refuge. The strains had already led to armed border clashes in 1975–1976 (see conflict 154), but despite a number of incidents along the Thai-Laos border in early 1982, relations between the two countries had generally been improving with the help of reciprocal ministerial visits.

This conflict began on June 16, 1982, when it was reported that Lao troops on the island of Don Sangkhi in the Mekong River had opened fire on the Thai village of Ban Mae, killing two villagers. The following day, when Thai patrol boats passed the island, they were shelled and one was sunk, while another ran aground, killing two more. After further shootings on June 22, the Thai ambassador to Laos made an official protest about the incidents and the border was closed. There were no attempts at peaceful conflict management throughout the dispute, and it eventually faded. In June 1984 fighting again broke out (see conflict 223).

For further information and background reading, see reference item numbers 663, 714, 728, 757, 778, 854, 865, 869.

205. SRI LANKA; TAMILS VS. SINHALESE
Communal violence, separatist fighting; the Tamil conflict (July 1982–)

Tensions had always existed between Sri Lanka's Buddhist Sinhalese population, who comprise more than 70 percent of the country's total population, and the Hindu Tamil minority, who live on the northern part of the island. The period following independence in 1948 had been relatively peaceful, but after outbreaks of communal violence, a separatist movement of sorts had arisen among the minority Tamils. This movement grew quickly when the government responded with widespread repression. In July 1982 a Tamil group calling itself the Liberation Tigers of Tamil Eelam (LTTE), led by Vellupillai Prabhakaran, began a low-level campaign of political violence against the regime.

The conflict began in earnest in July 1983, when Tamil guerrillas ambushed and killed thirteen soldiers in the Jaffna district. This was followed by massive communal violence and revenge attacks by government troops, which left more than four hundred people dead and underscored the issue of the Tamil minority's political future. The government responded by declaring a state of emergency, banning all expressions of separatism, and outlawing a number of Tamil political parties. After Indian mediation in August 1983, the Sri Lankan government called an all-party roundtable conference to deal with the problem in January 1984. Largely unsuccessful, it was dissolved in December 1984.

By this stage, the LTTE had formed itself into a fanatical, well-disciplined guerrilla army, and the north was in a virtual state of all-out war. The Tigers also began to campaign abroad, and as a result, Tamils from the south Indian state of Tamil Nadu began to agitate and attempted to aid the Sri Lankan Tamils, sending men and supplies in boats. Despite numerous mediations, negotiations, and all-party conferences, the war persisted until July 1987. The violence was intense, with continuous bombings, revenge attacks, and military clashes between guerrillas and government forces. Civilians were more often than not the target of attacks. Despite numerous government offensives in Jaffna, they were unable to defeat the Tamil separatists.

In July 1987 India and Sri Lanka signed an agreement that supposedly settled the Tamil issue and included the deployment of thousands of Indian troops as peace-keepers in Tamil areas. The plan proceeded relatively smoothly, with the LTTE's initial acceptance, until twelve Tamil Tigers committed suicide while in Indian custody. Their deaths provoked a wave of reprisal killings and a major Indian offensive on Tamil strongholds. Despite initial Indian successes and renewed offensives, the war continued. The Indian troops began to take heavy losses.

Meanwhile, the violence intensified when a banned leftist Sinhalese organization, called the Janatha Vimukthi Peramuna (People's Liberation Front, or JVP), staged a comeback by initiating a terrorist campaign against the government and the Tamils. Up to a thousand people per month were being killed as a result of the 1989 JVP campaign. Earlier that year, Indian troops began to withdraw from Sri Lanka because of rising losses and pressure from the new president, Ranasinghe Premadasa. Mutual accusations led to tension between the two countries and the threat of actual hostilities, but diplomatic moves defused the crisis, and the withdrawal continued. The last Indian troops left Sri Lanka in March 1990. At least one thousand Indian soldiers had been killed since their deployment in July 1987.

Soon after the Indian withdrawal, peace initiatives were abandoned and all-out war resumed. On May 1, 1993, President Premadasa was assassinated by a Tamil rebel. Despite numerous government offensives from 1990 to 1994, neither side was able to get the upper hand. At least 100,000 people have died in the conflict, many of them civilians killed in massacres and revenge attacks. In early 1995 peace talks between the government and the LTTE led to optimism that a negotiated settlement could be found, and a period of relative calm set in. Tamil intransigence, however, caused the peace process to break down in May. This was followed by a serious intensification of the war, especially by the Tamils, who launched several major suicide bomb attacks on the capital, Colombo. The government responded with an all-out offensive in July in which 2,500 people were killed and about 6,000 wounded. In November 1995 government forces surrounded and laid siege to the Tamil stronghold of Jaffna, capturing the town in December. The fall of Jaffna was a serious setback to the LTTE, but they continued to fight on from the jungle.

For further information and background reading, see reference item numbers 37, 682, 783, 794, 806, 836, 872, 881.

206. GHANA-TOGO
Territorial dispute; border incidents (August–October 1982)

Relations between Ghana and Togo had been strained ever since colonial boundaries had split Ewe tribal lands between the two countries, giving rise to an ongoing reunification campaign. Ghana's expansive policies had also caused regional instability, bringing about one armed conflict between Ghana and Togo in 1965 (see conflict 102).

Tensions rose dramatically in August 1982, when both sides accused the other of harboring each other's rebels. There were also several violations of airspace and a number of border incidents. One such incident left six people dead and several injured and resulted in the closure of the Ghana-Togo border. No peaceful conflict-management attempts were made during the dispute, and although the allegations and recriminations continued into 1983, the conflict lapsed. The underlying hostility remained, however, and there were further armed conflicts in 1986 (see conflict 237) and 1994 (see conflict 280).

For further information and background reading, see reference item numbers 46, 255, 297, 313.

207. GUATEMALA-MEXICO
Regional instability, Guatemalan civil war; border incidents (September 1982–January 1983)

Various guerrilla insurgencies throughout Latin America made the region unstable in the 1980s. Guatemala's brutal civil war in particular (see conflict 037), which began in 1961, led not only massive civilian casualties (100,000 dead, 40,000 missing) and refugee populations but also to a number of border incidents with surrounding states, as Guatemalan forces pursued leftist guerrillas, called the Guatemalan National Revolutionary Unity (URNG), across national boundaries.

With the outbreak of renewed fighting in 1982, thousands of Guatemalan refugees crossed into the Mexican border state of Chiapas. From September 1982 to January 1983, Guatemalan troops made frequent incursions into Mexican territory to harass, kill, or abduct refugees, purportedly in pursuit of URNG rebels. Mexico protested and then began to move the refugee camps farther away from the border area. No attempts at peaceful conflict management were made during the dispute, and it soon lapsed. Although Guatemalan and Mexican troops had not engaged in direct fighting, the regional instability made the incidents very serious. Another such armed conflict arose in 1984 (see conflict 222), when Guatemalan troops again crossed the border into Mexico.

For further information and background reading, see reference item numbers 255, 557, 560, 577, 607, 630.

208. SOUTH AFRICA–LESOTHO
Guerrilla insurgency fears; anti-ANC raid (December 1982)

Lesotho, a small enclave within the Republic of South Africa, had been an independent state since 1966. Although relations between the two states were generally cordial, they became strained in mid-1982 following a number of border incidents. Lesotho alleged that South Africa was supporting the rebel Lesotho Liberation Army (LLA) in its armed struggle against the government. Anxious about guerrilla infiltrations, South Africa responded that Lesotho was serving as a base for African National Congress (ANC) guerrillas planning terrorist attacks against the apartheid regime.

On December 9, 1982, South African commandos launched a raid on alleged ANC members in residential areas of Maseru, Lesotho's capital, which resulted in forty-two deaths. It was reported that 64 South African commandos were trapped in Lesotho for a few hours and had to be airlifted out. South African military commanders are said to have warned Lesotho security forces of massive retaliation if they interfered with the withdrawal.

The attack was widely condemned in the international community. There were no attempts at peaceful conflict management during the conflict. Although South Africa put Lesotho under increasing economic and political pressure, and there were continued allegations and recriminations, the conflict abated after the end of 1982. South Africa conducted similar raids against ANC bases in Botswana in 1984–1986 (see conflict 225) and Zambia in 1987 (see conflict 240).

For further information and background reading, see reference item numbers 255, 290, 299, 312, 317, 371, 384.

209. SUDAN

Secessionist fighting, civil war; the second Sudan civil war (January 1983–)

Sudan's predominantly Arab Muslim northern provinces had controlled the central government since the country's independence from Britain in 1956. As a consequence, the three southern provinces, populated largely by black Christians and animists, engaged in secessionist warfare from 1960 to 1972 (see conflict 087). Secessionist sentiment resurfaced in January 1983, when the southern rebels began attacking police stations and army patrols; southern army units began to stage mutinies.

The conflict escalated after President Gaafar Mohammed Numeiry announced a redivision of southern Sudan and the imposition of Islamic law (Shari`a) there, effectively rendering the southerners second-class citizens. Col. John Garang led the primary rebel group, the Sudan People's Liberation Army (SPLA), which attacked towns and government patrols and engaged in hijackings, sabotage, and other terrorist activities. Despite offensives by both sides and several peace initiatives, the war continued unabated into 1985. In 1985–1986 another rebel movement, Anya-Nya II, began to act as a progovernment militia, hampering the rebels' efforts to consolidate their successes.

Khartoum's brand of militant Islam hampered efforts to bring a peaceful end to the civil war. Persistent government moves to impose Shari`a in the south finally split the coalition government and ended numerous peace initiatives, including a number of signed agreements. The fighting continued in a cyclical fashion from 1987 to 1989. Typically, both sides would launch offensives during the dry season and consolidate their gains when the rains came. On June 30, 1989, the civilian government of Prime Minister Sadiq al-Mahdi was overthrown in a bloodless military coup. Negotiations were immediately opened with the SPLA, but these were unsuccessful.

Mediation by former U.S. president Jimmy Carter in December 1989 also failed—negotiations again broke down over the issue of Shari`a law. Fighting erupted again in January 1990 and continued without letup for the rest of the year. Both sides claimed victories, but in reality, neither side was able to gain the advantage. Beset by drought and famine that had claimed the lives of close to 300,000 people, Sudan also had to deal with numerous coup attempts.

In late 1991 the SPLA leadership split over the issue of southern secession, and intrafactional fighting broke out. This hampered both rebel efforts and the recently revived peace initiatives. The government launched a major offensive in late February 1992 that caused the United Nations to suspend aid to the south. In 1993 the Khartoum government was cited for gross human rights violations and "ethnic cleansing" against the southern Nuba people. There are reports of Kenyan, Ugandan, Ethiopian, and Eritrean support for the rebels based on the countries' distaste for Khartoum's militant Islam. Fierce fighting continued in a similar, cyclical fashion until the end of 1995. Kenya and Uganda attempted a major mediation between 1993 and 1994, as did Jimmy Carter, although these efforts met with no real success.

Deaths have been estimated at 1.5 million—many of war-induced famine and disease—and nearly 3 million southern Sudanese have been displaced. Khartoum's economic blockade of the south was particularly devastating.

For further information and background reading, see reference item numbers 255, 288, 289, 295, 304, 348, 386, 478, 479.

210. LIBERIA–SIERRA LEONE
Doe regime tensions (February 1983–March 1983)

Liberia, a West African state founded in 1822 by freed American slaves, had been independent since 1847 and had enjoyed a fairly peaceful existence until a bloody military coup in 1980 installed Sgt. Samuel K. Doe as head of state. Surrounding states had qualms about Doe's brutal regime, which were borne out after a story was published in Sierra Leone claiming that Doe had personally shot and killed his wife for taking part in an abortive coup. Relations between Sierra Leone and Liberia underwent a serious deterioration after this.

Doe recalled the Liberian ambassador to Sierra Leone, closed the border with Sierra Leone, and in a significant show of force deployed 3,500 troops along the border.

Tensions were extremely high, but after an offer of mediation by Guinean president Ahmed Sékou Touré on February 26, 1983, and negotiations on March 7–12, the conflict was resolved. Doe's regime continued to cause concern, however, and in 1989 Sierra Leone allowed a rebel force to invade Liberia from its territory in the start of what was to become the Liberian civil war (see conflict 254).

For further information and background reading, see reference item numbers 286, 287, 324.

211. CHINA-VIETNAM
Regional rivalry; border conflict (April 1983)

Sino-Vietnamese relations had been extremely hostile ever since a costly war in 1979 (see conflict 182). In Cambodia, the Vietnamese-backed Heng Samrin regime fought a running battle with Khmer Rouge guerrillas, which were supported by China. Troops engaged in a tense standoff on the Sino-Vietnam border, shelling each other's positions.

Repeated allegations of incursions and provocations by both sides escalated into fighting in April 1983. On April 16 Chinese soldiers in Guangxi Zhuangzu Autonomous Region shelled Vietnamese border positions; artillery bombardments and clashes spread to a second region on the border of Yunnan province the following day.

The fighting caused heavy casualties and coincided with a renewed Vietnamese offensive in Cambodia. There were no serious attempts at peaceful conflict management during the conflict, although Vietnam did adopt a conciliatory attitude toward China, apparently in response to pressure from the Soviet Union. The dispute gradually subsided in the following months but broke out into serious fighting again in January 1984 (see conflict 218).

For further information and background reading, see reference item numbers 255, 695, 696, 715, 735, 830, 878.

212. CHAD-NIGERIA
Boundary/resources dispute; the Lake Chad conflict (April–July 1983)

Both Chad and Nigeria had achieved independence in 1960, and relations between the two states were generally good during the 1960s and 1970s. Although both sides accepted colonial boundaries, areas of Lake Chad had not been demarcated, and a number of small islands had become the focus of ownership disputes. The conflict escalated in the late 1970s and early 1980s when oil exploration in the region began. Also, the Chadian civil war had resulted in Nigerian troops being stationed in Chad as part of an OAU peace-keeping force. When the Nigerian troops were forced out of Chad by a military coup, tensions were at an all-time high.

The focus of conflict moved to the Lake Chad islands, and a number of minor incidents escalated into a series of serious military clashes from April to July 1983. More than 370 soldiers are thought to have been killed in the fighting that occurred on the islands. Despite an agreement to end hostilities, which was signed in Lagos, Nigeria, on May 17, Chadian soldiers engaged in a major offensive backed by French mercenaries. Nigeria responded by bombing Chadian lakeside villages with MiG jet fighters. Negotiations between the two countries' presidents in July 1983 and early 1984 led to an end to the fighting and the reopening of the border, which had been closed for several months.

For further information and background reading, see reference item numbers 76, 255, 310, 469.

213. ISRAEL-LEBANON
Arab-Israeli hostilities, Muslim-Christian factional fighting; the security zone (mid-1983–)

Although this conflict was part of the almost continuous Arab-Israeli hostilities dating back to 1948, its immediate precursor was Israel's 1982 invasion of Lebanon (see conflict 199), during which the Jewish state a set up a "security zone" in southern Lebanon to protect its northern borders from infiltrators and cross-border raids. Israel further buttressed the zone by giving military support to the South Lebanon Army (SLA), a Christian faction, including air power, tanks, and IDF (Israeli Defense Force) troops. The SLA tried to counter the actions of extreme Muslim factions (such as Hezbollah and Amal) and PLO groups that were active among the local Shiite population.

The minority Lebanese Shiites initially welcomed the Israeli occupation because it countered PLO power in the area (although a secular organization, the Palestine Liberation Organization is composed primarily of majority Sunni Muslims). But the Shiites grew to resent the increasingly repressive Israeli occupation and began to support radical Muslim factions. From this time on, a growing cycle of violence ensued. This typically involved armed attacks on Israeli and SLA forces, which then retaliated against Shiite villages with raids and air attacks, followed by further revenge attacks on Israeli/SLA forces.

At various times the IDF mounted large-scale operations that moved troops into southern Lebanon in order to improve security. This led to the mobilization of Syrian forces and, on several occasions, Lebanese army regulars fired on

Israeli positions. As a result of the fighting, more than 300,000 Lebanese became refugees, and there were an estimated 3,000–4,000 fatalities. At the end of 1995, the fighting continued in its usual cyclical pattern, with no prospect of ending and no active measures to resolve the conflict peacefully. In early 1996 the IDF mounted a massive military operation to clear the security zone of Hezbollah fighters, causing heavy loss of life and displacing many people. The operation also caused massive infrastructural damage, as many Lebanese targets were attacked in an apparent effort to force the Lebanese government to exert pressure on Hezbollah.

For further information and background reading, see reference item numbers 1027, 1069, 1098, 1103, 1123, 1145, 1158, 1293.

214. ZAIRE-ZAMBIA
Regional tensions, deportations; border dispute
(September 1983–July 1984)

Following a 1982 Zaire-Zambia border conflict over Zambia's Lake Mweru region (see conflict 200), tensions were heightened dramatically in September 1983 when Zairean troops killed two Zambians in an ambush near the southwestern border town of Mufulira. Zambia deployed troops in the area, claiming the need to control widespread smuggling and banditry. A number of other border incidents followed.

Later, tensions rose again when Zambia announced it would deport thousands of Zairean nationals in July 1984. Zaire responded by deporting large numbers of Zambians living in Shaba province. Relations between the two countries improved in 1986 following talks between the two presidents, Kenneth Kaunda and Mobutu Sésé Séko, and the dispute lapsed.

For further information and background reading, see reference item numbers 290, 319, 383, 435, 469.

215. UNITED STATES–GRENADA
Anticommunist U.S. military invasion (October–December 1983)

The election of President Ronald Reagan in 1980 led to an intensification of the cold war. The new U.S. administration was particularly sensitive to Soviet forays into the Caribbean. Relations between the United States and the small island nation of Grenada deteriorated in early 1983 owing to Cuban participation in the construction of an airport on the island. The United States saw the airport as a potential military base, and President Reagan referred to it as part of the "Soviet-Cuban militarization of Grenada."

On October 25, 1983, on the heels of a Cuban-backed military coup in which Grenadian prime minister Maurice Bishop and many civilians were killed, the United States invaded the island with substantial forces. The huge U.S. contingent established control over the island within a few days of fighting, although fierce resistance occurred in some isolated areas. A contingent of three hundred soldiers from Jamaica, Barbados, Dominica, Antigua, St. Lucia and St. Vincent, and the Grenadines, also landed on the island at around the same time.

More than 250 people are estimated to have been killed in the invasion, including 42 U.S. soldiers and up to 70 Cubans. The coup leaders were subsequently arrested and imprisoned and the legitimate government restored. International criticism of the action was strong from some quarters. In December 1983 U.S. troops were withdrawn, although Caribbean troops remained for some time after. No peaceful conflict-management attempts were made during the conflict, and life on the island nation soon returned to normal.

For further information and background reading, see reference item numbers 517, 530, 590, 620, 621, 634, 650.

216. INDIA-BANGLADESH
Boundary dispute; border conflict (December 1983–June 1984)

The 1947 partition of the Subcontinent (see conflict 003) had left many borders unclear and thus in dispute. In fact, Indian-Bangladeshi relations had been characterized by border control and demarcation disputes ever since Bangladesh's independence in 1974 (see conflict 132). One such dispute had erupted into armed conflict in 1979 (see conflict 187), and relations between the two states were further strained by Indian support for Bangladeshi rebels in the Chittagong Hill Tracts (see conflict 149).

In December 1983 and January 1984, several people were killed in serious border incidents. The second incident involved an incursion into Bangladeshi territory by Indian security forces. At the same time, India attempted to construct a barbed-wire fence along their mutual border to prevent illegal immigration. This provoked a protest by Bangladesh, and when construction of the fence began in April 1984, a Bangladeshi border guard was killed. There were no attempts at peaceful conflict management throughout the dispute, but it eventually lapsed and normal relations resumed.

For further information and background reading, see reference item numbers 76, 661, 701, 743, 744, 844.

217. ECUADOR-PERU
Regional rivalry, territorial dispute; border conflict (January 1984)

Ecuador and Peru had been rivals since a long-standing border dispute erupt-ed into armed conflict in 1977 (see conflict 171) and 1981 (see conflict 193). The disputed territory in the Loreto region of northern Peru had been in con-tention for more than 150 years. Peru's claim was validated in a 1942 treaty, although Ecuador maintained it had been forced into signing the treaty.

Tensions between the two states were still high in the early 1980s. On January 15, 1984, fighting broke out at a frontier post on the Corrientes River (400 km southeast of Quito); one Ecuadoran soldier was killed. Given the his-tory of armed conflict between the two sides, the incident could easily have escalated into all-out war. As it was, neither side attempted any peaceful con-flict management, and the conflict subsided. Another conflict over the same piece of territory erupted in 1995, with much more serious consequences (see conflict 287).

For further information and background reading, see reference item numbers 46, 76, 255, 552, 633.

218. VIETNAM-CHINA
Regional rivalry; border conflict (January 1984–March 1987)

China and Vietnam had been rivals since Vietnam was reunified at the end of the Vietnam War (see conflict 069). They had fought an extremely bloody war in 1979 (see conflict 182) and in 1983 engaged in more fighting (see conflict 211). Strains increased in late 1983 after Sino-U.S. relations eased and Vietnam launched an offensive in Cambodia against the Chinese-backed Khmer Rouge. China and Vietnam also had a number of disputes over border demarcations.

From January to March 1984 there were many serious border incidents, with shellings and incursions by both sides. This was merely a precursor, how-ever, to a major intensification of the fighting in April. From this time, there were attempts to take high ground, massive shelling attacks, and some serious incursions. Tensions were further heightened in May, when the Chinese began to build up their troop concentrations along the border.

Clashes continued along the border until March 1987, with particularly heavy fighting in October 1986 and January 1987. Although China threatened to mount a serious attack on Vietnam, these threats never materialized. Most of the Chinese offensives coincided with Vietnamese offensives in Cambodia, and China insisted that any peace talks between the two countries could take place only after a Vietnamese withdrawal from Cambodia. Because of this pre-condition, there were never any attempts at peaceful conflict management, despite Vietnamese willingness. There were as many as three thousand fatalities in the conflict, most of them Chinese, and the hostilities tapered off after 1987.

For further information and background reading, see reference item numbers 255, 695, 696, 715, 736, 829, 878.

219. INDIA-PAKISTAN

Territorial dispute; the Siachen Glacier dispute, the India-Pakistan wars (April 1984–September 1985)

India and Pakistan had been adversaries since the 1947 partition of the Subcontinent, which displaced approximately 12 million people and resulted in intercommunal massacres of an estimated 300,000 people (see conflict 003). Disputed boundaries appear to have been the principal reason for the series of armed conflicts that followed (see conflicts 010, 056, 106, 195).

This particular conflict concerned the Siachen Glacier, which is in the Karakorum Range in northern Jammu and Kashmir—in the northernmost reaches of undemarcated territory along the India-Pakistan border. Because it was so inhospitable, the region had been left undemarcated after the 1947 partition as neither side thought it likely to become a matter of contention. Nevertheless, in early 1984 Indian troops occupied the northern end of the glacier and in April opened fire on a Pakistani helicopter. In June the Pakistanis launched an attack in an unsuccessful attempted to dislodge the Indian contingent.

Intermittent fighting followed, with several further Pakistani attempts to dislodge the Indian force. Perhaps as many as one hundred soldiers were killed in the conflict, and the dispute lapsed after September 1985. Although the two states undertook several negotiations, the issue was never resolved and remains in contention. Incidents continued in the area throughout the late 1980s and early 1990s, but in 1986 the locus of conflict between the two states returned to Kashmir (see conflict 231).

For further information and background reading, see reference item numbers 255, 667, 679, 684.

220. BURMA-THAILAND; THE KARENS

Karen separatist insurgency, counterinsurgency raids; border incidents (March 1984)

Burma had been fighting the separatist Karen guerrillas since 1949 (see conflict 018) in what has become the longest-running guerrilla insurgency in the world. Occupying positions on the Thai border, the Karen rebels would attack

Burmese targets and then withdraw across the border into the dense jungle. Relations between Burma and Thailand were quite strained owing to Burmese suspicions that the Thai government was actively aiding the rebels.

In March 1984 Burmese troops crossed the Moei River into Thailand in order to attack Karen rebel positions. Fighting broke out when the Burmese soldiers encountered a unit of Thai border police; two Thai border police were killed. Burmese troops withdrew before Thai reinforcements could arrive and the conflict escalate any further. There were no attempts at peaceful conflict management, and the dispute soon lapsed. More serious conflict had only narrowly been averted.

For further information and background reading, see reference item numbers 688, 706, 777, 843, 845, 860.

221. TURKEY-GREECE
Regional rivalry; naval incidents (March 1984–January 1988)

Turkey and Greece had been rivals in the region for some time, and previous conflict had erupted between the two countries in 1974–1978 over Cyprus (see conflict 143). Relations had been cool since. In March 1984 Greece protested an incident in which Turkish destroyers had fired on a Greek destroyer in the Aegean Sea. Greece placed its forces on alert, withdrew from NATO exercises, and protested U.S. efforts to rearm Turkey.

Tensions remained high throughout 1985 and 1986, with numerous incidents, including airspace violations, territorial waters violations, and an exchange of fire on the Thracian border. Greece announced its intention to rearm in view of the threat posed by Turkey. Threats were exchanged, and a border incident in the Thracian area left two Turkish infantrymen and one Greek soldier dead. The conflict threatened to escalate to all-out war. Relations were normalized in January 1988, however, after mediation by NATO and bilateral negotiations. The underlying rivalry between the two had not been addressed, however, and the basic relationship between the two countries remained sour.

For further information and background reading, see reference item numbers 887, 912, 916, 933, 969, 1009, 1012.

222. GUATEMALA-MEXICO
Regional instability, Guatemalan civil war; border incident (April 1984)

Guatemala's brutal civil war led not only to a huge number of refugees but also to regional tensions as Guatemalan troops pursued rebels from the Guatemalan National Revolutionary Unity (URNG) over national boundaries (see conflicts 037, 207).

In April 1984 an armed Guatemalan group crossed into Mexico and attacked a refugee camp, killing six people. The Mexican government protested and relocated its refugee camps farther away from the border. There were no attempts at peaceful conflict management and the dispute soon lapsed. Although direct fighting between Guatemala and Mexico had been avoided, the incident had given cause for alarm, given the general instability in Central America at the time.

For further information and background reading, see reference item numbers 255, 557, 560, 577, 607, 630.

223. THAILAND-LAOS
Boundary dispute; border war (June 1984–December 1988)

Thailand and Laos had a history of armed conflict going back to 1975, when the Pathet Lao's victory sent a flood of Laotians, most of them from the professional and commercial classes, across the border into Thailand (see conflicts 154, 204). Relations were also complicated by an ill-defined border and the consequent territorial disputes.

Following a number of border incidents earlier in the year, a serious Lao-Thai clash occurred in June 1984 over a proposed road through villages on the Thai border that Laos claimed as its own. Small-scale clashes continued in the area, despite ongoing bilateral negotiations, until 1986, when the fighting increased in intensity. Much more serious fighting broke out in late 1987, and in the early parts of 1988 the conflict threatened to escalate into all-out war, with air attacks and the use of heavy weaponry. However, negotiations in February 1988 led to a cease-fire, and the conflict was over by December. In all, more than seven hundred military personnel died in the fighting, which at its height was very intense.

For further information and background reading, see reference item numbers 663, 714, 728, 757, 778, 854, 865, 869.

224. THE KURDS–TURKEY
Kurdish separatist insurgency (August 1984–)

The Kurds, who inhabit a mountainous plateau region comprising parts of Turkey, Iran, and Iraq, have been struggling for an independent Kurdistan since the end of World War I, when the Treaty of Sèvres granted them autonomous status. The terms of the treaty were never implemented. Iranian Kurdistan had enjoyed a brief period of self-rule in 1945 (see conflict 005), while Iraqi Kurds had been waging an ongoing secessionist war since 1961 (see conflicts 071, 121, 144, 163).

This particular conflict is rooted in Turkey's oppression of its Kurdish population and the eruption of long-simmering nationalist passions. For many years, Turkey suppressed Kurdish language and culture and banned Kurdish organizations. In August 1984 the banned Kurdish Worker's Party (PKK), the Kurds' primary nationalist organization, launched attacks on government and civilian targets. In September Turkish troops pursued PKK rebels into Iraqi territory, provoking a storm of protest from Iraq. The PKK began serious guerrilla war in 1985, and smuggled weapons and fighters into Turkey via Iraq and Syria. It launched attacks from Syria on a number of occasions. Iran also suffered from Turkish troop incursions, and at various times Cyprus and Syria were thought to be aiding the Kurds. The fighting was intense, and by the end of 1988 more than three thousand people had been killed. Many of the casualties were civilians, killed by the PKK for being tacit government supporters, or by government troops for being potential PKK supporters. Brutal reprisals by government troops on civilian Kurds gave the PKK many new supporters.

From March 1990 the Kurdish insurgency in southeastern provinces escalated into a mass nationalist uprising. Thousands of people were killed in the government counterattack. In August 1991 and March 1992, Turkish forces made major incursions into Iraq in pursuit of PKK guerrillas, provoking Iraqi protests. The war escalated even further in 1992. In September, more than two hundred PKK and government soldiers were killed in a twelve-hour battle, while in October and November, a Turkish campaign into northern Iraq led to the threat of Turkey imposing a security zone in the area. Several thousand were reported to have been killed in this operation. Turkish incursions into northern Iraq continued for the next three years. In March 1995 more than 35,000 Turkish troops invaded northern Iraq in a series a search-and-destroy missions, withdrawing in May 1995 only after heavy international criticism.

The PKK also operated in Europe, where many Kurdish refugees had found asylum. Here they attacked Turkish embassies and businesses, often in well-coordinated campaigns across several countries. More than eighteen thousand people have been killed in the conflict, many of them civilians; two thousand Kurdish villages have been razed and hundreds of thousands of Kurds displaced. By the end of 1995 there was no sign that the fighting would abate. Neither side had initiated or accepted any serious attempts at peaceful conflict management, convinced as they were of ultimate victory. The Kurds were not prepared to lay down their arms, nor was the Turkish government prepared to offer autonomy.

For further information and background reading, see reference item numbers 1038, 1078, 1109, 1190, 1214, 1250, 1275, 1300.

225. SOUTH AFRICA–BOTSWANA
African nationalism; anti-ANC raids (October 1984–May 1986)

South Africa's white-minority government was fighting a guerrilla insurgency led by the African National Congress (ANC), whose leader, Nelson Mandela, had been sentenced in 1964 to life in prison. With a goal of establishing a majority-ruled state, the ANC guerrillas were aided by neighboring front-line states—Botswana, Mozambique, Tanzania, and Zambia—which allowed them to operate from their territory in addition to providing refuge for exiled ANC leaders. This made relations between South Africa and its neighbors very tense. South African commandos had already made raids into Lesotho in pursuit of ANC activists in 1982 (see conflict 208). Economic reprisals were also common practice by the South African regime.

This particular conflict began with an incident on the Botswana-Namibian border. The incident caused a rise in tensions, and this was exacerbated by South Africa's allegations that Botswana was being used as an infiltration route into South Africa by ANC fighters. South Africa threatened to invade Botswana if the infiltration was not stopped, and great pressure was put on Botswana to sign a nonaggression and security pact with South Africa, similar to the Nkomati accord signed with Mozambique (see conflict 160).

On June 14, 1985, seventy South African commando troops raided targets in Gaborone, killing twelve people in a firefight. Targeting ANC centers of activity, the raid was widely condemned by the international community as an act of aggression. Another such raid on Gaborone in May 1986 killed one more. Apart from unsuccessful negotiations in December 1984, February 1985, and September 1985, no other conflict-management efforts were undertaken, and the fighting eventually lapsed. A similar conflict involving a South African raid on ANC bases in Zambia occurred in 1987 (see conflict 240).

For further information and background reading, see reference item numbers 255, 290, 312, 313, 371, 384.

226. ZAIRE
Internal dissent; the third invasion of Shaba (November 1984)

The corrupt and authoritarian regime of President Mobutu Sésé Séko, in power since a 1965 military coup, had aroused both the dissent of Zaireans and the resentment of neighboring countries. Dissatisfaction with the Mobutu regime was most effectively expressed with invasions of Shaba, the mineral-rich southern province that accounted for two-thirds of Zaire's foreign earnings. The Mobutu regime prospered on graft skimmed off mining profits.

In the most serious disturbances in the province since the 1977 and 1978 invasions, rebels launched an invasion from Tanzanian territory and captured the town of Moba, 380 miles northeast of Lubumbashi, on November 13, 1984. The government counterattacked on November 13, and by November 15 the town was recaptured. At least 125 people were killed during the fighting. There were no attempts at managing the conflict peacefully, and another invasion was attempted in June 1985 (see conflict 229).

For further information and background reading, see reference item numbers 255, 305, 306, 349, 387.

227. NORTH KOREA–SOUTH KOREA
Cold war border incidents (November 1984)

Following World War II two separate regimes were established on the Korean peninsula: the communist Democratic People's Republic in the north, and the Republic of Korea in the south. Since the Korean War in 1950–1953 (see conflict 024), North and South Korean troops had faced each other along the 38th parallel in an intensely hostile standoff that had given rise to a number of armed conflicts from 1965 to 1968 (see conflict 105) and 1975 (see conflict 150).

This particular incident threatened to destroy a gradual improvement in relations. On November 23, 1984, shooting broke out between North and South Korean units when a Soviet citizen crossed the border at Panmunjom in an attempt to defect; three North Korean soldiers and one South Korean were killed in the fighting. The potential for serious escalation was always present in conflicts between these two states. No attempts were made to settle the conflict peacefully, and fighting broke out again in 1992 (see conflict 270).

For further information and background reading, see reference item numbers 255, 672, 675, 720, 804, 816, 848.

228. NICARAGUA–COSTA RICA
Regional rivalry; border incidents (May–June 1985)

Nicaragua and Costa Rica had been rivals since 1948, when Nicaragua intervened in the Costa Rican civil war (see conflict 011). Since then they had engaged in four militarized conflicts (see conflicts 017, 039, 174, 178). Tensions were high in 1985 as the war between Nicaragua's left-wing Sandinista government and the U.S.-backed right-wing contra rebels spread to surrounding states (see conflict 190).

The immediate context of this conflict was a diplomatic dispute concerning a Nicaraguan student who had taken refuge in the Costa Rican embassy in Managua but who had then been arrested. Relations between the two countries were then seriously strained following a number of border incidents and violations of airspace, including the killing of two Costa Rican civil guards on May 31, 1985, for which Nicaragua took responsibility. Following hostile diplomatic moves, the conflict was partially resolved after mediation by the Contadora Group (the foreign ministers of Colombia, Mexico, Panama, and Venezuela) on February 24, 1986. Costa Rica rejected the suggestion of the creation of a demilitarized zone between the two countries, though, and fighting broke out again in 1986 (see conflict 235).

For further information and background reading, see reference item numbers 255, 510, 511, 522, 523, 526, 546.

229. ZAIRE
Internal strife; the fourth invasion of Shaba (June 1985)

Zaire, the third-largest country in Africa, had been wracked by civil unrest since its independence from Belgium in 1960 (see conflict 067). The Mobutu regime, brought to power through a 1965 military coup, had spawned dissident movements, incessant rebellions, invasions, mercenary revolts, and trouble in most of the nine bordering nations (see conflicts 103, 119, 157, 169, 177, 200, and 226). Most of the invasions involved the cobalt- and copper-rich Shaba province.

In this particular conflict, a dissident group of exiles launched an attack on the town of Moba in Shaba on June 16–17, 1985, the second such attack in less than a year (see conflict 226). Invading from Tanzanian territory, the rebels were routed after five hours of fighting. Approximately fifty people were killed during the conflict, which was not considered as serious as the previous invasion. There were no attempts at peaceful conflict management during the conflict, and opposition to the government and civil unrest continued to plague the area. Relations with Tanzania were not greatly affected, but underlying tensions remained. Civil unrest in Zaire itself continued into the 1990s. In 1996 a rebel alliance led by Laurent Kabila began attacking government forces with the backing of Rwanda. Within a few months Mobutu's regime collapsed entirely, and Kabila took control of the country, now called the Democratic Republic of the Congo.

For further information and background reading, see reference item numbers 255, 305, 306, 349, 387.

230. MALI–BURKINA FASO

Territorial/resource dispute; border war
(December 1985–January 1986)

Mali and Burkina Faso both claimed a border area that contained a chain of pools through which flowed the Belí River, the only source of fresh water in the region. Mali claimed it was geographically and ethnically part of Mali, while Burkina Faso claimed the French colonial authorities had included it in Burkinabe territory. The dispute had already led to fighting in 1974 (see conflict 147).

Several months before this conflict erupted, Burkina had expelled Drissa Keita, the Malian secretary-general of the francophone West African Economic Community (CEAO). Burkina's attempts to carry out a census led to an outbreak of fighting on December 25, 1985, in the disputed Agacher border area. The fighting escalated quickly to all-out war. Air attacks and ground battles spread, and the fighting continued for five days. A cease-fire was arranged by members of the Non-Aggression and Defense Aid Agreement (ANAD) on December 31, 1985, and troops were withdrawn.

Further mediation was undertaken by ANAD in January 1986. The dispute was submitted to the International Court of Justice (ICJ) border commission in January 1986. The ICJ produced a settlement ending the conflict on January 18, 1986. As many as four hundred people were killed during the four days of fighting, many of them civilians.

For further information and background reading, see reference item numbers 76, 310, 354, 442, 469.

231. INDIA-PAKISTAN

Territorial dispute; the Siachen Glacier/Kashmir conflict, the India-Pakistan wars (1986–)

India and Pakistan's rivalry extended back to the 1947 partition of the Subcontinent (see conflict 003), which had left the borders between the two states ill-defined and thus open to dispute. The conflict over Kashmir and

Jammu began in 1947 (see conflict 010), and the two states had gone to war since then on a number of occasions. This conflict was preceded by fighting in the Siachen Glacier region in 1984–1985 (see conflict 219), Indian allegations of Pakistan involvement in Sikh extremist violence, and a number of border incidents. Tensions were high at the end of 1985.

Although there were clashes in several different border areas, the main fighting was concentrated in the disputed Siachen Glacier, which is in the northernmost reaches of undemarcated territory along the India-Pakistan border—the Karakorum Range in northern Jammu and Kashmir. Both sides began massing troops on their borders in December 1986, and particularly violent clashes occurred in September 1987 and May 1989. Further tensions between the two countries were heightened by massive unrest in Kashmir in January 1990 and the outbreak of a serious Muslim separatist insurgency. The unrest caused both sides to mobilize for war, and there were suspicions that both India and Pakistan were preparing nuclear devices. Forceful intervention by the United States, including threats, caused both sides to pull back, and a major war was narrowly averted.

Incidents and intermittent fighting continued into the 1990s, especially in the Siachen border areas and in Kashmir and Jammu. The fighting in Kashmir claimed as many as twenty thousand lives between 1989 and 1995 and was highlighted in the international media in 1994 when several Western hostages were taken by separatist rebels. Although India and Pakistan engaged in periodic negotiations, the issues in conflict remain unresolved.

For further information and background reading, see reference item numbers 255, 667, 679, 684, 765.

232. UNITED STATES–LIBYA
International terrorism fears; naval incidents (January–April 1986)

Relations between Libya and the United States were tense in the months leading up to January 1986. The Reagan administration was concerned about Libyan support for international terrorism and determined to curtail these activities by any means. Libya, meanwhile, engaged in inflammatory statements accusing the United States of terrorism and destabilization. Reports in November 1985 claimed that President Ronald Reagan had authorized a covert operation by the Central Intelligence Agency (CIA) against Col. Muammar Qaddafi's regime.

On December 27, 1985, gunmen attacked the Rome and Vienna international airports, killing twenty people. The United States blamed the Abu Nidal Palestinian group and Libyan government support for the attacks. In January 1986, as a direct result of these attacks, the United States sent naval forces to positions off the Libyan coast to perform maneuvers. At the same time, it imposed a set of economic sanctions on Libya. In response, Qaddafi placed Libyan forces on full alert.

U.S. naval maneuvers to the north of the Gulf of Sirte (or Sidra) in January 1986 produced several confrontations with Libyan forces, although no shots were fired until March 24, when both sides attacked each other's ships, planes, and shore batteries. Between 50 and 100 people were killed in the fighting. Following bomb explosions on April 2 on a TWA aircraft and in a West Berlin nightclub on April 5, speculation rose about a possible U.S. attack on Libya. On April 15, U.S. aircraft mounted air strikes on Tripoli and Benghazi that killed nearly 150 people. Libya responded with a botched attack on a U.S. Coast Guard station on the Italian island of Lampedusa in the southern Mediterranean, and revenge attacks on U.S. and British targets worldwide. International responses were mixed, with a hostile reaction from the Arab world. Neither side attempted to settle the conflict using peaceful methods, but over the next two years strains eased somewhat. The basic issues remained unresolved, however, and another serious armed confrontation occurred in 1989 (see conflict 248).

For further information and background reading, see reference item numbers 1097, 1141, 1220, 1305, 1307, 1315.

233. INDIA-BANGLADESH
Boundary dispute; the Muhuri River incidents
(February–April 1986)

Relations between India and its neighbors had been strained ever since the 1947 partition of the Subcontinent (see conflict 003). Ill-defined borders between India and Bangladesh had been a constant source of friction, and armed conflict had broken out in 1976 (see conflict 162), 1979 (see conflict 187), and 1983 (see conflict 216). Both sides accused each other of harboring rebels. In March and April 1986 a number of skirmishes erupted along the India-Bangladesh border, especially in the disputed Muhuri River area.

Following a two-day meeting to discuss border issues between Indian and Bangladeshi officials, Indian border personnel fired across the Muhuri River on April 9, killing two members of the Bangladesh Rifles. On April 22 forces stationed on both sides of the river withdrew to a "second line of defense," thereby vacating forward offensive positions. No other conflict-management attempts were made, and the dispute eventually lapsed, although border tensions remained.

For further information and background reading, see reference item numbers 76, 661, 701, 743, 744, 844.

234. QATAR-BAHRAIN
Sovereignty dispute; the Hawar Islands (April 1986)

The Hawar Islands are situated only 2.4 km off the coast of Qatar but are owned by Bahrain. Both countries had claimed them, however, and the disagreement had escalated into conflict on a number of occasions when Bahrain attempted to search for oil on the islands. Mediation by Saudi Arabia in the 1970s failed to find a solution.

The conflict escalated seriously in late 1985 when Bahrain began to erect military and coastguard installations on the islands and its accompanying reefs. On April 26, 1986, Qatari troops invaded the island of Fash al-Dibal and occupied it in an attempt to stop the work. After mediation by Omani, United Arab Emirates, and Saudi leaders on April 27, an agreement was reached providing for the withdrawal of Qatar's troops and the destruction of the installations. The agreement did not, however, deal with all the outstanding issues involved in the dispute. Negotiations were also held in August, and a further mediation attempt was made in October by Prince Sultan ibn Abdul Aziz, the Saudi defense minister, without success. Although there were no fatalities, the two states had come very close to all-out war.

For further information and background reading, see reference item numbers 76, 1022, 1023, 1094, 1142.

235. NICARAGUA–COSTA RICA
Regional rivalry; border incidents (April 1986)

Nicaragua and Costa Rica had been rivals for decades, starting a clash in 1948 (see conflicts 011, 017), 1955 (see conflict 039), 1977 (see conflict 174), 1978 (see conflict 178), and 1985 (see conflict 228). In recent years Costa Rica had allowed Nicaraguan right-wing contra rebels to operate from its territory. The contras were fighting a guerrilla insurgency with U.S. support against the Sandinista government in Nicaragua (see conflict 190).

Despite some recent improvement in relations, a Nicaraguan incursion into Costa Rican territory at the border post of Los Chiles on April 16, 1986, resulted in armed clashes between the two countries. The incident was not considered as serious as the previous conflict in May 1985, but the history of hostility between the two states made the potential for escalation very high. Neither side attempted to settle the conflict peacefully, and it subsided in the following months. In the 1990s the contra war ended, and relations improved between Nicaragua and Costa Rica.

For further information and background reading, see reference item numbers 255, 510, 511, 522, 523, 526, 546.

236. SURINAME
Guerrilla insurgency (July 1986–December 1992)

Suriname, on the northeastern coast of South America, gained its independence from the Netherlands in 1975 and since that time had been subject to civil unrest and a number of coups. The initial cause of this particular conflict was opposition to government plans to move thousands of so-called *boschnegers* out of the rainforests and into towns.[3] The *boschnegers* violently resisted government moves, and the rebellion soon took on a general opposition to Suriname's military regime. In July 1986 the *boschneger*-based Surinamese Liberation Army (SLA), led by Ronnie Brunswijk, attacked military bases in eastern Suriname and launched a guerrilla war. Initial army desertions to the rebels led to early successes, but army counterattacks led to fluctuating fortunes for the rebels from July 1986 to 1992.

From the beginning of the conflict, the SLA received massive financial and logistical support from the Amsterdam-based Movement for the Liberation of Suriname, who paid for British mercenaries to fight with the rebels. Beginning in December 1986 it became obvious that French Guyana was also aiding the rebels, allowing them to operate from French Guyanan territory. In July 1987 the conflict escalated when the French sent troop reinforcements to the border areas, warning Suriname not to pursue rebels into French territory.

In 1987 former president Hendrick R. Chin A Sen joined the SLA, and in April of that year the SLA declared a rival government administration in the territory they held. The army fueled the conflict by committing massive human rights violations. A peace accord with the SLA in August 1989 led to the outbreak of another insurgency in western Suriname among the Tucayana tribe. The Tucayana Amazonicas rebel group, led by Thomas Sabajo, was opposed to the peace accord. The fighting continued until May 1992, when both sides suspended their rebel activities. A peace agreement was signed in July 1992, but by the end of the year it had not been fully implemented, primarily because the rebels were refusing to disarm. The fighting ceased by December 1992, however, and the peace process moved forward from then on.

The few attempts at peaceful conflict management failed to resolve any of the underlying issues. Several hundred people were killed during the fighting. Although the insurgency was over by December 1992, civil unrest and instability continued to plague the country.

For further information and background reading, see reference item numbers 107, 255, 579.

---

[3] The *boschnegers*, or bush Negroes, are the descendants of escaped slaves who, since the 1760 treaties signed with the Dutch colonial authorities, have lived an autonomous existence in the rain forests and developed a unique tribal society with its own language, rituals, and political structure. With a population of 50,000, they make up 15 percent of the total population of Suriname.

237. TOGO-GHANA
Regional rivalry; attempted coup (September 1986)

Togo and Ghana had been rivals ever since the division of Togoland prior to its independence. Ghana absorbed the western part of the country (British Togoland), and the eastern half (French Togoland) became independent Togo. The partition split Ewe tribal lands between the two countries, giving rise to an ongoing and destabilizing unification campaign. Ghanaian leaders had for decades laid claim to Togo in an effort to reunite the two countries, and these efforts led to constant friction. Ghana attempted to undermine Togo, and armed conflict had broken out in 1965 (see conflict 102) and 1982 (see conflict 206). Tensions simmered in the months preceding this conflict, and Togo accused Ghana of harboring subversives.

On September 23, 1986, an armed commando unit of about sixty soldiers entered Togo from neighboring Ghana with the aim of overthrowing the regime of President Gnassingbé Eyadéma. By September 28 the commandos had been defeated, but only after France sent 150 paratroopers backed by a minesweeper and a Jaguar jet fighter, plus 350 Zairean troops. The borders with Ghana and Burkina Faso were closed. Togo claimed the attack was launched from Ghana, that Ghana had trained the insurgents, and that both Ghana and Burkina had massed troops on the Togo border in preparation for supporting the coup. Ghana and Burkina denied the allegations.

Up to thirty people are thought to have been killed in the conflict, and minor border incidents with Ghana continued for some time. On November 26, 1986, Ide Oumarou, secretary-general of the Organization of African Unity (OAU), attempted unsuccessfully to mediate the conflict, and President Félix Houphouët-Boigny of Ivory Coast attempted mediation in early January 1987. Although the conflict eased for some years, fighting broke out again in 1994 (see conflict 280).

For further information and background reading, see reference item numbers 255, 297, 313.

238. ZAIRE–PEOPLE'S REPUBLIC OF THE CONGO
Regional instability; border incident (January 1987)

Zaire (now called Congo, or the Democratic Republic of the Congo) and People's Republic of the Congo (formerly Middle Congo) had both attained independence in 1960 and since that time had been plagued by civil conflict and internal instability. Zaire in particular had been involved in numerous armed conflicts with its neighbors in recent years (see conflicts 200, 214, 226, 229). Only four months after the two countries agreed on measures to promote peace in the region, a conflict over security and territorial sovereignty erupted in mid-January 1987.

Fighting between the two countries broke out in the Mindouli region of the Congo, southwest of Brazzaville, when Zairean troops crossed the Zaire-Congo border and entered the village of Ngombe. At least three people were killed in the clash. No attempts were made to settle the dispute peacefully, and relations had normalized within a few months. Given the ongoing instability in the region, the conflict had the potential to escalate seriously.

For further information and background reading, see reference item numbers 286, 287, 365.

239. ETHIOPIA-SOMALIA
Somali expansionism; the third Ogaden war
(February 1987–April 1988)

When Somalia became independent from Britain in 1960, the new government began to claim the existence of a "Greater Somalia" owing to the presence of some 350,000 Somali tribes people in surrounding states. Such expansionist statements had already brought Somalia into armed conflict with Kenya from 1962 to 1967 (see conflict 085). Somalia's strongest claim, however, was to the vast Ogaden region of eastern Ethiopia inhabited primarily by Somalis (see map 10). Earlier Somali efforts to take the region had led to war with Ethiopia in 1964 (see conflict 090) and again from 1972 to 1985 (see conflict 139). Somalia continued to foment separatist passions among Ogaden tribesmen, arming and supplying them to attack Ethiopian targets.

Despite ongoing negotiations over the issue, tensions remained high, and the situation deteriorated in early 1987. On February 12, Ethiopian troops launched an air and ground attack on Somali positions. Intense fighting result-ed in heavy casualties, and there were reports of both sides building earthen ramparts on either side of the border, apparently in preparation for further offensives. Somali National Movement (SNM) rebels, who were opposed to the Somali government, operated jointly with the Ethiopian forces. The conflict lost some of its intensity, and only minor incidents occurred from this time until April 1988, when, as a result of numerous negotiations between President Mengistu Haile Mariam of Ethiopia and Gen. Muhammad Siad Barre of Somalia, a settlement was reached and both sides withdrew. More than three hundred people are thought to have been killed during the fighting.

For further information and background reading, see reference item numbers 255, 341, 352, 356, 363, 396, 421.

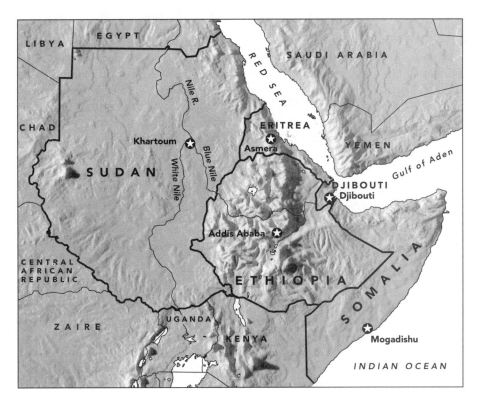

MAP 10. **Horn of Africa**

Somalia's desire to unite all Somali tribes under a single state has been a source of tension in East Africa since 1960, the year Somalia gained its independence. Its territorial claims fueled conflicts with Kenya and Ethiopia, both of which are inhabited by large Somali populations. The region was further destabilized by Eritrea's war of secession against Ethiopia (see conflicts 019 and 099).

240. SOUTH AFRICA–ZAMBIA
African nationalism, insurgency fears; anti-ANC raid (April 1987)

The white minority government in South Africa tried hard to protect its borders from attacks by African National Congress (ANC) guerrillas who were fighting for a majority-ruled South Africa. The front-line states—Angola, Botswana, Lesotho, Malawi, Mozambique, Swaziland, Tanzania, and Zambia—provided the ANC with military training and bases from which to operate. South African forces had already made raids into Lesotho in 1982 (see conflict 208) and Botswana in 1984–1986 (see conflict 225) to attack ANC bases and safehouses.

On April 25, 1987, a South African commando raid on Livingstone in southern Zambia, launched from northern Namibia, resulted in five fatalities.

South Africa claimed that the dead were all ANC "terrorists," while Zambia claimed they were Zambian citizens. The South African government's motive for the raid was thought to be an attempt to win right-wing votes in the forthcoming whites-only elections, although the South African Defence Forces (SADF) claimed it was only an "armed reconnaissance" mission. Neither side attempted to resolve their differences peacefully, and the conflict gradually lapsed. Reforms in South Africa eventually led to the release of Nelson Mandela, the legalization of the ANC, a new constitution, and a majority-elected ANC government.

For further information and background reading, see reference item numbers 255, 290, 312, 317, 371, 384.

241. PEOPLE'S REPUBLIC OF THE CONGO
Civil unrest; army rebellion (September 1987–July 1988)

People's Republic of the Congo gained independence from France in 1960, and its postindependence history is a litany of coups and civil unrest. The army was the source of much instability. In early September 1987 fighting broke out in the northern region of Curette between government troops and supporters of a former army officer, Capt. Pierre Anga, who had escaped to the region and taken up arms after refusing to be questioned as part of an inquiry into an antigovernment plot.

French army forces based in Gabon were sent to maintain order in the region after government troops failed to quell the uprising. Former military leader Joachim Yhombi-Opango, a close friend of Captain Anga, was arrested and brought to Brazzaville, the capital of the Congo, on September 8, 1987, in a government bid to suppress the rebellion. Intermittent clashes continued for several months, as Anga eluded capture.

No attempts at peaceful conflict management were made, and it was estimated that fifty lives were lost during the fighting. The rebellion ended on July 4, 1988, when Anga was killed during a clash with an army detachment near his hometown of Owando. His supporters fled or surrendered, and the French troops were withdrawn.

For further information and background reading, see reference item numbers 286, 287, 293, 316, 365, 456.

242. UGANDA-KENYA
Ugandan civil war, refugee influx; border conflict (December 1987)

Strains on the Kenya-Uganda border were heightened by the arrival of refugees fleeing the civil war in Uganda (see conflict 198). Both sides accused each other of harboring rebels and trying to undermine each other's regime. Alarmed by the large numbers of Ugandan troops stationed close to the Kenyan border in November 1987, the Kenyan government threatened to retaliate if Ugandan troops attempted to pursue rebels into its territory.

After numerous incidents in early December, a serious outbreak of fighting near the border at Busia in Kenya on December 14–16 left at least fifteen dead. Libyans were also thought to have been involved on the Ugandan side. The OAU president, Zambian president Kenneth Kaunda, offered to mediate the dispute, but his offer was rejected. Negotiations between President Daniel arap Moi of Kenya and President Yoweri Museveni of Uganda on December 28, 1987, led to an easing of tensions. Mutual suspicion remained, however, and another armed conflict broke out in 1989 (see conflict 249).

For further information and background reading, see reference item numbers 296, 376, 410, 453.

243. VIETNAM-CHINA
Regional rivalry, sovereignty dispute; the Spratlys dispute (March 1988)

China and Vietnam had been rivals in the region since the Vietnam War, when North Vietnam was closely allied with the Soviet Union. They fought a very bloody war in 1979 (see conflict 182) and had disputed the ownership of the Paracel and Spratly island chains for decades (see conflicts 045, 142). Both sides maintained that extensive oil reserves existed in the area, although this claim has never been proven. The real issue relates to their rivalry, and the dispute had simmered since the Vietnamese occupied the islands in 1975.

In early 1988 a Chinese military force went ashore on the Spratlys, and not long afterward, Chinese naval vessels sank a Vietnamese gunboat, killing more than seventy soldiers. Vietnam responded by sending naval reinforcements to the area, and the situation remained tense. Eventually, Vietnam withdrew unilaterally and the conflict lapsed. The islands remain in dispute, however, and some minor attempts at conflict management have failed to make any progress. China's aggressive actions caused a great deal of concern to other states in the region who feared China's expansionist designs. There were further armed conflicts over the islands in 1995 between China and the Philippines (see conflict 288) and Taiwan and Vietnam (see conflict 289).

For further information and background reading, see reference item numbers 695, 696, 715, 736, 829, 870, 878.

244. SOMALIA
Clan-based violence; the Somalian civil war (May 1988–)

Somalia, which gained its independence in 1960, is composed of many tribal clans and factions. In 1977 the socialist state broke its ties with the USSR over the issue of Soviet aid to Ethiopia, expelling more than six thousand Soviet advisers. Following the Soviet withdrawal, the loose alliance that constituted the government began to unravel. In May 1988 the Somali National Movement (SNM)—based in the northern, Issa-dominated region—launched a rebellion against Gen. Muhammad Siad Barre's despotic regime. The attack came after an Ethiopian-Somali agreement isolated the SNM, previously supported by Ethiopia. The SNM quickly took control of several important towns. A counterattack by the army took back the towns, but the rebels continued to control most of the countryside, engaging in guerrilla activities throughout 1988 and the first part of 1989. The initial fighting was intense, killing approximately fifty thousand people—many of these in army reprisals.

Throughout 1989 the Somali army was beset with mutinies, and antigovernment disturbances in the capital, Mogadishu, in July led to four hundred deaths. The SNM made significant gains in December 1989, although the army continued its violent repression. In August 1990 the SNM joined a number of other guerrilla groups, and by the end of 1990 they controlled most of the countryside; the government controlled only Mogadishu and its immediate surroundings. In December 1990 the United Somali Congress (USC), which was based in central Somalia and dominated by the Hawiye clan, also launched an assault on the Barre regime. By the end of January 1991 Barre had fled, Mogadishu had fallen, and the USC had installed an interim government. In the north, the SNM had taken the regional capital.

The USC immediately began fighting other southern, clan-based groups as well as Barre supporters, while the SNM in the north set up a rival administration in April 1991 and seceded in May. Calling itself Somaliland, the new entity essentially partitioned the country, but received no international recognition. In Mogadishu thousands were killed in September and November 1991 because of clan-based fighting within the United Somali Congress between President Ali Mohammed and Gen. Mohammed Farah Aidid. The fighting continued through 1992 and, combined with the general state of anarchy, led to the threat of mass starvation. Food and aid were being looted by armed gangs, and by August 1992 two thousand people were reported dying each day of starvation while hundreds were being killed in factional fighting.

The state of the country and the failure of numerous peace initiatives to resolve the conflict led to U.N. military intervention beginning in July 1992.

This culminated in a full-scale U.S.-led invasion in December 1992 by 28,000 U.S. troops; the objective was to restore law and order and protect aid convoys and food distribution. But unclear U.S. objectives, the reluctance of Somali clan leaders to negotiate, and intractable clan-based fighting meant that after nearly two years, anarchy still reigned in Somalia and no end to the fighting could be seen. Rising U.N. fatalities, especially among the U.S. forces, and the failure of U.N. mediation eventually saw the complete failure of the mission in late 1994, and the United Nations was forced to withdraw. The last U.N. forces withdrew in March 1995, and the country returned to full-scale clan-based fighting led by Gen. Mohammed Said Hirsi (a son-in-law of the former dictator, Barre) and Mohammed Haji Aden. Aidid was killed in 1996. Deaths from the civil war and resulting famine were in the hundreds of thousands.

For further information and background reading, see reference item numbers 255, 341, 356, 363, 396, 421.

245. BURUNDI
Tribal-based communal violence; the Hutu conflict (August 1988–)

Although the immediate causes of this conflict remain unclear, it is rooted in Burundian society and history. The Tutsi tribe in Burundi makes up only 15 percent of the population, yet Tutsis dominate the country's political, economic, and social institutions. This dominance was the result of deliberate colonial policies and led to a bitter history of ethnic rivalry. Previous conflict between the Tutsi and the majority Hutu in 1972 had caused more than 100,000 deaths, while in 1964 it had involved neighboring Rwanda in war (see conflict 092).

In August 1988 Hutu began attacking local Tutsi people in the northern districts, killing some two thousand people. The Tutsi-dominated army was sent in, and in a series of reprisal attacks, the army killed another three thousand, mainly Hutu villagers. More than fifty thousand Hutus then took refuge in southern Rwanda. It was suggested that the initial attacks were made from Rwandan territory. Although the government took a number of measures to defuse the situation and heal the rift between the two communities, these were unsuccessful. A number of killings and police operations continued throughout 1991, until another major rebellion took place between November and December 1991. Between five hundred and three thousand people are thought to have been killed in this instance.

In another coup attempt and period of turmoil in 1992–1993, about 100,000 people (most of them civilians and refugees) were killed in fighting between the Tutsi-dominated military and Hutu rebels. Throughout 1994 there was great strife, and the international community feared bloodletting on the scale of Rwanda (see conflict 263). To prevent this, the Organization of African

Unity (OAU) proposed sending in a peace-keeping force. No attempts at peaceful conflict management were ever undertaken owing largely to the ethnic-based nature of the fighting. The Hutu majority had few recognized leaders with whom the government could negotiate. In 1995 the ethnic violence claimed between ten thousand and fifteen thousand lives and created large numbers of refugees in the region. The United Nations stepped up efforts to reconcile the two communities, and the OAU threatened to intervene militarily. A proposal to create two separate, ethnically based states—effectively a Hutuland and a Tutsiland—was rejected by all sides, and the conflict remains unresolved.

For *further information and background reading, see reference item numbers 255, 397, 407, 440.*

246. BOUGAINVILLE–PAPUA NEW GUINEA
Separatist insurgency (October 1988–)

An island nation in the South Pacific, Papua New Guinea (PNG) comprises the eastern half of the mountainous island of New Guinea, in addition to the Bismarck archipelago, which includes New Britain and New Ireland; Bougainville and Buka, which form part of the West Solomon Islands; and other islands. Papua New Guinea gained its independence from Australia in 1975 and is sometimes described as "a mountain of gold floating in a sea of oil" because of its abundant natural resources.

This particular conflict flared after years of anger over the seizure of a Bougainville copper mine by an Australian firm. The Panguna mine, one of the world's largest copper mines, had accounted for about a third of PNG's income. But the Bougainville landowners had not been compensated by the Australian owners. Led by Francis Ona, a former mine employee, the landowners formed an insurgency and embarked on a sabotage campaign that led to several deaths and the deployment of the PNG army to quell the disturbances.

In May 1989 sabotage and violence closed the mine, and in July the government declared a state of emergency on Bougainville and withdrew government services. The government's brutal campaign to put down the rebellion actually redounded to the rebels' advantage. They called themselves the Bougainville Revolutionary Army (BRA), and the rebellion took on greater secessionist overtones. After failing to stop the rebellion, government forces withdrew from the island in March 1990 as a prelude to peace talks. In May 1990 the BRA declared independence for Bougainville; the PNG government responded with a total blockade of the island. No other states recognized Bougainville's independence. Although a number of agreements were signed between the protagonists, they inevitably broke down over the issue of independence. Government troops returned to the island in September 1990, April

1991, and May 1992. In October 1992 PNG forces launched a major offensive and began to make large gains on the island.

Although it refused to send troops, Australia provided helicopters and matériel to the PNG government starting in 1990. In late 1991 it became clear that the rebels were using the Solomon Islands not only as a base but also as a source of aid. This led to PNG raids on Solomon territory in March and September 1992. The Solomons responded by protesting and deploying troops in the region. The conflict continued in a similar manner throughout 1993 and 1994.

By the end of 1995, several hundred people had been killed as a direct result of the fighting, while up to three thousand had died as a consequence of the economic and medical blockade of the island. The terrain and the indigenous roots of the rebellion prevented both sides from gaining any significant advantage. A number of face-to-face peace talks in late 1994 and early 1995 led to some optimism about a peaceful resolution of the conflict, but the issue of Bougainville independence proved to be the main stumbling block. A surge in rebel activities in late 1995 led to the abandonment of the Bougainville peace negotiations and a new round of hostilities.

For further information and background reading, see reference item numbers 27, 36, 63, 107.

247. MALDIVES
Attempted coup; invasion (November 1988)

The Maldives, a small group of islands off the southwest coast of Sri Lanka, gained independence from Britain in 1965. For most of the period following independence, it led a peaceful existence. On November 3, 1988, some 150 Maldivian insurgents attacked the presidential palace and other government buildings in Male, the Maldives' capital, in an attempted coup. The attackers had arrived by boat from Sri Lanka and were headed by dissident Sri Lankan–based Maldivians led by Abdullah Luthufi and Sagar Ahmed Nasir. The remainder were Sri Lankan Tamil separatists recruited as mercenaries. About twenty people were killed in the fighting, which was fairly intense while the coup attempt was in progress.

The coup attempt was put down without further bloodshed by November 4 by a force of some 300 Indian paratroopers invited in by the Maldivian government. By November 8, 160 people had been rounded up and arrested in connection with the coup attempt. Many received severe prison terms. The Indian paratroopers returned home a year later. No peaceful conflict-management attempts were made by either party during the conflict.

For further information and background reading, see reference item numbers 671, 682, 783, 808.

248. UNITED STATES–LIBYA
Rabat chemical plant tensions; air incident (January 1989)

This conflict was the most serious confrontation between the United States and
Libya since the 1986 Tripoli bombings (see conflict 232). Libya was accused of
supporting worldwide terrorism, and the United States was actively seeking to
confront and destabilize the regime. This confrontation was the culmination of
tensions over the construction of a suspected Libyan chemical weapons plant
at Rabat, 60 km south of Tripoli. The United States again conducted naval
maneuvers in the area, provoking confrontations with Libyan forces.

On January 4, 1989, two U.S. planes shot down two Libyan jets over the
Mediterranean, and tensions rose dramatically. Although the dispute was
referred to the U.N. Security Council on January 6–11, 1989, nothing was
achieved, and the conflict gradually faded after that. Eventually, U.S. concerns
moved elsewhere, most notably to Saudi Arabia following Iraq's invasion of
Kuwait.

*For further information and background reading, see reference item numbers
1097, 1141, 1220, 1305, 1307, 1315.*

249. UGANDA-KENYA
Political turmoil, border conflict (March 1989)

Uganda's persistent civil war (see conflict 198) had led to strained border relations with Kenya, which played host to a steady flow of war-weary Ugandan
refugees. The situation had already led to military conflict fourteen months earlier (see conflict 242), and each side regularly accused the other of harboring
rebels.

But relations deteriorated still further when four hundred heavily armed
men in military uniform were reported to have invaded Kenya's West Pokot
area on March 2, 1989. Serious fighting ensued and more than seventy people
were killed in the battle. Kenya protested vigorously, but Uganda blamed
Karamojong cattle rustlers. On March 7 the Kenyan border town of
Lokichokio was bombed and five people killed. Kenya again blamed Uganda
and its collaborators, Sudan and Libya, for the attack and claimed Uganda was
massing troops in the region. As it was, relations eased in the following months
even though no attempts were made to resolve the conflict peacefully.

*For further information and background reading, see reference item numbers
296, 376, 410, 453.*

250. GEORGIA–SOUTH OSSETIA, ABKHAZIA
Post-Soviet political instability; separatist warfare (March 1989–)

In March 1989 thousands of ethnic Abkhazians began demonstrating for secession from Georgia, then part of the disintegrating Union of Soviet Socialist Republics. They further demanded Abkhazia's reinstatement as a full union republic, a status it had briefly held in the 1920s, before the Russian civil war. Abkhazia's ethnic Georgian population staged a counter-rally, however, which led to intercommunal clashes and further demonstrations. The leadership of Georgia declared Abkhazian separatist demands unconstitutional. Meanwhile, Georgian nationalists themselves were leading a massive campaign for Georgian independence, resulting in brutal repression by Soviet troops in the capital, Tbilisi. In July 1989 serious ethnic-based violence broke out in Abkhazia, which is in northwestern Georgia. Fighting among armed gangs caused dozens of deaths, and Russian interior ministry troops were brought in to restore order.

In October 1989 South Ossetia, with close ethnic ties to Russia, began to make similar secessionist demands. Separatists set up the Popular Front of South Ossetia, and police reinforcements were drafted to deal with the resulting demonstrations. Violence broke out in November when thousands of ethnic Georgians arrived in South Ossetia to protest the Ossetians' autonomy demands. At the same time, Georgia made further moves toward full independence from the old Soviet Union. South Ossetia declared itself a fully independent republic in September 1990, a move repudiated by Georgia. The violence intensified in December 1990 and January 1991, and a state of emergency was declared, followed by an economic blockade of the region by Georgian militants. By March 1991 Georgia was entrenched in a state of virtual war, and Georgia and Russia agreed to cooperate in an attempt to restore order.

Meanwhile, four months of violent confrontation in Tbilisi escalated into full-scale armed conflict in December 1991. President Zviad Gamsakhurdia fled and a military government was formed. In March 1992 Eduard Shevardnadze, the former Soviet foreign minister, agreed to head an interim government and was later elected president. Fighting continued, however, with Gamsakhurdia supporters holding positions in Abkhazia and elsewhere. These clashes continued until 1994, when the government forces routed Gamsakhurdian forces.

Abkhazia declared its independence from Georgia in July 1992, provoking a crisis that grew into all-out armed conflict by August. Fighting persisted into 1994, despite several cease-fire agreements; a cease-fire appeared to hold in South Ossetia after June. In 1994 Abkhazian rebels ousted Georgian forces, who were forced into a humiliating withdrawal. There were numerous mediations, negotiations, and multiparty talks throughout the conflict, especially by Russia, but with little success. At various times the conflict threatened to spread, with North Ossetians attempting to aid the South Ossetian separatists, rebel Abkhazians receiving arms and support from the Confederation of Caucasian Mountain People, and Russian troops aiding both the rebels and Georgian government forces at various times. Once the conflict began in earnest in 1992, the fighting was intense. More than five thousand people have been killed in the conflict, most of these from late 1992 onward. The fighting died down significantly after 1995.

In 1995 Georgia and Russia signed a military agreement under which Russia agreed to retain military bases in Georgia. Russia also pledged to aid Georgia in its attempts to reunify Abkhazia and South Ossetia with the Georgian state. Also in 1995, political instability and unrest within Georgia led to an attempt on President Shevardnadze's life on August 29, and the assassination of several other government officials.

For further information and background reading, see reference item numbers 890, 911, 920, 947, 956, 980, 998, 999.

251. MAURITANIA-SENEGAL
Ethnic violence (April 1989–January 1990)

Relations between these two West African countries were complicated by the many Senegalese nationals living and working in Mauritania and the numerous Mauritanians doing the same in Senegal. Mauritania, populated mostly by Arab-Berbers, also suspected Senegal of harboring black African opponents of its regime. The conflict began with the death of two individuals in a dispute on April 9, 1989, over competing claims to farming rights on the common border, the Senegal River. Both sides reinforced troops along the border, and two more fatal shootings occurred a few days later. This violence was followed by ethnically motivated rioting and attacks in both countries. Despite a state of emergency, the attacks continued. An airlift and repatriation exercise was undertaken in early May to deal with the crisis. Thousands had to be flown back to their country of origin, most leaving all their possessions behind.

Relations between the two countries deteriorated steadily after the repatriations, with hostile diplomatic moves, troop buildups along the border, and reports of expulsions and forced repatriations. Mediations by the Maghreb Union and the Organization of African Unity, plus a number of negotiations, failed to resolve the crisis. In January 1990 the conflict escalated with an exchange of heavy artillery fire across the Senegal River. The fighting subsided, however, and negotiations in July 1991 brought about a partial settlement to the conflict, although relations remained tense. In all, up to five hundred people are thought to have been killed during the conflict, most of these in the ethnic violence.

For further information and background reading, see reference item numbers 286, 287, 354, 399.

252. BOSNIA
Ethnic and religious warfare; the Balkans conflict (mid-1989–)

Yugoslavia was originally a federation of relatively autonomous republics dating back to the end of World War I, its constituent republics comprising Bosnia-Herzegovina, Croatia, Macedonia, Montenegro, Serbia, and Slovenia. In 1989, with the Soviet Union giving way to centrifugal forces, the republics began to voice their mistrust of Serbia, accusing the powerful republic of imposing its own rule on other regions under the guise of concern for the federation. The republics began to make moves toward secession, provoking violent incidents in most of the republics beginning in mid-1989.

Ethnic fighting broke out in September 1990 between Orthodox Serbs and Bosnian Muslims in Bosnia, and between Serbs and Catholic Croats in Croatia. Serbian enclaves in Croatia declared themselves independent, provoking further unrest. In January 1991 a major confrontation developed between the Croatian government and the Serb-dominated Yugoslav National Army (JNA) after the latter tried to disarm Croatian republican armed forces and militia. The conflict escalated in March when the JNA was used to put down Croat-Serb violence within Croatia itself. The Serbian republic threatened to arm Serbs living in Croatia if the Croatian authorities did not protect them from attacks by Croat paramilitary groups. The JNA came into direct conflict with Croatian forces in April and May 1991 after the JNA deployed further into Croatia to prevent fighting between Serb separatists and Croatian authorities.

In June 1991 the republics of Slovenia and Croatia both declared independence (see map 11). This provoked intense fighting in both republics between the JNA and the republican forces, with hundreds of fatalities. By July 1991 Yugoslavia was in a state of complete civil war, and by September the fighting had spread to the ports and to Bosnia. By this time, the JNA was openly identified with Serb nationalist forces. In November 1991, after Croat offensives, the fighting spread to Serbia itself.

The war threatened to spread in June 1991 when Austria dispatched hundreds of troops to border areas after JNA airspace violations. Hungary did the same in September 1991. From late 1991 the European Community (now called the European Union, or EU) imposed trade and arms sanctions on the protagonists in an attempt to end the conflict, while the United Nations sent more peace-keeping forces to the region from the beginning of 1992. The EC member states and many other countries accorded international recognition to Croatia and Slovenia in January 1992 and to Bosnia-Herzegovina in April 1992.

Fighting intensified in Bosnia from March 1992, and the siege of Sarajevo, the Bosnian capital, began in April. From mid-1992 the fighting in the region tended to center on the Muslim-dominated Bosnian republic, with the Serbs and the Croats making significant territorial gains. In May 1992 Bosnia's Serbian population declared itself independent, further complicating the situation.

MAP 11. **East Central Europe**

*In addition to the Balkans conflict, which resulted in the seces-
sion of Slovenia, Croatia, Bosnia-Herzegovina, and Macedonia
from the Yugoslav state, East Central Europe struggled to resolve
several other conflicts in the postwar period, including incidents
in Hungary (see conflict 048), Czechoslovakia (now the Czech
Republic and the Slovak Republic) (conflict 120), and Poland
(conflict 197).*

Throughout the conflict a multitude of organizations and countries made
intense diplomatic efforts—the European Community, the United Nations, the
Council on Security and Cooperation in Europe (now called the OSCE),
Russia, the United States, and other parties. Although dozens of cease-fires
were signed and numerous settlements announced, the fighting continued and
none of the outstanding issues was resolved. Even NATO air strikes failed to
deter the protagonists. In 1994 the fighting continued, with numerous fatali-

ties. Stepped-up NATO air strikes, territorial setbacks for Bosnian and Croat Serbs, and a major diplomatic initiative by U.S. mediators in 1995 eventually led to all-party talks in Dayton, Ohio, in November. The Dayton accord put an end to hostilities, although occasional violence still flared. In early 1996 thousands of U.S. troops were deployed in the former Yugoslavia as peace-keepers, and the political aspects of the Dayton accord were gradually implemented.

In all, the conflict created 3.3 million refugees and took more than sixty thousand lives, although some estimates are much higher. Many of the deaths were among civilians—victims of massacres, summary executions, large-scale disappearances, concentration camps, and other atrocities. The term "ethnic cleansing" came into use during 1992 to describe the policy of enforcing ethnically homogenous geographical zones by any means, though usually by extreme violence. In early 1996 the first war crimes trials got under way at the Hague, although many accused of war crimes remained at large in Bosnia, Serbia, and Croatia.

For further information and background reading, see reference item numbers 888, 898, 905, 910, 911, 914, 915, 919, 927, 928.

253. UNITED STATES–PANAMA
Anti-Noriega U.S. military invasion (December 1989)

Panama has occupied a strategic place in the U.S. economy, as much shipping passes through the Panama Canal. It has therefore been important to the United States to maintain good relations with the Panamanian government. Armed conflicts had soured U.S.-Panamanian relations in 1964 (see conflict 091). The relationship between the United States and Panamanian strongman, Gen. Manuel Antonio Noriega, had been severely strained for two years, despite Noriega's having once been on the payroll of U.S. intelligence organizations. General Noriega's human rights abuses angered the U.S. State Department, and he had also been indicted by two U.S. federal grand juries on drug charges.

Tensions rose significantly after Panamanian voters went to the polls to elect a new president in May 1989; although international observers declared an overwhelming victory for the opposition party, the government voided the elections. When Noriega announced a "state of war" with the United States, the United States responded on December 20, 1989, by invading Panama with 23,000 troops and massive air support. The primary military objective was to capture Noriega and overthrow his regime. The resistance to the invasion was strong, and more than 550 people were killed in the fighting, including 26 U.S. soldiers and a number of civilians. The invasion, however, was completed by December 23, 1989. Noriega himself took refuge in the Vatican diplomatic mission on December 24 and did not surrender until January 3, 1990. The general was then taken to the United States to stand trial on drugs-related charges. He was convicted on eight counts of racketeering and drug trafficking in 1992.

President George Bush said the motives for the invasion were to restore democracy, to protect the Panama Canal, to safeguard U.S. citizens in Panama, and to bring Noriega to trial. The action was widely condemned by the international community. Neither side sought to manage the conflict peacefully, and U.S. troops started to withdraw in January 1990 when the U.S.-installed regime stabilized.

For further information and background reading, see reference item numbers 541, 551, 582, 591.

254. LIBERIA
Civil war (December 1989–)

This conflict began in December 1989 when Charles Taylor led the previously unknown National Patriotic Forces of Liberia (NPFL) in an attack on government forces, launching the attack in northeastern Liberia from bases in Sierra Leone. A former government employee charged with theft, Taylor had escaped custody in the United States. The NPFL was composed of political dissidents and ex-soldiers who fled Liberia after a 1985 putsch failed to unseat President Samuel Doe; Libya and Burkina Faso had backed the coup attempt.

The fighting turned into a full-scale revolt against Doe's regime when government troops began to exact brutal punishment against local villagers. By May 1990 the rebels were moving south, and by mid-July fighting had moved into the capital, Monrovia. Doe's government was close to collapse. A splinter group from the NPFL emerged at this time led by Prince Yormie Johnson, who was opposed to both Taylor and President Doe. There were many atrocities and revenge attacks on civilians during the fighting, including a massacre of five hundred refugees in a church on July 29, 1990, by government troops. U.S. mediation in September 1990 failed to halt the bloodshed.

After the Economic Community of West African States (ECOWAS) emerged as the primary peace broker, it sent a peace keeping force to Liberia in August 1990 called the ECOWAS Monitoring Group (ECOMOG) to stop the war and oversee a cease-fire. The ECOMOG arranged a meeting between Doe and Johnson in September 1990, but fighting broke out at the meeting and Doe was killed. In October 1990 ECOMOG forces launched an offensive to separate the warring factions, which was largely successful. A cease-fire in November 1990 led to a wider peace agreement in February 1991.

By this stage four main factions all claimed leadership of the country: Brig. Gen. David Nimley, who was Doe's successor; Charles Taylor; Prince Johnson; and Amos Sawyer, an academic and lawyer who was the head of an ECOW-

AS-installed interim government. In November 1991 another group called the United Liberation Movement of Liberia for Democracy (ULIMO), made up of Doe supporters and based in Sierra Leone, also joined the war, attacking the NPFL.

Throughout 1991 and early 1992, the agreement was partially successful, but it stumbled on the intransigence of Taylor, who refused to disarm or join the interim government. Numerous incidents and atrocities continued, until full-scale fighting broke out between ULIMO and NPFL forces in August 1992. In October 1992 the NPFL attacked ECOMOG forces in Monrovia in an attempt to seize the capital. ECOMOG responded with massive air attacks.

Throughout 1993 and 1994 ULIMO and ECOMOG made significant gains against Taylor's NPFL, but not enough to dislodge him completely. In June 1993 a massacre of 450 refugees briefly focused world attention on the conflict. The United Nations sent an envoy but left the conflict largely in the hands of ECOWAS. In September 1993 Nigeria decided to withdraw its troops from ECOMOG, weakening it greatly and negating its gains. A cease-fire in December 1994 held until April 1995, when another brutal massacre claimed the lives of sixty-two people, mainly women and children. In August 1995 the end of the war appeared to be imminent with the signing of a peace accord in Abuja, the new Nigerian capital. A transitional government was formed, elections were planned, and all the warlords went to Monrovia to take their places in government. But in early 1996 the entire process unraveled when the transitional government tried to arrest a faction leader on murder charges and he resisted. Within days, the capital was engulfed in anarchy and factional fighting.

By the end of 1995 the war had cost upward of 150,000 lives, and despite numerous conflict-management attempts, peace had remained elusive. No side had either the ability to achieve a significant advantage nor the willpower to make any real concessions in the interest of peace. Many of the dead were civilians killed in grisly massacres, reprisals, or disease and starvation.

For further information and background reading, see reference item numbers 286, 287, 324.

255. USSR-LITHUANIA
Post-Soviet independence crisis (March 1990–late 1991)

Lithuania had been an independent nation at various times before 1945. The liberalization of Soviet society under Gorbachev saw Lithuanian nationalism take on new life in the late 1980s. Conflict between Lithuania and Russia was precipitated by Lithuania's unilateral declaration of independence on March 11, 1990, and its call for the removal of Soviet troops from Lithuanian soil. Moscow's reaction was hostile, declaring the independence declaration as unlawful. The Soviet authorities then began to apply intense political, economic, and military pressure on Lithuania.

In March the Soviet Union initiated provocative military moves, such as driving armored convoys through the capital, Vilnius. At the same time the Soviet Congress passed laws and declarations against Lithuanian independence. In April an intense economic blockade of the Baltic republic began, cutting off such vital supplies such as oil and foodstuffs. The crisis continued throughout 1990 with little international support for Lithuania and fruitless efforts at negotiations. The parties rejected an offer of mediation by French president François Mitterrand and German chancellor Helmut Kohl on April 2, 1990.

In January 1991 the Soviet military cracked down on Lithuania, seizing important facilities and attempting to round up Lithuanian deserters. There were eighteen fatalities in the violence, most of them civilians crushed by tanks as they passively resisted Soviet attempts to seize key buildings. Beginning in May 1991 Soviet OMON forces (the Otryad Militsii Osobogo Naznacheniya, or "Black Berets," were special-purpose militia detachments subordinate to the Soviet Ministry of Internal Affairs) made several attacks on Lithuanian customs control points on the Soviet-Lithuanian border, resulting in ten more fatalities. By the end of 1991 the conflict had died down somewhat, although Soviet troops remained in Lithuania. May 1992 saw a number of unsuccessful negotiations. Lithuania gradually gained international recognition, and Russian troops were withdrawn in following years.

For further information and background reading, see reference item numbers 890, 911, 920, 947, 956, 998, 999.

256. GUINEA-BISSAU–SENEGAL
Border conflict (April–May 1990)

Relations between the West African states of Senegal and Guinea-Bissau had been tense for some time. Both sides accused the other of harboring subversives, and there was a long-standing dispute over the demarcation of the maritime border. Serious border clashes in April and May 1990 and an exchange of artillery fire between border troops resulted in seventeen deaths. Pressures were extremely high, and there were fears of more serious conflict. But neither side wanted to go to war, and so they sought a peaceful solution to the conflict.

Following emergency talks in Paris and negotiations in São Domingo, Guinea-Bissau, the two sides agreed to maintain border troops at a reasonable distance, strengthen military cooperation, and refrain from harboring each other's rebels. Relations stabilized after this point.

For further information and background reading, see reference item numbers 286, 287, 354, 399, 469.

257. NIGER-TUAREGS
Sahel pastoralist separatism (May 1990–October 1994)

The Tuaregs, a Muslim nomadic tribe spread out over the Sahel region of north-central Africa, had a long history of grievances against the Niger government. These included overzealous army reprisals, development policies aimed primarily at urbanized inhabitants and settled agriculturalists, government neglect, broken promises regarding resettlement aid, and so forth. In May 1990 Tuareg nomads recruited and trained in Libya, attacked a gendarmerie in the region of Tchin-Tabaradene in Niger. The Tuaregs were returning refugees, and the fighting soon took on a separatist tone, as the Tuaregs blamed the government for failing to keep its promises. The death toll reached several hundred, and government troops were blamed for reprisal killings. The Tuaregs were organized into the Liberation Front of Air and Azawad (FLAA).

Although the conflict was fairly low level during 1991, attacks continued, and in early 1992 the new government was determined to find a solution without partitioning the country. In February 1992 the government closed the border with Algeria, possibly to stop the infiltration of arms to the Tuaregs. In May peace initiatives resulted in a truce and the agreement to pursue further talks. In September, however, some elements of the army took unauthorized reprisals against the Tuaregs and the conflict flared again. At the end of 1992 the government had released Tuaregs taken prisoner by rebellious army troops and the peace process resumed.

Peace efforts continued into 1993 and 1994, with intermittent clashes and outbreaks of fighting. Efforts by France, Algeria, and Burkina Faso led to a full settlement of the conflict in October 1994. At times throughout the conflict, the fighting was intense, and more than four hundred people were killed, many of them civilians in reprisals.

For further information and background reading, see reference item numbers 286, 287, 354, 399.

258. KYRGYZSTAN
Post-Soviet ethnic strife (June 1990)

With the disintegration of the Soviet Union, ethnic-based animosities (some going back a millennium) began to resurface in many of the former republics, particularly in the Caucasus and central Asia. This particular conflict began in the Kyrgyz city of Osh on June 4, 1990. Initially a dispute between ethnic Uzbeks and Kyrgyzis concerning the use of farmland for housing, the conflict soon turned into general ethnic-based violence in the form of riots, pogroms, clashes, and attacks on interior ministry buildings.

The conflict took on an international character and threatened to turn into a full-scale interrepublican armed conflict when up to fifteen thousand Uzbeks armed with makeshift weapons attempted to cross from Uzbekistan into southern Kyrgyzstan. Gangs of Kyrgyzis, similarly armed, were reported to be massing on their side of the border. The conflict eased after the border was closed and a state of emergency declared in both states. No peaceful conflict-management attempts were made during the conflict, and after two weeks of violence, it was estimated that nearly six hundred people had lost their lives. Animosities remained high for some years, and the problem of ethnic-based violence remained unsolved in the region.

For further information and background reading, see reference item numbers 890, 911, 920, 947, 956, 980, 998, 999.

259. MALI-TUAREGS
Sahel pastoralist rebellion, military coup (June 1990–)

A pastoral tribes people inhabiting the Sahel region in north-central Africa, the Tuaregs had nursed some long-standing grievances against their central governments of Mali and Niger (see conflict 257). Prompted by the Tuareg fighting in Niger, Tuaregs in Mali launched an attack in June 1990 at Menaka in the north, in which some twenty people died. The government declared a state of emergency and carried out reprisal attacks in July and August. In this case, it appeared that the Tuareg nomads were attempting to overthrow the government rather than simply secede. After Algerian mediation, a peace agreement was signed in January 1991, but there were reports of fighting again in May.

Meanwhile, the government was overthrown in March 1991 by a popular revolution and replaced by a transitional government. At this point, the Tuareg rebellion erupted in earnest, with rebel attacks and government reprisals. The renewed fighting caused refugees to flee into neighboring Algeria, worsening the strains between those two countries; there was also speculation about Libyan and French involvement in the rebellion. In addition, the refugees were thought to have established bases and launched attacks from Algerian territory.

The conflict was partly settled after an all-party conference in December 1991 and negotiations in January 1992, which produced a cease-fire. Another agreement was signed in March, but an attack on the Tuaregs in May underlined the fragility of the peace agreement. The Tuaregs responded with fresh rebel activity in July. At the end of 1992 the implementation of the agreement was going ahead, albeit with delays and continued strains. Tension and occasional violence were still present in 1993 and 1994, and despite negotiations leading to a number of minor agreements, the conflict remained unresolved at the end of 1995. In all, more than three hundred people were killed in the conflict.

For further information and background reading, see reference item numbers
286, 287, 354.

260. SENEGAL
*Secessionist armed insurrection; the Casamance rebellion
(mid-1990–)*

Casamance province in southern Senegal is nearly cut off from the rest of the
country by the Gambia. In 1982, complaining of government neglect, the people of Casamance organized the Movement of Democratic Forces of
Casamance (MFDC) to voice their demands for better treatment. When MFDC
demonstrations turned violent in 1982–1983, a brutal government crackdown
on the protesters allowed the movement to garner more sympathy and support.
As a consequence, the organization began to adopt secessionist aims. Low-level
agitation continued for the next few years.

In mid-1990 the MFDC launched a full-scale secessionist insurrection with
a series of attacks on civilian and army personnel. The government responded
by reinforcing troops in the Casamance, and a vicious guerrilla war ensued.
Largely made up of members of the Diola tribe, the MFDC often targeted
Muslim Madingos and Fulanis. In mid-1992 the conflict degenerated into
widespread ethnic violence, which the government had difficulty containing.
The violence continued into 1995, with spectacular MFDC attacks and brutal
government counterattacks—there were numerous reports of disappearances,
summary executions, and other human rights abuses.

The fighting led to thousands of refugees seeking safety in the Gambia, and
the war threatened to escalate in December 1992, when Senegalese infantry
forces bombarded MFDC rebel bases near São Domingo, Guinea-Bissau. A
number of Guinean civilians were killed in the attack, and the Guinea-Bissau
government protested. Senegalese aircraft also bombed targets in Guinea-
Bissau in February 1995, despite Guinean protestations that they were not aiding the rebels. Also in 1995, international attention was focused on the region
when the rebels began kidnapping foreign nationals.

In all, several hundred people have lost their lives in the conflict, and despite
a government peace commission set up in 1990, the fighting continued.
Mediation by Guinea-Bissau led to a number of short-lived cease-fires, but the
underlying issues remained unresolved. The conflict was complicated in mid-
1992 when the MFDC split, and a new faction emerged which was opposed to
the peace process.

For further information and background reading, see reference item numbers
286, 287, 354, 399.

261. IRAQ–COALITION FORCES

Territorial dispute, Iraqi expansionism; the Gulf war
(August 1990–March 1991)

In early August 1990 the Iraqi army invaded Kuwait, taking the oil sheikhdom's small army by complete surprise. Within days, Iraq had occupied the country, and by the end of the month it had absorbed Kuwait into its own territorial administration. The conflict was preceded by Iraqi accusations that Kuwaiti oil overproduction had depressed oil prices, but Iraqi debts to Kuwait and claims on Kuwaiti oil fields also played a role in the attack. Furthermore, Iraq had long claimed that Kuwait was part of Iraq, going back to Kuwaiti independence and before (see conflict 073). Following the invasion, there was a vicious crackdown on anti-Iraq elements in Kuwait and a troop buildup on the Kuwait–Saudi Arabian border.

Iraq's actions brought immediate worldwide condemnation, the imposition of massive sanctions, and the start of a massive buildup of troops in Saudi Arabia and surrounding states. Advanced industrial nations feared Iraqi designs on Saudi Arabia. With Kuwait under its control, Iraq now controlled a significant portion of the world's oil production. Despite numerous mediations and negotiations, the situation remained quite tense. An anti-Iraq coalition made up of the United States, a number of European states, and some Arab states began to take shape. On November 29, 1990, the United Nations passed a resolution authorizing the use of force to compel Iraq to withdraw, and set January 15, 1991, as the deadline for compliance.

On January 16, 1991, despite frantic last-minute diplomatic maneuvering by Russia, a massive allied bombing campaign of Iraqi positions began. Iraq responded with Scud missile attacks on Saudi Arabia and Israel in an attempt to draw Israel into the war and produce a wider regional conflict. This failed to occur, and within days the U.S.-led Coalition had complete air superiority. The Coalition fought off a small Iraqi invasion of Saudi Arabia on January 29, and on February 24 launched a full-scale ground invasion of Kuwait. Iraqi resistance was weak, and within days the Iraqis surrendered unconditionally. A formal cease-fire was declared on March 3, 1991.

In the wake of the Iraqi defeat, the Shiite community in the south and the Kurds in the north mounted a massive rebellion, but without foreign assistance they soon faltered and began to suffer brutal reprisals. The Coalition forces continued to occupy southern Iraq until May 1991, and in the north they set up safe havens for the Kurds. These lines of contact between the Coalition forces and the Iraqi army produced tensions that occasionally flared into armed confrontation (see conflicts 275, 284).

The number of fatalities was estimated at between 50,000 and 100,000; 200 Coalition soldiers were killed. After the conflict Iraq continued to defy the United States and the United Nations, prompting continued U.N. sanctions and military presence in the Gulf region (see conflicts 275, 284).

For *further information and background reading, see reference item numbers* 255, 1096, 1178, 1230, 1272, 1286, 1336.

262. AZERBAIJAN-ARMENIA
Post-Soviet strife, ethnic violence; the Nagorno-Karabakh conflict (August 1990–)

This conflict erupted in August 1990 when Armenia declared its independence from a disintegrating Soviet Union and laid claim to Nagorno-Karabakh—an ethnically Armenian and largely Christian enclave in the neighboring Soviet republic of Azerbaijan. The Azeris themselves are Turkic-speaking Shiite Muslims. Fighting broke out when Azeri and Soviet troops attempted to disarm Armenian militias in the enclave. Incidents occurred along the Azeri-Armenian border and within Nagorno-Karabakh until the violence underwent a serious escalation in April 1991, when Armenia accused Soviet troops of siding with Azeri forces. Despite a Soviet-negotiated cease-fire, ethnic-based violence continued along the border. Nearly eight hundred people had been killed in the conflict by this stage.

In September 1991 Nagorno-Karabakh declared its independence, with full Armenian support for the declaration. Azerbaijan responded by proclaiming direct presidential rule over the enclave. After the Soviet Union disbanded on December 26, 1991, all-out war started in January when Armenian forces invaded Nagorno-Karabakh. By May Armenian forces controlled the entire enclave. But an Azeri counteroffensive in June began to reverse some of the losses. By this time, many hundreds were being killed every month. The war continued without letup for the next two years, and neither side was able to totally defeat the other. Although a cease-fire was signed in May 1994, it eventually broke down. Fighting continued intermittently, as did peace talks, throughout 1995.

A wider regional conflict loomed in May 1992 when Turkey threatened to invade on the side of the Azeris, who had declared Azerbaijan's independence from the now-defunct Soviet Union. The Commonwealth of Independent States (CIS, the alliance of former Soviet republics) responded by saying its troops would defend Armenia in the event of Turkish military involvement. Given the specter of a wider Muslim-Christian conflict, a number of mediations were proffered during the course of the conflict, especially by Russia and Turkey. But despite many cease-fires, the conflict-management attempts failed. By the end of 1995 it was estimated that twenty thousand had been killed and 1 million people displaced as a result of the conflict. The war destabilized both states, which began to suffer serious civil unrest and political turmoil. Azerbaijan withstood a number of serious rebellions and coup attempts from 1993 to 1995.

For *further information and background reading, see reference item numbers 890, 911, 920, 930, 947, 956, 980, 998, 999.*

263. RWANDA
Tribal conflict, genocide, rebel invasion (September 1990–)

Intense tribal animosities between the Tutsi and Hutu people are at the root this conflict. These animosities deepened after a bloody 1959 coup ousted a Tutsi government, increasing even further after bloodshed in 1963 and 1973 sent Tutsi Rwandans flooding into neighboring countries. At present, more than seventy thousand Tutsi refugees reside in Uganda alone, and estimates state there are 1 million worldwide. Successive Rwandan governments had refused to acknowledge them as Rwandan nationals.

On the night of September 30, 1990, the Tutsi-dominated Rwandan Patriotic Front (RPF) invaded Rwanda from Uganda seeking to overthrow President Juvénal Habyarimana's regime and to repatriate all the refugees. The invasion was launched in the Mutara region in the north and was contained only after thousands of French, Belgium, and Zairean troops were dispatched to the fighting. Many hundreds of troops were killed in the initial clashes, which were intense. Diplomatic efforts by OAU and Belgian mediators failed to stop the fighting in the second half of October, and by the end of the month the government was claiming victory.

But RPF forces continued to invade from Uganda and engage government troops, particularly throughout December 1990 and January 1991. There were many fatalities. Fighting continued into March, despite peace initiatives, until Zairean president Mobutu Sésé Séko secured a shaky cease-fire on March 18. This soon collapsed, and low-level guerrilla fighting continued throughout the year. Numerous peace efforts during this period also failed. The formation of a transitional government in Rwanda in April 1992 saw the beginning of serious peace initiatives by the government, although fighting did intensify again in May and June.

In July 1992 the government and RPF began serious peace negotiations in Arusha, Tanzania. Despite continuous accusations of cease-fire violations, the two parties made great progress. In October both parties signed a power-sharing agreement and assented to end the war, but there was opposition to this, and sporadic ethnic violence was continuing at the end of 1992.

In early 1993 the RPF launched another major offensive after Hutu extremists killed fifty-three Tutsi. France sent in troops to protect its nationals. Peace talks continued, and although a settlement was signed in August 1993, it never took hold. On April 6, 1994, the presidents of Rwanda and Burundi were killed in a suspicious plane crash. This was followed immediately by a well-organized and systematic massacre of Tutsi civilians and opposition members by Hutu militias.

The RPF resumed its offensive in earnest, and although it made significant gains, it could not prevent the massacres of up to 500,000 Tutsi and Hutu opposition members by the gangs. Although the United Nations had observers on the ground and intelligence to suggest that the Hutu were waging a genocidal campaign, the world body vacillated, eventually doing nothing to prevent the mass killings. The RPF captured the whole country by mid-July 1994, but its victory caused more than 1 million Rwandans to flee the country, mainly ethnic Hutus who feared reprisals at the hands of the Tutsi-dominated rebels.

The repatriation of Rwandan refugees continued to vex the region throughout 1995, especially after a moderate Hutu political leader was assassinated in May in Kigali. The former Hutu government and its extremist militias also began to receive arms and organize for guerrilla warfare in 1995, and there were a number of clashes in border areas, culminating in an RPF government attack on a rebel training camp at Lake Kivu that left 141 rebels dead.

In all, as many as 1 million Rwandans were killed in the conflict—mainly of Tutsis by Hutu militias and Hutu colleagues and neighbors. Continued violence and animosity in refugee camps made the situation there extremely volatile. Despite frantic mediation efforts by the U.N., OAU, and Tanzanian officials during the worst of the fighting, no issues were resolved, and nothing could stop the violence. French troops in Rwanda were only partially successful in protecting civilians.

For further information and background reading, see reference item numbers 255, 397, 445.

264. MOLDOVA

Post-Soviet strife; Gagauz struggle for autonomy
(October 1990–July 1992)

With the disintegration of the Soviet Union in the early 1990s, ethnic minorities throughout the former Soviet republics began to agitate for secession (see conflicts 250, 252, 258, 262). This conflict began in Moldova, which is on the western fringes of the former Soviet Union, near Romania. About 65 percent of the country's population are Romanian-speaking ethnic Moldovans, another 25 percent are Ukrainians and Russians, and a small, Turkic-speaking Gagauz minority lives in the south. Given their strong ethnic and linguistic ties to Romania, the Moldovans were considering union with that country. Feeling oppressed by the Moldovan majority, the Gagauz called elections for their own leadership in October 1990; Moldova tried to forcibly quell these moves. Violence broke out when USSR interior ministry troops were brought in to calm the situation.

Matters worsened in November 1990 when the largely Russian-Ukrainian slice of eastern Moldova also declared independence as the "Trans-Dniester

Republic." Fearing Moldovan attempts to quell the region's moves toward autonomy, the separatists organized armed resistance. Fighting broke out when Moldovan units tried to retake control of the town of Dubossary. After diplomatic intervention by Soviet leader Mikhail Gorbachev, some calm returned to the republic in December 1990.

But when Moldova declared its own independence in August 1991, the Dniester region asked to remain part of Russia. In September Dniester reaffirmed its independence and began to assemble its own armed forces. The Gagauz region made similar moves in December. Fighting broke out again in Dniester and continued sporadically until March 1992, when fighting began in earnest. Russian Cossacks arrived in Dniester to fight on the side of the Russian minority, while Moldova received significant Romanian support. Meanwhile, Ukraine mobilized its border forces to prevent Cossack infiltration and defend its internal security.

Russia and the Conference for Security and Cooperation in Europe (CSCE, now the OSCE) made intense diplomatic efforts in April 1992 to end the conflict, but the skirmishes continued. In May the conflict intensified, as heavy weapons came into use and organized military units were deployed. Negotiations continued to fail. Moldova declared war on Russia in June after the former Soviet 14th Army, stationed in Dniester, began to intervene on the side of the separatist forces. The potential for a major regional conflict was high.

A peace accord was signed in July 1992, however, and began to take hold in August. A joint Russian, Moldovan, and Dniester peace-keeping force was deployed, negotiations were entered into, militias were disbanded, the 14th Army began to pull out, and a cease-fire started to take hold. Although no serious violence occurred for the rest of the year, there were problems in the negotiations over the Soviet 14th Army's withdrawal. The fighting ended in July 1992, but tensions remained. Negotiations over the withdrawal of the 14th Army and over political and constitutional arrangements continued for the next three to four years with only minor breakthroughs. But military conflict has not resumed. More than eight hundred people were killed during the course of the fighting.

For further information and background reading, see reference item numbers 890, 911, 920, 947, 956, 980, 998, 999.

265. USSR-LATVIA
Post-Soviet independence crisis (January 1991)

Like the other Baltic states, Estonia and Lithuania, Latvia had also been independent at various times before 1945. The liberalization of the Soviet Union under Mikhail Gorbachev saw a resurgence of Latvian nationalism in the late

1980s and early 1990s. In a case almost identical to Lithuania's independence crisis (see conflict 255), Latvia also experienced a crackdown by Soviet troops. Moves toward independence and calls for the removal of Soviet troops from Latvian soil had been building in previous weeks.

In early January 1991 Soviet troops attempted to enforce conscription and round up deserters. An assault on the Latvian interior ministry resulted in a gun battle between Soviet troops and Latvian police. There were other violent incidents when Soviet troops tried to disperse demonstrators. In all, four people were killed and a number injured. Worldwide condemnation of the crackdown eventually led to Soviet capitulation. Latvian independence soon followed, and Soviet troops were gradually withdrawn. At no time during the conflict did either side attempt to solve the conflict peacefully.

For further information and background reading, see reference item numbers 890, 911, 920, 956, 998, 999.

266. LIBERIA–SIERRA LEONE
Intervention, destabilization; Sierra Leone civil war (March 1991–)

While Liberia settled into an uneasy peace and tried to negotiate an end to its civil war (see conflict 254), members of Charles Taylor's National Patriotic Front of Liberia (NPFL) began cross-border raids into Sierra Leone in March 1991, killing numerous civilians. The NPFL wanted to destabilize Sierra Leone and take control of mineral-rich areas close to the Liberian border in order to finance their war in Liberia. By mid-April Sierra Leone forces were pursuing the raiders inside NPFL-held Liberian territory. Meanwhile, NPFL troops with heavy weapons were advancing into Sierra Leone, aided by a heavily armed Sierra Leone guerrilla movement, the Revolutionary United Front (RUF), led by Foday Sankoh. Although its specific aims were unclear, the RUF was opposed to the Sierra Leone government. The fighting was intense, and both sides claimed successes.

In May 1991 Nigerian and Guinean troops had been deployed in border areas to help Sierra Leone. By this stage, NPFL troops had advanced some 150 km into Sierra Leone territory. Burkinabe troops may also have been fighting for Taylor's group. The NPFL continued to fight alongside the Sierra Leone guerrillas for some time, partly because the Sierra Leone government had backed a rival Liberian faction that had invaded NPFL territory from Sierra Leone in September 1991.

Fighting continued until April 1992, when a coup in Sierra Leone led to renewed peace efforts by the new government. Although these were unsuccessful, the surge in fighting in Liberia itself compelled NPFL forces to shift their focus away from Sierra Leone. The RUF, however, continued to fight the government, leading to a general state of civil war. By this stage, their only discernible aim was to rid the country of foreign troops. Nigerian and Guinean peace-keepers began to take mounting casualties, as the government was unable to contain rebel activities.

   Throughout the conflict the fighting was intense, and more than 4,600 people were killed, many in grisly massacres. There were no actual incidents of peaceful conflict management, even though the Sierra Leone government had offered negotiations. The United Nations sent a mediator, who had been unable to contact rebel leaders. Sierra Leone was in a general state of anarchy by the end of 1995, with inter- and intrafactional fighting complicating the conflict. Since the civil war broke out in 1991, more than 100,000 people have been killed. There are 1.2 million internal refugees, most of whom are suffering from malnutrition, and the countryside is reported to be empty owing to the severe security problems. Banditry is also rife, and in 1995 the rebels began to receive international attention when they started kidnapping foreign nationals. A military coup in May 1997 unseated President Ahmad Tejan Kabbah, elected in 1996. Coup leaders claimed he had failed to consolidate the peace.

For further information and background reading, see reference item numbers 286, 287, 295, 296.

267. DJIBOUTI
Ethnic-based violence; civil war (November 1991–July 1993)

The Djibouti civil war began in early November 1991 as a revolt by the Front for the Restoration of Unity and Democracy (FRUD) against the Issa-dominated central government (the Issas are ethnically related to Somalis). The Afars, who have strong ethnic ties to the Ethiopians, comprise 35 percent of the Djibouti population and had long been mistreated by the majority Issas. Ethiopia assisted the Afar rebel movement by providing training and support, and Afars living in both Ethiopia and Somalia joined the guerrilla group as fighters. The Djibouti government claimed early on that FRUD was a foreign invasion force.

   The rebels' aim was to replace "the tribalist regime of President Hassan Gouled Aptidon with a government of national unity that represents equally the Issas, the Afaris, and other communities." Fighting centered on the northern coastal towns of Tadjoura and Obock and was intense during late November and December 1991. Despite several French attempts at mediation, fighting continued into January 1992.

   French diplomatic efforts produced a cease-fire and moves toward a negotiated end to the conflict in February 1992, as well as the deployment of a French peace-keeping force. This broke down in mid-June, and high civilian casualties began to result from a government blockade of the rebel areas in the north, leading to starvation and disease. The fighting continued into 1993, but ended in July when negotiations between government ministers and FRUD leaders resulted in a full settlement of the conflict. FRUD joined the political process, and the Afar fighters were integrated into the army. There were hundreds of fatalities during the conflict.

For further information and background reading, see reference item numbers 286, 287, 293, 327.

268. BURMA-BANGLADESH
Rohingya Muslim rebellion; border incidents (December 1991)

The Burmese government had been fighting Rohingya Muslim rebels in the province of Arakan for years. A brutal offensive against the rebels in late 1991 caused more than sixty thousand civilian refugees to cross into neighboring Bangladesh. Border relations became strained as a result, culminating in an incident on December 21, 1991. Burmese border guards fired on a Bangladesh Rifles camp near Ukhia Upazila, killing one soldier and wounding seven others. Both countries then began massing troops in the region.

The dispute subsided in the following months, however, and agreement was reached on several important issues after negotiations in December 1991 and January and April 1992. The border in the region was ill-defined and frequently used by smugglers, and the continued presence of numerous refugees led to a similar armed conflict in 1994 (see conflict 282).

For further information and background reading, see reference item numbers 688, 706, 777, 843, 845.

269. IRAN–UNITED ARAB EMIRATES
Territorial dispute; the Tunb islands dispute (April 1992)

The conflict over the Abu Musa and Tunb islands in the Persian Gulf had simmered between Iran and the United Arab Emirates (U.A.E.) for years. In 1971 Iran seized the smaller Tunb islands despite competing ownership claims (see conflict 134). In April 1992 Iran invaded and seized the island of Abu Musa and in August declared an air-exclusion zone over the area, threatening to shoot down any foreign planes. The invasion was condemned by many nations in the region. They saw it as a threat to shipping lanes and their own security because of the islands' strategic location in the Gulf.

The conflict had potential for escalation when Russia announced it would defend the United Arab Emirates in the event of any aggression. Mediation and negotiation in September 1992 failed to resolve the crisis, and pressures increased again when Iran installed pads for Silkworm surface-to-surface missiles on the islands. By late 1992, however, Iran was beginning to make peace moves in an attempt to repair relations with the U.A.E. The dispute remains unresolved and the source of potential future conflict.

For further information and background reading, see reference item numbers 76, 1021, 1022, 1023, 1028, 1034, 1150, 1267.

270. NORTH KOREA–SOUTH KOREA
Historical enmity; border incident (May 1992)

Relations between North Korea and South Korea were in a constant state of hostility. This conflict was the most serious border incident in several years and followed the pattern of earlier conflicts between the two countries since the Korean War (see conflict 105, 150, 227).

A heavily armed North Korean patrol was said to have infiltrated the demilitarized zone, where it encountered a South Korean unit. Three North Koreans were killed in the ensuing skirmish; two South Korean soldiers were wounded. There were no attempts at peaceful conflict management, and in the following months, the conflict lapsed without any great concern. Given the history of conflict between the two states, however, this incident could easily have escalated into much more serious fighting.

For further information and background reading, see reference item numbers 255, 672, 675, 720, 804, 816, 848.

271. TAJIKISTAN
Post-Soviet strife, ethnic-based civil war (May 1992–)

After the disintegration of the Soviet Union and the independence of Tajikistan in September 1991, violent conflict broke out in the capital, Dushanbe, between heavily armed supporters President Rakhman Nabiyev's regime and its pro-Islamic opponents. The independence agreement had included Russian promises to protect Tajikistan, and Russia still maintained significant forces in the country. Negotiations and intervention by Commonwealth of Independent States (CIS, the alliance of former Soviet republics) and KGB forces resulted in the formation of a coalition government.

Fighting broke out again in the south, however, and it was suppressed only with the aid of Russian interior ministry troops. A cease-fire was negotiated in late July, but it soon broke down. President Nabiyev was ousted by opposition forces in September, but the new government was unable to prevent further bloodshed. Alarmed by the military success of Islamic forces, Russia and central Asian states sent reinforcements to the region bordering Afghanistan.

Rebels were receiving arms, supplies, and some fighters from inside Afghanistan, and Iran is also thought to have been involved in a similar fashion.

In October 1992 the government lost control over the southern provinces of Kulyab and Kurgan-Tyube (Qurghonteppa), these being held by pro-Nabiyev supporters. The rebels advanced toward Dushanbe and briefly took control of the capital before being driven out by government forces. As Dushanbe was under siege, the coalition government resigned and a new government took over. A brief cease-fire came into effect in November but was overtaken by disturbances in early December, which were continuing by the end of the year.

The conflict escalated in 1993, when in March 1993 Russian/CIS troops were deployed along the Afghan border to prevent Afghan fighters from infiltrating and joining the rebels. The rebels themselves established bases just inside Afghan territory and launched a series of strikes resulting in high Russian fatalities. This escalated the conflict further, and provoked serious strains between Russia and Kabul. This pattern of warfare continued throughout 1994 and 1995, and Russian fatalities continued to mount. Although the United Nations made some attempts at peaceful conflict management, these were largely ineffectual.

Throughout the fighting, interior ministry troops tried unsuccessfully to mediate and to keep the peace. The fighting was intense, and as many as fifty thousand people are thought to have been killed in the conflict.

For further information and background reading, see reference item numbers 890, 911, 920, 956, 980, 998, 999.

272. SAUDI ARABIA–QATAR
Post–Gulf war tensions; border incidents (September–October 1992)

In the months leading up to this conflict, relations between Saudi Arabia and Qatar became strained owing primarily to Qatari agreements signed with Iran, which had refused to join the anti-Iraq coalition in the Gulf war (see conflict 261). Qatar was also alarmed by Saudi preparations for building military installations on its side of the border.

The increased tension led to an incident on September 30, 1992, which caused three fatalities. Qatar claimed Saudi troops had attacked a Qatari border post. As a result, Qatar suspended a 1965 border agreement with Saudi Arabia. Pressures mounted in October when Qatar claimed that Saudi forces had launched further attacks. Iran expressed support for Qatar, and Qatar withdrew from the joint Gulf security force. After frantic mediation attempts by other Arab states, including Egypt, Kuwait, Morocco, U.A.E., and Oman, tensions were eased. Direct talks then resulted in an agreement to withdraw forces and renew friendship.

For further information and background reading, see reference item numbers 76, 1022, 1023, 1094, 1142.

273. RUSSIA-CHECHNYA, THE CAUCASUS

Post-Soviet lawlessness, separatist fighting; the Chechen war, the Caucasus conflict (October 1992–)

The breakup of the Soviet Union led to unprecedented internal instability in Russia, as nationalist groups emerged almost daily. Law and order broke down in many parts of the country, and ethnic animosities came to the fore. This conflict began as ethnic violence between Ingush people, a Muslim people who had lived in North Ossetia since the time of Stalin, and the largely Christian North Ossetians (see map 12). About three hundred people were killed in ethnic attacks, and there were claims of atrocities on both sides. Approximately fifty thousand people were displaced as a result of the fighting.

MAP 12. **The Caucasus**

Within the Russian Federation, the republics of the Caucasus, which straddle the Caucasus Mountains, include Adygey, Armenia, Azerbaijan, Chechnya, Dagestan, Georgia, Ingushetia, Kabardino-Balkaria, Karachay-Cherkessia, and North Ossetia. The Russia-Chechnya war began in 1992 as an ethnic conflict in North Ossetia.

Russia responded by sending in three thousand elite troops to the area, and the conflict threatened to spread when neighboring Chechnya demanded that the Russian troops withdraw from its borders or face retaliation. Chechen forces then gathered on the border. Despite an agreement for both Chechnya and Russia to withdraw its troops from the border areas, the situation remained tense. Chechnya had designs on forming an extended state by uniting with the Ingush area of North Ossetia.

From here the center of conflict in the Caucasus moved to Chechnya, which had defied Moscow since declaring independence in October 1991. Russia tried to declare a state of emergency in the region in late 1991 owing to increasing lawlessness by Chechen gunmen and bandits, but had been forced into a humiliating retreat when President Dzhokhar M. Dudayev's forces blocked the airport to prevent the arrival of Russian troops. From this time Russia began to actively support Chechen opposition parties.

In mid-October the Russian-backed Chechen opposition attacked President Dudayev's forces in an effort to topple him. When this failed, Russia sent in warplanes and threatened to invade. There was a huge troop buildup in late November, and an ultimatum was issued. On December 10, 1994, Russian forces invaded Chechnya and a bloody war ensued. The fighting was extremely intense, with hundreds of fatalities on both sides, but Russian forces took the capital Grozny in February 1995. A number of belated attempts at negotiation between Boris Yeltsin and President Dudayev had failed to prevent the invasion by Russian forces.

Throughout 1995 the two sides held numerous peace talks under the auspices of the Organization for Security and Cooperation in Europe (OSCE, formerly the CSCE) in Grozny. Largely unsuccessful, these often broke down completely. The fighting continued unabated, with separatist forces launching attacks from mountain bases. Chechen rebels twice invaded Russian territory and took Russian civilians as hostages, leading to heavy loss of life. For its part, Russian forces were unable to defeat the Chechens and by the end of 1995 had suffered more than two thousand fatalities. The Chechen rebels had lost as many as eleven thousand men. In early 1996, Russian aircraft killed Dudayev in a carefully planned surprise attack. In May 1997 Russian president Boris N. Yeltsin and Aslan Maskhadov, the Chechen president, signed a peace treaty.

For further information and background reading, see reference item numbers 890, 911, 920, 947, 956, 980.

274. EGYPT-SUDAN
Territorial/resource dispute; the Halaib dispute (December 1992)

Relations between Egypt and Sudan had been tense since Sudan's adoption of a more militant style of Islamic fundamentalist government. Egypt was trying to contain a deadly fundamentalist rebellion at home. The Halaib, a largely empty desert triangle on the border between Egypt and Sudan, was potentially rich in oil and minerals and had been a source of friction and conflict since before the turn of the century. Following a border incident in April 1991, on December 9, 1992, Sudan accused Egypt of sending more troops to the area. It lodged a complaint with the United Nations that Egypt had invaded Sudanese territory with more than six hundred troops. Egypt continued to build up its troops in the area until by February 1993 it had more two thousand troops stationed there.

Both sides claimed the other had training camps for dissidents and was engaging in destabilizing tactics. Tensions were raised in April and May when Sudan said it would mobilize to counter Egyptian provocation. An all-out border war was feared. Some negotiations were broached, and the fighting eased after this time. But the issues of border demarcation and Sudanese support for Islamic fundamentalist forces remained unresolved, leaving room for future conflict.

For further information and background reading, see reference item numbers 76, 1106, 1147, 1207, 1221.

275. IRAQ–THE COALITION
Post–Gulf war incidents (December 1992–July 1993)

Following Iraq's defeat in the Gulf war, the Coalition forces established air-exclusion (or "no fly") zones and safe havens for the Kurds (see conflict 261). Iraq responded to this imposition on its sovereignty with a series of provocations. In December 1992 Iraqi planes entered the no-fly zone, and in a confrontation with Coalition jet fighters, an Iraqi MiG-25 was shot down. In response to the downing of the aircraft, Iraq installed antiaircraft missiles inside the exclusion zone, but was soon forced to remove them in January 1993 following Coalition threats. Also in January, Iraqi troops invaded Kuwaiti territory in an attempt to retrieve weapons.

On January 13, 1993, 114 Coalition jet fighters attacked missile sites and air defense systems in southern Iraq after Iraqi officials banned U.N. flights carrying weapons inspectors. Later in January another MiG was shot down, and 40 cruise missiles were launched at the Iraqi nuclear weapons facility at Zafaraniych. Further armed incidents occurred until July. The most serious of these was a missile attack on Iraqi intelligence headquarters in Baghdad after an Iraqi plot to assassinate U.S. president George Bush was uncovered. Typically, Iraqi provocations led to swift retaliation by Coalition forces.

Although the number of fatalities was relatively low throughout the conflict, tensions were high, and despite many negotiations between senior U.N. officials and the Iraqi foreign minister, Tariq Aziz, little was resolved. After July the conflict subsided somewhat, until another crisis was precipitated in July 1994 (see conflict 284).

For further information and background reading, see reference item numbers 1096, 1178, 1229, 1272, 1286, 1336.

276. BURMA-BANGLADESH
Border incidents (March–September 1993)

On March 21, 1993, Burmese border guards infiltrated Bangladeshi territory and attacked a number of villages, killing one person and wounding five others. Bangladesh responded to the incident with a storm of protest. The enormous Burmese refugee population in Bangladesh (some estimates put the number as high as 288,000) was already straining relations between the two countries, and the border incidents only made matters worse. Burma (called Myanmar by the military regime that came to power in 1988) then accused Bangladesh of allowing Burmese rebels to operate from its territory. Tensions remained high throughout April and May, especially after Burmese troops abducted a number of Bangladeshi fishermen and refused to release them.

The conflict escalated alarmingly in July when Bangladesh began deploying large numbers of troops along the border with Burma after the country refused to release Bangladeshi smugglers it had taken into custody. Burma responded by reinforcing its troops in the area as well. In early September, Burmese border guards fired on a group of Bangladeshi fishermen, killing one and wounding four others. The conflict dissipated after this time. There were no attempts at peaceful conflict management, and a similar conflict broke out in 1994 (see conflict 282).

For further information and background reading, see reference item numbers 688, 706, 777, 843, 845, 859.

277. CYPRUS
Ethnic-based tensions (April 1993)

The problem of Cyprus remained unresolved in the 1990s despite years of U.N.-sponsored talks on the island state's constitutional arrangements. Despite the presence of U.N. peace-keepers, strains persisted between the two communities—the majority Greeks and the minority Turks. In April 1993 two armed incidents raised tensions in Cyprus. On April 8, 1993, a Greek Cypriot conscript was shot dead in the U.N.-controlled buffer zone in Nicosia. This led to Greek Cypriots firing on Turkish Cypriot border posts a few days later.

Tensions were raised even higher when in late April, a Greek Cypriot gun-boat fired on a Turkish freighter in the Mediterranean, wounding two aboard. There were no attempts to peacefully settle the conflict, but strains eased in May and the dispute lapsed. Given the history of violent conflict on the island, these incidents were cause for serious international concern.

For further information and background reading, see reference item numbers 255, 887, 900, 912, 916, 921, 924, 933, 934.

278. YEMEN
Unification difficulties; civil war (November 1993–July 1994)

Yemen had originally been two separate states, both of which experienced civil conflict. North Yemen and South Yemen had also had several violent conflicts since the 1960s, which had drawn international intervention. Talks aimed at unifying the two states had gotten under way in the 1980s, proving successful toward the end of the decade. But the unification process was plagued with dif-ficulties: the armies and police forces of both sides were never fully integrated, and the respective leaders, President Ali Abdullah Saleh in the north and Vice President Ali Salem al-Beidh in the south, maintained a turbulent relationship. These problems, plus the discovery of oil deposits in the south, which would have made seceding an economically viable option, led to a serious breakdown in north-south relations in 1993.

The crisis began with the vice president's failure to take up his government post in Sanaa, the northern capital. As the feud developed, both sides began to move troops into position in November 1993, and there were a number of armed clashes. In January 1994 the conflict escalated with the political killings of southern leaders. The first serious clashes between the two armies erupted in February, but frantic mediation by Middle Eastern leaders led to a cease-fire and the beginnings of a settlement. An uneasy peace took hold in March. In late April, however, fighting began in earnest with large-scale battles leaving hundreds dead. The south formally seceded on May 21, receiving some recog-nition from the United Arab Emirates and Saudi Arabia, traditional allies of the south. But the south was losing ground, and in July Aden fell to northern forces and southern leaders were forced to flee. The war was over; it was a complete northern victory.

The conflict caused thousands of fatalities, and despite many mediation attempts by Middle Eastern nations and the United States, these failed to reunite the two estranged leaders. Yemen remained united at the end of 1995 and was rebuilding. No serious opposition movement had been formed by exiled southern leaders, and the regime seemed secure.

For further information and background reading, see reference item numbers 1060, 1143, 1167, 1188, 1238, 1253, 1316, 1317, 1333.

279. NIGERIA-CAMEROON
Border dispute; the Diamond Islands (December 1993–March 1994)

Following a long history of border disputes, the Diamond and Djabane Islands in the Gulf of Guinea, off the coast of West Africa, became the source of serious conflict in late 1993. These areas provided good fishing grounds and were thought to contain oil deposits. On December 30, 1993, five hundred Nigerian troops invaded and occupied the islands; six Cameroon soldiers were killed. Cameroon responded with a number of incursions of its own, and there was a serious battle on February 19, 1994, on the Bakassi peninsula, where up to twenty soldiers were killed.

The conflict escalated even further when France sent troops and a frigate to bolster Cameroon's forces in late February. Numerous negotiations failed to stop the conflict, but following mediation by African leaders from the region and the OAU, the dispute abated beginning in March. French forces were withdrawn and troops maintained separation. Cameroon did attempt to have the dispute submitted to the ICJ in April, but Nigeria refused, and the basic issues remained unresolved into 1995.

For further information and background reading, see reference item numbers 76, 310, 469.

280. GHANA-TOGO
Border incidents (January–February 1994)

Relations between these two West African states had been strained for some time. After armed conflict between Togo and Ghana in 1982 (see conflict 206), Ghana backed a 1986 coup attempt against the Togolese government (see conflict 237). The two regimes constantly traded accusations of harboring each other's rebels.

Armed conflict broke out in January 1994 when government forces and an armed group engaged in serious fighting in Lomé, Togo's capital. Nearly one hundred people were killed. Claiming that Ghana had trained and then infiltrated Togolese rebels into the capital, Togo responded by shelling Ghana across the border. There had been evidence for some time of Ghanaian support for Togolese opposition forces. A number of serious border incidents occurred in the following days, and the situation was complicated by an outbreak of ethnic-based fighting in northern Ghana in February, which left one thousand dead. More than six thousand refugees fled to Togo. Although no serious attempts were made at peaceful conflict management, the fighting stopped. After a few months, relations returned to their usual state.

For further information and background reading, see reference item numbers 255, 297, 313.

281. GREECE-ALBANIA
Border tensions (April 1994)

The root of this conflict lay in the northern Ipiros region of southern Albania, which Greece claimed held up to 200,000 ethnic Greeks. The Albanian government feared Greek designs on the territory and countered that there were no more than 90,000 ethnic Greeks resided there. On April 10, 1994, in a training camp near the border two Albanian soldiers were killed by masked raiders said to be wearing Greek army uniforms. A vicious diplomatic row ensued and troops were reinforced along border areas.

The foreign ministers of both countries met in Zurich in early May in an effort to calm the situation, and although no specific agreements were made, the fighting eased after this. The basic issue presented by Albania's large and increasingly nationalistic Greek minority was not resolved. This conflict had potential for a much more serious armed confrontation given the violent civil war in the Balkans (see conflict 252).

For further information and background reading, see reference item numbers 997, 998, 1016, 1018.

282. BURMA-BANGLADESH
Border incidents (May–August 1994)

Like the previous fighting between Burma and Bangladesh (see conflict 276), this conflict began when Burmese border guards abducted a number of Bangladeshi fishermen. Ill-defined and densely vegetated, the border between the two countries was used extensively by fishermen and smugglers. Tensions were high between the two states because of the large numbers of Burmese refugees who had fled to Bangladesh to escape the military junta. Burma, which was renamed Myanmar by the State Law and Order Restoration Council (SLORC, as the junta called itself), often accused Bangladesh of allowing Burmese rebels to operate from its territory.

In May 1994 Bangladeshi border guards fired on Burmese border guards. The conflict escalated with a troop buildup in the area and the reinforcement of border garrisons. Further incidents in June and August—including the killing of a Bangladeshi fisherman and the laying of mines on Bangladeshi territory by Burmese troops—kept the tension high. No serious attempts were made to manage the conflict peacefully, and the dispute eventually faded.

For further information and background reading, see reference item numbers 688, 706, 777, 843, 845, 859.

283. UNITED STATES–HAITI
U.S. military invasion, reinstallation of Aristide (September 1994)

In December 1990 Father Jean-Bertrand Aristide became Haiti's first democratically elected president. But Aristide was forced into exile after a September 1991 military coup. Amid concerns over human rights abuses and alarm about Haitian refugees trying to reach U.S. waters by boat, the United States and the United Nations began putting pressure on the Haitian military junta to step down and allow Aristide to return to office. The United Nations declared a worldwide oil, arms, and financial embargo on the island and dispatched human rights monitors. After a tense standoff with Haiti's military leaders, the U.N. gave the go-ahead for restoring democracy in Haiti using "all necessary means."

In early September the United States built up an invasion force of some twenty thousand troops and twenty naval vessels in the area. A "last chance" mission to Haiti led by former U.S. president Jimmy Carter on September 18 produced a compromise agreement whereby the military leader agreed to step down. U.S. troops entered Haiti on September 19 unopposed by the military. In subsequent weeks the U.N. sanctions were lifted, Aristide was restored to the presidency, and more troops were deployed. By September 27 there were 15,700 U.S. troops in Haiti. The apparent suicide of a U.S. soldier on guard duty was the only U.S. fatality in the operation.

After the invasion, violence between the police and pro-Aristide supporters led to dozens of deaths, while efforts to disarm paramilitary and police groups by civilians and U.S. soldiers also resulted in numerous fatalities. Policing remained in the hands of U.S. troops in the following months, and by the end of 1995 Aristide was making a concerted effort to rebuild the country's economy and its shattered democratic institutions, although with only varying degrees of success.

For further information and background reading, see reference item numbers 549, 573.

284. IRAQ–THE COALITION
Post–Gulf war border tensions (October 1994)

Following its defeat in the Gulf war (see conflict 261) and confrontation with the Coalition forces in 1992–1993 (see conflict 275), Iraq provoked a major crisis with the prospect of war in October 1994 when it massed eighty thousand troops on the Kuwaiti border in an apparently hostile move. The Coalition forces responded by sending massive numbers of troops, aircraft, and a naval task force to the area. The tension remained extremely high for several weeks, but mediation by Andrei Kosirev, the Russian foreign minister, eventually led to Iraq's official recognition of Kuwait in November 1994. The troops were withdrawn and the conflict abated. Although no shots had been fired, a return to all-out war was a clear possibility given Iraq's unpredictability and the hard-line approach of the U.S.-led Coalition.

For *further information and background reading, see reference item numbers 1096, 1178, 1229, 1272, 1286, 1336.*

285. TAIWAN-CHINA
Communist-Nationalist dispute; shelling incident (November 1994)

A series of dangerous conflicts had plagued Taiwanese-Chinese relations for the past four decades. China had repeatedly expressed its intention to unite all the offshore islands, including Taiwan, with the mainland. An incident heightened tensions between the two countries when twenty-four Taiwanese tourists were murdered in China in March 1994.

In mid-November Taiwanese troops stationed in Lesser Quemoy, an island less than two km off the Chinese mainland, fired at least a dozen shells into a suburb of Xiamen. Several people were injured, and China put its forces on alert. There were grave fears of Chinese retaliation and a major escalation of the conflict. However, the Taiwanese government quickly apologized for the incident, claiming it was an accident, and offered to pay compensation to the victims. Although tensions remained high for a time, the conflict gradually eased. There were no other attempts at conflict management, and although there were only a few casualties, the history of bloodshed between the two states meant there was a much greater likelihood of serious conflict.

For *further information and background reading, see reference item numbers 255, 698, 718, 852, 866, 878.*

286. SAUDI ARABIA–YEMEN
Post–Gulf war border conflict (December 1994)

Some ill-defined border areas between Saudi Arabia and Yemen had been a source of some friction between the two countries. Further, these tensions were exacerbated by Yemen's support for Iraq during the Gulf war (see conflict 261). A dispute over potentially oil-rich territory led to strains in March 1992, but no military confrontation. Oil exploration had been suspended, and several rounds of unsuccessful negotiations followed.

In early December 1994, however, Yemen accused Saudi Arabia of erecting observation posts and building roads in the disputed areas. On December 7, 1994, a clash between border troops left three Yemeni officers dead. Although tensions remained extremely high for a while, the dispute lapsed, with both sides deciding to engage in negotiations rather than violent confrontation.

For further information and background reading, see reference item numbers 1060, 1167, 1188, 1238, 1316.

287. ECUADOR-PERU
Regional rivalry; border conflict (January–March 1995)

Ecuador and Peru had been rivals since 1977, when a long-standing territorial dispute over the Loreto region of northern Peru erupted into armed conflict (see conflict 171). Skirmishes in 1981 and 1984 (see conflicts 193 and 217) had created a tense and hostile border situation. Although a 1942 treaty had validated Peru's sovereignty over the region, Ecuador maintained it had been forced into signing the agreement.

In early January 1995 fighting erupted once again in the Loreto region when Ecuadoran helicopters attacked and destroyed a Peruvian border post. Both sides quickly called up reserves and mobilized their forces in the area. A virulent propaganda war ensued, and each side threatened total war. This escalation of tensions flared into full-scale offensives involving tanks and air support in late January. Heavy fighting continued into February, and several planes were shot down.

Neighboring states and the guarantor nations of the 1942 treaty sought a peaceful resolution to the fighting, and their efforts produced a cease-fire in February. Skirmishes continued into March, however, and it was not until April 1995 that both sides agreed to end the fighting and withdraw their forces from the area. In all, an estimated one hundred troops were killed in the fighting, and efforts to resolve the underlying dispute continued throughout the rest of the year.

For further information and background reading, see reference item numbers 46, 76, 255, 552, 633.

288. CHINA–THE PHILIPPINES
Territorial dispute; the Paracel and Spratly Islands (January–February 1995)

The Paracel and Spratly island groups, which lie in the South China Sea, had been disputed for decades by China, Taiwan, Vietnam, the Philippines, Malaysia, and Brunei. Thought to contain valuable mineral deposits, the Spratly and Paracel islands were the source of armed conflict in 1956 (see conflict 045), 1974 (see conflict 142), and 1988 (see conflict 243). Ongoing discussions among the claimants had resolved none of the issues, and the islands were a constant source of tension in the region.

In late January 1995 Chinese troops, supported by eight naval ships, occupied Mischief Reef, which was only 200 km from the Philippine island of Palawan. The Philippines lodged a formal protest and began to step up its patrols in the area. Philippine troops reinforced other islands already held by the Philippines in the event of further Chinese attacks, and tensions remained high.

In March 1995 Philippine patrols arrested more than sixty Chinese fishermen and detained a number of Chinese vessels said to be violating Philippine waters. The conflict escalated even further when Philippine patrols began to destroy Chinese territorial markers in the area. The conflict died down after this, although there was another armed clash between Spratly island claimants in March 1995 (see conflict 289).

For further information and background reading, see reference item numbers 76, 255, 870.

289. TAIWAN-VIETNAM
Territorial dispute; the Spratlys clash (March 1995)

Chinese-Philippine fighting over the disputed Spratly island chain in January 1995 (see conflict 288) led to a heightened state of tension in the area. The islands were claimed in whole or in part by China, Taiwan, Vietnam, the Philippines, Malaysia, and Brunei. Armed conflict had broken out over either the Spratlys or the other disputed island chain in the region, the Paracels, in 1956 (see conflict 045), 1974 (see conflict 142), and 1988 (see conflict 243). Although it was never proven, the island chain was thought to contain valuable mineral deposits.

The territorial dispute heated up in early 1995, when Taiwan started building outposts on the disputed Ban Than island. Ban Than was claimed by Vietnam, but Taiwan announced plans to rename it Taiping. On March 25 Taiwanese troops fired on a Chinese freighter as it passed the island. Vietnam protested the incident and demanded the withdrawal of Taiwan from Ban Than, while also reinforcing its presence in the area.

Tensions remained high, especially after Vietnam reasserted its claim to the islands in mid-April, but there were no further incidents and the conflict eased after this. The islands remained a potential flashpoint in the region throughout the rest of 1995.

For further information and background reading, see reference item numbers 76, 255, 870.

290. BELIZE-GUATEMALA
Postindependence territorial dispute; border incidents (August 1995)

A British colony in the nineteenth century, the tiny Central American country of Belize became fully independent in 1981. Guatemala had long claimed Belize as part of its own territory, but preindependence negotiations had never resolved the issue. Britain had agreed to guarantee Belizean security immediately following the country's independence and had left a military force there. Belize took over full responsibility for its own defense in 1990.

Friendly relations between Belize and Guatemala were hindered by Guatemala's refusal to recognize Belizean independence and a poorly demarcated border. Tensions escalated alarmingly in August 1995, when Belizean army units crossed the border into Guatemala and began harassing local villagers. Guatemala promptly reinforced its troops in border areas and threatened violent retaliation if there were any further territorial violations.

Tensions remained high, and there were fears of war. There were no further incidents, however, and the conflict lapsed after this time.

For further information and background reading, see reference item numbers 76, 521.

291. COMOROS
Attempted coup (September–October 1995)

The Comoros Islands, off the Mozambican coast of Africa, had become French protectorates at the end of the nineteenth century; they were granted independence in 1975. The Comoros had been wracked by political instability since independence—withstanding up to sixteen coup attempts by 1995, several of them undertaken with the help of mercenaries. In 1989 President Ahmed Abdallah was assassinated and his government overthrown with the help of mercenaries led by Bob Dénard, who had fought in many African conflicts.

In late September 1995 the previously unknown Capt. Ayouba Combo staged a coup to overthrow the regime of President Said Mohammed Djohar, ostensibly to restore the conditions for a return to democracy. The rebels were aided by Dénard and a force of mercenaries. In fierce fighting, they managed to capture the presidential palace and disarm government troops. The coup collapsed, however, when France sent in nine hundred antiterrorist troops, which surrounded Dénard and his men in October 1995. Dénard surrendered without resistance and was flown to France to stand trial.

In all, two Comoran soldiers and one civilian were killed. Following the coup, some confusion and political uncertainty prevailed about who was actually in control of the government. Negotiations throughout the rest of the year finally led to the return of President Djohar in early 1996.

For further information and background reading, see reference item numbers 286, 287, 293, 327, 456, 464.

292. ERITREA-YEMEN
Invasion of the Hanish Islands (November–December 1995)

After a long and bloody war in 1993 (see conflict 099), Eritrea finally won its independence from Ethiopia and promptly laid claim to the three Hanish islands in the Red Sea on the historical basis that they had been variously owned by the Ottoman Empire, Italy, Britain, and Ethiopia. The islands were strategically situated near important shipping lanes. Yemen disputed Eritrea's claims, and a Yemeni fishing community occupied one of the islands. Negotiations failed to find any solution.

Following a Yemeni attempt to build tourist facilities on one of the islands, Eritrean troops invaded the islands in early November 1995. Eritrea claimed the islands as its own and demanded Yemen's withdrawal from the area. Yemen responded by reinforcing its troops, and the conflict escalated alarmingly. On December 15, 1995, Eritrean forces attacked Yemeni positions and a full-scale battle erupted, with both sides using aircraft, battleships, and troops. After three days of fierce fighting, Eritrea seized the Greater Hanish Island and took two hundred Yemeni soldiers prisoner.

Frantic mediation efforts by Algeria, Ethiopia, Egypt, the OAU, and U.N. secretary-general Boutros Boutros-Ghali managed to secure a cease-fire. The conflict ended when Yemen agreed to withdraw its troop presence from the islands and submit to international arbitration. In all, twelve soldiers were killed in the fighting.

For further information and background reading, see reference item numbers 286, 287, 293.

References

GENERAL

1. Acharya, A. 1993. *Third World Conflicts and International Order After the Cold War.* Working Paper #134. Canberra: Peace Research Center, Australian National University.

2. Adelman, J. R. 1985. *Revolutions, Armies and War: A Political History.* Boulder, Colo.: Lynne Rienner.

3. Arno, A., and W. Dissanayake. 1984. *The News Media in National and International Conflict.* Boulder, Colo.: Westview.

4. Atwater, E., K. Forster, and J. S. Prybyla. 1972. *World Tensions: Conflict and Communication.* 2d ed. New York: Appleton-Century-Crofts.

5. Avruch, K., P. W. Black, and J. A. Scimecca, eds. 1991. *Conflict Resolution: Cross-Cultural Perspectives.* New York: Greenwood.

6. Ayoob, M., ed. 1986. *Regional Security in the Third World: Case Studies From South East Asia and the Middle East.* London: Croom Helm.

7. ———. 1995. *The Third World Security Predicament: Statemaking, Regional Conflict, and the International System.* Boulder, Colo.: Lynne Rienner.

8. Ayoob, M., and K. Subrahmanyhan. 1972. *The Liberation War.* New Delhi: S. Chand.

9. Azar, E. E. 1990. *The Management of Protracted Social Conflict: Theory and Cases.* Aldershot (Hants), Eng.: Dartmouth.

10. Azar, E. E., and J. W. Burton, eds. 1986. *International Conflict Resolution: Theory and Practice.* Boulder, Colo.: Lynne Rienner.

11. Bailey, S. D. 1971. *Peaceful Settlement of International Disputes: Some Proposals for Research.* 3d ed. New York: UNITAR.

12. ———. 1982. *How Wars End: The United Nations and the Termination of Armed Conflict, 1946–1964.* 2 vols. Oxford: Clarendon.

13. Banks, M., and J. W. Burton, eds. 1984. *Conflict in World Society: A New Perspective on International Relations.* New York: St. Martin's.

14. Barkat, A. M. ed. 1970. *Conflict, Violence, and Peace.* Geneva: World Council of Churches.

15. Barringer, R. 1972. *War: Patterns of Conflict.* Cambridge: MIT Press.

16. Barth, F. 1969. *Ethnic Groups and Boundaries.* Boston: Little, Brown.

17. Bartlett, C. J. 1994. *The Global Conflict: The International Rivalry of Great Powers, 1880–1990.* 2d ed. London: Longman.

18. Bar-Yaacov, N. 1974. *The Handling of International Disputes by Means of Inquiry.* London: Royal Institute of International Affairs, Oxford University Press.

19. Baylis, J., and N. J. Rengger, eds. 1992. *Dilemmas of World Politics*. Oxford: Oxford University Press.

20. Beer, F. A. 1981. *Peace Against War: The Ecology of International Conflict*. San Francisco: W. H. Freeman.

21. Berman, M. R., and J. E. Johnson, eds. 1977. *Unofficial Diplomats*. New York: Columbia University Press.

22. Berridge, G. R. 1987. *International Politics: States, Power, and Conflict Since 1945*. New York: St. Martin's.

23. Bertram, C., ed. 1982. *Third World Conflict and International Security*. London: Macmillan.

24. Betts, R. K. 1977. *Soldiers, Statesmen, and Cold War Crises*. Cambridge: Harvard University Press.

25. Blainey, G. 1973. *The Causes of War*. New York: Free Press.

26. Bonoma, T. V. 1975. *Conflict: Escalation and Deescalation*. Beverly Hills: Sage.

27. Boucher, J., D. Landis, and K. A. Clark, eds. 1987. *Ethnic Conflict: International Perspectives*. Newbury Park, Calif.: Sage.

28. Boudreau, T. 1991. *Sheathing the Sword: The United Nations Secretary-General and the Prevention of International Conflict*. New York: Greenwood.

29. Boulding, E. 1992. *New Agendas for Peace Research: Conflict and Security Reexamined*. Boulder, Colo.: Lynne Rienner.

30. Boulding, E., J. R. Passmore, and R. S. Gassler, comps. 1979. *Bibliography on World Conflict and Peace*. 2d ed. Boulder, Colo.: Westview.

31. Brams, S. J. 1985. *Superpower Games: Applying Games Theory to Superpower Conflict*. New Haven, Conn.: Yale University Press.

32. Braudel, F. 1979. *The Perspective of the World*. London: Fontana.

33. Brecher, M., J. Wilkenfeld, and P. James. 1989. *Crisis, Conflict, and Instability*. Oxford: Pergamon.

34. Brecher, M., J. Wilkenfeld, and S. Moser. 1988. *Crises in the Twentieth Century*. New York: Pergamon.

35. Bremer, S. A. 1990. "The Contagiousness of Coercion: The Spread of Serious International Disputes, 1900–1976." *International Interactions* 91: 29–55.

36. Brogan, P. 1990. *The Fighting Never Stopped: A Comprehensive Guide to World Conflicts Since 1945*. New York: Vintage.

37. ———. 1989. *World Conflicts: Why and Where They Are Happening*. London: Bloomsbury.

38. Brown, J., and W. P. Snyder, eds. 1985. *The Regionalization of Warfare: The Falklands/Malvinas Islands, Lebanon, and the Iran-Iraq Conflicts*. New Brunswick, N.J.: Transactions.

39. Bull, H., and A. Watson, eds. 1984. *The Expansion of International Society*. Oxford: Clarendon.

40. Burton, J. W. 1969. *Conflict and Communication: The Use of Controlled Communication in International Relations*. London: Macmillan.

41. ———. 1979. *Deviance, Terrorism, and War.* Oxford: Martin Robertson.

42. ———. 1984. *Global Conflict: The Domestic Sources of International Crisis.* Brighton (Sussex), Eng.: Wheatsheaf.

43. Burton, J. W., and F. Dukes. 1990. *Conflict: Practices in Management, Settlement, and Resolution.* New York: St. Martin's.

44. ———, eds. 1990. *Conflict: Readings in Management and Resolution.* New York: St. Martin's.

45. Burton, J. W., F. Dukes, and G. Mason. 1990. *Conflict: Resolution and Prevention.* Basingstoke (Hants), Eng.: Macmillan.

46. Butterworth, R. L. 1976. *Managing Interstate Conflict, 1945–1974.* Pittsburgh: Center for International Studies, University of Pittsburgh.

47. ———. 1978. *Moderation From Management: International Organizations and Peace.* Pittsburgh: University of Pittsburgh Center for International Studies.

48. Buzan, B. 1988. *National Security in the Third World.* Aldershot (Hants), Eng.: Edward Elgar.

49. Calvocressi, P. 1962. *World Order and New States.* London: Chatto and Windus.

50. Canciam, F. M., and J. W. Gibson, eds. 1990. *Making War/Making Peace: The Social Foundations of Violent Conflict.* Belmont, Calif.: Wadsworth.

51. Carter, J. 1982. *Keeping the Faith: Memoirs of a President.* New York: Bantam.

52. Chanda, N. 1986. *Brother Enemy: The War After the War.* San Diego, Calif.: Harcourt Brace Jovanovich.

53. Chay, J., and T. E. Ross, eds. 1986. *Buffer States in World Politics.* Boulder, Colo.: Westview.

54. Chisholm, M., and D. M. Smith. 1990. *Shared Space, Divided Space: Essays on Conflict and Territorial Organization.* London: Unwin Hyman.

55. Chourcri, N. 1975. *Nations in Conflict: National Growth and International Violence.* San Francisco: W. H. Freeman.

56. Cimbala, S. J., and K. A. Dunn, eds. 1986. *Conflict Termination and Military Strategy: Coercion, Persuasion, and War.* Boulder, Colo.: Westview.

57. Cimbala, S. J., and S. R. Waldman, eds. 1992. *Controlling and Ending Conflict: Issues Before and After the Cold War.* New York: Greenwood.

58. Claude, I. L. Jr. 1962. *Power and International Relations.* New York: Random House.

59. Clutterbuck, R. 1993. *International Crisis and Conflict.* New York: St. Martin's.

60. Coakley, J., ed. 1993. *The Territorial Management of Ethnic Conflict.* London: F. Cass.

61. Cohen, R. 1979. *Threat Perception and International Crisis.* Madison: University of Wisconsin Press.

62. ———. 1987. *Theatre of Power.* London: Longman.

63. Conner, W. 1994. *Ethnonationalism: The Quest for Understanding.* Princeton, N.J.: Princeton University Press.

64. Cox, K. R., D. R. Reynolds, and S. Rokkan, eds. 1974. *Locational Approaches to Power and Conflict.* Beverly Hills: Sage.

65. Craig, G. A., and A. L. George. 1983. *Force and Statecraft: Diplomatic Problems of Our Time.* New York: Oxford University Press.

66. Crozier, B. 1974. *A Theory of Conflict.* London: Hamilton.

67. Cukwurah, A. O. 1967. *The Settlement of Boundary Disputes in International Law.* Manchester, Eng.: Manchester University Press; Dobbs Ferry, N.Y.: Oceana.

68. Cusack, T. R., and W. D. Eberwein. 1982. "Prelude to War: Incidence, Escalation, and Intervention in International Disputes, 1900–1976." *International Interactions* 91: 9–28.

69. Dac, A. S., ed. 1982. *Border and Territorial Disputes.* Detroit: Gale Research Co.

70. Daniel, C., ed. 1987. *Chronicles of the Twentieth Century.* Mount Kisco, N.Y.: Chronicle Publications.

71. David Davies Memorial Institute of International Studies. 1972. *International Disputes: The Legal Aspects.* London: Europa.

72. David, K., and S. Kadirgamar. 1989. *Ethnicity: Identity, Conflict, and Crisis.* Hong Kong: Arena.

73. David, S. 1985. *Defending Third World Regimes From Coups d'Etat.* Lanham, Md.: Harvard University Center for International Affairs/University Press of America.

74. ———. 1987. *Third World Coups d'Etat and International Security.* Baltimore: Johns Hopkins University Press.

75. Davison, W. P. 1974. *Mass Communication and Conflict Resolution: The Role of the Information Media in the Advancement of International Understanding.* New York: Praeger.

76. Day, A., ed. 1987. *Border and Territorial Disputes.* 2d ed. Burnt Mill, Harlow (Essex), Eng.: Longman.

77. Day, A. R., and M. W. Doyle, eds. 1986. *Escalation and Intervention: Multilateral Security and Its Alternatives.* Boulder, Colo.: Westview.

78. De Silva, K. M., and R. J. May, eds. 1991. *Internationalization of Ethnic Conflict.* New York: St. Martin's.

79. Diehl, P. 1993. *International Peacemaking.* Baltimore: Johns Hopkins University Press.

80. Diehl, P., and G. Goertz. 1985. "Territorial Changes and Militarized Conflict." *Journal of Conflict Resolution* 32 (March): 103–122.

81. Donelan, M. D., and M. J. Grieve. 1973. *International Disputes: Case Histories, 1945–1970.* New York: St. Martin's.

82. Doran, C. F. 1976. *Domestic Conflict in State Relations: The American Sphere of Influence.* Beverly Hills: Sage.

83. Dowling, D. 1980. *An Atlas of Territorial and Border Disputes.* London: New English Library.

84. Druckman, D. 1973. *Human Factors in International Negotiations: Social-Psychological Aspects of International Conflict.* Beverly Hills: Sage.

85. Dupuy, R., and T. Dupuy. 1986. *The Encyclopedia of Military History.* 2d rev. ed. New York: Harper and Row.

86. Eagleton, C. 1972. *Analysis of the Problem of War.* New York: Garland.

87. Eberwein, W. D. 1982. "The Seduction of Power: Serious International Disputes and the Power Status of Nations, 1900–1976." *International Interactions* 91: 57–74.

88. Edmead, F. 1971. *Analysis and Prediction in International Mediation.* New York: UNITAR Study.

89. Enloe, C. H. 1973. *Ethnic Conflict and Political Development.* Boston: Little, Brown.

90. Esman, M. J. 1977. *Ethnic Conflict in the Western World.* Based on a conference on Ethnic Pluralism and Conflict in Contemporary West Europe and Canada, in Ithaca, New York, 1975. Ithaca, N.Y.: Cornell University Press.

91. Esman, M. J., and S. Telhami. 1995. *International Organizations and Ethnic Conflict.* Ithaca, N.Y.: Cornell University Press.

92. Etzioni, A., and Wenglinsky, M. 1970. *War and Its Prevention.* New York: Harper and Row.

93. Fallers, L. A. 1974. *The Social Anthropology of the Nation-State.* Chicago: Aldine.

94. Fauré, G., and J. Z. Rubin, eds. 1993. *Culture and Negotiation: The Resolution of Water Disputes.* Newbury Park, Calif.: Sage.

95. Fermann, G. 1992. *International Peacekeeping, 1956–1990: Comparative Analysis.* Defence Study #5. Oslo: Institute for Defence Studies.

96. Findlay, T. 1992. *Conflict Resolution and Peacekeeping in the Post–Cold War Era: Implications for Regional Security.* Canberra: Peace Research Center, Australian National University.

97. Folberg, J., and A. Taylor. 1984. *Mediation: A Comprehensive Guide to Resolving Conflicts Without Litigation.* San Francisco: Jossey-Bass.

98. Franck, T. M. 1985. *Nation Against Nation.* London: Oxford University Press.

99. Frankel, J. 1969. *International Politics: Conflict and Harmony.* London: Allen Lane.

100. Galtung, J. 1977. "Patterns of Conflict and Prospects for Peace." Third Annual Peace Lecture, New Zealand Foundation for Peace Studies, University of Auckland, June 23, 1977.

101. Gilpin, R. 1981. *War and Change in World Politics.* Cambridge: Cambridge University Press.

102. Gochman, C. S., and Z. Maoz. 1984. "Militarized Interstate Disputes, 1916–1975." *Journal of Conflict Resolution* 103: 585–615.

103. Goertz, G. 1992. *Territorial Changes and International Conflict.* London: Routledge.

104. Goodman, A. E. , and S. Clemens Bogart, eds. 1992. *Making Peace: The United States and Conflict Resolution.* Boulder, Colo.: Westview.

105. Graebner, N. A., ed. 1976. *The Cold War: A Conflict of Ideology and Power.* 2d ed. Lexington, Mass.: D.C. Heath.

106. Gulliver, P. A. 1987. *Disputes and Negotiations.* New York: Academic.

107. Gurr, T. R. 1993. *Minorities at Risk: A Global View of Ethnopolitical Conflicts.* Washington, D.C.: U.S. Institute of Peace Press.

108. ———. 1994. *Ethnic Conflict in World Politics*. Boulder, Colo.: Westview.

109. Haas, M. 1974. *International Conflict*. Indianapolis, Ind.: Bobbs-Merrill.

110. Haass, R. 1990. *Conflicts Unending: The United States and Regional Disputes*. New Haven, Conn.: Yale University Press.

111. Harkavy, R. E., and S. G. Neuman, eds. 1985. *The Lessons of Recent Wars in the Third World*. Lexington, Mass.: Lexington Books.

112. Hass, E., R. L. Butterworth, and J. S. Nye. 1972. *Conflict Management by International Organizations*. Morristown, N.J.: General Learning.

113. Heisler, M. O. 1977. *Ethnic Conflict in the World Today*. Vol. 433 of *The Annals of American Academy of Political and Social Science*. Philadelphia: Academy of Political and Social Science.

114. Heraclides, A. 1991. *The Self-Determination of Minorities in International Politics*. London and Portland, Ore.: F. Cass.

115. Holbraad, C. 1979. *Superpowers and International Conflict*. New York: St. Martin's.

116. Holsti, K. J. 1991. *Peace and War: Armed Conflicts and International Order, 1648–1989*. New York: Cambridge University Press.

117. Holsti, O. R. 1972. *Crisis, Escalation, War*. Montreal: McGill–Queen's University Press.

118. Holsti, O. R., R. M. Siverson, and A. L. George, eds. 1980. *Change in the International System*. Boulder, Colo.: Westview.

119. Horowitz, D. L. 1985. *Ethnic Groups in Conflict*. Berkeley and Los Angeles: University of California Press.

120. Houweling, H. W., and J. G. Siccama. 1985. "The Epidemiology of War, 1816–1980." *Journal of Conflict Resolution* 29 (December): 641–663.

121. Howard, M. 1983. *The Causes of War*. London: Unwin.

122. ———, ed. 1979. *Restraints on War: Studies in the Limitation of Armed Conflict*. Oxford: Oxford University Press.

123. Hybel, A. R. 1986. *The Logic of Surprise in International Conflict*. Lexington, Mass.: Lexington Books.

124. International Institute for Strategic Studies (IISS). 1981. "Third World Conflict and International Security." Adelphi Papers #166–167. Based on IISS conference held in Stressa, Italy, 1980. London: IISS.

125. Intrilligator, M. D., and H. A. Jacobsen. 1988. *East-West Conflict: Elite Perception and Political Options*. Boulder, Colo.: Westview.

126. Isand, W., and Y. Nagao, eds. 1983. *International and Regional Conflict: Analytic Approaches*. Cambridge, Mass.: Ballinger.

127. Janowitz, M. 1975. *Military Conflict: Essays in the Institutional Analysis of War and Peace*. Beverly Hills: Sage.

128. Jervis, R. 1976. *Perception and Misperception in International Politics*. Princeton, N.J.: Princeton University Press.

129. Kacowicz, A. M. 1994. *Peaceful Territorial Change*. Columbia: University of South Carolina Press.

130. Kahng, T. J. 1970. *Law, Politics and the Security Council: An Inquiry into the Handling of Legal Questions Involved in International Disputes and Situations.* 2d ed. The Hague: M. Nijhoff.

131. Karnes, M. P., ed. 1986. *Persistent Patterns and Emergent Structures in a Waning Century.* New York: Praeger.

132. Keegan, J., ed. 1983. *World Armies.* 2d ed. Detroit: Gale Research Co.

133. *Keesings Contemporary Archives.* Weekly and monthly, 1931–1987.

134. *Keesings Record of World Events.* Monthly, 1987– (continues *Keesings Contemporary Archives*).

135. Kegley, C. W., and Raymond, G. A. 1990. *When Trust Breaks Down: Alliance Norms and World Politics.* Columbia: University of South Carolina Press.

136. Kelman, H., ed. 1965. *International Behavior.* New York: Holt, Rinehart, and Winston.

137. Kennedy, P. M. 1987. *The Rise and Fall of the Great Powers: Economic Change and Military Conflict From 1500 to 2000.* New York: Random House.

138. Keohane, R. O., and J. Nye, eds. 1972. *Transnational Relations and World Politics.* Cambridge: Harvard University Press.

139. ———. 1977. *Power and Independence: World Politics in Transition.* Boston: Little, Brown.

140. Kidron, M., and D. Smith. 1983. *The War Atlas: Armed Conflict, Armed Peace.* New York: Simon and Schuster.

141. Kliot, N., and S. Waterman, eds. 1991. *The Political Geography of Conflict and Peace.* London: Belhaven.

142. Kohn, G. C., ed. 1986. *Dictionary of Wars.* New York: Facts on File.

143. Kolb, D. 1983. *The Mediators.* Cambridge: MIT Press.

144. Kremenyuk, V., ed. 1991. *International Negotiation: Analysis, Approaches, Issues.* San Francisco: Jossey-Bass.

145. Kriesburg, L., T. A. Northrup, and S. J. Thorson, eds. 1989. *Intractable Conflicts and Their Transformation.* Syracuse, N.Y.: Syracuse University Press.

146. Laffin, J. 1986. *The World in Conflict, 1987, War Annual 1.* London: Brassey's.

147. ———. 1987. *The World in Conflict, 1988, War Annual 2.* London: Brassey's.

148. ———. 1989. *The World in Conflict, 1989: War Annual 3.* London: Brassey's.

149. Lebow, R. N. 1981. *Between Peace and War: The Nature of International Crisis.* Baltimore: Johns Hopkins University Press.

150. Lederach, J. P. 1994. *Building Peace: Sustainable Reconciliation in Divided Societies.* Tokyo: United Nations University Press.

151. Leurdijk, J. H. 1986. *Intervention in International Politics.* Leeuwarden, Netherlands: Eisema.

152. Le Vine, R. A., and D. T. Campbell. 1972. *Ethnocentrism: Theories of Conflict, Ethnic Attitudes, and Group Behavior.* New York: Wiley.

153. Levy, J. S. 1981. "Alliance Formation and War Behavior: An Analysis of the Great Powers, 1495–1975." *Journal of Conflict Resolution* 25 (December): 581–613.

154. ———. 1983. *War in the Modern Great Power System, 1495–1975*. Lexington: University of Kentucky Press.

155. Lewis, S., ed. 1991. *Conflict Management for the Future*. Washington, D.C.: U.S. Institute of Peace Press.

156. Lider, J. 1977. *On the Nature of War*. Farnborough, Eng.: Saxon House.

157. Luard, E. 1970. *Conflict and Peace in the Modern International System*. London: University of London Press.

158. ———. 1970. *The International Regulation of Frontier Disputes*. London: Thames and Hudson.

159. ———. 1986. *War in International Society*. New Haven, Conn.: Yale University Press.

160. ———. 1988. *Conflict and Peace in the Modern International System: A Study of the Principles of International Order*. 2d ed. Basingstoke (Hants), Eng.: Macmillan.

161. Maniruzzaman, T. 1982. *The Security of Small States in the Third World*. Working Paper #25. Canberra: Strategic and Defence Studies Center, Australian National University.

162. Maoz, Z. 1982. *Paths to Conflict: International Dispute Initiation, 1816–1976*. Boulder, Colo.: Westview.

163. Matthews, R. O., A. G. Rubinoff, and J. G. Stein, eds. 1989. *International Conflict and Conflict Management: Readings in World Politics*. 2d ed. Scarborough, Ont.: Prentice-Hall Canada.

164. Maull, H. W. 1984. *Raw Materials, Energy, and Western Security*. International Institute for Strategic Studies #22. London: Macmillan.

165. Mautner-Mankhof, E., ed. 1989. *Process of International Negotiations*. Boulder, Colo.: Westview.

166. McGarrt, J., and B. O'Leary, ed. 1993. *The Politics of Ethnic Conflict Regulation: Case Studies of Protracted Ethnic Conflicts*. London: Routledge.

167. McWhinney, E. 1991. *Judicial Settlement of International Disputes: Jurisdiction, Justiciability, and Judicial Lawmaking on the Contemporary International Court*. Dordrecht, The Netherlands: M. Nijhoff.

168. Merritt, R. C., ed. 1972. *Communication in International Politics*. Urbana-Champaign: University of Illinois Press.

169. Merritt, R. L., and B. Russett, eds. 1981. *From National Development to Global Community*. London: George Allen and Unwin.

170. Miall, H. 1988. *Non-Government Third-Party Intervention in Conflicts: A Review of Four Approaches*. Oxford: Oxford Research Group.

171. ———. 1992. *The Peacemakers: Peaceful Settlement of Disputes Since 1945*. New York: St. Martin's.

172. ———. 1988. *The Onset of World War*. Boston: Allen and Unwin.

173. ———, ed. 1986. *The Disintegration of Political Systems: War and Revolution in Comparative Perspective*. Columbia: University of South Carolina Press.

174. ———. 1989. *Handbook of War Studies*. Boston: Unwin Hyman.

175. ———. 1990. "Big Wars, Little Wars—A Single Theory?" Special Issue of *International Interactions* 163: 157–224.

176. Midlarsky, M. I., ed. 1992. *The Internationalization of Communal Strife.* London: Routledge.

177. Millar, B. 1995. *When Opponents Cooperate: Great Power Conflict and Collaboration in World Politics.* Ann Arbor: University of Michigan Press.

178. Millar, T. B. 1983. *The Resolution of Conflict and the Study of Peace.* Canberra: Strategic and Defence Studies Center, Australian National University.

179. Minority Rights Group. 1989. *World Directory of Minorities.* Harlow (Essex), Eng.: Longman.

180. Mitchell, A. D., A. D. Grant, and E. J. Edmond, eds. 1981. *Major Armed Conflict: A Compendium of Interstate and Intrastate Conflict, 1730–1980.* Ottawa, Ont.: May.

181. Mitchell, C. R. 1981. *The Structure of International Conflict.* London: Macmillan.

182. Montville, K. V., ed. 1990. *Conflict and Peacemaking in Multiethnic Societies.* Lexington, Mass.: Lexington Books.

183. Moore, C. W. 1986. *The Mediation Process: Practical Strategies for Resolving Conflict.* San Francisco: Jossey-Bass.

184. Munro, D., and A. J. Day. 1990. *A World Record of Major Conflict Areas.* Chicago: St. James Press.

185. Mushkat, M. 1982. *The Third World and Peace: Some Aspects of the Interrelationship of Underdevelopment and International Security.* New York: St. Martin's.

186. Natkiel, R., and J. Pimlott, eds. 1988. *Atlas of Warfare.* Greenwich, Conn.: Bison Books.

187. Nettleship, M. A., R. D. Givens, and A. Nettleship, eds. 1975. *War, Its Causes and Correlates.* The Hague: Mouton.

188. Nicholson, M. 1970. *Conflict Analysis.* London: English Universities Press.

189. Nijman, J. 1993. *The Geopolitics of Power and Conflict: Superpowers in the International System, 1945–1992.* London: Belhaven.

190. Nordstrom, C. *War Zones: Cultures of Violence, Militarism, and Peace.* Working Paper #145. Canberra: Peace Research Center, Australian National University.

191. Northedge, F. S., and M. D. Donelan. 1971. *International Disputes: The Political Aspects.* London: Europa.

192. Northedge, F. S., ed. 1974. *The Use of Force in International Relations.* London: Faber.

193. Paarlberg, R. L., E. Y. Park, and D. L. Wyman. 1978. *Diplomatic Disputes: United States Conflict With Iran, Japan, and Mexico.* Cambridge: Center for International Affairs, Harvard University Press.

194. Paget, J. 1967. *Counter-Insurgency Operations: Techniques of Guerrilla Warfare.* New York: Walker.

195. Patchen, M. 1988. *Resolving Disputes Between Nations: Coercion or Conciliation.* Durham, N.C.: Duke University Press.

196. Payne, R. 1973. *Massacre.* New York: Macmillan.

197. Pechota, V. 1971. *Complementary Structures of Third-Party Settlement and International Disputes.* New York: UNITAR.

198. Pillar, P. R. 1983. *Negotiating Peace.* Princeton, N.J.: Princeton University Press.

199. Plascov, A. 1982. *Modernization, Political Development, and Stability.* Aldershot (Hants), Eng.: Gower.

200. Princen, T. 1992. *Intermediaries in International Conflict.* Princeton, N.J.: Princeton University Press.

201. Rabi, M. 1994. *Conflict Resolution and Ethnicity.* Westport, Conn.: Praeger.

202. Rahim, M. A., ed. 1989. *Managing Conflict: An Interdisciplinary Approach.* New York: Praeger.

203. Raman, K. V. 1975. *The Ways of the Peacemaker: A Study of the United Nations Intermediary Assistance in the Peaceful Settlement of Disputes.* New York: UNITAR.

204. Rangarajan, L. N. 1985. *The Limitations of Conflict: A Theory of Bargaining and Negotiation.* London: Croom Helm.

205. Rapport, A. 1989. *The Origins of Violence: Approaches to the Study of Conflict.* New York: Paragon House.

206. Rice, E. E. 1988. *Wars of the Third Kind: Conflict in Underdeveloped Countries.* Berkeley and Los Angeles: University of California Press.

207. Richardson, J. L., and R. Leaver, ed. 1993. *The Post–Cold War Order: Diagnoses and Prognoses.* St. Leonards (NSW), Australia: Allen and Unwin.

208. Richardson, L. F. 1960. *Statistics of Deadly Quarrels.* Pittsburgh: Boxwood.

209. Roberts, A., and B. Kingsbury, eds. 1988. *United Nations, Divided World: The United Nations' Role in International Relations.* Oxford: Clarendon.

210. Rosenau, J. N., and H. Tromp, eds. 1989. *Interdependence and Conflict in World Politics.* Aldershot (Hants), Eng.: Avebury.

211. Rothman, J. 1992. *From Confrontation to Cooperation: Resolving Ethnic and Regional Conflict.* Newbury Park, Calif.: Sage.

212. Rothschild, J. 1981. *Ethnopolitics: A Conceptual Framework.* New York: Columbia University Press.

213. Royce, A. P. 1982. *Ethnic Identity: Strategies of Diversity.* Bloomington: Indiana University Press.

214. Rubinstein, A. Z. 1988. *Moscow's Third World Strategy.* Princeton, N.J.: Princeton University Press.

215. Rubinstein, R. A., and M. L. Foster, eds. 1988. *The Social Dynamics of Peace and Conflict: Culture in International Security.* Boulder, Colo.: Westview.

216. Rummel, R. 1981. *Understanding Conflict and War: The Just Peace.* Beverly Hills: Sage.

217. Rupesinghe, K., ed. 1992. *Internal Conflict and Governance.* London: Macmillan.

218. ———. 1994. *Conflict Transformation.* London: Macmillan.

219. Russett, B., ed. 1972. *Peace, War, and Numbers.* Beverly Hills: Sage.

220. Ryan, S. 1990. *Ethnic Conflict in International Relations.* Brookfield, Vt.: Gower.

221. Sabrosky, A. N., ed. 1985. *Polarity and War: The Changing Structure of International Conflict.* Boulder, Colo.: Westview.

222. Samarasinghe, S. W. R., and R. Coughlan. 1991. *Economic Dimensions of Ethnic Conflict.* London: Pinter.

223. Sandole, D. J. D., and H. vander Merwe. 1993. *Conflict Resolution Theory and Practice: Integration and Application.* Manchester, Eng.: Manchester University Press.

224. Schechterman, B., and M. W. Slann, eds. 1993. *The Ethnic Dimension in International Relations.* Westport, Conn.: Praeger.

225. Schere, K. R., R. P. Abeles, and C. S. Fischer. 1975. *Human Aggression and Conflict: Interdisciplinary Perspectives.* Englewood Cliffs, N.J.: Prentice-Hall.

226. Schofield, C. H., ed. 1994. *Global Boundaries.* London: Routledge.

227. Singer, J. D. 1972. *The Wages of War, 1916–1965.* New York: Wiley.

228. ———, ed. 1980. *The Correlates of War.* New York: Free Press.

229. Singer, J. D., and M. Small. 1984. *The Wages of War, 1816–1980.* Ann Arbor, Mich.: Inter-University Consortium for Political and Social Research.

230. Singer, M. R. 1972. *Weak States in a World of Power.* New York: Free Press.

231. SIPRI (Stockholm International Peace Research Institute). *World Armaments and Disarmament: SIPRI Year Book.* Stockholm: SIPRI.

232. Sivard, R. L. 1987. *World Military and Social Expenditures.* Washington, D.C.: World Priorities.

233. Sloss, L., and M. Scott Davis, eds. 1986. *A Game of High Stakes: Lessons Learned in Negotiating With the Soviet Union.* Cambridge, Mass.: Ballinger.

234. Slow, P. M. 1990. *Geography and Political Power: The Geography of Nations and States.* London: Routledge.

235. Small, M., and D. Singer. 1982. *Resort to Arms: International and Civil Wars, 1816–1980.* Beverly Hills: Sage.

236. Smith, C. G. 1971. *Conflict Resolution: Contributions of the Behavioral Sciences.* South Bend, Ind.: University of Notre Dame Press.

237. Snyder, G. H., and P. Diesing. 1977. *Conflict Among Nations: Bargaining, Decision Making, and System Structure in International Crises.* Princeton, N.J.: Princeton University Press.

238. Spiegel, S. L., and K. N. Waltz, eds. 1971. *Conflict in World Politics.* Cambridge, Mass.: Winthrop.

239. Stavenhagen, R. 1991. *The Ethnic Question: Conflicts, Development, and Human Rights.* Tokyo: United Nations University Press.

240. Steinbruner, J. D., ed. 1980. *Restructuring American Foreign Policy.* Washington, D.C.: Brookings.

241. Stoessinger, J. G. 1982. *Why Nations Go to War.* 3d ed. New York: St. Martin's.

242. Stone, J. 1954. *Legal Controls of International Conflict: A Treatise on the Dynamics of Disputes and War-Law.* New York: Rinehart.

243. Stulberg, J. B. 1987. *Taking Charge, Managing Conflict.* Lexington, Mass.: Lexington Books.

244. *Survey of International Affairs.* Annual. London: Royal Institute of International Affairs.

245. Susskind, L., and J. Cruikshank, 1987. *Breaking the Impasse.* New York: Basic Books.

246. Suter, K. D. 1986. *Alternatives to War: Conflict Resolution and the Peaceful Settlement of International Disputes.* 2d ed. Sydney: Women's International League for Peace and Freedom.

247. Tacsan, J. T. 1992. *The Dynamics of International Law in Conflict Resolution.* Dordrecht, the Netherlands, and Boston: M. Nijhoff.

248. Tanca, A. 1993. *Foreign Armed Intervention in International Conflict.* Boston: M. Nijhoff.

249. Taylor, C. F., and D. A. Jodice. 1983. *World Handbook of Political and Social Indicators.* 3d ed. New Haven, Conn.: Yale University Press.

250. Taylor, W. J., and S. A. Maaranen, eds. 1982. *The Future of Conflict in the 1980s.* Lexington, Mass.: Lexington Books.

251. Taylor, W. J., S. A. Maaranen, and G. W. Gong, eds. 1984. *Strategic Responses to Conflict in the 1980's.* Lexington, Mass.: Lexington Books.

252. Thakar, R. C., ed. 1988. *International Conflict Resolution.* Dunedin, N.Z.: University of Otago Press.

253. Tharp, P. A. 1971. *Regional International Organizations: Structures and Functions.* New York: St. Martin's.

254. Thompson, R., ed. 1981. *War in Peace: Conventional and Guerrilla Warfare Since 1945.* London: Orbis.

255. Tillema, H. K. 1991. *International Armed Conflict Since 1945: A Bibliographic Handbook of Wars and Military Interventions.* Boulder, Colo.: Westview.

256. Tinker, H. 1977. *Race, Conflict, and the International Order: From Empire to United Nations.* London: Macmillan.

257. Tunnicliff, K. H. 1984. *The United Nations and the Mediation of International Conflicts.* Ann Arbor: University of Michigan Press.

258. Valents, J. 1989. *Gorbachev's New Thinking and Third World Conflicts.* New York: Transaction.

259. Vance, C. 1983. *Hard Choices: Critical Years in America's Foreign Policy.* New York: Simon and Schuster.

260. Van den Berghe, P., ed. 1990. *State Violence and Ethnicity.* Niwot: University Press of Colorado.

261. Vayrynen, R., ed. 1991. *New Directions in Conflict Theory: Conflict Resolution and Conflict Transformation.* London: Sage.

262. Venn, F. 1986. *Oil Diplomacy in the Twentieth Century.* London: Macmillan.

263. Vital, D. 1971. *The Survival of Small States: Studies in Small Power/Great Power Conflict.* London: Oxford University Press.

264. Volkan, V. D., J. V. Montville, and D. A. Julius, eds. 1991. *Unofficial Diplomacy at Work.* Vol. 2 in *The Psychodynamics of International Relationships.* Lexington, Mass.: Lexington Books.

265. Waldock, C. H. M. 1972. *International Disputes: The Legal Aspects.* London: David Davies Memorial Institute of International Studies/Europa.

266. Wallace, M. 1973. *War and Rank Among Nations.* Lexington, Mass.: D. C. Heath.

267. Wallensteen, P., J. Galtung, and C. Portales, eds. 1985. *Global Militarism.* Boulder, Colo.: Westview.

268. Walt, S. M. 1987. *The Origins of Alliances.* Ithaca, N.Y.: Cornell University Press.

269. Wehr, P. 1979. *Conflict Regulation.* Boulder, Colo.: Westview.

270. Westing, A. H., ed. 1986. *Global Resources and International Conflict: Environmental Factors in Strategic Policy and Action.* New York: Oxford University Press.

271. Whelan, J. G. 1983. *Soviet Diplomacy and Negotiating Behavior.* Boulder, Colo.: Westview.

272. White, N. D. *Keeping the Peace: The United Nations and the Maintenance of International Peace and Security.* New York: St. Martin's.

273. Wilkenfeld, J., ed. 1973. *Conflict Behavior and Linkage Politics.* New York: David McKay.

274. Williams, C. H., and E. Kofman, eds. 1989. *Community Conflict: Partition and Nationalism.* New York: Routledge.

275. Woito, R. S., and R. Pickus. 1982. *To End War: A New Approach to International Conflict.* New York. Pilgrim.

276. Wolfers, A. 1962. *Discord and Collaboration.* Baltimore: Johns Hopkins University Press.

277. Wood, D. 1968. *Conflict in the Twentieth Century.* Adelphi Papers #48. London: IISS.

278. Yarrow, C. H. M. 1978. *Quaker Experiences in International Conciliation.* New Haven, Conn.: Yale University Press.

279. Zacher, M. W. 1979. *International Conflict and Collective Security, 1946–1977.* New York: Praeger.

280. Zagare, F. C., ed. 1990. *Modeling International Conflict.* New York: Gordon and Breach Science Publishers.

281. Zartman, I. W., and M. R. Berman. 1982. *The Practical Negotiator.* New Haven, Conn.: Yale University Press.

282. Zartman, I. W., ed. 1991. *Resolving Regional Conflict: International Perspectives.* Newbury Park, Calif.: Sage.

283. ———. 1995. *Collapsed States: The Disintegration and Restoration of Legitimate Authority.* Boulder, Colo.: Lynne Rienner.

284. Zimmerman, W., and H. K. Jacobson, eds. 1993. *Behavior, Culture, and Conflict in World Politics.* Ann Arbor: University of Michigan Press.

AFRICA

285. Abi-Saab, G. 1978. *The U.N. Operation in the Congo, 1960–1964.* Oxford: Oxford University Press.

286. *Africa Contemporary Record.* Annual. 1968/1969–.

287. *African Recorder.* Weekly. 1962–.

288. Albino, O. 1970. *The Sudan: A Southern Viewpoint.* London: Institute of Race Relations, Oxford University.

289. Alport, C. J. M. 1965. *The Sudden Assignment: Being a Record of Service in Central Africa During the Last Controversial Years of the Federation of Rhodesia and Nyasaland, 1961–1963.* London: Hodder and Stoughton.

290. Aluko, O., and T. Shaw, eds. 1985. *Southern Africa in the 1980s.* London: Allen and Unwin.

291. Amate, C. O. C. 1986. *Inside the OAU.* New York: St. Martin's.

292. Andemicael, B. 1972. *Peaceful Settlement Among African States: Roles of U.N. and OAU.* New York: UNITAR.

293. Andereggen, A. 1994. *France's Relationship With Sub-Saharan Africa.* Westport, Conn.: Praeger.

294. Andrews, W. G. 1962. *French Politics and Algeria: The Process of Policy Formations, 1954–1962.* New York: Appleton-Century-Crofts.

295. Assefa, H. 1987. *Mediation of Civil Wars: Approaches and Strategies—The Sudan Conflict.* Boulder, Colo.: Westview.

296. Avirgan, T., and M. Honey. 1982. *War in Uganda: The Legacy of Idi Amin.* Westport, Conn.: Lawrence Hill.

297. Awoonor, K. 1990. *Ghana: A Political History From Pre-European to Modern Times.* Accra, Ghana: Sedco.

298. Barber, J. 1967. *Rhodesia: The Road to Rebellion.* London: Oxford University Press.

299. Bardill, J., and H. Cobbe. 1985. *Lesotho: Dilemmas of Dependence in Southern Africa.* Boulder, Colo.: Westview.

300. Behr, E. 1961. *The Algerian Problem.* Harmondsworth (Middlesex), Eng.: Penguin.

301. Bender, G. J. 1978. *Angola Under the Portuguese: The Myth and the Reality.* London: Heinemann.

302. Berman, B., and J. Lonsdale. 1992. *Unhappy Valley: Conflict in Kenya and Africa.* London: J. Currey.

303. Beshir, M. O. 1968. *The Southern Sudan: Background to Conflict.* New York: Praeger.

304. ———. 1974. *Revolution and Nationalism in the Sudan.* London: Rex Collings.

305. Biebuyck, D., and M. Douglas. 1961. *Congo Tribes and Parties.* London: Royal Anthropological Institute.

306. Birmingham, D. 1992. *Front-line Nationalism in Angola and Mozambique.* London: J. Currey.

307. Boatena, E. A. 1978. *A Political Geography of Africa.* Cambridge: Cambridge University Press.

308. Bozzoli, B., ed. 1987. *Class, Community, and Conflict: South African Perspectives.* Johannesburg: Ravan.

309. Brown, M. 1979. *Madagascar Rediscovered: A History From Early Times to Independence.* Hamden, Conn.: Archon.

310. Brownlie, I. 1963. *African Boundaries: A Legal and Diplomatic Encyclopedia.* Berkeley and Los Angeles: University of California Press.

311. Bruce, N. 1975. *Portugal: The Last Empire.* New York: Wiley.

312. Burchett, W. 1978. *Southern Africa Stands Up: The Revolutions in Angola, Mozambique, Zimbabwe, Namibia, and South Africa.* New York: Urizen Books.

313. Carmichael, J. 1993. *African Eldorado: Gold Coast to Ghana.* London: Duckworth.

314. Carmoy, G. de. 1970. *The Foreign Policies of France, 1944–1968.* Chicago: University of Chicago Press.

315. Carter, G. M., and P. O'Meara, eds. 1982. *International Politics in Southern Africa.* Bloomington: Indiana University Press.

316. Carter, G. M., ed. 1964. *Five African States: Responses to Diversity: The Congo, Dahomey, the Cameroon Federal Republic, the Rhodesias, and Nyasaland, South Africa.* London: Pall Mall.

317. Cawthra, G. 1986. *Brutal Force: The Apartheid War Machine.* London: International Defence and Aid Fund for Southern Africa.

318. Cervenka, Z. 1969. *The Organization of African Unity and Its Charter.* New York: Praeger.

319. Chan, S. 1992. *Kaunda and Southern Africa: Image and Reality in Foreign Policy.* London: British Academic Press.

320. Chan, S., and V. Jabri, eds. 1993. *Mediation in Southern Africa.* London: Macmillan.

321. Charlton, M. 1990. *The Last Colony in Africa: Diplomacy and the Independence of Rhodesia.* Oxford: B. Blackwell.

322. Chilcote, R. H., ed. 1972. *Protest and Resistance in Angola and Brazil: Comparative Studies.* Berkeley and Los Angeles: University of California Press.

323. Cilliers, J. 1985. *Counter-Insurgency in Rhodesia.* London: Croom Helm.

324. Clapham, C. S. 1976. *Liberia and Sierra Leone: Essay in Comparative Politics.* Cambridge: Cambridge University Press.

325. Clark, M. 1960. *Algeria in Turmoil—The Rebellion: Its Causes, Its Effects, Its Future.* New York: Grosset and Dunlap.

326. Clayton, A. 1984. *Counter-Insurgency in Kenya: A Study of Military Operations Against the Mau Mau.* Manhattan, Kan.: Sunflower University Press.

327. ———. 1988. *France, Soldiers, and Africa.* London: Brassey's.

328. Cliffe, L., and R. Bush. 1994. *The Transition to Independence in Namibia.* Boulder, Colo.: Lynne Rienner.

329. Cloete, S. 1956. *Storm Over Africa: A Study of the Mau Mau Rebellion, Its Causes, Effects, and Implications in Africa South of the Sahara.* Cape Town: Culemborg.

330. Cohen, M. A. 1974. *Arab Policy and Political Conflict in Africa: A Study of the Ivory Coast.* Chicago: University of Chicago Press.

331. Coker, C. 1985. *NATO, the Warsaw Pact, and Africa.* New York: St. Martin's.

332. ———. 1987. *South Africa's Security Dilemmas.* New York: Praeger.

333. Cooley, J. 1982. *Libyan Sandstorm.* New York: Holt, Rinehart, and Winston.

334. Damis, J. 1983. *Conflict in North West Africa.* Stanford, Calif.: Hoover.

335. Davidson, B. 1972. *In the Eye of the Storm: Angola's People.* London: Longman.

336. Decalo, S. 1976. *Coups and Army Rule in Africa: Studies in Military Style.* New Haven, Conn.: Yale University Press.

337. ———. 1987. *Historical Dictionary of Chad.* 2d ed. Metuchen, N.J.: Scarecrow.

338. Delarue, J. 1994. *L'OAS contre de Gaulle.* Paris: Fayard.

339. Deng, F., ed. 1991. *Conflict Management in Africa.* Washington, D.C.: Brookings.

340. Doob, L. W. 1970. *Resolving Conflict in Africa: The Fermeda Workshop.* New Haven, Conn.: Yale University Press.

341. Doornbos, M. B., ed. 1992. *Beyond Conflict in the Horn: Prospects for Peace, Recovery, and Development in Ethiopia, Somalia, and the Sudan.* Trenton, N.J.: Red Sea.

342. Dugard, C., ed. 1973. *The South West Africa/Namibia Dispute: Documents and Scholarly Writings on the Controversy Between South Africa and the United Nations.* Berkeley and Los Angeles: University of California Press.

343. Edgerton, R. 1989. *Mau Mau: An African Crucible.* New York: Free Press.

344. Ekpebu, L. B. 1989. *Zaire and the African Revolution.* Ibadan, Nigeria: Ibadan University Press.

345. Ekwe-Ekwe, H. 1990. *Conflict and Intervention in Africa: Nigeria, Angola, Zaire.* Basingstoke (Hants), Eng.: Macmillan.

346. El-Ayouty, Y., and I. W. Zartman, eds. 1984. *The OAU After Twenty Years.* New York: Praeger.

347. El-Ayouty, Y., ed. 1975. *The OAU After Ten Years.* New York: Praeger.

348. Eprile, C. 1974. *War and Peace in the Sudan.* Newton Abbot: David and Charles.

349. Epstein, H., ed. 1965. *Revolt in Congo, 1960–1964.* New York: Facts on File.

350. Erlikh, H. 1983. *The Struggle Over Eritrea, 1962–1978: War and Revolution in the Horn of Africa.* Stanford, Calif.: Hoover.

351. ———. 1994. *Ethiopia and the Middle East.* Boulder, Colo.: Lynne Rienner.

352. Farer, T. 1979. *War Clouds on the Horn of Africa: The Widening Storm.* 2d rev. ed. New York: Carnegie Endowment for International Peace.

353. Fitzgerald, M. 1980. *Drought, Famine, and Revolution in Ethiopia.* Occasional Paper #1. School of Oriental and African Studies. London: University of London.

354. Folz, W. J. 1965. *From French West Africa to the Mali Federation.* New Haven, Conn.: Yale University Press.

355. Fraenkkel, P. J. 1978. *The Namibians of South West Africa.* Minority Rights Group Report #19. London: Minority Rights Group.

356. Fukin, K., and J. Markakis, eds. 1994. *Ethnicity and Conflict in the Horn of Africa.* Athens: Ohio University Press.

357. Gann, L., and T. Hendriksen. 1981. *The Struggle for Zimbabwe: Battle in the Bush.* New York: Praeger.

358. Gauze, R. 1973. *The Politics of Congo, Brazzaville.* Translated and edited by V. B. Thompson and R. Adloff. Hoover Institution Publications #129. Stanford, Calif.: Hoover.

359. Gavshon, A. 1984. *Crisis in Africa: Battleground of East and West.* Boulder, Colo.: Westview.

360. Getachew, M. 1977. *An Inside View of the Ethiopian Revolution.* #39. Pasadena: Munger Africana Library, California Institute of Technology.

361. Gillespie, J. 1960. *Algeria, Rebellion, and Revolution.* New York: Praeger.

362. Gonidec, P. F. 1981. *African Politics.* The Hague: M. Nijhoff.

363. Gorman, R. 1981. *Political Conflict on the Horn of Africa.* New York: Praeger.

364. Gran, G., and G. Hill, eds. 1979. *Zaire: The Political Economy of Underdevelopment.* New York: Praeger.

365. Great Britain Central Office of Information, Reference Division. 1961. *Congo, Gabon, Central African Republic, and Chad.* London: (n. p.).

366. Halliday, F., and M. Molyneux. 1981. *The Ethiopian Revolution.* London: NLB.

367. Hanlon, J. 1984. *Mozambique: The Revolution Under Fire.* London: Zed.

368. Harbeson, J., and D. Rothchild, eds. 1991. *Africa in World Politics.* Boulder, Colo.: Westview.

369. Harsch, E. 1978. *The Ethiopian Revolution.* New York: Pathfinder.

370. Harsch, E., and T. Thoma. 1976. *Angola: The Hidden History of Washington's War.* New York: Pathfinder.

371. Heitman, H. 1985. *South African War Machine.* Novato, Calif.: Presidio.

372. Henderson, W. 1967. *The Rhodesian-U.K. Conflict: The Constitutional Issue.* Klemzig, South Aust.: South Australia–Rhodesia Association.

373. Henissart, P. 1971. *Wolves in the City: The Death of French Algeria.* London: Hart-Davis.

374. Herbstein, D., and J. A. Evenson. 1989. *The Devils Are Among Us: The War for Namibia.* London: Atlantic Highlands.

375. Heseltine, N. 1971. *Madagascar.* New York: Praeger.

376. Hooper, E., and L. Pirouet. 1989. *Uganda.* Minority Rights Group Report #66. London: Minority Rights Group.

377. Horne, A. 1987. *A Savage War of Peace: Algeria, 1954–1962.* Rev. ed. New York: Penguin.

378. Hoskyns, C., ed. 1969. *The Ethiopian-Somalia-Kenya Dispute, 1960–1967.* Dar es Salaam, Tanzania: Oxford University Press/Institute of Public Administration, University College, Tanzania.

379. Humbaraci, A., and N. Muchnik. 1974. *Portugal's African Wars: Angola, Guinea-Bissau, Mozambique.* New York: Third Press.

380. International Defence and Aid Fund. 1973. *The Rhodesia-Zambia Border Closure, January–February 1973.* London: International Defence and Aid Fund.

381. Jabri, V. 1990. *Mediating Conflict: Decision-Making and Western Intervention in Namibia.* Manchester, Eng.: Manchester University Press.

382. Jaster, R. S. 1985. *South Africa in Namibia: The Botha Strategy.* Lanham, Md.: University Press of America.

383. ———. 1986. *South Africa and Its Neighbours: The Dynamics of Regional Conflict.* Adelphi Papers #209. London: IISS/Jane's.

384. ——— .1989. *The Defence of White Power: South African Foreign Policy Under Pressure.* New York: St. Martin's.

385. ———. 1990. *The 1988 Peace Accords and the Future of South-Western Africa.* Adelphi Papers #253. London: Brassey's.

386. Johnson, D. H. 1988. *The Southern Sudan.* Minority Rights Group Report #78. London: Minority Rights Group.

387. Kalb, M. 1982. *The Congo Crisis: The Cold War in Africa From Eisenhower to Kennedy.* New York: Macmillan.

388. Kapungu, L. T. 1974. *Rhodesia: The Struggle For Freedom.* Maryknoll, N.Y.: Orbis.

389. Katjavivi, P. 1988. *A History of Resistance in Namibia.* Paris: UNESCO Press.

390. Keller, E. J., and D. S. Rothchild, eds. 1987. *Afro-Marxist Regimes: Ideology and Public Policy.* Boulder, Colo.: Lynne Rienner.

391. Kelley, M. 1986. *A State in Disarray: Conditions of Chad's Survival.* Boulder, Colo.: Westview.

392. Kitchen, H. A., ed. 1987. *Angola, Mozambique, and the West.* Washington Papers #130. New York: CSIS/Praeger.

393. Koig, B. 1983. *Namibia, The Ravages of War: South Africa's Onslaught on the Namibian People.* London: International Defence and Aid Fund for Southern Africa.

394. LeGoyet, P. 1989. *La guerre d'Algerie.* Paris: Perrin.

395. Legum, C., and B. Lee. 1977. *Conflict in the Horn of Africa.* New York: Africana.

396. Legum, C., and T. Hodges. 1978. *After Angola: The War Over Southern Africa.* 2d ed. New York: Africana.

397. Lemarchand, R. 1970. *Rwanda and Burundi.* New York: Praeger.

398. Leonard, R. 1983. *South Africa at War: White Power and the Crisis in Southern Africa.* Westport, Conn.: Lawrence Hill.

399. LeVine, V. T. 1967. *Political Leadership in Africa: Post-Independence Generational Conflict in Upper Volta, Senegal, Niger, Dahomey, and the Central African Republic.* Stanford, Calif.: Hoover.

400. Leys, C., J. S. Saul, and S. Brown. 1995. *Namibia's Liberation Struggle: The Two-Edged Sword.* London: J. Currey.

401. Ling, D. 1967. *Tunisia: From Protectorate to Republic.* Bloomington: Indiana University Press.

402. Loey, M. 1975. *Rhodesia: White Racism and Imperial Response.* Harmondsworth (Middlesex), Eng.: Penguin.

403. Makinda, S. 1982. *Kenya's Role in the Somali-Ethiopian Conflict.* Working Paper #55. Canberra: Center for Strategic and Defence Studies, Australian National University.

404. Marcum, J. 1969–1978. *The Angolan Revolution.* Cambridge: MIT Press.

405. Markakis, J. 1987. *National and Class Conflict in the Horn of Africa.* African Studies Series #55. New York: Cambridge University Press.

406. Markovitz, I. L. 1977. *Power and Class in Africa: An Introduction to Change and Conflict in African Politics.* Englewood Cliffs, N.J.: Prentice-Hall.

407. Melady, T. 1974. *Burundi: The Tragic Years.* Maryknoll, N.Y.: Orbis.

408. Merriam, A. 1961. *Congo: Background to Conflict.* Evanston, Ill.: Northwestern University Press.

409. Minority Rights Group. 1983. *Eritrea and Tigray.* London: Minority Rights Group.

410. Mittleman, J. 1975. *Ideology and Politics in Uganda.* Ithaca, N.Y.: Cornell University Press.

411. Mondlane, E. 1983. *The Struggle for Mozambique.* London: Zed.

412. Morris, M. S. L. 1974. *Armed Conflict in Southern Africa: A Survey of Regional Terrorisms From Their Beginnings to the Present, With a Comprehensive Examination of the Portuguese Position.* Cape Town: J. Spence.

413. Mungazi, D. A. 1992. *Colonial Policy and Conflict in Zimbabwe: A Study of Cultures in Collision, 1890–1979.* New York: Crane, Russak.

414. Munslow, B. 1983. *Mozambique: The Revolution and Its Origins.* London: Longman.

415. Murray, J., ed. 1988. *Cultural Atlas of Africa.* Oxford: Phaidon.

416. Nafziger, E. W. 1983. *The Economics of Political Instability: The Nigerian-Biafran War.* Boulder, Colo.: Westview.

417. Naidoo, P. 1992. *Le Rona Re Batho: An Account of the 1982 Masera Massacre.* Verulam, South Africa: P. Naidoo.

418. Niven, R. 1970. *The War of Nigerian Unity, 1967–1970.* Ibadan, Nigeria: Evans Brothers.

419. Nnoli, O. 1978. *Self-Reliance and Foreign Policy in Tanzania: The Dynamics of the Diplomacy of a New State, 1961 to 1971.* New York: NOK.

420. Nyangoni, W. 1985. *Africa in the United Nations System.* London: Associated University Press.

421. Nzongola-Ntalaja, G., ed. 1991. *Conflict in the Horn of Africa.* Atlanta, Ga.: African Studies Association Press.

422. O'Ballance, E. 1967. *The Algerian Insurrection, 1954–1962.* Hamden, Conn.: Archon.

423. ———. 1977. *The Secret War in the Sudan, 1955–1972.* Hamden, Conn.: Archon.

424. Obozuwa, A. U. 1973. *The Namibian Question: Legal and Political Aspects.* Benin City, Nigeria: Ethiope.

425. Odom, T. 1988. *Dragon Operations: Hostage Rescues in the Congo, 1964–1965.* Leavenworth, Kan.: Combat Studies Institute, U.S. Army Command and General Staff College.

426. Ojo, O. J. C. B., D. K. Orwa, and C. M. B. Utete. 1985. *African International Relations.* London and New York: Longman.

427. Olou, S. L. O. 1982. *Conflict Management of the OAU in Intra-African Conflicts, 1963–1980.* Ann Arbor, Mich.: University Microfilms International.

428. Oluleye, J. 1985. *Military Leadership in Nigeria, 1966–1979.* Ibadan, Nigeria: Ibadan University Press.

429. O'Meara, P. 1975. *Rhodesia: Racial Conflict or Coexistence?* Ithaca, N.Y.: Cornell University Press.

430. Onwuka, R. I., and T. M. Shaw, eds. 1989. *Africa in World Politics: Into the 1990s.* New York: St. Martin's.

431. Onwuka, R. I., O. Abegunrin, and D. N. Ghista, eds. 1985. *African Development: The OAU/ECA Lagos Plan of Action and Beyond.* Lawrenceville, Va.: Brunswick.

432. Ottaway, D., and M. Ottaway. 1970. *Algeria: The Politics of a Socialist Revolution.* Berkeley and Los Angeles: University of California Press.

433. Ottaway, M. 1982. *Soviet and American Influence in the Horn of Africa.* New York: Praeger.

434. Paret, P. 1964. *French Revolutionary Warfare From Indochina to Algeria: The Analysis of a Political and Military Doctrine.* London: Centre for International Studies.

435. Pettman, J. 1974. *Zambia: Security and Conflict.* Lewes (Sussex), Eng.: J. Friedman.

436. Picard, L. A., ed. 1985. *The Evolution of Modern Botswana.* London: Rex Collings.

437. Post, K. W. J., and M. Vickers. 1973. *Structure and Conflict in Nigeria, 1960–1966.* London: Heinemann.

438. Quandt, W. B. 1969. *Revolution and Political Leadership: Algeria, 1954–1968.* Cambridge: MIT Press.

439. Ranger, T. O. 1985. *Peasant Consciousness and Guerrilla War in Zimbabwe: A Comparative Study.* London: J. Currey.

440. Reyntjens, F. 1995. *Burundi: Breaking the Cycle of Violence.* London: Minority Rights Group.

441. Rosberg, C., and J. Nottingham. 1966. *The Myth of the "Mau Mau": Nationalism in Kenya.* New York: Praeger.

442. Sankara, T. 1988. *Thomas Sankara Speaks: The Burkina Faso Revolution, 1983–1987.* Translated by S. Anderson. New York: Pathfinder.

443. Saul, J. S. 1979. *The State and Revolution in East Africa.* London: Heinemann.

444. Schaller, G. B. 1964; 1988. *The Year of the Gorilla.* Chicago: University of Chicago Press.

445. Segal, A. 1964. *Massacre in Rwanda.* Fabian Research Series #240. London: Fabian Society.

446. Selassie, B. 1980. *Conflict and Intervention on the Horn of Africa.* New York: Monthly Review Press.

447. Shamayarira, N. M. 1981. *National Liberation Through Self-Reliance in Rhodesia, 1956–1972.* Ann Arbor, Mich.: University Microfilms.

448. Shepherd, J. 1975. *The Politics of Starvation.* New York: Carnegie Endowment for International Peace.

449. Sherman, R. 1980. *Eritrea, the Unfinished Revolution.* New York: Praeger.

450. Skinner, E. P., ed. 1986. *Beyond Constructive Engagement: U.S. Foreign Policy Toward Africa.* New York: Paragon House.

451. Slater, M. 1975. *The Trial of Jomo Kenyatta.* 2d rev. ed. London: Heinemann.

452. Smith, A. D. 1983. *State and Nation in the Third World: The Western State and African Nationalism.* Brighton, Eng.: Wheatsheaf.

453. Smith, G. 1980. *Ghosts of Kampala.* New York: St. Martin's.

454. Smith, S. 1990. *Front-line Africa: The Right to a Future: An Oxfam Report on Conflict and Poverty in South Africa.* Oxford: Oxfam.

455. Soggot, D. 1986. *Namibia: The Violent Heritage.* London: Rex Collings.

456. Somerville, K. 1990. *Foreign Military Intervention in Africa.* London: Pinter.

457. Steadman, S. J. 1991. *Peacemaking in Civil War: International Mediation in Zimbabwe, 1974–1980.* Boulder, Colo.: Lynne Rienner.

458. Steenkamp, W. 1976. *Adeus Angola.* Cape Town: H. Timmins.

459. Stockholm International Peace Research Institute (SIPRI). 1976. *Southern Africa: The Escalation of a Conflict: A Politico-Military Study.* New York: Praeger.

460. Stoneman, C., ed. 1982. *Zimbabwe's Inheritance.* New York: St. Martin's.

461. Stremlai, J. 1977. *The International Politics of the Nigerian Civil War.* Princeton, N.J.: Princeton University Press.

462. SWAPO of Namibia, Department of Information and Publicity. 1981. *To Be Born a Nation: The Liberation Struggle for Namibia.* London: Zed.

463. Talbott, J. 1980. *The War Without a Name: France in Algeria, 1954–1962.* New York: Knopf.

464. Thomas, G. 1985. *Mercenary Troops in Modern Africa.* Boulder, Colo.: Westview.

465. Thompson, V. B., and R. Adloff. 1965. *The Malagasy Republic: Madagascar Today.* Stanford, Calif.: Stanford University Press.

466. ———. 1981. *Conflict in Chad.* Berkeley: Institute of International Studies, University of California.

467. Thomson, B. 1975. *Ethiopia: The Country That Cut Off Its Head: A Diary of the Revolution.* London: Robson.

468. Tillan, G. 1958. *Algeria: The Realities.* London: Eyre and Spottiswoode.

469. Touval, S. 1972. *The Boundary Politics of Independent Africa.* Cambridge: Harvard University Press.

470. Trevaskis, G. K. N. 1960. *Eritrea: A Colony in Transition, 1941–1952.* London: Oxford University Press.

471. Trout, F. 1969. *Morocco's Saharan Frontiers.* Geneva: Droz.

472. Ungar, S. J. 1985. *Africa: The People and Politics of an Emerging Continent.* New York: Simon and Schuster.

473. University of London, Center for African Studies. 1972. *Conflicts in Africa.* Adelphi Papers #93. London: IISS.

474. Utete, C. M. B. 1979. *The Road to Zimbabwe: The Political Economy of Settler, Colonialism, National Liberation, and Foreign Intervention.* Washington, D.C.: American University Press.

475. Vansina, J. 1990. *Paths in the Rainforests: Toward a History of Political Tradition in Equatorial Africa.* London: J. Currey.

476. Venter, A. J. 1973. *Portugal's Guerrilla War: The Campaign for Africa.* Cape Town, South Africa: J. Malherbe.

477. Venys, L. 1970. *A History of the Mau Mau Movement in Kenya.* Prague: Charles University.

478. Verney, P. 1995. *Sudan: Conflict and Minorities.* London: Minority Rights Group.

479. Wai, D. 1981. *The African-Arab Conflict in the Sudan.* New York: Africana.

480. Waring, R. 1961. *The War in Angola, 1961.* Lisbon: s. n.

481. Whiteman, K. 1988. *Chad.* Minority Rights Group Report #80. London: Minority Rights Group.

482. Williams, P. M. 1960. *De Gaulle's Republic.* London: Longman.

483. Wilson, A. 1991. *The Challenge Road: Women and the Eritrean Revolution.* London: Earthscan.

484. Windrich, E. 1975. *The Rhodesian Problem: A Documentary Record, 1923–1973.* London: Routledge and Kegan Paul.

485. ———. 1978. *Britain and the Politics of Rhodesian Independence.* London: Croom Helm.

486. ———. 1992. *The Cold War Guerrilla: Jonas Savimbi, the U.S. Media, and the Angolan War.* New York: Greenwood.

487. Wiseman, H., and A. Taylor. 1981. *From Rhodesia to Zimbabwe: The Politics of Transition.* New York: Pergamon.

488. Wolfers, M. 1976. *Politics in the OAU.* London: Methuen.

489. Wolfers, M., and J. Bergerol. 1983. *Angola in the Front-Line.* London: Zed.

490. Woodward, P., and M. Forthsyth, eds. 1994. *Conflict and Peace in the Horn of Africa: Federalism and Its Alternatives.* Aldershot (Hants), Eng.: Dartmouth.

491. Woronoff, J. 1970. *Organization of African Unity.* Metuchen, N.J.: Scarecrow.

492. Wight, J. L. 1989. *Libya, Chad, and the Central Sahara.* Totowa, N.J.: Barnes and Noble.

493. Young, K. 1967. *Rhodesia and Independence: A Study in British Colonial Policy.* London: Eyre and Spottiswoode.

494. Zartman, I. W. 1964. *Morocco: Problems of New Power.* New York: Atherton.

495. ———. 1966. *Government and Politics in Northern Africa.* London: Methuen.

496. ———. 1966. *International Relations in the New Africa.* Englewood Cliffs, N.J.: Prentice-Hall.

497. ———. 1987. *International Relations in the New Africa.* 2d ed. Lanham, Md.: University Press of America.

498. ———. 1989. *Ripe for Resolution: Conflict and Intervention in Africa.* Rev. ed. New York: Oxford University Press.

499. ———, ed. 1993. *Europe and Africa: The New Phase.* Boulder, Colo.: Lynne Rienner.

500. Zewde, B. 1991. *A History of Modern Ethiopia, 1855–1974.* London: J. Currey.

THE AMERICAS

501. Allison, G. T. 1971. *Essence of Decision: Explaining the Cuban Missile Crisis.* Boston: Little, Brown.

502. Ameringer, C. D. 1978. *Don Pepe: A Political Biography of José Figueres of Costa Rica.* Albuquerque: University of New Mexico Press.

503. Anderson, T. 1981. *The War of the Dispossessed: Honduras and El Salvador, 1969.* Lincoln: University of Nebraska Press.

504. Bagley, B., ed. 1987. *Contadora and the Diplomacy of Peace in Central America.* Boulder, Colo.: Westview.

505. Bailey, N. A., ed. 1966. *Latin America: Politics, Economics and Hemispheric Security.* New York: Praeger.

506. Baloyra, E. A. 1982. *El Salvador in Transition.* Chapel Hill: University of North Carolina Press.

507. Baloyra, E. A., and J. A. Morris, eds. 1993. *Conflict and Change in Cuba.* Albuquerque: University of New Mexico Press.

508. Bell, J. 1971. *Crisis in Costa Rica: The 1948 Revolution.* Austin: University of Texas Press.

509. Benjamin, J. R. 1970. *The United States and the Origins of the Cuban Revolution: An Empire of Liberty in an Age of National Liberation.* Princeton, N.J.: Princeton University Press.

510. Bird, L. A. 1984. *Costa Rica, the Unarmed Democracy.* London: Sheppard.

511. Black, G. 1981. *Triumph of the People: The Sandinista Revolution in Nicaragua.* London: Zed.

512. Blackman, M. J., and R. G. Hellman, eds. 1977. *Terms of Conflict: Ideology in Latin American Politics*. Philadelphia: Center for Inter-American Relations, Institute for the Study of Human Issues.

513. Blasier, C., and C. Mesa-Lago, eds. 1979. *Cuba in the World*. Pittsburgh: University of Pittsburgh Press.

514. Bonachea, R. L., and M. San Martin. 1974. *The Cuban Insurrection, 1952–1959*. New Brunswick, N.J.: Transaction.

515. Bonsal, P. W. 1971. *Cuba, Castro, and the United States*. Pittsburgh: University of Pittsburgh Press.

516. Brown, J., and W. P. Snyder, eds. 1985. *The Regionalization of Warfare: The Falklands/Malvinas, Lebanon, and the Iran-Iraq Conflicts*. New Brunswick, N.J.: Transaction.

517. Burrowes, R. 1988. *Revolution and Rescue in Grenada: An Account of the U.S.-Caribbean Invasion*. New York: Greenwood.

518. Calvert, P. 1969. *Latin America: Internal Conflict and International Peace*. London: Macmillan.

519. ———. 1982. *The Falklands Crisis: The Rights and the Wrongs*. London: Pinter.

520. Central Office of Information Reference Division. 1982. *The Falkland Islands: The Facts*. London: HMSO.

521. Child, J. 1985. *Geopolitics and Conflict in South America: Quarrels Among Neighbors*. New York: Praeger.

522. Christian, S. 1985. *Nicaragua: Revolution in the Family*. New York: Random House.

523. Cockburn, L. 1987. *Out of Control: The Story of the Reagan Administration's Secret War in Nicaragua*. New York: Atlantic Monthly Press.

524. Coleman, K. M., and G. C. Herring. 1985. *The Central American Crisis: Sources of Conflict and the Failure of U.S. Policy*. Wilmington, Del.: Scholarly Resources.

525. Coll, A. R., and A. C. Arend, eds. 1985. *The Falklands War: Lessons for Strategy, Diplomacy, and International Law*. Boston: Allen and Unwin.

526. Crawley, E. 1984. *Nicaragua in Perspective*. Rev. ed. New York: St. Martin's.

527. Curry, E. R. 1979. *Hoover's Dominican Diplomacy and the Origins of the Good Neighbor Policy*. New York: Garland.

528. Dabat, A. 1984. *Argentina, the Malvinas, and the End of Military Rule*. Translated by Ralph Johnstone. New York and London: Verso.

529. Danchev, A. 1992. *International Perspective on the Falklands Conflict: Matter of Life and Death*. Basingstoke (Hants), Eng.: Macmillan.

530. Davidson, S. 1987. *Grenada: A Study in Politics and the Limits of International Law*. Aldershot (Hants), Eng.: Gower.

531. Debray, R. 1967. *Revolution in the Revolution? Armed Struggle and Political Struggle in Latin America*. New York: Monthly Review Press.

532. Debray, R., and R. Blackburn, eds. 1970. *Strategy for Revolution*. London: Cape.

533. Del Aguila, J. M. 1984. *Cuba: Dilemmas of a Revolution.* Boulder, Colo.: Westview.

534. Denton, C. F. 1971. *Patterns of Costa Rican Politics.* Boston: Allyn and Bacon.

535. Didion, J. 1982. *Salvador.* New York: Simon and Schuster.

536. Dillon, G. 1989. *The Falklands, Politics, and War.* New York: St. Martin's.

537. Diskin, M., and K. Sharpe. 1986. *The Impact of U.S. Policy in El Salvador, 1979–1985.* Berkeley: Institute of International Studies, University of California.

538. Dominguez, J. I. 1989. *To Make a World Safe for Revolution: Cuba's Foreign Policy.* Cambridge: Harvard University Press.

539. Draper, T. 1968. *The Dominican Revolt: A Case Study in American Policy.* New York: Commentary Report.

540. Dreier, J. C. 1962. *The Organization of American States and the Hemisphere Crisis.* New York: Harper and Row.

541. Dubois, J. 1964. *Danger in Panama.* Indianapolis, Ind.: Bobbs-Merrill.

542. Dunkerley, J. 1984. *Rebellion in the Veins: Political Struggle in Bolivia, 1952–1982.* New York and London: Verso.

543. ———. 1985. *The Long War: Dictatorship and Revolution in El Salvador.* New York and London: Verso.

544. ———. 1988. *Power in the Isthmus: A Political History of Modern Central America.* New York and London: Verso.

545. Durham, W. H. 1979. *Scarcity and Survival in Central America: Ecological Origins of the Soccer War.* Stanford, Calif.: Stanford University Press.

546. Earley, S. 1982. *Arms and Politics in Costa Rica and Nicaragua, 1948–1981.* Albuquerque: Latin American Institute/University of New Mexico Press.

547. Eddy, P., and M. Linklater, eds. 1982. *The Falklands War.* London: André Deutsch.

548. English, A. 1984. *Armed Forces of Latin America.* London: Jane's.

549. Fagen, R. 1987. *Forging Peace: The Challenge of Central America.* New York: B. Blackwell.

550. ———. 1969. *The Transformation of Political Culture in Cuba.* Stanford, Calif.: Stanford University Press.

551. Farnsworth, D. N., and J. W. McKenney. 1983. *U.S.-Panama Relations, 1903–1978: A Study in Linkage Politics.* Boulder, Colo.: Westview.

552. Fitch, J. S. 1977. *The Military Coup d'Etat as a Political Process: Ecuador, 1948–1966.* Baltimore: Johns Hopkins University Press.

553. Franks, O. 1983. "Falkland Island Review: Report of a Committee of Privy Councillors." London: Falkland Islands Review Committee/HMSO.

554. Freedman, L. 1988. *Britain and the Falklands War.* Oxford: B. Blackwell.

555. ———. 1991. *Signals of War: The Falkland Conflict of 1982.* Princeton, N.J.: Princeton University Press.

556. Freedman, L., and O. Gamba-Stonehouse. 1991. *Signals of War: The Falklands Conflict of 1982.* Princeton, N.J.: Princeton University Press.

557. Fried, J. L., ed. 1983. *Guatemala in Rebellion: Unfinished History.* New York: Grove.

558. Gamba, V. 1987. *The Falklands/Malvinas War: A Model for North-South Crisis Prevention.* Boston: Allen and Unwin.

559. Gleijeses, P. 1978. *The Dominican Crisis: The 1965 Constitutionalist Revolt and American Intervention.* Translated by Lawrence Lipson. Baltimore: Johns Hopkins University Press.

560. ———. 1991. *Shattered Hope: The Guatemalan Revolution and the United States, 1944–1954.* Princeton, N.J.: Princeton University Press.

561. Goldblat, J., and V. Millan. 1983. *The Falklands/Malvinas Conflict: A Spur to Arms Build-Up.* Solna, Sweden: SIPRI.

562. Goldenberg, B. 1965. *The Cuban Revolution and Latin America.* London: Allen and Unwin.

563. Gonzalez, E. 1974. *Cuba Under Castro: The Limits of Charisma.* Boston: Houghton Mifflin.

564. Gopal, M. M. 1992. *Politics, Race, and Youth in Guyana.* San Francisco: Mellen Research University Press.

565. Griffiths, J., and P. Griffiths, eds. 1979. *Cuba: The Second Decade.* London: Writers and Readers Publishing Cooperative.

566. Gutierrez, C. M. 1972. *The Dominican Republic: Rebellion and Repression.* Translated by R. E. Edwards. New York: Monthly Review Press.

567. Gutman, R. 1988. *Banana Diplomacy: The Making of American Policy in Nicaragua, 1981–1987.* New York: Simon and Schuster.

568. Hadar, A. 1981. *The United States and El Salvador: Political and Military Involvement.* Berkeley: U.S.–El Salvador Research and Information Center.

569. Halebsky, S., and J. M. Kirk, eds. 1985. *Cuba: 25 Years of Revolution, 1959–1984.* New York: Praeger.

570. Halebsky, S., R. Hernandez, and J. M. Kirk, eds. 1990. *Transformation and Struggle: Cuba Faces the 1990s.* New York: Praeger.

571. Hartlyn, J. 1988. *The Politics of Coalition Rule in Colombia.* Cambridge: Cambridge University Press.

572. Hastings, M., and S. Jenkins. 1983. *The Battle for the Falklands.* London: Michael Joseph.

573. Heinl, R. D., and N. G. Heinl. 1978. *Written in Blood: The Story of the Haitian People, 1492–1971.* Boston: Houghton Mifflin.

574. Higgins, T. 1987. *The Perfect Failure: Kennedy, Eisenhower, and the CIA at the Bay of Pigs.* New York: Norton.

575. Horowitz, I. L. 1993. *The Conscience of Worms and the Cowardice of Lions: Cuban Politics and Culture in an American Context.* University of Miami Lectures, North-South Center, Coral Gables, Florida. New Brunswick, N.J.: Transaction.

576. ———, ed. 1978. *Castro's Cuba in the 1970s.* 3d ed. New Brunswick, N.J.: Transaction.

577. Immerman, R. H. 1982. *The CIA in Guatemala: The Foreign Policy of Intervention.* Austin: University of Texas Press.

578. Jackson, D. B. 1969. *Castro, the Kremlin, and Communism in Latin America.* Baltimore: Johns Hopkins University Press.

579. Jeffrey, H., and C. Baber. 1986. *Guyana: Politics, Economics, and Society.* London: Pinter.

580. Karol, K. S. 1970. *Guerrillas in Power: The Course of the Cuban Revolution.* Translated by A. Pomerans. New York: Hill and Wang.

581. Kirk, J. M. 1989. *Between God and the Party: Religion and Politics in Revolutionary Cuba.* Gainesville: University of Florida Press.

582. Kitchel, D. 1978. *The Truth About the Panama Canal.* New Rochelle, N.Y.: Arlington House.

583. Kornbluh, P., 1987. *Nicaragua: the Price of Intervention: Reagan's Wars Against the Sandinistas.* Washington, D.C.: Institute for Policy Studies.

584. LaFeber, W. 1993. *Inevitable Revolutions: The United States in Central America.* 2d ed. New York: Norton.

585. Langley, L. D. 1968. *The Cuban Policy of the U.S.: A Brief History.* New York: Wiley.

586. ———, ed. 1970. *The U.S., Cuba and the Cold War: American Failure or Communist Conspiracy?* Lexington, Mass.: D.C. Heath.

587. Lernoux, P. 1982. *Cry of the People: The Struggle for Human Rights in Latin America—the Catholic Church in Conflict With U.S. Policy.* Harmondsworth (Middlesex), Eng.: Penguin.

588. Levine, D. H. 1981. *Religion and Politics in Latin America: The Catholic Church in Venezuela and Colombia.* Princeton, N.J.: Princeton University Press.

589. ———, ed. 1986. *Religion and Political Conflict in Latin America.* Chapel Hill: University of North Carolina Press.

590. Lewis, G. 1987. *Grenada: The Jewel Despoiled.* Baltimore: Johns Hopkins University Press.

591. Liss, S. 1967. *The Canal: Aspects of United States–Panamanian Relations.* South Bend, Ind.: University of Notre Dame Press.

592. Llerena, M. 1978. *The Unsuspected Revolution: The Birth and Rise of Castroism.* Ithaca, N.Y.: Cornell University Press.

593. Lopes, C. 1987. *Guinea-Bissau: From Liberation Struggle to Independent Statehood.* Translated by Michael Wolfers. Boulder, Colo.: Westview.

594. Lowenthal, A. F. 1972. *The Dominican Intervention.* Cambridge: Harvard University Press.

595. Lowenthal, A. F. 1987. *Partners in Conflict: The United States and Latin America.* Baltimore: Johns Hopkins University Press.

596. Malloy, J. M. 1970. *Bolivia: The Uncompleted Revolution.* Pittsburgh: University of Pittsburgh Press.

597. Malloy, J. M., and E. Gramarra. 1988. *Revolution and Reaction: Bolivia, 1964–1985.* New Brunswick, N.J.: Transaction.

598. Malloy, J. M., and R. S. Thorn, eds. 1971. *Beyond the Revolution: Bolivia Since 1952.* Pittsburgh: University of Pittsburgh Press.

599. Manley, R. 1979. *Guyana Emergent: The Post-Independence Struggle for Nondependent Development*. Boston: G. K. Hall.

600. Mansback, R. W. 1971. *Dominican Crisis, 1965*. New York: Facts on File.

601. Martin, J. B. 1966. *Overtaken by Events: The Dominican Crisis From the Fall of Trujillo to the Civil War*. Garden City, N.Y.: Doubleday.

602. Matthews, H. L. 1975. *Revolution in Cuba: An Essay in Understanding*. New York: Scribner's.

603. McClintock, M. 1985. *State Terror and Popular Resistance in El Salvador*. Vol. 1 of *The American Connection*. London: Zed.

604. ———. 1985. *The American Connection*. London: Zed.

605. Mechan, J. L. 1967. *The United States and Inter-American Security, 1889–1960*. Austin: University of Texas Press.

606. Medin, T. 1990. *Cuba: The Shaping of Revolutionary Consciousness*. Boulder, Colo.: Lynne Rienner.

607. Melville, T., and M. Melville. 1971. *Guatemala—Another Vietnam?* Harmondsworth (Middlesex), Eng.: Penguin.

608. Mesa-Lago, C. 1971. *Revolutionary Change in Cuba*. Pittsburgh: University of Pittsburgh Press.

609. Middlebrook, M. 1985. *Operation Corporate: The Falklands War, 1982*. London: Viking.

610. Mitchell, C. 1977. *The Legacy of Populism in Bolivia: From the MNR to Military Rule*. New York: Praeger.

611. Montaner, C. A. 1958. *Cuba, Castro, and the Caribbean: The Cuban Revolution and the Crisis in Western Consciousness*. Translated by N. Duran. New Brunswick, N.J.: Transaction.

612. Montgomery, T. 1982. *Revolution in El Salvador: Origins and Evolution*. Boulder, Colo.: Westview.

613. Morley, M. T. T. 1987. *Imperial State and Revolution: The U.S. and Cuba, 1952–1986*. Cambridge: Cambridge University Press.

614. Moro, R. 1989. *The History of the South Atlantic Conflict: The War for the Malvinas*. New York: Praeger.

615. Morris, J. A. 1984. *Honduras: Caudillo Politics and Military Rulers*. Boulder, Colo.: Westview.

616. Mujal-Leon, E. M. 1989. *European Socialism and the Conflict in Central America*. Washington Papers #138. New York: CSIS/Praeger.

617. Munck, R. 1984. *Revolutionary Trends in Latin America*. Montreal: Centre for Developing Area Studies, McGill University.

618. Nelson, L. 1972. *Cuba, The Measure of Revolution*. Minneapolis: University of Minnesota Press.

619. Nelson, W. J. 1990. *Almost a Territory: America's Attempt to Annex the Dominican Republic*. Newark: University of Delaware Press.

620. O'Shaughnessy, H. 1984. *Grenada: An Eyewitness Account of the U.S. Invasion and the Caribbean History That Provoked It*. New York: Dodd, Mead.

621. ———. 1984. *Grenada: Revolution, Invasion, and Aftermath*. London: Hamilton/The Observer.

622. Palmer, B. 1989. *Intervention in the Caribbean: The Dominican Crisis of 1965*. Lexington: University Press of Kentucky.

623. Pastor, R. 1987. *Condemned to Repetition: The United States and Nicaragua*. Princeton, N.J.: Princeton University Press.

624. Pear, R., and E. E. Larson. 1983. *The Falkland Islands Dispute in International Law and Politics: A Documentary Source Book*. London: Oceana.

625. Pike, F. B. 1964. *The Conflict Between Church and State in Latin America*. New York: Knopf.

626. Purcell, S. K. 1992. *Cuba at the Turning Point: A Conference Report, 1992*. New York: Americas Society.

627. Rabkin, R. P. 1991. *Cuban Politics: The Revolutionary Experiment*. New York: Praeger.

628. Ropp, S. C., and J. A. Morris. 1984. *Central America: Crisis and Adaption*. Albuquerque: University of New Mexico Press.

629. Sater, W. F. 1990. *Chile and the United States: Empires in Conflict*. Athens: University of Georgia Press.

630. Schlesinger, S. C., and S. Kinzer. 1982. *Bitter Fruit: The Untold Story of the American Coup in Guatemala*. Garden City, N.Y.: Doubleday.

631. Schmitt, K. M. 1974. *Mexico and the United States, 1821–1973: Conflict and Coexistence*. New York: Wiley.

632. Schmitter, P. C. 1971. *Interest, Conflict, and Political Change in Brazil*. Stanford, Calif.: Stanford University Press.

633. Schodt, D. W. 1987. *Ecuador: An Andean Enigma*. Boulder, Colo.: Westview.

634. Schoenhals, K. P., and R. A. Melanson. 1985. *Revolution and Intervention in Grenada: The New Jewel Movement, the United States, and the Caribbean*. Boulder, Colo.: Westview.

635. Schooley, H. 1987. *Conflict in Central America*. Burnt Mill, Harlow (Essex), Eng.: Longman.

636. Schulz, D. E., ed. 1994. *Cuba and the Future*. Westport, Conn.: Greenwood.

637. Shearman, P. 1987. *The Soviet Union and Cuba*. London: Routledge and Kegan Paul.

638. Simon, J. 1988. *Guatemala: Eternal Spring, Eternal Tyranny*. New York: Norton.

639. Slater, J. 1970. *Intervention and Negotiation: The United States and the Dominican Revolution*. New York: Harper and Row.

640. Sobel, L. A. 1964. *Cuba, the United States, and Russia, 1960–1963*. New York: Facts on File.

641. ———, ed. 1978. *Castro's Cuba in the 1970s*. New York: Facts on File.

642. Somoza Debayle, A. 1980. *Nicaragua Betrayed*. Boston: Western Islands.

643. Spinner, T. J. 1984. *A Political and Social History of Guyana, 1945–1983*. Boulder, Colo.: Westview.

644. Stockwell, J. 1978. *In Search of Enemies: A CIA Story.* New York: Norton.

645. Stoll, D. 1993. *Between Two Armies in the Ixil Towns of Guatemala.* New York: Columbia University Press.

646. Stubbs, J. 1989. *Cuba: The Test of Time.* London: Latin America Bureau.

647. Suarez, A. 1967. *Castroism and Communism, 1959–1966.* Cambridge: MIT Press.

648. Suchlicki, J., ed. 1972. *Cuba, Castro, and Revolution.* Coral Gables, Fla.: University of Miami Press.

649. Szulc, T. 1965. *Dominican Diary.* New York: Delacorte.

650. Thorndike, T. 1985. *Grenada: Politics, Economics, and Society.* Boulder, Colo.: Lynne Rienner.

651. Tillema, H. 1973. *Appeal to Force: American Military Intervention in the Era of Containment.* New York: Crowell.

652. Turner, R. 1987. *Nicaragua v. United States: A Look at the Facts.* Washington, D.C.: Pergamon-Brassey's.

653. U.S. Department of State. 1976. *Intervention on International Communism in Guatemala.* Westport, Conn.: Greenwood.

654. Vanderlaan, M. 1986. *Revolution and Foreign Policy in Nicaragua.* Boulder, Colo.: Westview.

655. Vasques, C., and M. Garcia y Griego. 1983. *Mexican-U.S. Relations: Conflict and Convergence.* Los Angeles: UCLA Latin American Center Publications.

656. Weinstein, M., ed. 1979. *Revolutionary Cuba in the World Arena.* Philadelphia: Institute for the Study of Human Issues.

657. Weintraub, S. 1978. *Conflict, Order and Peace in the Americas.* Austin: Lyndon B. Johnson School of Public Affairs, University of Texas Press.

658. Welch, R. E. 1985. *Response to Revolution: The United States and the Cuban Revolution, 1959–1961.* Chapel Hill: University of North Carolina Press.

659. White, A. 1973. *El Salvador.* London: E. Benn.

660. Wydem, P. 1980. *Bay of Pigs: The Untold Story.* New York: Simon and Schuster.

ASIA AND PACIFIC

661. Ahmed, M. 1978. *Bangladesh: Constitutional Quest for Autonomy, 1950–1971.* Wiesbaden: Steiner.

662. Aijmer, G., ed. 1984. *Leadership on the China Coast.* London: Curzon.

663. Alagappa, M. 1987. *The National Security of Developing States: Lessons From Thailand.* Dover: Auburn House.

664. Allen, R. 1968. *Malaysia—Prospect and Retrospect: The Impact and Aftermath of Colonial Rule.* New York: Oxford University Press.

665. Amnesty International. 1985. *East Timor: Violations of Human Rights: Extrajudicial Executions, "Disappearances," Torture, and Political Imprisonment, 1975–1984.* London: Amnesty International.

666. An, T. 1973. *The Sino-Soviet Territorial Dispute.* Philadelphia: Westminister.

667. Appadorai, A. 1981. *The Domestic Roots of India's Foreign Policy, 1947–1972.* Delhi: Oxford University Press.

668. Asprey, R. B. 1976. *War in the Shadows: The Guerrilla in History.* London: MacDonald/Jane's.

669. Aung San Suu Kyi. 1995. *Freedom From Fear, and Other Writings.* Edited with an introduction by Michael Aris. Rev. ed. New Delhi and New York: Penguin.

670. Aung San U. 1972. *The Political Legacy of Aung San.* Compiled by Josef Silverstein. Ithaca, N.Y.: Southeast Asian Program, Cornell University.

671. Babbage, R., and A. D. Gordon. 1992. *India's Strategic Future: Regional, State, or Global Power?* Auckland, New Zealand: Oxford University Press.

672. Baldwin, F. 1974. *Without Parallel: The American-Korean Relationship Since 1945.* New York: Pantheon.

673. Ballhatchet, K., and D. D. Taylor, eds. 1984. *Changing South Asia: Politics and Government.* Honk Kong: Centre of South Asian Studies, School of Oriental and African Studies, University of London/Asian Research Service.

674. Barnds, W. J. 1972. *India, Pakistan, and the Great Powers.* London: Pall Mall.

675. ———. 1976. *The Two Koreas in East Asian Affairs.* New York: New York University Press.

676. Beasant, J. 1984. *The Santo Rebellion: An Empirical Reckoning.* Richmond (Victoria), Australia: Heinemann.

677. Beg, A. 1966. *Pakistan Faces India.* Lahore: Babur and Amer.

678. Bharagava, G. S. 1976. *India's Security in the 1980s.* Adelphi Papers #125. London: IISS.

679. Blinkenberg, L. 1972. *India-Pakistan: The History of Unsolved Conflicts.* Copenhagen: Munksgaard.

680. Borisov, O., and B. Koloskov. 1975. *Soviet-Chinese Relations, 1945–1970.* Bloomington: Indiana University Press.

681. Bradnock, R. W. 1990. *India's Foreign Policy Since 1971.* London: Royal Institute of International Affairs; New York: Council of Foreign Relations Press.

682. Braun, D. 1983. *The Indian Ocean: Region of Conflict or "Peace Zone"?* London: C. Hurst.

683. Brecher, M. 1968. *India and World Politics: Krishna Menon's View of the World.* New York: Praeger.

684. Brines, R. 1968. *The Indo-Pakistani Conflict.* London: Pall Mall.

685. Budiardjo, C., and L. Liong. 1984. *The War Against East Timor.* London: Zed.

686. Burchett, W. G. 1970. *The Second Indo-China War: Cambodia and Laos.* New York: International Publishers.

687. ———. 1981. *The China-Cambodia-Vietnam Triangle.* Chicago: Vanguard.

688. Cady, J. 1958. *A History of Modern Burma.* Ithaca, N.Y.: Cornell University Press.

689. Caldwell, M., and L. Tan. 1973. *Cambodia in the Southeast Asian War.* New York: Monthly Review Press.

690. Cao, V., and D. Khuyen. 1980. *Reflections on the Vietnam War*. Washington, D.C.: U.S. Army Center of Military History.

691. Chakravarti, P. C. 1971. *The Evolution of India's Northern Borders*. New York: Asia Publishing.

692. Chandler, D. P. 1991. *The Tragedy of Cambodian History: Politics, War, and Revolution Since 1945*. New Haven, Conn.: Yale University Press.

693. ———. 1992. *Brother Number One: A Political Biography of Pol Pot*. Boulder, Colo.: Westview.

694. Chang, P. 1985. *Kampuchea Between China and Vietnam*. Singapore: Singapore University Press.

695. ———. 1986. *The Sino-Vietnamese Territorial Dispute*. Washington Papers 118. New York: CSIS/Praeger.

696. Chen, K. 1987. *China's War With Vietnam, 1979: Issues, Decisions, and Implications*. Stanford, Calif.: Hoover.

697. Chen, M. 1992. *The Strategic Triangle and Regional Conflicts: Lessons From the Indochina Wars*. Boulder, Colo.: Lynne Rienner.

698. Chiu, H., ed. 1979. *China and the Taiwan Issue*. New York: Praeger.

699. Chomsky, N. 1970. *At War With Asia*. London: Fontana/Collins.

700. Choudhury, G. 1968. *Pakistan's Relations With India, 1947–1966*. New York: Praeger.

701. ———. 1974. *The Last Days of United Pakistan*. London: C. Hurst.

702. Clements, K. P., ed. 1993. *Peace and Security in the Asia Pacific Region: Post–Cold War Problems and Prospects*. Palmerston North, New Zealand: Dunmore.

703. Clough, R. 1978. *Island China*. Cambridge: Harvard University Press.

704. ———. 1987. *Embattled Korea: The Rivalry for International Support*. Boulder, Colo.: Westview.

705. Clutterbuck, R. 1985. *Conflict and Violence in Singapore and Malaysia, 1945–1983*. Boulder, Colo.: Westview.

706. Collis, M. 1975. *Trials in Burma*. New York: AMS.

707. Crossette, B. 1993. *India: Facing the Twenty-first Century*. Bloomington: Indiana University Press.

708. Cumings, B. 1981. *Liberation and the Emergence of Separate Regimes*. Vol. 1 of *The Origins of the Korean War*. Princeton, N.J.: Princeton University Press.

709. ———. 1990. *The Roaring of the Cataract*. Vol. 2 of *The Origins of the Korean War*. Princeton, N.J.: Princeton University Press.

710. Dahm, B. 1971. *History of Indonesia in the Twentieth Century*. Translated by P. S. Falla. New York: Praeger.

711. Davidson, P. 1988. *Vietnam at War: The History, 1946–1975*. Novato, Calif.: Presidio.

712. Deane, H. 1963. *The War in Vietnam*. New York: Monthly Review Press.

713. Devillers, P., and J. Lacouture. 1969. *End of a War: Indochina 1954*. London: Pall Mall.

714. Dommen, A. J. 1971. *Conflict in Laos.* Rev. ed. New York: Praeger.

715. Duiker, W. 1986. *China and Vietnam: The Roots of Conflict.* Berkeley: Institute of East Asian Studies, University of California.

716. Elliot, D. W. P. 1981. *The Third Indochina Conflict.* Boulder, Colo.: Westview.

717. Evans, G., and K. Rowley. 1984. *Red Brotherhood at War: Indochina Since the Fall of Saigon.* London: Verso.

718. Fairbank, J. K. 1971. *The United States and China.* Cambridge: Harvard University Press.

719. Falk, R. A., ed. 1976. *The Vietnam War and International Law.* Princeton, N.J.: Princeton University Press.

720. Foot, R. 1985. *The Wrong War: American Policy and the Dimensions of the Korean Conflict, 1950–1953.* Ithaca, N.Y.: Cornell University Press.

721. Gelb, L., and R. Betts. 1979. *The Irony of Vietnam: The System Worked.* Washington, D.C.: Brookings.

722. Georges, A. 1974. *Charles de Gaulle et la guerre d'Indochine.* Paris: Nouvelles Editions Latines.

723. Ginsburg, G., and M. Mathos. 1964. *Communist China and Tibet: The First Dozen Years.* The Hague: M. Nijhoff.

724. Gordon, B. K. 1966. *The Dimensions of Conflict in South East Asia.* Englewood Cliffs, N.J.: Prentice-Hall.

725. Grinter, L. E., and Y. W. Kihl, eds. 1987. *East Asian Conflict Zones: Prospects for Regional Stability and Deescalation.* New York: St. Martin's.

726. Grover, B. 1974. *Sikkim and India: Storm and Consolidation.* New Delhi: Jain Brothers.

727. Gulhati, N. D. 1973. *Indus Waters Treaty: An Exercise in International Mediation.* New York: Allied Publishers.

728. Gunn, G. C. 1990. *Rebellion in Laos: Peasant and Politics in a Colonial Backwater.* Boulder, Colo.: Westview.

729. Gurtov, M., and Byong-Moo Hwang. 1980. *China Under Threat: The Politics of Strategy and Diplomacy.* Baltimore: Johns Hopkins University Press.

730. Haas, M. 1991. *Cambodia, Pol Pot, and the United States: The Faustian Pact.* New York: Praeger.

731. Heder, S. R. 1991. *Reflections on Cambodian Political History: Background to Recent Developments.* Canberra: Strategic and Defence Studies Center, Australian National University.

732. Henderson, W. 1973. *West New Guinea: The Dispute and Its Settlement.* South Orange, N.J.: Seton Hall University/American-Asian Educational Exchange.

733. Hess, G. R. 1990. *Vietnam and the United States: Origins and Legacy of War.* Boston: Wayne.

734. Hildebrand, G. C., and G. Porter. 1976. *Cambodia: Starvation and Revolution.* New York: Monthly Review Press.

735. Hinton, H. C. 1966. *Communist China in World Politics.* New York: Houghton Mifflin.

736. ———. 1972. *China's Relations With Burma and Vietnam: A Brief Survey.* Ann Arbor, Mich.: University Microfilms.

737. Hodson, H. 1985. *The Great Divide: Britain, India, Pakistan.* New York: Oxford University Press.

738. Hoffman, S. 1990. *India and the China Crisis.* Berkeley and Los Angeles: University of California Press.

739. Huxley, T. 1983. *Indochina and the Insurgency in the ASEAN States, 1975–1981.* Working Paper #67. Canberra: Strategic and Defence Studies Center, Australian National University.

740. International Commission of Jurists Secretariat. 1972. *The Events in East Pakistan, 1971: A Legal Study.* Geneva: International Commission of Jurists Secretariat.

741. Isaacs, A. 1983. *Without Honor: Defeat in Vietnam and Cambodia.* Baltimore: Johns Hopkins University Press.

742. Jackson, K., ed. 1989. *Cambodia, 1975–1978: Rendezvous With Death.* Princeton, N.J.: Princeton University Press.

743. Jackson, R. V. 1975. *South Asian Crisis: India-Pakistan-Bangladesh.* London: Chatto and Windus.

744. Jagdev Singh. 1988. *The Dismemberment of Pakistan: 1971 Indo-Pak War.* New Delhi: Lancer International.

745. Jolliffe, J. 1978. *East Timor: Nationalism and Colonialism.* St. Lucia, Australia: University of Queensland Press.

746. Jones, H. 1971. *Indonesia: The Possible Dream.* New York: Harcourt, Brace, Jovanovich.

747. Kahin, G. 1952. *Nationalism and Revolution in Indonesia.* Ithaca, N.Y.: Cornell University Press.

748. ———. 1986. *Intervention: How America Became Involved in Vietnam.* New York: Knopf.

749. Karnow, S. 1983. *Vietnam: A History.* New York: Viking.

750. Kaul, B. M. 1972. *Confrontation With Pakistan.* London: Vikas.

751. Kelly, G. A. 1965. *Lost Soldiers: The French Army and Empire in Crisis, 1947–1962.* Cambridge: MIT Press.

752. Kerr, G. 1965. *Formosa Betrayed.* Boston: Houghton Mifflin.

753. Kesaris, P. 1982. "Transcripts and Files of the Paris Peace Talks on Vietnam, 1968–1973." Microfilm. Frederick, Md.: University Publications of America.

754. Kiernan, B. 1985. *How Pol Pot Came to Power: A History of Communism in Kampuchea, 1930–1975.* London: Verso.

755. Kiernan, B., and C. Boua. 1982. *Peasants and Politics in Kampuchea, 1942–1981.* London: Zed.

756. Kiljunen, K., ed. 1984. *Kampuchea: Decade of the Genocide: Report of a Finnish Inquiry Commission.* London: Zed.

757. Kirk, D. 1971. *Wider War: The Struggle for Cambodia, Thailand, and Laos.* New York: Praeger.

758. Klintworth, G. 1989. *The Vietnamese Achievement in Kampuchea.* Working Paper #181. Canberra: Strategic and Defence Studies Center, Australian National University.

759. ———. 1989. *Vietnam's Intervention in Cambodia in International Law.* Canberra: AGPS.

760. ———. 1990. *Vietnam's Withdrawal From Cambodia: Regional Issues and Realignments.* Working Paper #64. Canberra: Strategic and Defence Studies Center, Australian National University.

761. Kosut, H., ed. 1971. *Cambodia and the Vietnam War.* New York: Facts on File.

762. Kolko, G. 1986. *Vietnam: Anatomy of a War 1940–1975.* London: Allen and Unwin.

763. Kroef, J. 1979. "The Cambodian-Vietnamese War: Some Origins and Implications." *Asia Quarterly* 2: 83–94.

764. Lagerberg, K. 1979. *West Irian and Jakarta Imperialism.* New York: St. Martin's.

765. Lamb, A. 1967. *The Kashmir Problem: A Historical Survey.* New York: Columbia University Press.

766. Lancaster, D. 1961. *The Emancipation of French Indochina.* New York: Oxford University Press.

767. Langley, G. 1992. *A Decade of Dissent: Vietnam and the Conflict on the Australian Home Front.* North Sydney: Allen and Unwin.

768. Leifer, M. 1980. *Conflict and Regional Order in South East Asia.* Adelphi Papers #162. London: IISS.

769. Leonard, K. I. 1978. *Social History of an Indian Caste: The Kayasths of Hyderabad.* Berkeley and Los Angeles: University of California Press.

770. Lewy, G. 1978. *America in Vietnam.* New York: Oxford University Press.

771. Li, S. 1971. *The Ageless Chinese: A History.* New York: Charles Scribner and Sons.

772. Lijphart, A. 1966. *The Trauma of Decolonization: The Dutch and West New Guinea.* New Haven, Conn.: Yale University Press.

773. Ling, T. 1979. *Buddhism, Imperialism, and War: Burma and Thailand in Modern History.* London: Allen and Unwin.

774. Lintner, B. 1990. *Land of Jade: A Journey Through Insurgent Burma.* Bangkok: White Lotus.

775. ———. 1990. *Outrage: Burma's Struggle for Democracy.* 2d ed. London: White Lotus.

776. ———. 1990. *The Rise and Fall of the Communist Party of Burma (CPB).* Ithaca, N.Y.: South East Asian Program, Cornell University.

777. ———. 1994. *Burma in Revolution: Opium and Insurgency Since 1948.* Boulder, Colo.: Westview.

778. Lissak, M. 1976. *Military Roles in Modernization: Civil-Military Relations in Thailand and Burma.* Beverly Hills: Sage.

779. Lockhart, G. 1985. *"Strike in the South, Clear in the North": The "Problem of Kampuchea" and the Roots of Vietnamese Strategy There.* Clayton (Victoria), Australia: Monash University.

780. Low, A. D. 1987. *The Sino-Soviet Confrontation Since Mao Zedong: Dispute, Detente, or Conflict?* Boulder, Colo.: Social Science Monographs.

781. Lu, C. 1986. *The Sino-Indian Border Dispute: A Legal Study.* New York: Greenwood.

782. Mackle, J. 1974. *Konfrontasi: The Indonesia-Malaysia Dispute, 1963–1966.* New York: Oxford University Press.

783. Manogaran, C. 1987. *Ethnic Conflict and Reconciliation in Sri Lanka.* Honolulu: University of Hawaii Press.

784. Matray, J. I. 1985. *The Reluctant Crusade: American Foreign Policy in Korea, 1941–1950.* Honolulu: University of Hawaii Press.

785. Maung, M. 1991. *The Burma Road to Poverty.* New York: Praeger.

786. Maung Maung, G. 1983. *Burmese Political Values: The Socio-Political Roots of Authoritarianism.* New York: Praeger.

787. Maung Maung, U. 1980. *From Sangha to Laity: Nationalist Movements of Burma, 1920–1940.* New Delhi: Manohar.

788. Maxwell, N. 1972. *India's China War.* Garden City, N.Y.: Doubleday.

789. McDougall, H., and J. Want. 1985. "Burma in 1984: Political Stasis or Political Renewal?" *Asian Survey,* 25 February, 241–248, 789.

790. McMullen, C. J. 1981. *Mediation of the West New Guinea Dispute, 1962: A Case Study.* Washington, D.C.: Institute for the Study of Diplomacy, Georgetown University.

791. Menon, V. 1961. *The Story of the Integration of the Indian States.* 3d ed. Bombay: Orient Longman.

792. Millar, T. B., ed. 1983. *International Security in the South-East Asia and South-West Pacific Region.* St. Lucia, Australia: University of Queensland Press.

793. Mobbed, I. W., and D. P. Chandler. 1995. *The Khmers.* Oxford: B. Blackwell.

794. Muni, S. D. 1993. *Pangs of Proximity: India and Sri Lanka's Ethnic Crisis.* Oslo, Norway: PRIO; New Delhi and Newbury Park, Calif.: Sage.

795. Mya Sein, D. 1973. *The Administration of Burma.* Introduction by Josef Silverstein. Kuala Lumpur: Oxford University Press.

796. Nair, K. K. 1984. *ASEAN-Indochina Relations Since 1979: The Politics of Accommodation.* Working Paper #30. Canberra: Strategic and Defence Studies Center, Australian National University.

797. Naumkin, V. V., ed. 1994. *Central Asia and Transcaucasia: Ethnicity and Conflict.* Westport, Conn.: Greenwood.

798. Neemia, U. F. 1986. *Cooperation and Conflict: Costs, Benefits, and National Interests in Pacific Regional Cooperation.* Suva, Fiji: Institute of Pacific Studies, University of the South Pacific.

799. New Zealand Prime Minister's Office. 1965. *Vietnam: Background to the Conflict.* Wellington, New Zealand: Government Printer.

800. Nguyen-Vo, T. H. 1992. *Khmer-Viet Relations and the Third Indochina Conflict*. Jefferson, N.C.: McFarland.

801. Nu, U. 1975. *U Nu: Saturday's Son*. Translated by U Law Yone. New Haven, Conn.: Yale University Press.

802. O'Ballance, E. 1964. *The Indo-China War, 1945–1954: A Study in Guerrilla Warfare*. London: Faber and Faber.

803. ———. 1966. *Malaya: The Communist Insurgent War, 1948–1960*. Hamden, Conn.: Archon.

804. ———. 1969. *Korea: 1950–1953*. Hamden, Conn.: Archon.

805. ———. 1981. *The Wars in Vietnam, 1954–1980*. New enlarged ed. New York: Hippocrene.

806. ———. 1989. *The Cyanide War: Tamil Insurrection in Sri Lanka, 1973–1988*. Washington, D.C.: Brassey's.

807. O'Neill, R. J. 1984. *Security in East Asia*. New York: St. Martin's.

808. Ostheimer, J. N. 1975. *The Politics of the West Indian Ocean Islands*. New York: Praeger.

809. Paige, G. 1968. *The Korean Decision, June 24-30, 1950*. New York: Free Press.

810. Palit, D. K. 1972. *The Lightning Campaign: The Indo-Pakistan War, 1971*. Salisbury, Eng.: Compton.

811. Pavet, P. 1964. *French Revolutionary Warfare From Indochina to Algeria: The Analysis of a Political and Military Doctrine*. London: Pall Mall.

812. Peace, Power, and Politics in Asia Conference Committee. 1968. *Peace, Power, and Politics in Asia: The Background*. Wellington, New Zealand: the Committee.

813. Pettman, R. H. 1973. *China in Burma's Foreign Policy*. Canberra: Australian National University Press.

814. Pike, D. E. 1969. *War, Peace, and the Viet Cong*. Cambridge: MIT Press.

815. Pillai, K. R. 1970. *The Political Triangle: Pakistan, India, and Britain*. New Delhi: Young India.

816. Polomka, P. 1986. *The Two Koreas: Catalyst for Conflict in East-Asia?* Adelphi Papers #208. London: IISS.

817. Premdas, R. 1978. "Papua New Guinea in 1977: Elections and Relations With Indonesia." *Asian Survey*, 18 January, 58–67.

818. Project Maje. 1992. *Deadly Enterprises: A Burma-India Situation Report*. December. Cranford, N.J.: Project Maje.

819. Ramazani, P. 1978. *Sikkim: The Story of Its Integration With India*. New Delhi: Cosmo.

820. Ranjit Singh, D. 1984. *Brunei, 1839–1983: The Problems of Political Survival*. Singapore and New York: Oxford University Press.

821. Rao, R. 1963. *Portuguese Rule in Goa, 1510–1961*. New York: Asia Publishing.

822. Ray, H. 1983. *China's Strategy in Nepal*. New Delhi: Radiant Publishers.

823. Razvi, M. 1971. *The Frontiers of Pakistan*. Karachi: National Publishing.

824. Rees, D. 1964. *Korea: The Limited War.* New York: St. Martin's.

825. Reid, A. 1974. *The Indonesian National Revolution, 1945–1950.* Hawthorne, Australia: Longman.

826. Richards, J. F. 1975. *Mughal Administration in Golconda.* Oxford: Clarendon.

827. Richardson, H. 1984. *Tibet and Its History.* 2d ed. Boulder, Colo.: Shambhala.

828. Rizvi, H. 1981. *Internal Strife and External Intervention: India's Role in the Civil War in East Pakistan/Bangladesh.* Lahore: Progressive Publishers.

829. Ross, R. 1988. *The Indochina Tangle: China's Vietnam Policy, 1975–1979.* New York: Columbia University Press.

830. Rossow, R. 1956. "The Battle of Azerbaijan, 1946." *Middle East Journal* 10 (Winter): 17–32.

831. Rowland, J. 1967. *A History of Sino-Indian Relations.* Princeton, N.J.: Van Nostrand.

832. Rubinoff, A. 1971. *India's Use of Force in Goa.* Bombay: Popular Prakashan.

833. Sakamoto, Y. 1988. *Asia, Militarization, and Regional Conflict.* New York: Zed.

834. Savage, P. 1978. *The National Liberation Struggle in West Irian: From Millenarianism to Socialist Revolution.* Wellington, New Zealand: South Pacific Action Network.

835. Scalapino, R. A., Seizaburo Sato, and Jusuf Wanandi, eds. 1986. *Internal and External Security Issues in Asia.* Berkeley: Institute of East Asian Studies, University of California.

836. Schwarz, W. 1975. *The Tamils of Sri Lanka.* Minority Rights Group Report #25. London: Minority Rights Group.

837. Segal, G. 1985. *Defending China.* New York: Oxford University Press.

838. Sen Gupta, J. 1974. *History of the Freedom Movement in Bangladesh, 1943–1973.* Calcutta: Naya Prokash.

839. Shakabpa, T. 1967. *Tibet: A Political History.* New Haven, Conn.: Yale University Press.

840. Shawcross, W. 1979. *Sideshow: Kissinger, Nixon, and the Destruction of Cambodia.* London: André Deutsch.

841. Short, A. 1975. *The Communist Insurrection in Malaya, 1948–1960.* New York: Crane, Russak.

842. Sievers, A. M. 1974. *The Mystical World of Indochina: Culture and Economic Development in Conflict.* Baltimore: Johns Hopkins University Press.

843. Silverstein, J. 1977. *Burma: Military Rule and the Politics of Stagnation.* Ithaca, N.Y.: Cornell University Press.

844. Sisson, R., and L. E. Rose. 1990. *War and Secession: Pakistan, India, and the Creation of Bangladesh.* Berkeley and Los Angeles: University of California Press.

845. Smith, M. 1991. *Burma: Insurgency and the Politics of Ethnicity.* London: Atlantic Highlands.

846. Snitwongse, K. 1991. *South East Asia Beyond a Cambodian Settlement:*

Conflict or Cooperation? Working Paper #223. Canberra: Strategic and Defence Studies Center, Australian National University.

847. Sondi, M. L. 1972. *Non-Appeasement: A New Direction for Indian Foreign Policy.* New Delhi: Abhinav.

848. Srivastava, M. P. 1982. *The Korean Conflict: Search for Unification.* New Delhi: Prentice-Hall of India.

849. Starobin, J. R. 1954. *Eyewitness in Indo-China.* New York: Cameron and Kahn.

850. Steinberg, D. I. 1981. *Burma's Road Toward Development: Growth and Ideology Under Military Rule.* Boulder, Colo.: Westview.

851. Steinberg, D. J. 1959. *Cambodia: Its People, Its Society, Its Culture.* New Haven, Conn.: HRAF.

852. Stolper, T. 1985. *China, Taiwan, and the Offshore Islands.* Armonk, N.Y.: M. E. Sharpe.

853. Stone, I. 1952. *The Hidden History of the Korean War.* New York: Monthly Review Press.

854. Stuart-Fox, M. 1986. *Laos: Politics, Economics, and Society.* Boulder, Colo.: Lynne Rienner.

855. Summers, H. 1985. *Vietnam War Almanac.* New York: Facts on File.

856. Suter, K. D. 1979. *West Irian, East Timor, and Indonesia.* London: Minority Rights Group.

857. Tan, S. K. 1989. *Decolonization and Filipino Muslim Identity.* Quezon City, the Philippines: Diliman.

858. Taylor, R. H. 1983. *An Undeveloped State: The Study of Modern Burma's Politics.* London: Department of Economics and Political Studies, School of Oriental and African Studies, University of London.

859. ————. 1988. *The State in Burma.* Honolulu: University of Hawaii Press.

860. ————. 1973. *Foreign and Domestic Consequences of the KMT Intervention in Burma.* Ithaca, N.Y.: Southeast Asian Program, Department of Asian Studies, Cornell University.

861. Tho, T. 1979. *The Cambodian Incursion.* Washington, D.C.: U.S. Army Center of Military History.

862. Thompson, R. 1966. *Defeating Communist Insurgency: Experiences From Malaya and Vietnam.* London: Chatto and Windus.

863. Tinker, H. 1967. *The Union of Burma: A Study of the First Years of Independence.* 4th ed. London: Oxford University Press.

864. ————, ed. 1984. *Burma: The Struggle for Independence, 1944–1948: Documents From Official and Private Sources.* London: HMSO.

865. Toye, H. 1968. *Laos: Buffer State or Battleground?* London: Oxford University Press.

866. Tsou, T. 1959. *The Embroilment Over Quemoy: Mao, Chiang, and Dulles.* Salt Lake City: Institute of International Studies, University of Utah.

867. Turley, W. 1986. *The Second Indochina War: A Short Political and Military History, 1954–1975.* Boulder, Colo.: Westview.

868. Turner, M. M., R. J. May, and L. Turner. 1992. *Mindanao: Land of Unfulfilled Promise.* Quezon City, the Philippines: New Day.

869. Turton, A., J. Fast, and M. Caldwell, eds. 1978. *Thailand: Roots of Conflict.* Nottingham: Spokesman Books.

870. Valencia, M. J. 1995. *China and the South China Sea Disputes.* Adelphi Papers #298. London: IISS.

871. VanDyke, J. M. 1972. *North Vietnam's Strategy for Survival.* Stanford, Calif.: Pacific Books.

872. Vanniasingham, S. 1988. *Sri Lanka: The Conflict Within.* New Delhi: Lancer.

873. Vertzberger, Y. 1984. *Misperception in Foreign Policy Making: The Sino-Indian Conflict, 1959–1962.* Boulder, Colo.: Westview.

874. Vickery, M. 1984. *Cambodia, 1975–1982.* Boston: South End.

875. Vidyarthi, L. P., ed. 1969. *Conflict, Tension, and Cultural Trend in India.* Calcutta: Punthi Pustak.

876. Vo, N. G. 1971. *National Liberation War in Vietnam: General Line, Strategy, Tactics.* Hanoi: Foreign Languages Publishing House.

877. Walt van Praag, M. C. Van. 1987. *The Status of Tibet: History, Rights, and Prospects in International Law.* Boulder, Colo.: Westview.

878. Watson, F. 1966. *The Frontiers of China.* New York: Praeger.

879. Wehl, D. 1948. *The Birth of Indonesia.* London: Allen and Unwin.

880. White, R. K. 1970. *Nobody Wanted War: Misperception in Vietnam and Other Wars.* Garden City, N.Y.: Doubleday.

881. Wilson, A. J. 1988. *The Break-Up of Sri Lanka: The Sinhalese-Tamil Conflict.* Honolulu: University of Hawaii Press.

882. Wroth, J. 1968. "Korea: Our Next Vietnam." *Military Review* 48 (November): 34–40.

883. Yasmeen, S. 1987. *India and Pakistan: Why the Latest Exercise in Brinkmanship?* Working Paper #125. Canberra: Strategic and Defence Studies Center, Australian National University.

884. Young, M. B. 1991. *The Vietnam Wars, 1945–1990.* New York: HarperCollins.

885. Zagoria, O. S. 1964. *The Sino-Soviet Conflict, 1956–1961.* New York: Atheneum.

886. Zakaria, H. A. 1984. *War and Conflict Studies in Malaysia: The State of the Art.* Working Paper #76. Canberra: Strategic and Defence Studies Center, Australian National University.

EUROPE

887. Adams, T. W., and A. J. Cottrell. 1968. *Cyprus Between East and West.* Baltimore: Johns Hopkins University Press.

888. Akhavan, P., and R. Howse, eds. 1995. *Yugoslavia, the Former and Future: Reflections by Scholars From the Region.* Washington, D.C.: Brookings; Geneva: United Nations Research Institute for Social Development.

889. Allison, R. 1988. *The Soviet Union and the Strategy of Non-Alignment in the Third World.* Cambridge: Cambridge University Press.

890. ———. 1993. *Military Forces in the Soviet Successor States: An Analysis of the Military Policies, Force Dispositions, and Evolving Threat Perceptions of the Former Soviet States.* Adelphi Papers #280. London: Brassey's.

891. Allison, R., and P. Williams. 1990. *Superpower Competition and Crisis Prevention in the Third World.* Cambridge: Cambridge University Press.

892. An, T. 1973. *The Sino-Soviet Territorial Dispute.* Philadelphia: Westminister.

893. Andric, I. 1977. *The Bridge on the Drina.* Translated by L. Edwards. Chicago: University of Chicago Press.

894. Anwar, R. 1988. *The Tragedy of Afghanistan: A First-hand Account.* Translated by Khalid Hasan. New York: Verso.

895. Arnold, A. 1985. *Afghanistan: The Soviet Invasion in Perspective.* Stanford, Calif.: Hoover.

896. Barber, N. 1974. *Seven Days of Freedom: The Hungarian Uprising, 1956.* New York: Stein and Day.

897. Barta, I., contr. 1975. *A History of Hungary.* Edited by Ervin Pamlenyi. London: Collet's.

898. Bennett, C. 1995. *Yugoslavia's Bloody Collapse: Causes, Course, and Consequences.* New York: New York University Press.

899. Bhasin, V. 1984. *Soviet Intervention in Afghanistan: Its Background and Implications.* New Delhi: S. Chand.

900. Bitsios, D. 1975. *Cyprus: The Vulnerable Republic.* Thessalonike: Institute for Balkan Studies.

901. Blaxland, G. 1971. *The Regiments Depart: A History of the British Army, 1945–1970.* London: Kimber.

902. Borisov, O., and B. Koloskov. 1975. *Soviet-Chinese Relations, 1945–1970.* Bloomington: Indiana University Press.

903. Bradsher, H. 1985. *Afghanistan and the Soviet Union.* Expanded ed. Durham, N.C.: Duke University Press.

904. Brzezinski, Z. 1967. *The Soviet Bloc: Unity and Conflict.* Cambridge: Harvard University Press.

905. Burg, S. L. 1983. *Conflict and Cohesion in Socialist Yugoslavia: Political Decision-Making Since 1966.* Princeton, N.J.: Princeton University Press.

906. Campbell, J. C., ed. 1976. *Successful Negotiation, Trieste 1954: An Appraisal by Five Participants.* Princeton, N.J.: Princeton University Press.

907. Chandler, G. 1959. *The Divided Land: An Anglo-Greek Tragedy.* London: Macmillan.

908. Close, D. H., ed. 1993. *The Greek Civil War, 1943–1950: Studies of Polarization.* London: Routledge.

909. Cohen, L. J. 1995. *Broken Bonds: Yugoslavia's Disintegration and Balkan Politics in Transition.* 2d ed. Boulder, Colo.: Westview.

910. Cohen, L. J., and P. Warwick. 1983. *Political Cohesion in a Fragile Mosaic: The Yugoslav Experience.* Boulder, Colo.: Westview.

911. Colton, T. J., and R. Legvold, eds. 1992. *After the Soviet Union: From Empire to Nations.* New York: Norton.

912. Crawley, N. 1978. *The Cyprus Revolt: An Account of the Struggle for Union With Greece.* Boston: Allen and Unwin.

913. Dawisha, K. 1984. *The Kremlin and the Prague Spring.* Berkeley and Los Angeles: University of California Press.

914. Denitch, B. 1990. *Limits and Possibilities: The Crisis of Yugoslav Socialism and State Socialist Systems.* Minneapolis: University of Minnesota Press.

915. ———. 1994. *Ethnic Nationalism: The Tragic Death of Yugoslavia.* Minneapolis: University of Minnesota Press.

916. Denktash, R. 1982. *The Cyprus Triangle.* Boston: Allen and Unwin.

917. Dewar, M. 1984. *Brush Fire Wars: Minor Campaigns of the British Army Since 1945.* New York: St. Martin's.

918. Djilas, M. 1977. *Wartime.* Translated by M. B. Petrovich. New York: Harcourt Brace Jovanovich.

919. Donia, R. J., and J. V. A. Fine Jr. 1994. *Bosnia and Hercegovina: A Tradition Betrayed.* New York: Columbia University Press.

920. Duncan, W. R., and G. P. Holman Jr. 1994. *Ethnic Nationalism and Regional Conflict: The Former Soviet Union and Yugoslavia.* Boulder, Colo.: Westview.

921. Ehrlich, T. 1974. *Cyprus, 1958–1967.* London: Oxford University Press.

922. Emsley, C., ed. 1979. *Conflict and Stability in Europe.* London: Croom Helm.

923. Eyal, J. 1993. *Europe and Yugoslavia: Lessons From a Failure.* Whitehall Paper #19. London: Royal United Services Institute for Defence Studies.

924. Foley, C., and W. Scobie. 1975. *The Struggle for Cyprus.* Stanford, Calif.: Hoover.

925. Gablentz, O. M. van der. 1964. *The Berlin Question in Its Relations to World Politics, 1944–1963.* Munich: Oldenbourg.

926. Ghaus, A. S. 1988. *The Fall of Afghanistan: An Insider's Account.* Washington, D.C.: Pergamon-Brassey's.

927. Glenny, M. 1993. *The Fall of Yugoslavia: Third Balkan War.* New York: Penguin.

928. Gow, J. 1992. *Legitimacy and the Military: The Yugoslav Crisis.* London: Pinter.

929. Griffiths, S. I. 1993. *Nationalism and Ethnic Conflict: Threats to European Security.* Oxford: Oxford University Press.

930. Gunter, M. M. 1986. *Pursuing the Just Cause of Their People: A Study of Contemporary Armenian Terrorism.* New York: Greenwood.

931. Hakovira, H. 1988. *East-West Conflict and European Neutrality.* Oxford: Clarendon.

932. Hammond, T. 1984. *Red Flag Over Afghanistan: The Communist Coup, the Soviet Invasion, and the Consequences.* Boulder, Colo.: Westview.

933. Hare, A. P. 1974. *Cyprus—Conflict and Its Resolution.* Cape Town: University of Cape Town.

934. Hart, P. T. 1990. *Two NATO Allies at the Threshold of War: Cyprus, A Firsthand Account of Crisis Management, 1965–1968.* Institute for the Study of Diplomacy. Durham, N.C.: Duke University Press.

935. Heidelmeyer, W., and G. Hindrichs, eds. 1963. *Documents on Berlin, 1943–1963.* 2d ed. Munich: Oldenbourg.

936. Heinrich, H. G. 1986. *Hungary: Politics, Economics, and Society.* Boulder, Colo.: Lynne Rienner.

937. Hill, J. 1977. *Soviet Political Elites: The Case of Tiraspil.* New York: St. Martin's.

938. Hitchens, C. 1984. *Cyprus.* London: Quartet.

939. Hodnett, G., and P. J. Potichnyj. 1976. *The Ukraine and the Czechoslovak Crisis.* Occasional Paper #6. Canberra: Department of Political Science, Australian National University.

940. Institute for European Studies. 1993. *Interethnic Conflict and War in the Former Yugoslavia.* Working Paper #140. Canberra: Australian National University.

941. International Commission of Jurists. 1957. *The Hungarian Situation and the Rule of Law.* The Hague: ICJ.

942. James, R. R. 1969. *The Czechoslovak Crisis, 1968.* London: Weidenfeld and Nicolson.

943. Kaplan, S., ed. 1981. *Diplomacy of Power: Soviet Armed Forces as a Political Instrument.* Washington, D.C.: Brookings.

944. Kay, H. 1970. *Salazar and Modern Portugal.* New York: Hawthorn Books.

945. Keesings Research Report. 1973. *Germany and Eastern Europe Since 1945: From the Potsdam Agreement to Chancellor Brandt's "Ostpolitik."* New York: Scribner's.

946. Khan, R. M. 1991. *Untying the Afghan Knot: Negotiation and Soviet Withdrawal.* Institute for the Study of Diplomacy. Durham, N.C.: Duke University Press.

947. King, R. R. 1973. *Minorities Under Communism.* Cambridge: Harvard University Press.

948. Kiraly, B. K., and P. Jonas, eds. 1978. *The Hungarian Revolution of 1956 in Retrospect.* New York: Columbia University Press.

949. Kohout, P. 1972. *From the Diary of a Counterrevolutionary.* Translated by G. Theiner. New York: McGraw-Hill.

950. Kousoulas, D. 1965. *Revolution and Defeat: The Story of the Greek Communist Party.* New York: Oxford University Press.

951. Kovacs, I., ed. 1958. *Facts About Hungary: The Fight for Freedom.* Written by Magyar Bizottsag. New York: Hungarian Committee.

952. ———, comp. 1966. *Facts About Hungary: The Fight for Freedom.* Rev. ed. Written by Magyar Bizottsag. New York: Hungarian Committee.

953. Lasky, M. J., ed. 1957. *The Hungarian Revolution: A White Book.* New York: Praeger.

954. Littell, R. 1969. *The Czech Black Book.* Prepared by the Institute of History, Czechoslovak Academy of Sciences. New York: Praeger.

955. Lomax, W. 1976. *Hungary 1956.* London: Allen and Busby.

956. Maclean, F. 1992. *All the Russias.* New York: Smithmark.

957. Magas, B. 1993. *The Destruction of Yugoslavia: Tracking the Breakup, 1980–1992.* London: Verso.

958. Miall, H., ed. 1994. *Redefining Europe: New Patterns of Conflict and Cooperation.* New York: Pinter.

959. Markides, K. 1977. *The Rise and Fall of the Cyprus Republic.* New Haven, Conn.: Yale University Press.

960. McInnes, E. 1960. *The Shaping of Postwar Germany.* London: Dent.

961. Mikes, G. 1957. *The Hungarian Revolution.* London: André Deutsch.

962. Mojzes, P. 1994. *The Yugoslavian Inferno: Ethnoreligious Warfare in the Balkans.* New York: Continuum.

963. Molnar, M. 1971. *Budapest, 1956: A History of the Hungarian Revolution.* Translated by Jennetta Ford. London: Allen and Unwin.

964. Novak, B. 1970. *Trieste, 1941–1954: The Ethnic, Political, and Ideological Struggle.* Chicago: University of Chicago Press.

965. O'Ballance, E. 1966. *The Greek Civil War, 1944–1949.* New York: Praeger.

966. Oleser, A. 1995. *Islam and Politics in Afghanistan.* Richmond (Surrey), Eng.: Curzon.

967. Pajic, Z. 1993. *Violation of Fundamental Rights in the Former Yugoslavia.* Occasional Paper #2. London: David Davies Memorial Institute of International Studies.

968. Patrick, R. A., J. H. Bater, and R. Preston, eds. 1976. *Political Geography and the Cyprus Conflict, 1963–1971.* Publication Series #4. Waterloo, Ont.: Department of Geography, Faculty of Environmental Studies, University of Waterloo.

969. Polyviou, P. 1975. *Cyprus: The Tragedy and the Challenge.* Washington, D.C.: American Hellenic Institute.

970. Psomiades, H. J. 1968. *The Eastern Question: The Last Phase—A Study in Greek-Turkish Diplomacy.* Thessalonike: Institute for Balkan Studies.

971. Rabel, R. G. 1988. *Between East and West: Trieste, the United States and the Cold War, 1941–1954.* Durham, N.C.: Duke University Press.

972. Radvanyi, J. 1972. *Hungary and the Superpowers: The 1956 Revolution and Realpolitik.* Stanford, Calif.: Hoover.

973. Ramazani, R. K. 1966. *The Northern Tier: Afghanistan, Iran, and Turkey.* Princeton, N.J.: Van Nostrand.

974. Ramet, S. P. 1992. *Nationalism and Federalism in Yugoslavia, 1962–1991.* 2d ed. Bloomington: Indiana University Press.

975. Ramet, S. P., and L. S. Adamovich, eds. 1995. *Beyond Yugoslavia: Politics, Economics, and Culture in a Shattered Community.* Boulder, Colo.: Westview.

976. Randle, M. 1968. *Support Czechoslovakia.* London: Housemans.

977. Remington, R. 1969. *Winter in Prague: Documents on Czechoslovak Communism in Crisis.* Cambridge: MIT Press.

978. Roberts, A. 1969. *Czechoslovakia 1968.* London: Chatto and Windus.

979. Roy, O. 1991. *The Lessons of the Soviet-Afghan War.* Adelphi Papers #259. London: Brassey's.

980. Rupesinghe, K., P. King, and O. Vorkunova, eds. 1992. *Ethnicity and Conflict in a Post-Communist World: The Soviet Union, Eastern Europe, and China.* New York: St. Martin's.

981. Rusinow, D. 1977. *The Yugoslav Experiment, 1948–1974.* Berkeley and Los Angeles: University of California Press.

982. ———, ed. 1988. *Yugoslavia: A Fractured Federalism.* Washington, D.C.: Wilson Center Press.

983. Salem, N., ed. 1992. *Cyprus: A Regional Conflict and Its Resolution.* New York: St. Martin's.

984. Salomon, M. 1971. *Prague Notebook: The Strangled Revolution.* Translated by H. Eustis. Boston: Little, Brown.

985. Schmid, A. P. 1985. *Soviet Military Interventions Since 1945.* With case studies by E. Berends. New Brunswick, N.J.: Transaction.

986. Schwartz, H. 1969. *Prague's 200 Days: The Struggle for Democracy in Czechoslovakia.* New York: Praeger.

987. Sena, C. 1986. *Afghanistan: Politics, Economics, and Society: Revolution, Resistance, Intervention.* Boulder, Colo.: Lynne Rienner.

988. Simecka, M. 1984. *The Restoration of Order: The Normalization of Czechoslovakia, 1969–1976.* Translated by A. G. Brain. London: Verso.

989. Simes, D. K. 1977. *Detente and Conflict: Soviet Foreign Policy, 1972–1977.* Beverly Hills: Sage.

990. Skilling, H. G. 1976. *Czechoslovakia's Interrupted Revolution.* Princeton, N.J.: Princeton University Press.

991. Smith, J. E. 1963. *The Defense of Berlin.* Baltimore: Johns Hopkins University Press.

992. Stephens, R. H. 1966. *Cyprus: A Place of Arms: Power Politics and Ethnic Conflict in the Eastern Mediterranean.* London: Pall Mall.

993. Stern, L. M. 1977. *The Wrong Horse: The Politics of Intervention and Failure of American Diplomacy.* New York: Times Books.

994. Suda, Z. 1969. *The Czechoslovak Socialist Republic.* Baltimore: Johns Hopkins University Press.

995. Sugar, P., P. Harak, and T. Frank. 1990. *A History of Hungary.* Bloomington: Indiana University Press.

996. Svitak, I. 1971. *The Czechoslovak Experiment, 1968–1969.* New York: Columbia University Press.

997. Sword, K., ed. 1991. *The Times's Guide to Eastern Europe: Inside the Other Europe.* London: Times Books.

998. Szajkowski, B. 1993. *Encyclopaedia of Conflicts, Disputes, and Flashpoints in Eastern Europe, Russia, and the Successor States.* Harlow (Essex), Eng.: Longman.

999. Szporluk, R., ed. 1994. *National Identity and Ethnicity in Russia and the New States of Russia.* Armonk, N.Y.: M. E. Sharpe.

1000. Tanter, R. 1974. *Modeling and Managing International Conflicts: The Berlin Crisis*. Beverly Hills: Sage.

1001. Tigrid, P. 1971. *Why Dubcek Fell*. London: MacDonald and Company.

1002. Toma, P. A. 1988. *Socialist Authority: The Hungarian Experience*. New York: Praeger.

1003. Toma, P. A., and I. Volyges. 1977. *Politics in Hungary*. San Francisco: W. H. Freeman.

1004. Tornaritis, C. G. 1975. *The Turkish Invasion of Cyprus and Legal Problems Arising Therefrom*. Nicosia: (s. n.)

1005. Urban, M. 1989. *War in Afghanistan*. New York: St. Martin's.

1006. Valenta, J. 1979. *Soviet Intervention in Czechoslovakia, 1968: Anatomy of a Decision*. Baltimore: Johns Hopkins University Press.

1007. Vali, F. 1961. *Rift and Revolt in Hungary: Nationalism Versus Communism*. Cambridge: Harvard University Press.

1008. Vanezis, P. 1977. *Cyprus: The Unfinished Agony*. London: Abelard-Schuman.

1009. Volkan, V. D., and N. Itzkowitz. 1994. *Turks and Greeks: Neighbours in Conflict*. Huntingdon, Eng.: Eothen.

1010. Warnes, K. 1994. *Developing More Effective Regional Peacemaking Structures: Western European Intercession in the Yugoslav Conflict, 1990–1993*. Working Paper #153. Canberra: Peace Research Center, Australian National University.

1011. Willerton, J. P. 1992. *Patronage and Politics in the USSR*. Cambridge: Cambridge University Press.

1012. Wilson, A. 1979. *The Aegean Dispute*. Adelphi Papers #155. London: IISS.

1013. Wilson, D. 1979. *Tito's Yugoslavia*. Cambridge: Cambridge University Press.

1014. Wirsing, R. G. 1981. *The Baluchis and Pathans*. Minority Rights Group Report #48. London: Minority Rights Group.

1015. Woodhouse, C. 1976. *The Struggle for Greece, 1941–1949*. London: Hart-Davis, MacGibbon.

1016. Woodward, S. L. 1995. *Balkan Tragedy: Chaos and Dissolution After the Cold War*. Washington, D.C.: Brookings.

1017. Xydris, S. G. 1973. *Cyprus: Reluctant Republic*. The Hague: Mouton.

1018. Zametica, J. 1992. *The Yugoslav Conflict: An Analysis of the Causes of the Yugoslav War, the Policies of the Republic, and the Regional and International Implications of the Conflict*. Adelphi Papers #270. London: Brassey's.

1019. Zeman, Z. A. B. 1969. *Prague Spring*. New York: Hill and Wang.

MIDDLE EAST

1020. Abdulghani, J. 1984. *Iraq and Iran: The Years of Crisis*. Baltimore: Johns Hopkins University Press.

1021. Abdullah, M. 1978. *The United Arab Emirates: A Modern History*. London: Croom Helm.

1022. Abir, M. 1974. *Oil, Power, and Politics: Conflict in Arabia, the Red Sea, and the Gulf.* London: F. Cass.

1023. Adkin, M. 1989. *Oil, Power and Politics: Conflict in Arabia, the Red Sea and the Gulf.* London: F. Cass.

1024. Agha, H., and A. S. Khalidi. 1995. *Syria and Iran: Rivalry and Cooperation.* New York: Council on Foreign Relations Press for the Royal Institute of International Affairs

1025. Agha, U. H. 1978. *The Role of Mass Communications in Inter-State Conflict: The Arab-Israeli War of October 1973.* Cairo: American University in Cairo.

1026. Ahrari, M. E., ed. 1989. *The Gulf and International Security: The 1980s and Beyond.* Basingstoke (Hants), Eng.: Macmillan.

1027. Alamuddin, N. 1993. *Turmoil: The Druzes, Lebanon, and the Arab-Israeli Conflict.* London: Quartet.

1028. Alkim, H. H. 1989. *The Foreign Policy of the United Arab Emirates.* London: Saqi.

1029. Allen, D., and A. Pijpers, eds. 1984. *European Foreign Policy Making and the Arab-Israeli Conflict.* The Hague: M. Nijhoff.

1030. Allen, P. 1982. *The Yom Kippur War.* New York: Scribner's.

1031. Al Madfai, M. R. 1993. *Jordan, the United States, and the Middle East Peace Process, 1974–1991.* Cambridge: Cambridge University Press.

1032. Alon, H. 1980. *Countering Palestinian Terrorism in Israel: Toward a Policy Analysis of Countermeasures.* Rand Report #1567. Santa Monica, Calif.: Rand.

1033. Amirahmadi, H., and N. Entessar, eds. 1992. *Reconstruction and Regional Diplomacy in the Persian Gulf.* London and New York: Routledge.

1034. ———. 1993. *Iran and the Arab World.* New York: St. Martin's.

1035. Amos, J. W. 1979. *Arab-Israeli Military-Political Relations: Arab Perceptions and the Politics of Escalation.* New York: Pergamon.

1036. Anderson, L. 1986. *The State and Social Transformation in Tunisia and Libya, 1830–1980.* Princeton, N.J.: Princeton University Press.

1037. Anderson, R., R. F. Seibert, and J. G. Wagner. 1990. *Politics and Change in the Middle East: Sources of Conflict and Accommodation.* Englewood Cliffs, N.J.: Prentice-Hall.

1038. Arfa, H. 1966. *The Kurds: A Historical and Political Study.* London: Oxford University Press.

1039. Aronoff, M. J. 1989. *Israeli Visions and Division: Cultural Change and Political Conflict.* New Brunswick, N.J.: Transaction.

1040. Aronson, S. 1978. *Conflict and Bargaining in the Middle East: An Israeli Perspective.* Baltimore: Johns Hopkins University Press.

1041. Assiri, A. 1990. *Kuwait's Foreign Policy: City-State in World Politics.* Boulder, Colo.: Westview.

1042. Ayoob, M. 1981. *Defusing the Middle East Time Bomb: A State for the Palestinians.* Working Paper #35. Canberra: Strategic and Defence Studies Center, Australian National University.

1043. ———, ed. 1986. *Regional Security in the Third World: Case Studies From South East Asia and the Middle East.* London: Croom Helm.

1044. Ayubi, N. N. M. 1980. *Bureaucracy and Politics in Contemporary Egypt.* London: Ithaca Press.

1045. Badeeb, S. 1986. *The Saudi-Egyptian Conflict Over North Yemen, 1962–1970.* Boulder, Colo.: Westview/American-Arab Affairs Council.

1046. Bailey, C. 1984. *Jordan's Palestinian Challenge, 1948–1983: A Political History.* Boulder, Colo.: Westview.

1047. Bailey, S. 1990. *Four Arab-Israeli Wars and the Peace Process.* New York: St. Martin's.

1048. Baker, R. W. 1990. *Sadat and After: Struggles for Egypt's Political Soul.* Cambridge: Harvard University Press.

1049. Barnett, M. N. 1992. *Confronting the Costs of War: Military Power, State, and Society in Egypt and Israel.* Princeton, N.J.: Princeton University Press.

1050. Bar-Simon-Tov, Y. 1983. *Linkage Politics in the Middle East: Syria Between Domestic and External Conflict, 1961–1970.* Boulder, Colo.: Westview.

1051. Bar-Yaacov, N. 1967. *The Israel-Syrian Armistice: Problems of Implementation, 1949–1966.* Jerusalem: Magnes.

1052. Beauré, A. 1969. *The Suez Expedition.* London: Faber.

1053. Becker, J. 1984. *The PLO: The Rise and Fall of the Palestine Liberation Organization.* New York: St. Martin's.

1054. Beirut Institute for Palestine Studies. 1982. *U.N. Resolutions on Palestine and Arab-Israeli Conflict, 1981.* New York: United Nations.

1055. Bell, C. 1986. *Politics, Diplomacy, and Islam: Four Case Studies.* Canberra Studies in World Affairs #21. Canberra: International Relations, Research School of Pacific Studies, Australian National University.

1056. Ben-Dor, G. 1983. *State and Conflict in the Middle East: Emergence of the Post-Colonial State.* New York: Praeger.

1057. Ben-Dor, G., and D. B. Dewitt, eds. 1987. *Conflict Management in the Middle East.* Lexington, Mass.: Lexington Books.

1058. Ben Rafael, E. 1987. *Israel-Palestine: A Guerrilla Conflict in International Politics.* New York: Greenwood.

1059. Beschorner, N. 1992. *Water and Instability in the Middle East.* Adelphi Papers #273. London: Brassey's.

1060. Bidwell, R. 1983. *The Two Yemens.* New York: Longman.

1061. Bill, J. A. 1988. *The Eagle and the Lion: The Tragedy of American-Iranian Relations.* New Haven, Conn.: Yale University Press.

1062. Binder, L. 1978. *In a Moment of Enthusiasm: Political Power and the Second Stratum in Egypt.* Chicago: University of Chicago Press.

1063. Blechman, B. 1972. "The Impact of Israel's Reprisals on Behavior of the Bordering Arab Nations Directed at Israel." *Journal of Conflict Resolution* 16 (June): 155–181.

1064. Boasson, C., and M. Nurock, eds. 1974. *The Changing International Community: Some Problems of Its Laws, Structures, Peace Research and the Middle East Conflict.* Essays in honor of Marion Mushkat. The Hague: Mouton.

1065. Boulding, E. 1994. *Building Peace in the Middle East: Challenges for States and Civil Society.* Boulder, Colo.: Lynne Rienner.

1066. Bowie, R. R. 1974. *Suez 1956.* London: Oxford University Press.

1067. Brown, L. C. 1984. *International Politics and the Middle East: Old Rules, Dangerous Game.* London: I. B. Tauris.

1068. Browne, H. 1971. *Suez and Sinai.* London: Longman.

1069. Brynen, R. 1990. *Sanctuary and Survival: The PLO in Lebanon.* Boulder, Colo.: Westview.

1070. Bull, O. 1976. *War and Peace in the Middle East.* London: Leo Cooper.

1071. Burns, E. 1963. *Between Arab and Israeli.* New York: Ivan Obelinsky.

1072. Burrell, R. M., and A. J. Cottrell. 1974. *Iran, Afghanistan, Pakistan: Tension and Dilemmas.* Beverly Hills: Sage.

1073. Burrell, R. M., and A. Kelidar. 1977. *Egypt: The Dilemmas of a Nation, 1970–1977.* Beverly Hills: Sage.

1074. Butterworth, C. E., and I. W. Zartman, eds. 1992. *Political Islam.* Newbury Park, Calif.: Sage.

1075. Capitanchik, D. B. 1991. *The Middle East: Conflict and Stability.* Oxford: B. Blackwell.

1076. Carlton, D. 1989. *Britain and the Suez Crisis.* Oxford: B. Blackwell.

1077. Cattan, H. 1976. *Palestine and International Law: The Legal Aspects of the Arab-Israeli Conflict.* 2d ed. London: Longman.

1078. Chliand, G., ed. 1993. *A People Without a Country: The Kurds and Kurdistan.* New York: Olive Branch.

1079. Chomsky, N. 1975. *Peace in the Middle East?: Reflections on Justice and Nationhood.* London: Fontana/Collins.

1080. Christopher, W., and P. Kreisberg, eds. 1985. *American Hostages in Iran: The Conduct of a Crisis.* New Haven, Conn.: Yale University Press.

1081. Chubin, S. 1980. *Soviet Policy Towards Iran and the Gulf.* Adelphi Papers #157. London: IISS.

1082. Cobban, H. 1983. *The Palestinian Liberation Organization.* Cambridge: Cambridge University Press.

1083. ———. 1985. *The Making of Modern Lebanon.* Boulder, Colo.: Westview.

1084. ———. 1991. *The Superpowers and the Syrian-Israeli Conflict.* New York: Praeger.

1085. Cohen, R. I., ed. 1985. *Vision and Conflict in the Holy Land.* New York: St. Martin's.

1086. ———. 1990. *Culture and Conflict in Egyptian-Israeli Relations: A Dialogue of the Deaf.* Bloomington: Indiana University Press.

1087. Comay, M. 1976. *U.N. Peace-Keeping in the Israel-Arab Conflict, 1948–1975: An Israel Critique.* Jerusalem Papers on Peace Problems #17–18. Jerusalem: Leonard Davis Institute for International Relations, Hebrew University of Jerusalem.

1088. Cooley, J. 1973. *Green March, Black September: The Story of the Palestinian Arabs.* London: F. Cass.

1089. ———. 1982. *Libyan Sandstorm.* New York: Holt, Rinehart, and Winston.

1090. Cooper, M. N. 1982. *The Transformation of Egypt.* Baltimore: Johns Hopkins University Press.

1091. Cordesman, A. H. 1987. *The Iran-Iraq War and Western Security, 1984–1987: Strategic Implications and Policy Options.* London: Jane's.

1092. ———. 1984. *The Gulf and the Search for Strategic Stability: Saudi Arabia, the Military Balance in the Gulf, and Trends in the Arab-Israeli Military Balance.* Boulder, Colo.: Westview.

1093. Cotlan, R. W. 1977. *Foreign Policy Motivation: A General Theory and a Case Study.* Pittsburgh: University of Pittsburgh Press.

1094. Cyrsal, J. 1990. *Oil and Politics in the Gulf: Rulers and Merchants in Kuwait and Qatar.* Cambridge: Cambridge University Press.

1095. Dann, U. 1969. *Iraq Under Qassem: A Political History, 1958–1963.* New York: Praeger.

1096. Dannreuther, R. 1992. *The Gulf Conflict: A Political and Strategic Analysis.* Adelphi Papers #264. London: Brassey's.

1097. Davis, B. L. 1990. *Qaddafi, Terrorism, and the Origins of the U.S. Attack on Libya.* New York: Praeger.

1098. Davis, L., E. Rozeman, and J. Z. Rubin, eds. 1988. *Myths and Facts 1989: A Concise Record of the Arab-Israeli Conflict.* Washington, D.C.: Near East Report.

1099. Dawisha, A. 1976. *Egypt in the Arab World: The Elements of Foreign Policy.* London: Macmillan.

1100. ———. 1980. *Saudi Arabia's Search for Security.* Adelphi Papers #158. London: IISS.

1101. Dawisha, A., and I. W. Zartman, eds. 1988. *Beyond Coercion: The Durability of the Arab State.* London: Croom Helm.

1102. Dayan, M. 1981. *Break Through: A Personal Account of the Egypt-Israel Peace Negotiations.* London: Weidenfeld and Nicolson.

1103. Deeb, M. 1980. *The Lebanese Civil War.* New York: Praeger.

1104. Dekmejian, R. H. 1971. *Egypt Under Nasir: A Study in Political Dynamics.* Albany: State University of New York Press.

1105. Dowty, A. 1984. *Middle East Crisis: U.S. Decision-Making in 1958, 1970, and 1973.* Berkeley and Los Angeles: University of California Press.

1106. Drysdale, A., and G. H. Blake. 1985. *The Middle East and North Africa: A Political Geography.* New York: Oxford University Press.

1107. Eden, A. 1968. *The Suez Crisis of 1956.* Boston: Beacon Press.

1108. Eknes, A. 1989. *From Scandal to Success: The United Nations and the Iran-Iraq War, 1980–1988.* Working Paper #406. Oslo: Norwegian Institute of International Affairs.

1109. Entessaur, N. 1992. *Kurdish Ethnonationalism.* Boulder, Colo.: Lynne Rienner.

1110. Epstein, L. D. 1964. *British Politics in the Suez Crisis.* London: Pall Mall.

1111. Evron, Y. 1987. *War and Intervention in Lebanon: The Israeli-Syrian Deterrence Dialogue.* Baltimore: Johns Hopkins University Press.

1112. Fahmy, I. 1983. *Negotiation for Peace in the Middle East.* London: Croom Helm.

1113. Farah, N. R. 1986. *Religious Strife in Egypt: Crisis and Ideological Conflict in the 1970s.* New York: Gordon and Breach Science Publishers.

1114. Fatemi, F. S. 1980. *The USSR in Iran.* South Brunswick, N.J.: A. S. Barnes.

1115. Feste, K. A. 1991. *Plans for Peace: Negotiation and the Arab-Israeli Conflict.* New York: Greenwood.

1116. Finer, H. 1964. *Dulles Over Suez: The Theory and Practice of His Diplomacy.* London: Heinemann.

1117. Fischer, S. 1994. *Securing Peace in the Middle East.* Cambridge: MIT Press.

1118. Fitzsimons, M. A. 1957. *The Suez Crisis and the Containment Policy.* Indianapolis: Bobbs-Merrill.

1119. Foot, M., and M. Jones. 1957. *Guilty Men 1957.* London: Gollancz.

1120. Freiberger, S. Z. 1992. *Dawn Over Suez: The Rise of American Power in the Middle East.* Chicago: I. R. Dee.

1121. Freidlander, M. A. 1983. *Sadat and Begin: The Domestic Politics of Peacemaking.* Boulder, Colo.: Westview.

1122. Fullick, R., and G. Powell. 1979. *Suez: The Double War.* London: Hamish Hamilton.

1123. Gabriel, R. 1984. *Operation Peace for Galilee: The Israeli-PLO War in Lebanon.* New York: Hill and Wang.

1124. Gainsborough, J. R. 1986. *The Arab-Israeli Conflict: A Politico-Legal Analysis.* Aldershot (Hants), Eng.: Gower.

1125. Gause, F. 1990. *Saudi-Yemeni Relations: Domestic Structures and Foreign Policies.* New York: Columbia University Press.

1126. Gavin, R. 1975. *Aden Under British Rule, 1839–1967.* New York: Barnes and Noble.

1127. George, A. L. 1993. *Bridging the Gap: Theory and Practice in Foreign Policy.* Washington, D.C.: U.S. Institute for Peace Press.

1128. Ghareeb, E. 1981. *The Kurdish Question in Iraq.* Syracuse, N.Y.: Syracuse University Press.

1129. Gilbert, M. *Atlas of the Arab-Israeli Conflict.* New York: Macmillan.

1130. Gilboa, E. 1980. *Simulation of Conflict and Conflict Resolution in the Middle East.* Jerusalem Papers on Peace Problems #30. Jerusalem: Magnes.

1131. ———. 1987. *American Public Opinion Toward Israel and Arab-Israeli Conflict.* Lexington, Mass.: Lexington Books.

1132. Gilmour, D. 1980. *Dispossessed: The Ordeal of the Palestinians.* London: Shere.

1133. ———. 1984. *Lebanon: The Fractured Country.* New York: St. Martin's.

1134. Golan, G. 1977. *Yom Kippur and After: The Soviet Union and the Middle East Crisis.* Cambridge: Cambridge University Press.

1135. ———. 1992. *Moscow and the Middle East: New Thinking on Regional Conflict.* London: Pinter.

1136. Golan, M. 1976. *The Secret Conversations of Henry Kissinger: Step-by-Step Diplomacy in the Middle East.* New York: Quadrangle/New York Times Book Co.

1137. Gordon, M. 1981. *Conflict in the Persian Gulf.* London: Macmillan.

1138. Grossier, P. L. 1982. *The United States and the Middle East.* Albany: State University of New York Press.

1139. Grummon, S. R. 1982. *The Iran-Iraq War: Islam Embattled.* Washington Papers #92. New York: CSIS/Praeger.

1140. Gustave, E., and G. L. Tikku, 1971. *Islam and Its Cultural Divergence.* Urbana-Champaign: University of Illinois Press.

1141. Haley, P. E. 1984. *Qaddafi and the United States Since 1969.* New York: Praeger.

1142. Halliday, F. 1974. *Arabia Without Sultans: A Political Survey of Instability in the Arab World.* New York: Random House.

1143. ———. 1990. *Revolution and Foreign Policy: The Case of South Yemen, 1967–1987.* New York: Cambridge University Press.

1144. Hamezeh, F. S. 1968. *U.N. Conciliation for Palestine, 1949–1967.* Beirut: Institute for Palestine Studies.

1145. Hamizrachi, B. 1988. *The Emergence of the South Lebanon Security Belt: Major Saad Haddad and the Ties With Israel, 1975–1978.* New York: Praeger.

1146. Handel, M. I. 1976. *Perception, Deception, and Surprise: The Case of the Yom Kippur War.* Jerusalem Papers on Peace Problems #19. Jerusalem: Leonard Davis Institute for International Relations, Hebrew University of Jerusalem.

1147. Harris, L. C., ed. 1988. *Egypt: Internal Challenges and Regional Stability.* London: Routledge and Kegan Paul.

1148. Harris, W. W. 1981. *Taking Root: Israeli Settlement in the West Bank, the Golan, and Gaza-Sinai, 1967–1980.* Chichester, Eng.: Research Studies Press.

1149. Hart, A. 1989. *Arafat: A Political Biography.* Bloomington: Indiana University Press.

1150. Hashim, A. 1995. *The Crisis of the Iranian State: Domestic, Foreign, and Security Policies in Post-Khomeini Iran.* Oxford: Oxford University Press.

1151. Hassouna, H. 1975. *The League of Arab States and Regional Disputes: A Study of Middle East Conflicts.* Dobbs Ferry, N.Y.: Oceana.

1152. Haykal, M. H. 1975. *The Road to Ramadan.* New York: Quadrangle/New York Times Book Co.

1153. Hazon, B. 1976. *Soviet Propaganda: A Case Study of the Middle East Conflict.* New York: Wiley.

1154. Heard-Bey, F. 1982. *From Trucial States to United Arab Emirates: A Society in Transition.* New York: Longman.

1155. Heikal, M. 1975. *The Road to Ramadan.* London: Collins.

1156. Heller, M., and S. Nusseibeh. 1991. *No Trumpets, No Drums: A Two-State Settlement of the Israeli-Palestinian Conflict.* New York: Hill and Wang.

1157. Herzog, C. 1975. *The War of Atonement, October 1973.* Boston: Little, Brown.

1158. ———. 1984. *The Arab-Israeli Wars: War and Peace in the Middle East From the War of Independence to Lebanon.* Rev. ed. London: Arms and Armour.

1159. Hiro, D. 1991. *The Longest War: The Iran-Iraq Military Conflict.* New York: Routledge.

1160. Hofstadter, D. 1973. *Egypt and Nasser.* New York: Facts on File.

1161. Hollis, R. 1993. *Gulf Security: No Consensus.* Whitehall Paper #20. London: Royal United Services Institute for Defence Studies.

1162. Hopwood, D. 1991. *Egypt, Politics, and Society, 1945–1990.* 3d ed. London: HarperCollins Academic.

1163. Howard, M., and R. E. Hunter. 1967. *Israel and the Arab World: The Crisis of 1967.* Adelphi Papers #41. London: IISS.

1164. Insight Team of the London Sunday *Times.* 1974. *The Yom Kippur War.* Garden City, N.Y.: Doubleday.

1165. International Institute for Strategic Studies (IISS). 1975. *The Middle East and the International System: Part I: The Impact of the 1973 War.* Adelphi Papers #114. London: IISS.

1166. Ismael, T. Y. 1971. *The UAR in Africa: Egypt's Policy Under Nasser.* Evanston, Ill.: Northwestern University Press.

1167. Ismael, T. Y., and J. Ismael, 1986. *The People's Democratic Republic of Yemen: Politics, Economics, and Society—the Politics of Socialist Transformation.* Boulder, Colo.: Lynne Rienner.

1168. Jackson, E. I. 1983. *Middle East Mission: The Story of a Major Bid for Peace in the Time of Nasser and Ben-Gurion.* New York: Norton.

1169. Jansen, J. J. G. 1986. *The Neglected Duty: The Creed of Sadat's Assassins and Islamic Resurgence in the Middle East.* New York: Macmillan.

1170. Jawad, S. 1981. *Iraq and the Kurdish Question, 1958–1970.* London: Ithaca Press.

1171. Kadi, L. S. 1973. *The Arab-Israeli Conflict: The Peaceful Proposals, 1948–1972.* Beirut: Palestine Research Center.

1172. Kamil, M. I. 1986. *The Camp David Accords: A Testimony.* Boston: Routledge and Kegan Paul.

1173. Karpat, K. H. 1975. *Turkey's Foreign Policy in Transition, 1950–1974.* Leiden: Brill.

1174. Kaufman, E., S. Abed, and R. L. Rothstein, eds. 1993. *Democracy, Peace, and the Israeli-Palestinian Conflict.* Boulder, Colo.: Lynne Rienner.

1175. Kedourie, E. 1992. *Politics in the Middle East.* Oxford: Oxford University Press.

1176. Kellerman, B., and J. Z. Rubin, eds. 1988. *Leadership and Negotiation in the Middle East.* New York: Praeger.

1177. Kelly, J. 1980. *Arabia, the Gulf and the West.* New York: Basic Books.

1178. Kettle, T. J., and S. Dowrick. 1991. *After the Gulf War, for Peace in the Middle East.* Leichhardt (NSW), Australia: Pluto Press.

1179. Khadduri, M. 1969. *Republican Iraq: A Study in Iraqi Politics Since the Revolution of 1958.* New York: Oxford University Press.

1180. ———. 1988. *The Gulf War: The Origins and Implications of the Iraq-Iran Conflict.* New York: Oxford University Press.

1181. Khalidi, W. 1983. *Conflict and Violence in Lebanon: Confrontation in the Middle East.* Cambridge: Center for International Affairs, Harvard University.

1182. Khouri, F. 1985. *The Arab-Israeli Dilemma.* 3d ed. Syracuse, N.Y.: Syracuse University Press.

1183. Kienle, E. 1990. *Bath vs. Bath: The Conflict Between Syria and Iraq, 1968–1989.* London: I. B. Tauris.

1184. Kimmerling, B. 1979. *A Conceptual Framework for the Analysis of Behaviour in a Territorial Conflict: The Generalization of the Israeli Case.* Jerusalem Papers on Peace Problems #25. Jerusalem: Leonard Davis Institute for International Relations, Hebrew University of Jerusalem.

1185. King, R. 1987. *The Iran-Iraq War: The Political Implications.* Adelphi Papers #219. London: IISS.

1186. Kissinger, H. 1982. *Years of Upheaval.* Boston: Little, Brown.

1187. Klieman, A. S. 1981. *Israel, Jordan, Palestine: The Search for a Durable Peace.* Beverly Hills: Sage.

1188. Kostiner, J. 1984. *The Struggle for South Yemen.* London: Croom Helm.

1189. Kosut, H. 1968. *Israel and the Arabs: The June 1967 War.* New York: Facts on File.

1190. Kreyenbroek, P. G., and S. Sperl, eds. 1992. *The Kurds: A Contemporary Overview.* London: Routledge.

1191. Kriesberg, L. 1992. *International Conflict Resolution: The US-USSR and Middle East Cases.* New Haven, Conn.: Yale University Press.

1192. Kunz, D. B. 1991. *The Economic Diplomacy of the Suez Crisis.* Chapel Hill: University of North Carolina Press.

1193. Kurzman, D. 1970. *Genesis 1948: The First Arab-Israeli War.* New York: World Publishing Co.

1194. Kyle, K. 1991. *Suez.* New York: St. Martin's.

1195. Lackner, H. 1978. *A House Built on Sand: A Political Economy of Saudi Arabia.* London: Ithaca Press.

1196. ———. 1985. *P. D. R. Yemen: Outpost of Socialist Development.* London: Ithaca Press.

1197. Landau, J. M., ed. 1972. *Man, State, and Society in the Contemporary Middle East.* New York: Praeger.

1198. Lapidoth, R. E., and M. Hirsch. 1992. *The Arab-Israel Conflict and Its Resolution: Selected Documents.* Boston: M. Nijhoff.

1199. Laqueur, W. 1969. *The Road to War: The Origin and Aftermath of the Arab-Israeli Conflict, 1967–1968*. Harmondsworth (Middlesex), Eng.: Penguin.

1200. ———. 1974. *Confrontation: The Middle East and World Politics*. London: Wildwood House.

1201. Lauterpacht, E. 1960. *The Suez Canal Settlement*. London: Stevens.

1202. Lenczowski, G. 1968. *Russia and the West in Iran, 1918–1948*. New York: Greenwood.

1203. Lesh, A. M., and M. A. Tessler. 1989. *Israel, Egypt, and the Palestinians: From Camp David to Intifada*. Bloomington: Indiana University Press.

1204. Lissak, M., ed. 1984. *Israeli Society and Its Defence Establishment: The Social and Political Impact of a Protracted Violent Conflict*. London: F. Cass.

1205. Little, D., J. Kelsay, and A. A. Sucedina. 1988. *Human Rights and the Conflict of Cultures: West and Islamic Perspectives on Religious Liberty*. Columbia: University of South Carolina Press.

1206. Litwak, R. 1981. *Sources of Inter-State Conflict*. Vol. 2 of *Security in the Persian Gulf*. Aldershot (Hants), Eng.: IISS/Gower.

1207. Long, D. E., and B. Reich, eds. 1980. *The Government and Politics of the Middle East and North Africa*. Boulder, Colo.: Westview.

1208. Lorch, N. 1968. *Israel's War of Independence, 1947–1949*. 2d rev. ed. Hartford, Conn.: Hartmore House.

1209. Louis, W. R., and E. R. J. Owen, eds. 1989. *Suez 1956: The Crisis and Its Consequences*. Oxford: Clarendon.

1210. Love, K. 1969. *Suez—The Twice-Fought War: A History*. New York: McGraw-Hill.

1211. Lucas, W. S. 1991. *Divided We Stand: Britain, the United States, and the Suez Crisis*. London: Hodder and Stoughton.

1212. Lukacs, Y., ed. 1984. *Documents on the Israel-Palestine Conflict, 1967–1983*. Cambridge: Cambridge University Press.

1213. ———, ed. 1992. *The Israeli-Palestinian Conflict: A Documentary Record*. Cambridge: Cambridge University Press.

1214. Mango, A. 1994. *Turkey: The Challenge of a New Role*. Westport, Conn.: Praeger.

1215. MacDowell, D. 1986. *Lebanon: A Conflict of Minorities*. London: Minority Rights Group.

1216. Mackinlay, J. 1989. *The Peacemakers: An Assessment of Peacemaking Operations at the Arab-Israel Interface*. London: Unwin Hyman.

1217. Margold, P. 1978. *Superpower Intervention in the Middle East*. New York: St. Martin's.

1218. Marlowe, J. 1965. *Anglo-Egyptian Relations, 1800–1956*. 2d ed. London: F. Cass.

1219. Marr, P. 1985. *The Modern History of Iraq*. Boulder, Colo.: Westview.

1220. Martin, L. 1984. *The Unstable Gulf: Threats From Within*. Lexington, Mass.: Lexington Books.

1221. McDermott, A. 1988. *Egypt From Nasser to Mubarak: A Flawed Revolution.* London: Croom Helm.

1222. McLauren, R. D., M. Mughisuddin, and A. R. Wagner. 1977. *Foreign Policy Making in the Middle East: Domestic Influences on Policy in Egypt, Iraq, Israel and Syria.* New York: Praeger.

1223. McLeish, R. 1968. *The Sun Stood Still: Perspectives on the Arab-Israeli Conflict.* London: Macdonald and Co.

1224. Meo, L. 1965. *Lebanon, Improbable Nation: A Study in Political.* Bloomington: Indiana University Press.

1225. Messenger, C. 1982. *The Tunisian Campaign.* London: I. Allan.

1226. Micaud, C. A. 1964. *Tunisia: The Politics of Modernization.* London: Pall Mall.

1227. *Middle East Contemporary Survey,* annual 1976/1977–.

1228. Miller, A. D. 1983. *The PLO and the Politics of Survival.* New York: Praeger.

1229. Miller, J., and L. Mylroe. 1990. *Saddam Hussein and the Crisis in the Gulf.* New York: Times Books.

1230. Monroe, E., and A. Farrar-Hockley. 1975. *The Arab-Israel War, October 1973: Background and Events.* Adelphi Papers #111. London: IISS.

1231. Moore, J. N., ed. 1977. *The Arab-Israeli Conflict: Readings and Documents.* Princeton, N.J.: Princeton University Press.

1232. Mor, B. D. 1993. *Decision and Interaction in Crisis: A Model of International Crisis Behavior.* Westport, Conn.: Praeger.

1233. Naff, T., and M. E. Wolfgang. 1985. *Changing Patterns of Power in the Middle East.* Beverly Hills: Sage.

1234. Nassar, J. R. 1991. *The PLO: From Armed Struggle to the Declaration of Independence.* New York: Praeger.

1235. Neuberger, B. 1982. *Involvement, Invasion, and Withdrawal: Qaddafi's Libya and Chad, 1969–1981.* Shiloah Center Studies #83. Tel Aviv: Shiloah Center.

1236. Nutting, A. 1967. *No End of a Lesson: The Story of Suez.* London: Constable.

1237. O'Ballance, E. 1959. *The Sinai Campaign, 1956.* New York: Praeger.

1238. ———. 1971. *The War in the Yemen.* Hamden, Conn.: Archon.

1239. ———. 1972. *The Third Arab-Israeli War.* Hamden, Conn.: Archon.

1240. ———. 1973. *The Kurdish Revolt: 1961–1970.* Hamden, Conn.: Archon.

1241. ———. 1978. *No Victor, No Vanquished: The Yom Kippur War.* San Rafael, Calif.: Presidio.

1242. ———. 1988. *The Gulf War.* London: Brassey's.

1243. Obieta, J. A. 1970. *The International Status of the Suez Canal.* 2d ed. The Hague: M. Nijhoff.

1244. Oded, A. 1987. *Africa and the Middle East Conflict.* Boulder, Colo.: Lynne Rienner.

1245. Odeh, B. J. 1985. *Lebanon: Dynamic of Conflict.* London: Zed.

1246. O'Neill, B. 1978. *Armed Struggle in Palestine: A Political-Military Analysis.* Boulder, Colo.: Westview.

1247. Pappe, I. 1988. *Britain and the Arab-Israeli Conflict, 1948–1951.* New York: St. Martin's.

1248. ———. 1992. *The Making of the Arab-Israeli Conflict, 1947–1951.* London: I. B. Tauris.

1249. Parker, R. B. 1993. *The Politics of Miscalculation in the Middle East.* Bloomington: Indiana University Press.

1250. Pelletière, S. 1984. *The Kurds: An Unstable Element in the Gulf.* Boulder, Colo.: Westview.

1251. Peters, J. 1984. *From Time Immemorial: The Origins of the Arab-Jewish Conflict Over Palestine.* New York: Harper and Row.

1252. Peterson, J. 1978. *Oman in the Twentieth Century: Political Foundations of an Emerging State.* London: Croom Helm.

1253. ———. 1981. *Conflict in the Yemens and Superpower Involvement.* Washington, D.C.: Center for Contemporary Arab Studies, Georgetown University.

1254. Petran, T. 1972. *Syria.* New York: Praeger.

1255. Pieragostini, K. 1991. *Britain, Aden and South Arabia: Abandon and Empire.* Basingstoke (Hants), Eng.: Macmillan.

1256. Pogany, I. S. 1984. *The Security Council and the Arab-Israeli Conflict.* New York: St. Martin's.

1257. Polk, W. R. 1979. *The Elusive Peace: The Middle East in the Twentieth Century.* London: Croom Helm.

1258. Price, D. 1975. *Oman: Insurgency and Development.* London: Institute for the Study of Conflict.

1259. Quandt, W. B. 1977. *Decade of Decisions: American Policy Toward the Arab-Israeli Conflict, 1967–1976.* Berkeley and Los Angeles: University of California Press.

1260. ———. 1986. *Camp David: Peacemaking and Politics.* Washington, D.C.: Brookings.

1261. ———. 1988. *The Middle East: Ten Years at Camp David.* Washington, D.C.: Brookings.

1262. ———. 1993. *Peace Process: American Diplomacy and the Arab-Israeli Conflict Since 1967.* Washington, D.C.: Brookings.

1263. Qubain, F. 1961. *Crisis in Lebanon.* Washington, D.C.: Middle East Institute Press.

1264. Rabinovich, I. 1985. *The War for Lebanon, 1970–1985.* Rev. ed. Ithaca, N.Y.: Cornell University Press.

1265. Ramazani, R. K. 1975. *Iran's Foreign Policy, 1941–1973: A Study of Foreign Policy in Modernizing Nations.* Charlottesville: University Press of Virginia.

1266. ———. 1979. *The Persian Gulf and Straits of Hormuz.* Alphen aan den Rijn, the Netherlands: Sijthoff and Noordhoff.

1267. ———. 1986. *Revolutionary Iran: Challenge and Response in the Middle East.* Baltimore: Johns Hopkins University Press.

1268. Rapaport, I. 1971. *Israel in Courage and in Faith*. Melbourne: Hawthorn Press.

1269. Rasmussen, J. L., and R. B. Oakley. 1992. *Conflict Resolution in the Middle East: Simulating a Diplomatic Negotiation Between Israel and Syria*. Washington, D.C.: U.S. Institute of Peace Press.

1270. Reilly, B. 1960. *Aden and the Yemen*. London: HMSO.

1271. Rejwan, N. 1974. *Nasserist Ideology: Its Exponents and Critics*. New York: Wiley.

1272. Renshon, S. A. 1993. *The Political Psychology of the Gulf War: Leaders, Publics, and the Process of Conflict*. Pittsburgh, Penn.: University of Pittsburgh Press.

1273. Riad, M. 1981. *The Struggle for Peace in the Middle East*. London: Quartet.

1274. Robertson, T. 1965. *Crisis: The Inside Story of the Suez Conspiracy*. New York: Atheneum.

1275. Robins, P. 1991. *Turkey and the Middle East*. London: Pinter.

1276. Rosen, B., ed. 1985. *Iran Since the Revolution: Internal Dynamics, Regional Conflict and the Superpowers*. New York: Columbia University Press.

1277. Rosen, S. J. 1977. *Military Geography and the Military Balance in the Arab-Israel Conflict*. Jerusalem Papers on Peace Problems #21. Jerusalem: Leonard Davis Institute for International Relations, Hebrew University of Jerusalem.

1278. Roth, S. J, ed. 1988. *The Impact of the Six-Day War: A Twenty-Year Assessment*. Basingstoke (Hants), Eng.: Macmillan.

1279. Rothenberg, G. 1979. *The Anatomy of the Israeli Army: The Israel Defence Force, 1948–78*. New York: Hippocrene.

1280. Rubin, B. 1990. *Islamic Fundamentalism in Egyptian Politics*. New York: St. Martin's.

1281. Rubin, J., ed. 1981. *Dynamics of Third-Party Intervention: Kissinger in the Middle East*. New York: Praeger.

1282. Rubinstein, A. Z., ed. 1991. *The Arab-Israeli Conflict: Perspectives*. 2d ed. New York: HarperCollins.

1283. Sachar, H. 1976. *A History of Israel: From the Rise of Zionism to Our Time*. New York: Knopf.

1284. Safran, N. 1969. *From War to War: the Arab-Israeli Confrontation*. New York: Pegasus.

1285. Safty, A. 1992. *From Camp David to the Gulf: Negotiations, Language and Propaganda, and War*. Montreal, N.Y.: Black Rose Books.

1286. Saikal, A., and R. King. 1991. *The Gulf Crisis: Testing a New World Order*. Working Paper #233. Canberra: Strategic and Defence Studies Center, Australian National University.

1287. Saivetz, C. R. 1989. *The Soviet Union and the Gulf in the 1980s*. Boulder, Colo.: Westview.

1288. Salibi, K. 1976. *Crossroads to Civil War: Lebanon, 1958–1976*. London: Ithaca Press.

1289. Sandler, S., and H. Frisch. 1984. *Israel, the Palestinians, and the West Bank: A Study in Intercommunal Conflict*. Lexington, Mass.: Lexington Books.

1290. Satloff, R. B. 1986. *Troubles on the East Bank: Challenges to the Domestic Stability of Jordan.* New York: Praeger.

1291. Saunders, H. 1985. *The Other Walls—The Politics of the Arab-Israeli Peace Process.* Washington, D.C.: American Enterprise Institute for Public Policy Research.

1292. Schiff, Z. 1993. *Peace and Security: Israel's Minimal Security Requirements in Negotiations With Syria.* Washington, D.C.: Washington Institute for Near East Policy.

1293. Schiff, Z., and E. Yaari. 1984. *Israel's Lebanon War.* Edited and translated by Ina Friedman. New York: Simon and Schuster.

1294. Schonfield, H. 1969. *The Suez Canal in Peace and War, 1869–1969.* Coral Gables, Fla.: University of Miami Press.

1295. Seale, P. 1965. *The Struggle for Syria: A Study of Post-War Arab Politics, 1945–1958.* New York: Oxford University Press.

1296. Shamir, S. ed. 1981. *Self-Views in Historical Perspective in Egypt and Israel.* Proceedings of an Israeli-Egyptian Colloquium held at the Tel Aviv University, April 15, 1980.

1297. Shazly, S. 1980. *The Crossing of the Suez.* San Francisco: American Mideast Research.

1298. Sheehan, E. R. R. 1976. *The Arabs, Israelis, and Kissinger—A Secret History of American Diplomacy in the Middle East.* New York: Reader's Digest Press.

1299. Shehadi, N., and D. H. Mills, eds. 1988. *Lebanon: A History of Conflict and Consensus.* London: I. B. Tauris.

1300. Short, M., and A. McDermott. 1985. *The Kurds.* London: Minority Rights Group.

1301. Shuckburgh, E., and J. Charmley. 1987. *Descent to Suez: Diaries, 1951–1956.* New York: Norton.

1302. Shulimson, J. 1966. *Marines in Lebanon 1958.* Washington, D.C.: U.S. Marine Corps Headquarters, G-3 Division, Historical Branch.

1303. Shwardran, B. 1960. *The Power Struggle in Iraq.* New York: Council for Middle Eastern Affairs.

1304. Sick, G. 1985. *All Fall Down: America's Tragic Encounter With Iran.* New York: Random House.

1305. Sicker, M. 1987. *The Making of a Pariah State: The Adventurist Politics of Muammar Qaddafi.* New York: Praeger.

1306. ———. 1989. *Between Hashemites and Zionists: The Struggle for Palestine, 1908–1988.* New York: Holmes and Meier.

1307. Simons, G. L. 1993. *Libya: The Struggle for Survival.* New York: St. Martin's.

1308. Sirriyeh, H. 1989. *Lebanon: Dimensions of Conflict.* London: Brassey's.

1309. Skeet, I. 1992. *Oman: Politics and Development.* New York: St. Martin's.

1310. Smith, C. D. 1992. *Palestine and the Arab-Israeli Conflict.* 2d ed. New York: St. Martin's.

1311. Smolansky, O. M., and B. M. Smolansky. 1991. *The USSR and Iraq: The Soviet Quest for Influence.* Durham, N.C.: Duke University Press.

1312. Sobel, L. A., ed. 1974. *Israel and the Arabs: The October 1973 War.* New York: Facts on File.

1313. Spiegel, S. L. 1992. *Conflict Management in the Middle East.* Boulder, Colo.: Westview.

1314. ———, ed. 1992. *The Arab-Israeli Search for Peace.* Boulder, Colo.: Lynne Rienner.

1315. St. John, R. B. 1987. *Qaddafi's World Design: Libyan Foreign Policy, 1969–1987.* London: Atlantic Highlands.

1316. Stookey, R. 1978. *Yemen: The Politics of the Yemen Arab Republic.* Boulder, Colo.: Westview.

1317. ———. 1982. *South Yemen: Marxist Republic in Arabia.* Boulder, Colo.: Westview.

1318. Taheri, A. 1988. *Nest of Spies: America's Journey to Disaster in Iran.* New York: Pantheon.

1319. Talhami, G. H. 1992. *Palestine and Egyptian National Identity.* New York: Praeger.

1320. Thomas, H. 1967. *The Suez Affair.* London: Weidenfeld and Nicolson.

1321. Tibi, B. 1993. *Conflict and War in the Middle East, 1967–1991: Regional Dynamic and the Superpowers.* New York: St. Martin's.

1322. Touval, S. 1982. *The Peace-Brokers: Mediators in the Arab-Israeli Conflict, 1948–1979.* Princeton, N.J.: Princeton University Press.

1323. Townsend, J. 1977. *Oman: The Making of a Modern State.* London: Croom Helm.

1324. Tripp, C., ed. 1984. *Regional Security in the Middle East.* Aldershot (Hants), Eng.: Gower.

1325. Troen, S. I., and M. Shemesh. 1990. *The Suez-Sinai Crisis, 1956: Retrospective and Reappraisal.* New York: Columbia University Press.

1326. Udovitch, A. L, ed. 1976. *The Middle East: Oil, Conflict, and Hope.* Lexington, Mass.: Lexington Books.

1327. Van Creveld, M. L. 1975. *Military Lessons of the Yom Kippur War: Historical Perspectives.* Beverly Hills: Sage.

1328. Vatikiotis, P. J. 1984. *Arab and Regional Politics in the Middle East.* London: Croom Helm.

1329. Wagner, A. R. 1974. *Crisis Decision-Making: Israel's Experience in 1967 and 1973.* New York: Praeger.

1330. Waterbury, J. 1978. *Egypt: Burdens of the Past, Options for the Future.* Bloomington: Indiana University Press.

1331. ———. 1983. *The Egypt of Nasser and Sadat: The Political Economy of Two Regimes.* Princeton, N.J.: Princeton University Press.

1332. Watt, D. C. 1971. *Documents on the Suez Crisis, 26 July to 6 November 1956.* London: Royal Institute of International Affairs.

1333. Wenner, M. 1967. *Modern Yemen, 1918–1966.* Baltimore: Johns Hopkins University Press.

1334. Whetten, L. 1974. *The Canal War: Four-Power Confrontation in the Middle East.* Cambridge: MIT Press.

1335. Wilson, K. M., ed. 1983. *Imperialism and Nationalism in the Middle East: The Anglo-Egyptian Experience, 1882–1982.* London: Mansell.

1336. Wood, J. 1992. *Mobilization: The Gulf War in Retrospective.* Working Paper #250. Canberra: Strategic and Defence Studies Center, Australian National University.

1337. Wright, J. L. 1989. *Libya, Chad, and the Central Sahara.* Totowa, N.J.: Barnes and Noble.

1338. Yodaf, A. 1984. *The Soviet Union and Revolutionary Iran.* London: Croom Helm.

1339. Yorke, V. 1988. *Domestic Politics and Regional Security: Jordan, Syria and Israel: The End of an Era?* Aldershot (Hants), Eng.: Gower.

1340. Zabih, S. 1988. *The Iranian Military in Revolution and War.* London: Routledge.

1341. Zakaria, R. 1989. *The Struggle Within Islam: The Conflict Between Religion and Politics.* London: Penguin.

Index

Page references followed by *t*, *f*, or *n* indicate tables, figures, or notes, respectively. Those in *italics* indicate maps.